CW01665973

WELCOME TO

HOW IT WORKS Annual

Welcome to the seventh volume of the How It Works Annual, where your burning questions about how the world ticks finally get answers. Feed your mind, indulge your curiosity, get answers to your strangest questions and uncover the truth behind the greatest misconceptions. We delve deep into the mysteries of our world with in-depth and entertaining articles, accompanied by cutaways, illustrations and incredible images to show you exactly what goes on inside. The How It Works Annual explores the universe through six areas of knowledge: technology, transport, the environment, history, science and space. Our subjects run from the smallest of things in the natural world, like the Venus flytrap, to huge architectural accomplishments like the Palais Garnier opera house. We also uncover the things we cannot touch, like the science of fear, and the technology behind virtual reality. We go back in time to meet Egyptians and early humans, and gaze into our crystal ball to see what the future holds, like miraculous medicine and interstellar travel. Are you ready to learn more about the world around you? Then read on and be amazed.

HOW IT WORKS Annual

Imagine Publishing Ltd
Richmond House
33 Richmond Hill
Bournemouth
Dorset BH2 6EZ
☎ +44 (0) 1202 586200
Website: www.imagine-publishing.co.uk
Twitter: @Books_Imagine
Facebook: www.facebook.com/ImagineBookazines

Publishing Director
Aaron Asadi

Head of Design
Ross Andrews

Editor in Chief
Jon White

Production Editor
Ross Hamilton

Senior Art Editor
Greg Whitaker

Assistant Designer
Briony Duguid

Photographer
James Sheppard

Additional cover images courtesy of
Thinkstock, Getty, Alamy, DK images

Printed by
William Gibbons, 26 Planetary Road, Willenhall, West Midlands, WV13 3XT

Distributed in the UK, Eire & the Rest of the World by:
Marketforce, 5 Churchill Place, Canary Wharf, London, E14 5HU
Tel 0203 787 9060 www.marketforce.co.uk

Distributed in Australia by:
Gordon & Gotch Australia Pty Ltd, 26 Rodborough Road, Frenchs Forest, NSW 2086, Australia
Tel +61 2 9972 8800 www.gordongotch.com.au

Part of the HOW IT WORKS bookazine series

IMAGINE PUBLISHING

CONTENTS

TRANSPORT

TECHNOLOGY

ENVIRONMENT

048

066

027

028
Super submarines

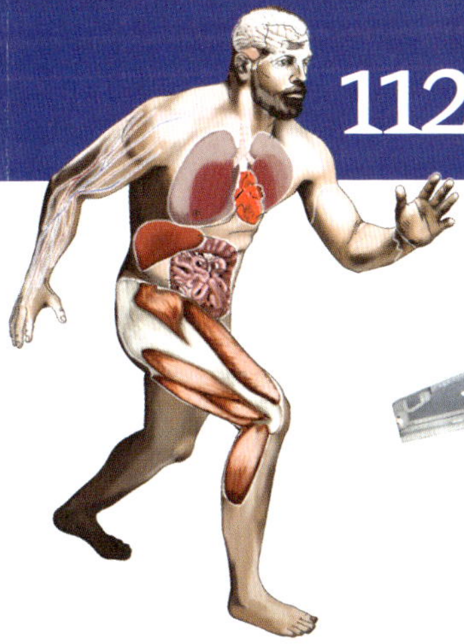

112

010
Become a top gun

110

SCIENCE

SPACE

HISTORY

143
Cannibal galaxies

088
The Galapagos Islands

157

TRANSPORT

028
Super submarines

018
Inside the Airbus A380

"Today's fighter jets are configured for a variety of missions, engaging in air superiority operations and ground targeting"

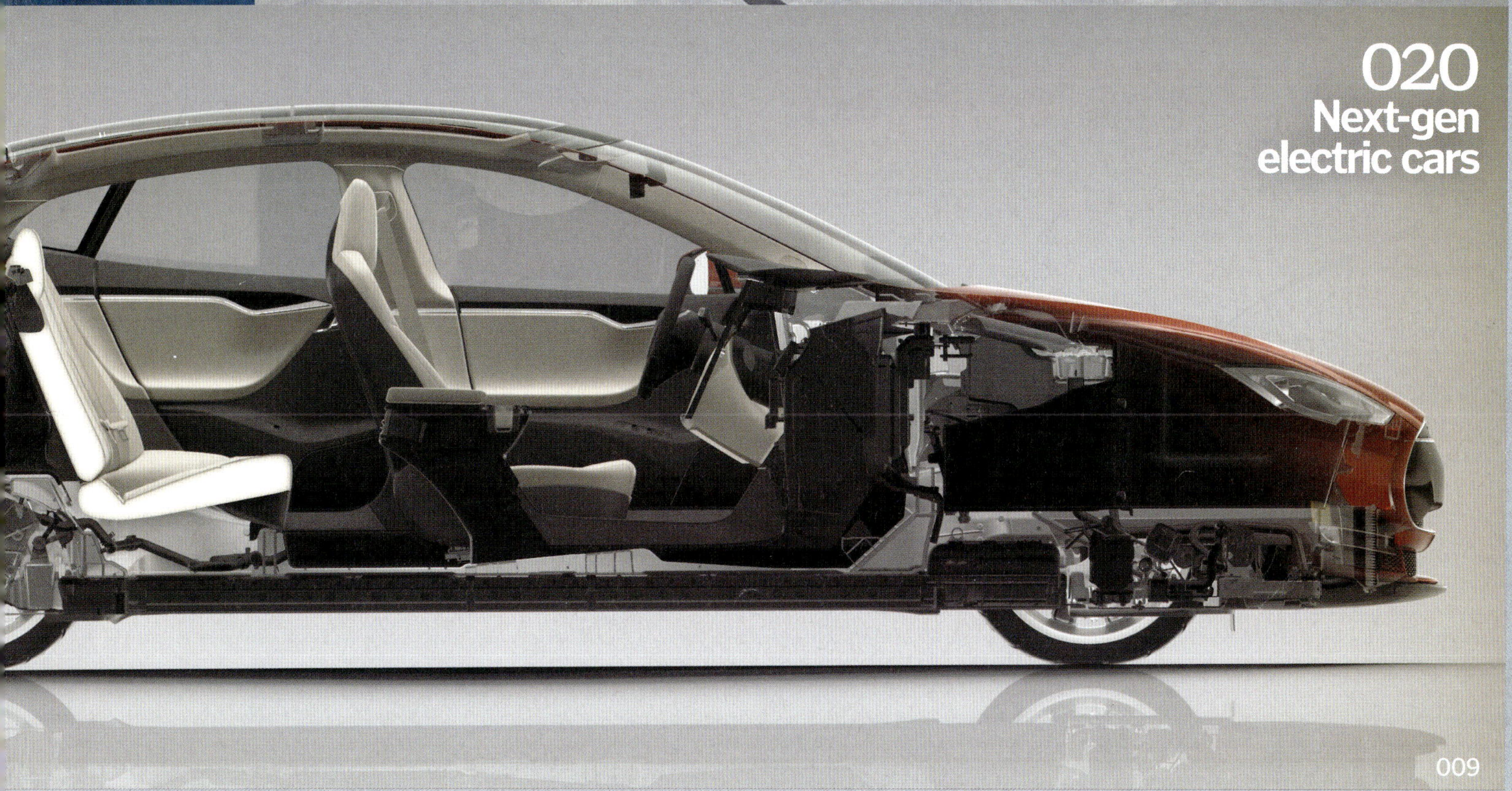

BECOME A TOP GUN

FROM COCKPIT LAYOUT TO COMBAT MANOEUVRES

DISCOVER WHAT IT TAKES TO FLY A FIGHTER JET

The life of a fighter pilot requires courage, commitment and energy. While flying one of the most complex military machines in the world, monitoring and manipulating multiple systems, a pilot's training, intelligence and sharply honed skills work seamlessly. However, pilots never stop learning, growing and pushing themselves to the limit – both physically and mentally.

"Complete dedication is required outside the cockpit too," says US Navy Lieutenant Joshua S Bettis. "The choice to fly jets for the Navy is life-consuming. The jets are expensive and dangerous. So, when a pilot isn't actually flying he is practising flying or studying. The current ratio of maintenance hours per flight hour also means that many sailors spend long days preparing jets to fly for short periods. In a training environment, if a slip-up doesn't end in a mishap, it will affect a pilot's grades. There is seemingly an inexhaustible supply of young officers that would jump at the opportunity to take his spot."

Fighter pilot training is intense and ongoing. Young jet pilot candidates complete initial flight screening in propeller-driven aircraft such as the Cessna 172. US Navy pilots progress through primary and advanced flight training, familiarising themselves with additional aircraft such as the conventional Beechcraft T-34C Turbomentor and the McDonnell Douglas/Boeing T-45C two-seat advanced jet trainer.

Fighter pilots complete up to three years of training before earning their wings. During that time they spend countless hours in the classroom, respond to emergency situations in the simulator and endure the centrifuge, which spins the pilot vigorously to replicate the intense G-forces they will encounter during the majority of in-flight manoeuvres.

"The training we receive is everything from basic airmanship to air-to-ground munitions delivery and air-to-air combat," explains Lieutenant Commander Josh Denning. "We also train to land on aircraft carriers and refuel in flight. Flying is hard work. It requires hours of preparation for each flight. A typical 1.5-hour flight would consist of approximately two hours of briefing before the flight, the flight itself, and then anywhere from one hour to many hours for a debrief of the event."

Navy fighter pilots are constantly reminded that the success of a mission depends on them. Once they've mastered a fighter capable of flashing into combat at more than 1,600 kilometres per hour, the fighter pilot must be ready to spring into action at a moment's notice.

FLIGHT GEAR

Fighter pilots require specialist equipment to tackle death-defying manoeuvres

Suiting up is a critical aspect of the job. Fighter pilots' equipment is often tailored to their mission, whether the jet aircraft is flying faster than the speed of sound, engaging hostile targets or the pilot is on the ground, evading capture or fighting for survival.

"A pilot wears a helmet and visor, a mask which is worn at all times with a radio incorporated, a flight suit made from aramid (Nomex) – a material that is not fireproof but will char instead of melt – gloves, steel-toed boots, a G-suit, harness and survival vest," explains Lieutenant Bettis. "Other types of equipment vary depending on your mission, whether it is peacetime training or combat."

The flight suit is ideal for protecting the fighter pilot in case of an onboard fire. "It's like zip-up pyjamas with a few pockets. It's pretty simple," Bettis describes. "The G-suit, on the other hand, is an expensive piece of gear that plugs into a receptacle in the cockpit." Heavy acceleration can generate high G-forces on the pilot, sending blood rushing towards their head or their feet. Either scenario can cause a pilot to pass out, so pressurised G-suits are worn to combat this.

In cold weather, pilots don a rubber-lined exposure suit that functions much like a diver's wetsuit, providing insulation and retaining body warmth if they land in water after a forced ejection. Gloves are made of Nomex material similar to the flight suit, and are both fire-resistant and warm in cold weather.

"We carry a large assortment of mostly survival gear on our vest," explains Lieutenant Commander Denning, "in case we ever have to eject." The survival vest contains a hand-held GPS for orientation, waterproof matches, thimble-like lights that turn fingertips into miniature flashlights, camouflage paint, a tourniquet for wound treatment and more.

Every pilot's outfit is meticulously thought out for their safety

Meet the pilots

Lieutenant Joshua S Bettis, US Navy

Lieutenant Bettis graduated from the US Naval Academy in 2006 and was designated a student naval aviator. He earned his wings in 2009, subsequently serving with Squadron VFA-125 in Lemoore, California, flying the F/A-18C Hornet fighter. In 2011, he transitioned to the Civil Engineer Corps and currently serves with Naval Facilities Engineering Command in Washington, DC.

Lieutenant Commander Josh Denning, US Naval Reserve

Lieutenant Commander Josh Denning was commissioned in the US Navy through Officer Candidate School in 2007. He earned his wings in 2009, serving at naval air stations in Florida, Texas, and California. He flew the F/A-18E and F/A-18F Hornet fighters. He works as a police officer and as a reserve staff supply officer for the Seventh Fleet.

Next-gen helmets

What tech makes the F-35 Gen III a pilot's ultimate wingman?

Quiet flight
Active noise reduction allows the pilot to focus and operate the F-35 with minimal distractions.

Night vision
Integrated digital night vision technology provides superior awareness while flying in darkness.

Camera
Video recording helps to monitor the pilots' performance on missions and identifies training opportunities.

Blind spots
The headset provides a wide, unrestricted field of view, giving the pilot a clear view of their setting.

Visor
The F-35 pilot's £275,000 ($400,000) visor functions as a head-up display with six high-res cameras embedded on the outside of the plane.

Lightweight
The F-35 helmet shell is constructed of carbon graphite, reducing weight to 2.3 kilograms.

Precise fit
A pupilometer calculates the distance between the pilot's eyes, and a dozen other measurements help provide an exact fit. This avoids the helmet causing motion sickness.

G-suit integration
Custom fitted hoses and cables, integrated with the pilot's G-suit, allow freedom of movement.

The flight suit's transparent thigh pockets usually hold the flight plan and a map

IN THE COCKPIT

The fighter pilot monitors and operates scores of switches, controls and buttons

During all phases of operation, pre-flight, in-flight, and post-flight, the fighter pilot is constantly aware of their surroundings, and the command centre of the jet aircraft is the cockpit. To those who have not trained as pilots, the confusing mass of control panels is overwhelming, but to seasoned professionals the operation of these instruments is second nature, thanks to years of training.

"Pilots develop a cockpit scan over time, where each instrument is monitored at an appropriate interval," relates Lieutenant Joshua Bettis. "The scan varies depending on the pilot's mission. Pilots also spend a significant amount of time in the books. They must know the proper use and limitations of every piece of gear on the jet."

Today's fighter jets are configured for a variety of missions, engaging in air superiority operations and ground targeting. "Everything in the cockpit is as streamlined as possible for the pilot to operate the systems, their hands never leaving the controls," says Lieutenant Commander Josh Denning. "Before we even learn to fly airplanes we go through many hours of cockpit familiarisation, learning the systems and their respective controls in the cockpit."

The pilot has to know their stuff when a split second could be the difference between being the hunter or the hunted. "Training depends on the complexity of the gear the pilot is learning," Bettis continues. "Ground school covers complex instrument function and theory, followed by simulators with seasoned instructor pilots. Next, the instruments are utilised in manoeuvres and tactics in the aircraft – normally in a 'demo-do' format, where the instructor demonstrates proper usage before the student makes an attempt."

Scores of knobs, buttons and switches govern the function of at least 20 systems, each of them

Staying in control

Fighter pilots must know their cockpit layout and the function of every console in it

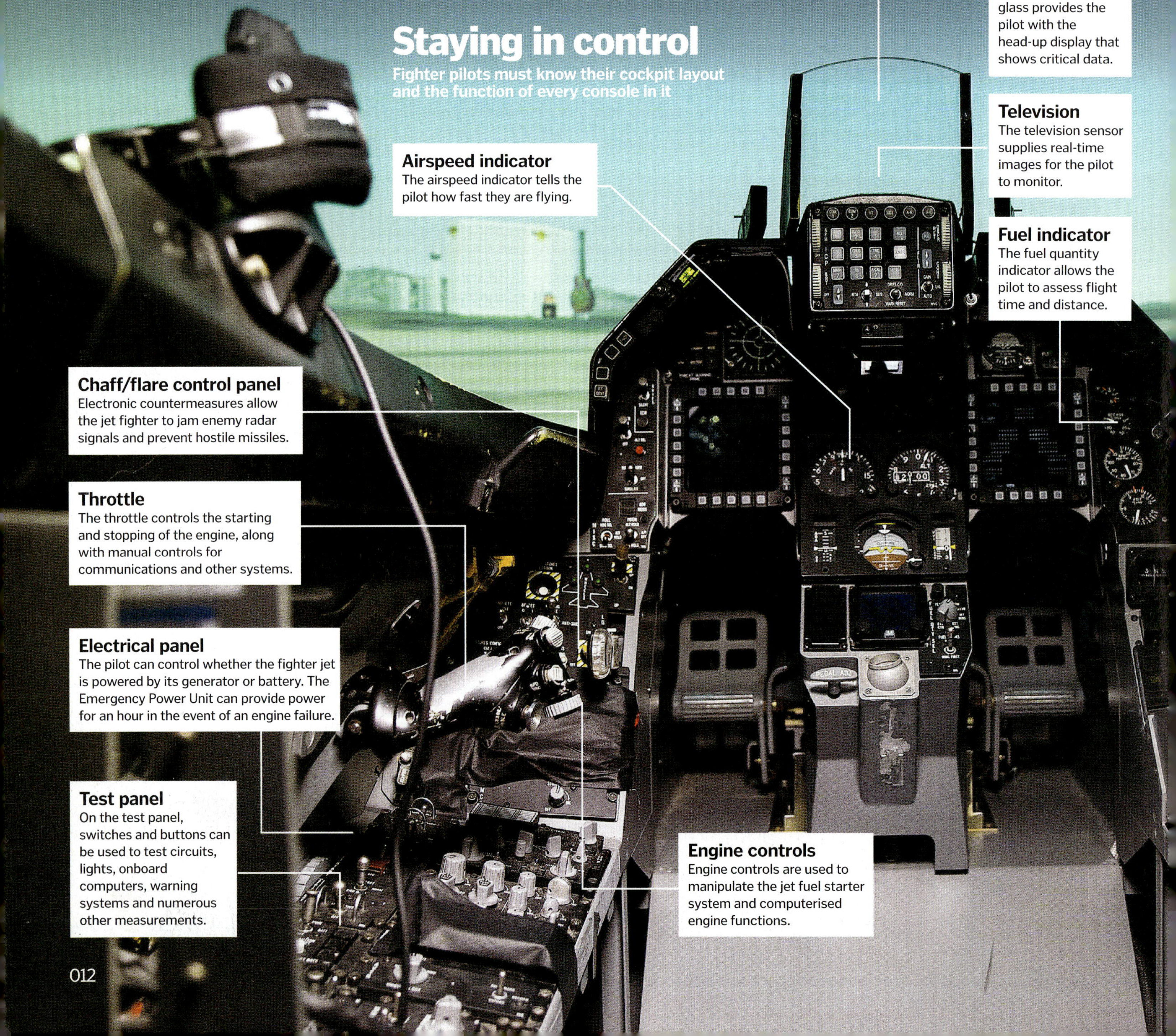

critical to the fighter's performance and the survival of the pilot. These include the engine along with other systems related to fuel, environment and temperature, electrical systems, flight control, hydraulics, landing gear, autopilot, lighting, communications, navigation, IFF (Identification, Friend or Foe), weapons, radar and more.

"As pilots progress in their careers and aircraft get more expensive to fly, the learning curve gets steeper," explains Lieutenant Bettis. "Students work through 20 or more flights in primary flight training just to be able to solo a T-34C. Conversely, a newly winged aviator that is transitioning into the Hornet is expected to solo on his third or fourth flight. Simulators are an excellent tool used to teach pilots and evaluate their performance in a low risk setting. They allow instructors to create emergency situations that otherwise wouldn't be feasible, and adjust conditions such as weather to challenge a pilot that is working on instrument flight."

The jets' quick acceleration can generate high G-forces

Mastering the cockpit controls of a fighter jet takes years of training

All good in the HUD

The head-up display shows pilots their essential real-time data

The fighter jet head-up display (HUD) presents data to the pilot in their forward field of view through the integration of three basic components: the projector unit, combiner and video generation computer. This setup means they don't have to divert their eyes while in flight, which minimises the distractions of looking down or away from the front of the aircraft, and avoids the pilot having to refocus their eyesight when assessing data. A typical HUD provides the airspeed, altitude, horizon line and global positioning, as well as navigational and aerial combat information. This includes data such as angle of attack, number of available weapons, range to target and whether or not they are locked onto an enemy aircraft.

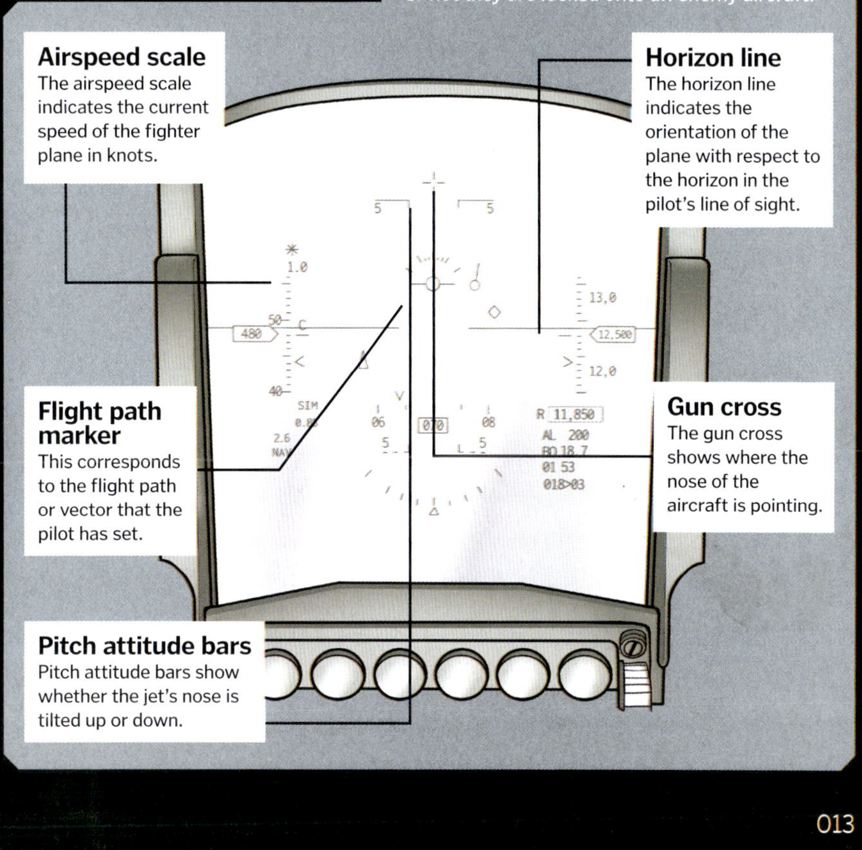

> "A split second could be the difference between being the hunter or the hunted"

The F-35B is specially designed to take off over short distances

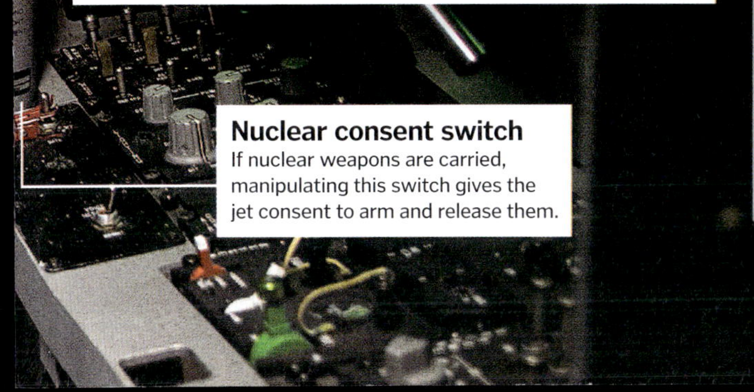

IN FLIGHT

With great power comes great responsibility: how to handle a fighter jet like a pro

Few fighter pilots would deny that the adrenaline rush of take-off, flight and landing is exhilarating, but they are also clear that the experience comes with significant responsibility. "Inside the cockpit there can be no complacency," warns Lieutenant Bettis. "Even the greatest pilots are one mistake away from demonstrating their mortality."

The fighter jet is designed for speed and manoeuvrability, and pilots feel they are on the aircraft rather than inside it, surrounded by the cockpit. "You literally strap the plane on to you," says David Collette, a former F-16 pilot in the US Air Force. "The plane is your life, but you are the brain."

The F-22 Raptor can cruise at supersonic speeds

In contrast to the wrangling of a fighter jet, commercial aircraft are designed for stability, a smooth ride and passenger comfort. In a fighter jet there are no passengers, just highly skilled professionals who are trained to complete dangerous missions. The fighter jet accelerates like a race car, and the characteristics of the aircraft shape and mould the flight experience. The shake of turbulence is never cushioned.

"Flying a fighter is the most exhilarating feeling I have ever had," explains Lieutenant Commander Denning. "There is an absolute sense of freedom while flying, especially in a high performance airplane such as the Hornet. G-forces feel as if you have weight pressing down on every part of your body. It takes a lot of practice to master the physiology of fighting the forces you experience in the cockpit to maintain consciousness and continue your mission. It is a very intense workout, and sweating out as much as five pounds [2.3 kilograms] of body weight is not uncommon under our most physically stressful missions."

The force is strong

Tight turns, steep dives and swift climbs are all in a day's work for the fighter pilot, and the laws of physics take their toll. The power of gravity exerted on the human body during acceleration, deceleration and turning is known as G-force (G). Standing still you experience 1G under gravitational pressure, but when flying the Gs that pilots feel are directly proportional to the jet's changing velocity. Ordinary activities like riding a roller coaster, or heavily accelerating or braking in a car, could generate up to 3Gs. Fighter pilots, flying at tremendous speeds may 'pull' up to 9Gs, restricting the normal flow of blood and potentially causing a blackout. During manoeuvres the pilot is at great risk when blood pools in the lower extremities and the brain is starved of oxygen. To ward off the effects of G-forces, pilots wear a G-suit that provides a continuous flow of air, operating like a large blood pressure cuff.

A US Marine Corps fighter pilot dons gear, including the G-suit, prior to a mission

Aerial combat manoeuvres

Fighter pilots execute precise moves to gain the decisive edge on an adversary

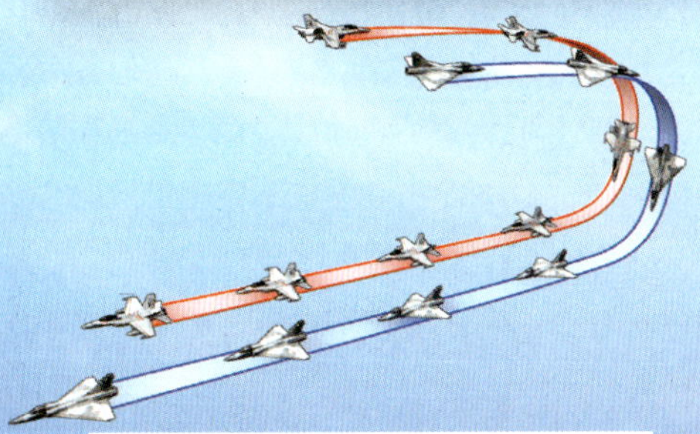

Turning in
A pilot seeking the most advantageous firing position on the tail of their adversary may execute this turn to close in.

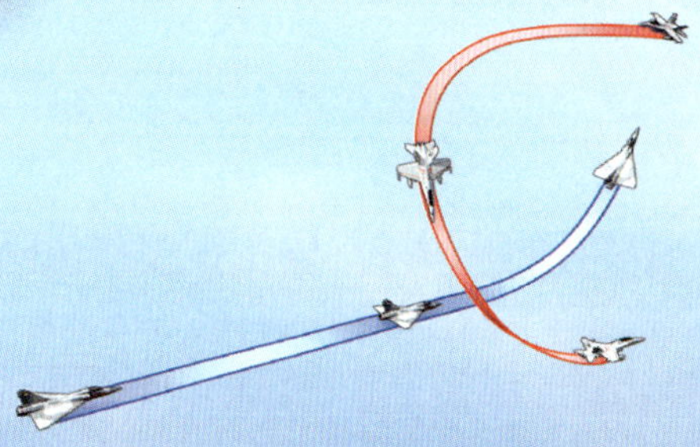

Lead turn
This move enables a pursuing fighter pilot to close in on their opponent by starting to turn before the planes pass each other.

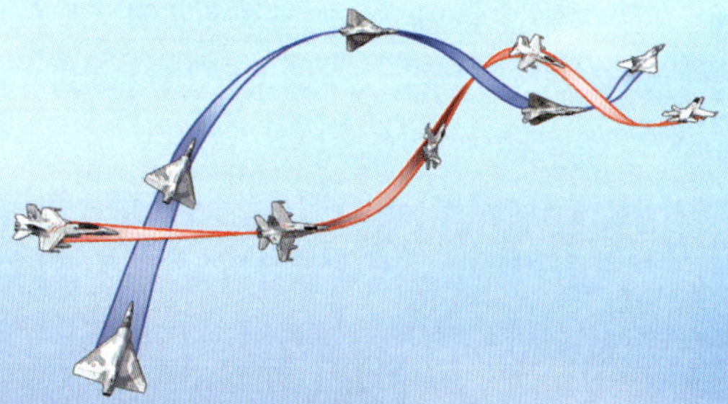

Rolling scissors
Often following a high-speed overshoot, an evader reverses into a vertical climb and barrel roll, compelling the pursuer to follow.

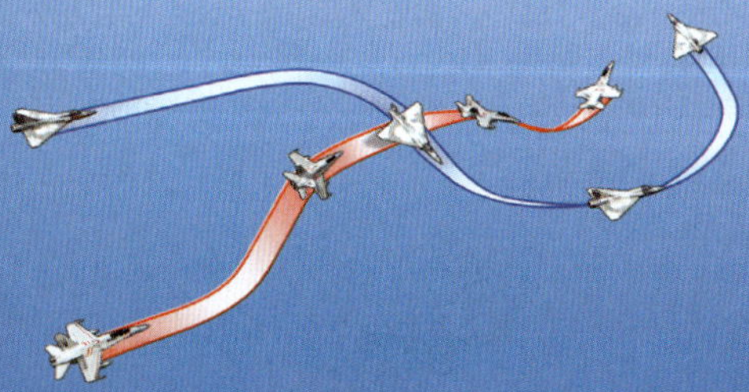

Flat scissors
This manoeuvre involves two planes weaving from side to side as they each try to get behind the other.

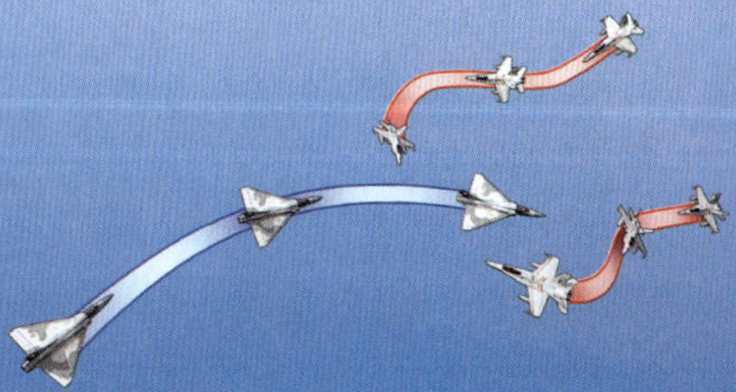

Bracket
Two pursuers launching a pincer attack force the evader to choose which opponent they will engage.

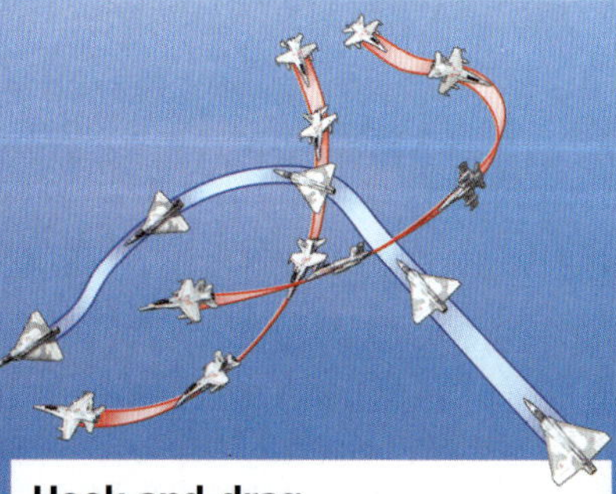

Hook-and-drag
Two persuers launching a pincer attack can take advantage of an evader's turn towards either of them.

Ejecting is always a last resort for fighter pilots

SAFETY FIRST

Fighter pilots must be vigilant at all times

The warning light flashes. Sights, sounds and sensors alert of potential disaster. Instinctively, the pilot takes action, as safety is second nature. Then, the exercise is over. The flight simulator has done its job so the pilot will know how to do theirs. "The simulators are run by former pilots with a breadth and depth of experience," remarks Lieutenant Bettis. "However, nothing replaces seat time in the jet."

During that "seat time" the pilot is constantly alert, blending their knowledge with onboard systems that keep both pilot and plane safe. Flying is a risky business. Not only does the pilot's life depend on it, the fate of a jet aircraft worth millions is also in their hands.

"Flying an airplane like the Hornet demands 100 per cent of your focus and situational awareness for 100 per cent of the time," relates Lieutenant Commander Denning. "Flying is terribly unforgiving for any carelessness, incapacity or neglect. There are systems in the airplane that alert us to several different types of emergencies, but most importantly it's the focus you must maintain that keeps a pilot safe."

Safety begins with pilot awareness and follows established procedures. From suiting up with indispensable gear to a huge range of pre-flight checks, the pilot works to minimise risk, through take-off, mission fulfilment and landing.

"Flying a fighter is the most exhilarating feeling I have ever had" – Lieutenant Commander Denning

The last resort

Pilots only eject from their jets when all other options are exhausted

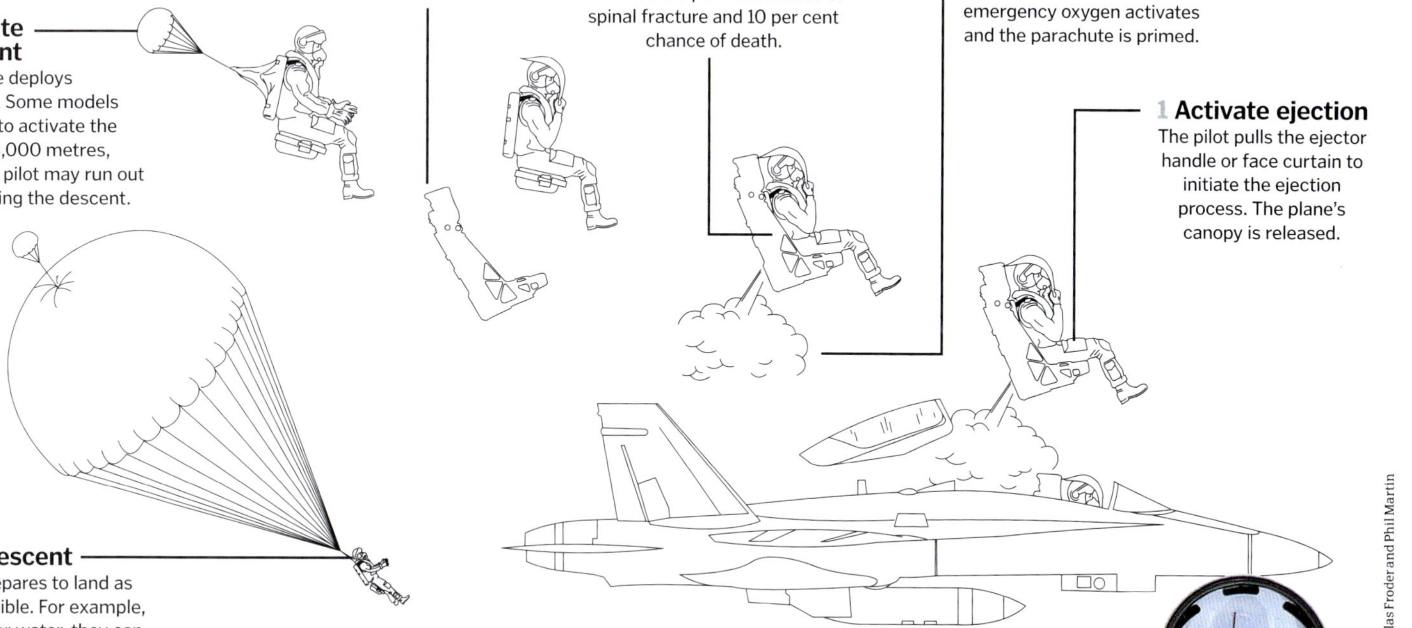

Man versus machine

Military applications of drones are revolutionising the future of the fighter pilot. The virtually silent, sophisticated drone removes the risk to human life, and executes its lethal task with pinpoint accuracy. However, the human element may never completely disappear from the sphere of aerial combat.

"Manned combat aircraft will be around for the foreseeable future," asserts Lieutenant Commander Denning. "Today's unmanned aircraft mainly focus on intelligence and surveillance missions with the capability to launch some limited air-to-ground missions, but as far as fighter aircraft are concerned, there are no limits."

While engineers may one day remove the fighter pilot from the cockpit, a new breed of expert fliers will remain, stationed at remote locations on the ground, handling the drone, watching and waiting, locking onto targets and firing.

Unmanned aerial vehicles like the MQ-9 Reaper can carry out missions via remote control

An F-35B undertakes one of its many test flights before being assigned to a fleet

F-35 jets have clocked up a total of 60,000 flight hours since 2006

Pilots flying the F-35 have a 360-degree view of their surroundings

Pilots can communicate securely with commanders on the ground

Huge tanker aircraft can refuel fighter jets in mid-air

Two F-35C Lightning II jets (foreground) fly alongside two F/A-18 Super Hornets

© WIKI; Lockheed Martin

The Airbus A380 is greener and quieter than many other passenger jets

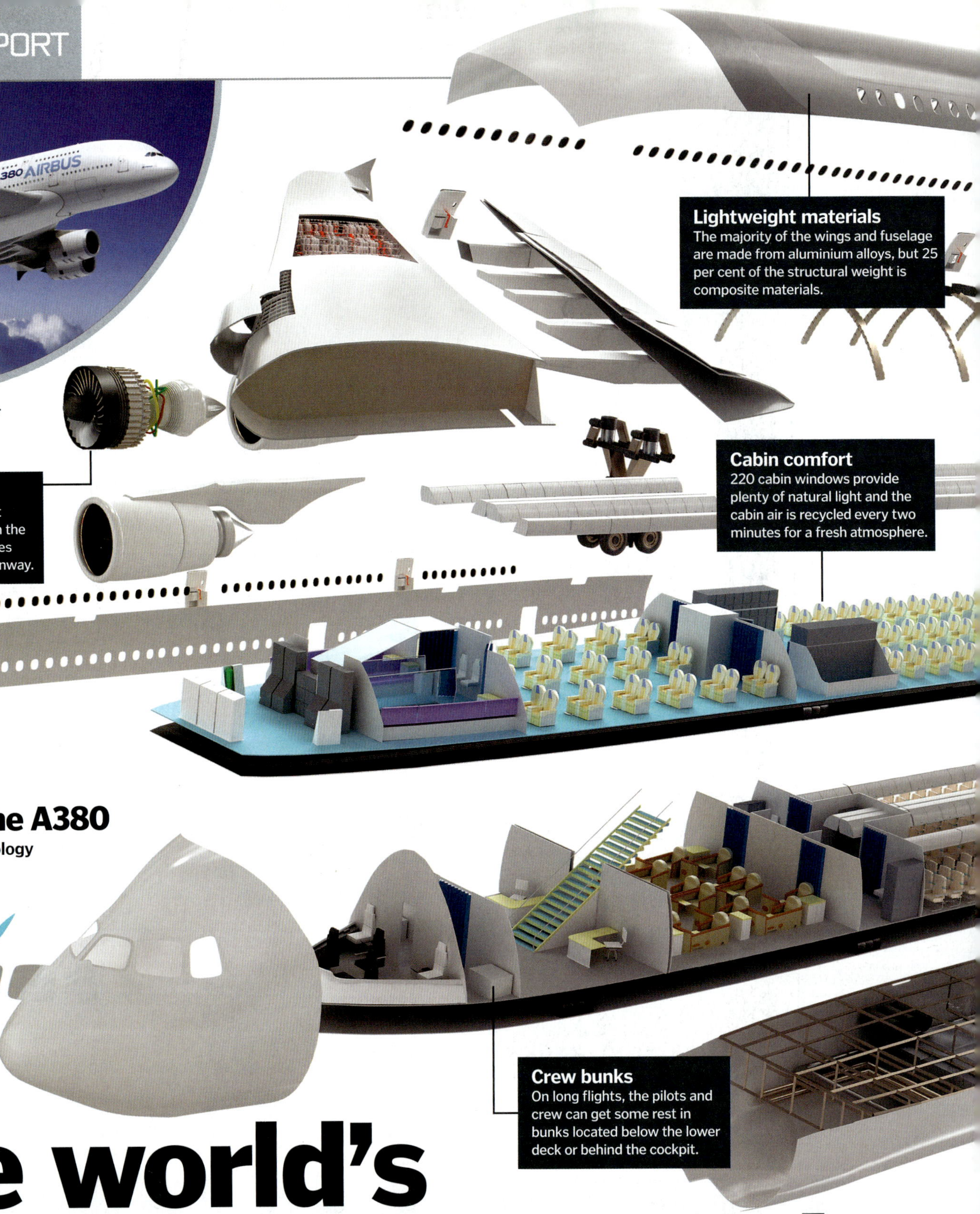

Boarding the A380

The incredible technology inside this sky giant

The world's largest passenger jet

How does the enormous double-decker Airbus A380 get off the ground?

Ferrying travellers all over the globe is an expensive business for the world's airlines, so it makes sense that they would want to pack as many passengers as possible onto each aircraft, reducing the number of flights they need to make. Thanks to its double-decker design, the Airbus A380 is capable of carrying up to 853 passengers at a time, if it is in a single-class cabin configuration. That's over 150 more than the aircraft's competitor, the Boeing 747-8. Most A380s, however, feature four separate classes, with economy and premium economy on the lower deck of the airplane and the more spacious business and first class upstairs, which reduces the passenger number to 544. This is still a 40 per cent increase on the 747-8's four-class capacity.

As well as being the largest passenger jet, the A380 is one of the quietest, with dampeners reducing engine noise to half that of other jets. It is also more environmentally friendly, because it needs to take fewer flights to deliver the same amount of passengers, and the fuel-efficient engines are claimed to give off 22 per cent fewer CO_2 emissions than the jet's closest competitor.

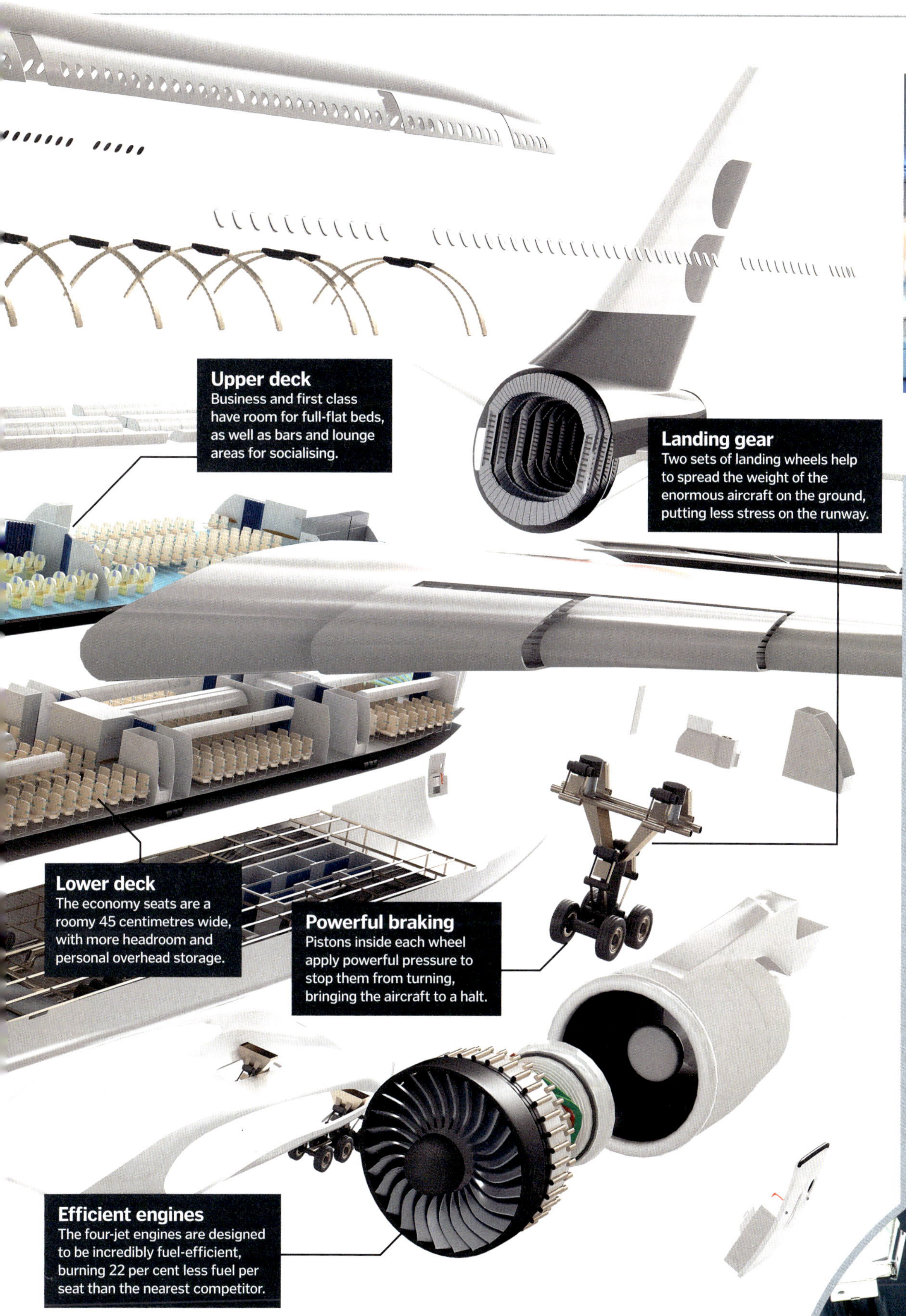

Two staircases provide access to the aircraft's upper and lower decks

Next-gen flight deck

The cockpit of the A380 is designed to be very similar to that of other Airbus aircraft, minimising the amount of time that pilots have to spend training to fly it. It features an instrument panel with eight large, interactive liquid crystal display units showing navigation, engine and systems information, as well as a transparent head-up display that superimposes information over the pilot's view. An electronic library also replaces the traditional paper documentation used by pilots, allowing them to locate operational information more easily and analyse the aircraft's performance. As the plane prepares for landing, the process is made easier as the flight crew can pre-select the optimum runway exit at their destination airport, and leave the autopilot to regulate deceleration after touchdown accordingly. This helps to reduce runway occupancy time and therefore increase the number of aircraft the airport can handle at any given time.

The A380's cockpit is designed to make Airbus pilots feel at home

Building an aircraft of this enormous size does present a few problems, though. Many airlines have had to modify their aircraft hangers to accommodate the increased height and wingspan of the A380, and some airports just don't have enough space for them to park. Also, to speed up the process of boarding and offloading such a large number of passengers, two gangways from the aircraft to the terminal building are needed – a set-up that only certain airports are capable of.

As a result, the A380 can usually be found travelling to and from the world's biggest international airports, making the most of its 15,200-kilometre range to deliver passengers to far-flung destinations in style.

INSIDE THE TESLA MODEL S

They're the most talked-about electric car manufacturer in the world, but just what makes Tesla Motors so innovative?

The concept of an electric car is not a new idea. Manufacturers were building them as far back as the 19th century, with Porsche building their first car, the electric P1, in 1898. Despite its deep-rooted foundation with vehicles, electricity was never substantially developed enough to become the power of choice for cars. Instead, vehicles have been powered by igniting fuel in internal combustion engines. However, this petroleum – a product of crude oil – is in limited supply, prompting car manufacturers to look at alternative forms of power, such as hydrogen and hybrid systems. Electricity has once again come to the fore, and California-based Tesla Motors is leading the charge for this viable, greener technology in our modern world. Unlike other manufacturers, Tesla (led by renowned entrepreneur and CEO Elon Musk) is a relatively new company that specifically produces electric vehicles. Their innovation and commitment to making futuristic cars has ensured that this small Californian company has garnered an impressive reputation across the globe, and we will show you why...

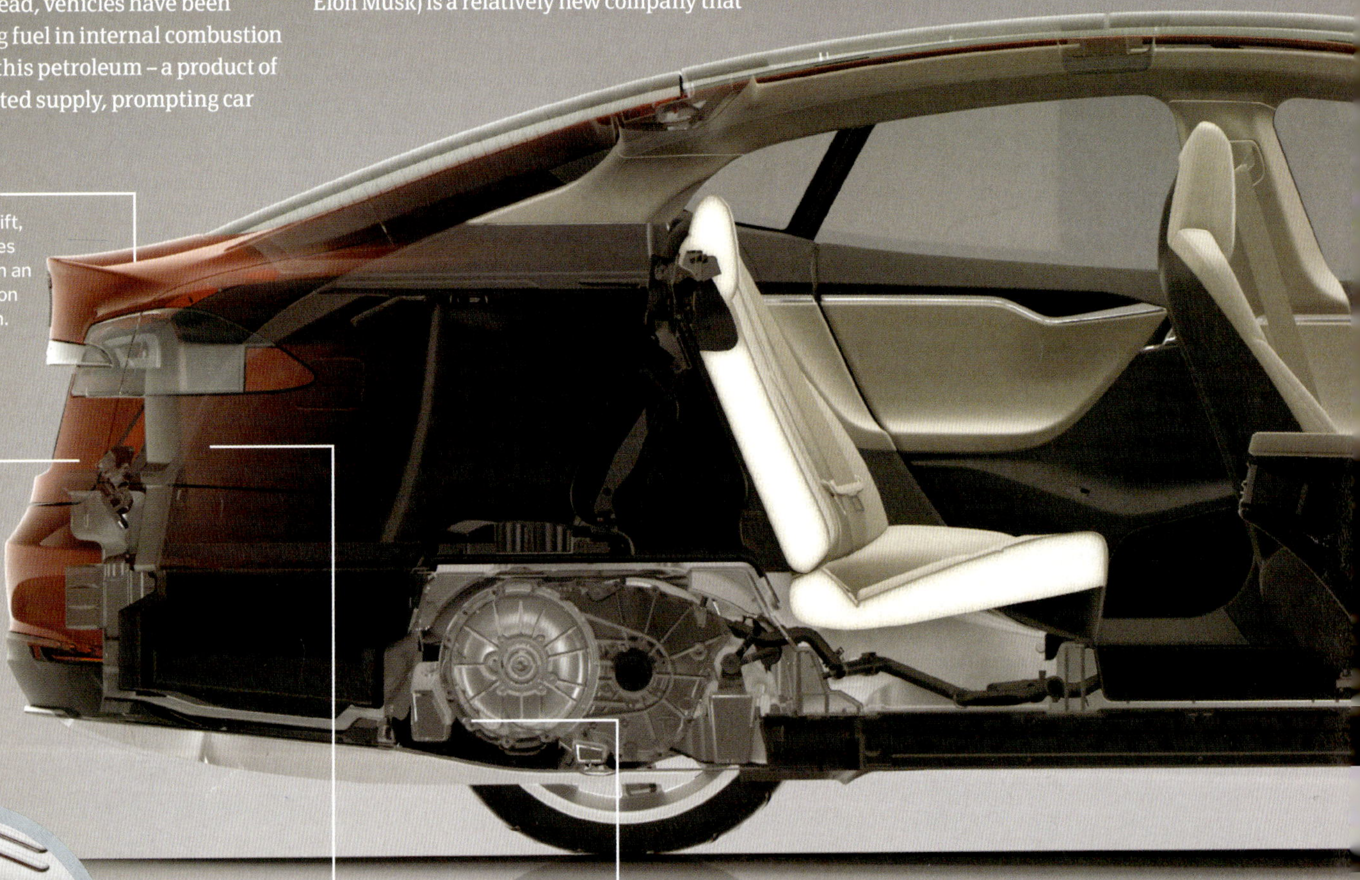

Auto-close boot
Boots can be heavy to lift, but the Model S provides the perfect answer with an auto-open/close function at the touch of a button.

Rear-view camera
Mounted above the rear licence plate, a camera passes a live feed through to the large interior screen, so the driver can see behind the car when reversing.

More storage space
With no engine to speak of, the Model S actually has two luggage storage compartments: one in the front of the car under the conventional 'hood', and the other in the rear.

"Tesla Motors is leading the charge for this viable, greener technology"

Regenerative brakes

As well as using electricity, the Model S is also able to generate it while driving through town. When a driver lifts off the accelerator pedal, gentle braking is automatically applied, and the energy harvested by the brakes is then fed back into the motor to reuse. This is a key component in helping the Model S to maintain its exceptional range.

Software updates

One of the most creative innovations over a conventional car is Tesla's use of software updates. This is all done over-the-air, meaning cool new features can be added to the Model S overnight. An example of this is the addition of the 'creep' function when releasing the brake pedal in traffic, which was added after Tesla consulted with Model S owners on how to improve the driving experience.

Preconditioning

Thanks to the intuitive Tesla Model S app, owners can precondition the on-board climate of their vehicle remotely, so the car reaches the perfect temperature by the time they enter.

No more keys!

The Model S doesn't use a conventional car key as we know it. Instead, owners are presented with a small fob – sculpted to mimic the shape of the car itself – which has a built-in transmitter that talks to the car via onboard sensors. This means an owner only needs to have the key on their person and, when they approach the car, the door handles pop out and the car is ready to start.

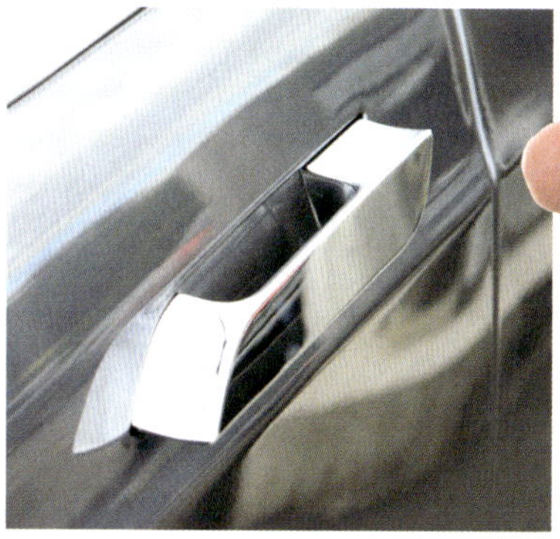

Interactive interface

The huge dash-mounted touchscreen is the technological epicentre, providing access to navigation, entertainment, HVAC controls and more.

Air suspension

Want to lower the Model S for sportier handling or raise it to clear a steep driveway? This can be done with a tap of the dash-mounted touchscreen.

Quiet tyres

With a noisy engine replaced by a beautifully silent motor, the Model S glides along the road with virtually no audible soundtrack. From inside the car, the only noise that remains (with the radio switched off) is rolling road noise. To combat this, ContiSilent tyres from Continental are used, which have an extra layer of foam inside to reduce the noise it produces when rolling along a surface.

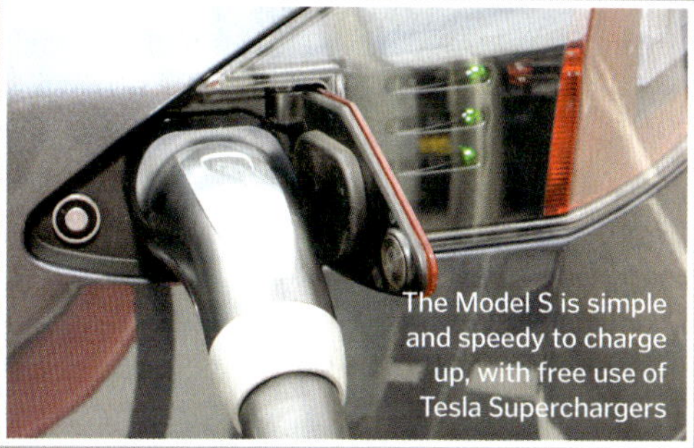

The Model S is simple and speedy to charge up, with free use of Tesla Superchargers

INSIDE THE TESLA FACTORY

See how the Model S is assembled in Fremont, CA

Tesla Motors can lay claim to producing some of the most innovative and technically advanced electric vehicles on the planet. Currently, Tesla produce one car – the Model S – which is available with a variety of power and drive options, however, a Model X SUV is planned for 2016. This Model X will be manufactured alongside the existing Model S from Tesla's main factory in Fremont, California.

The facility was once home to General Motors and Toyota, producing half a million vehicles per year. Tesla purchased the premises on Fremont Boulevard in 2010. They transformed the building into a factory that's as advanced as the cars that roll out of it, all on a site that covers an area of 492,000 square metres (5.3 million square feet), used for both manufacturing and office space. Old assembly equipment was torn out and robots were installed that can perform complex functions, from assembling the chassis to welding and laser-cutting parts. Each one is named after an *X-Men* character, as they have the 'superpowers' to lift and manoeuvre entire cars with ultimate precision.

The factory floor itself is split down into five sections: stamping, assembly, body, paint and plastics. Every part of the Model S build process is carried out at the factory in California, from the early panel beating to final test-driving. State-of-the-art technology used by Tesla in the production of its cars also means high efficiency, reducing its carbon footprint. This includes basic measures, such as replacing fluorescent lights with energy-saving LED lamps, all the way to using ultrasonic waves inside the car instead of wasting gallons of water for a leak test. They also use powder coatings for the primer and clear coat layers instead of traditional liquid paints (which contain harmful compounds), another modification that helps lower emissions.

The addition of advanced robots and conveyors enables the factory to process one million battery cells every day. Soon it is hoped that the robots will also be able to install the battery packs in the cars, which will relieve factory workers of one of the most labour-intensive jobs in the process. Currently, Tesla can produce up to 100,000 vehicles annually. Not bad for a company that is less than 15 years old.

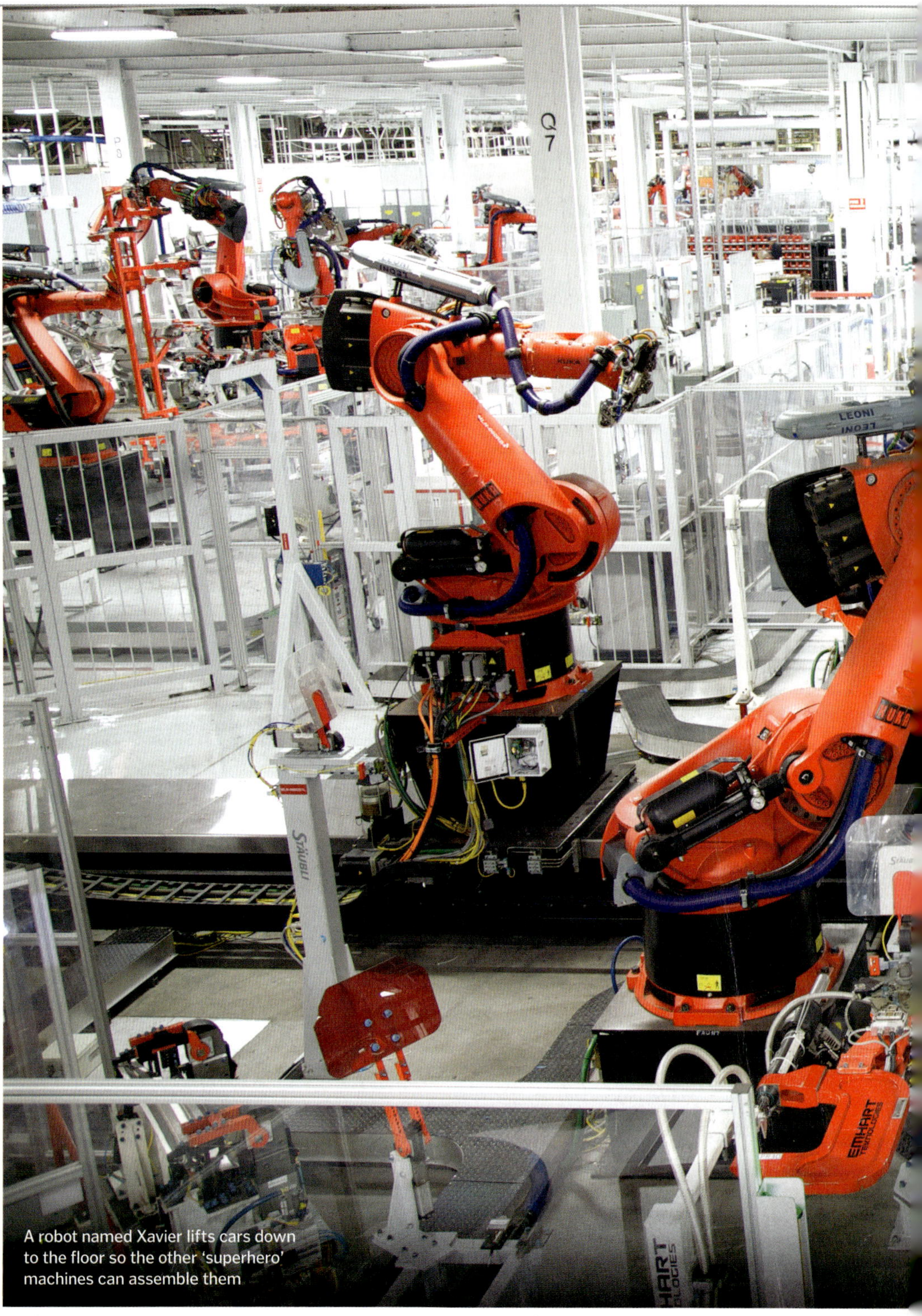

A robot named Xavier lifts cars down to the floor so the other 'superhero' machines can assemble them

From factory floor to your driveway

Discover what it takes to create a Tesla Model S

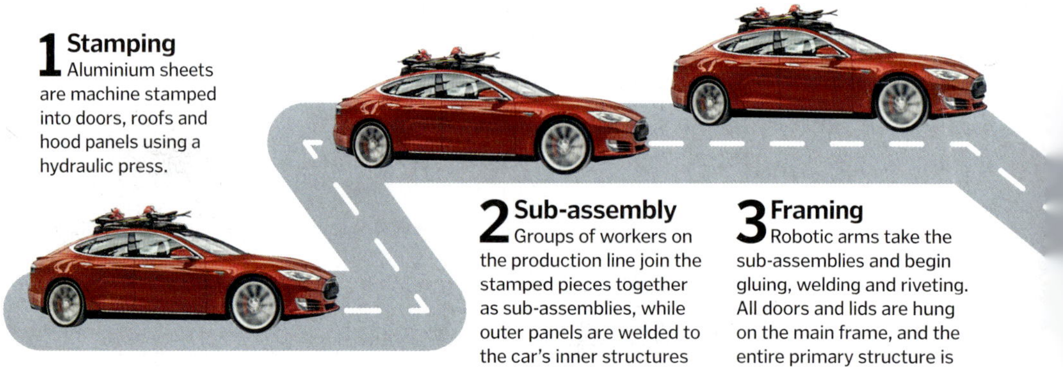

1 Stamping Aluminium sheets are machine stamped into doors, roofs and hood panels using a hydraulic press.

2 Sub-assembly Groups of workers on the production line join the stamped pieces together as sub-assemblies, while outer panels are welded to the car's inner structures for strength and safety.

3 Framing Robotic arms take the sub-assemblies and begin gluing, welding and riveting. All doors and lids are hung on the main frame, and the entire primary structure is checked for imperfections.

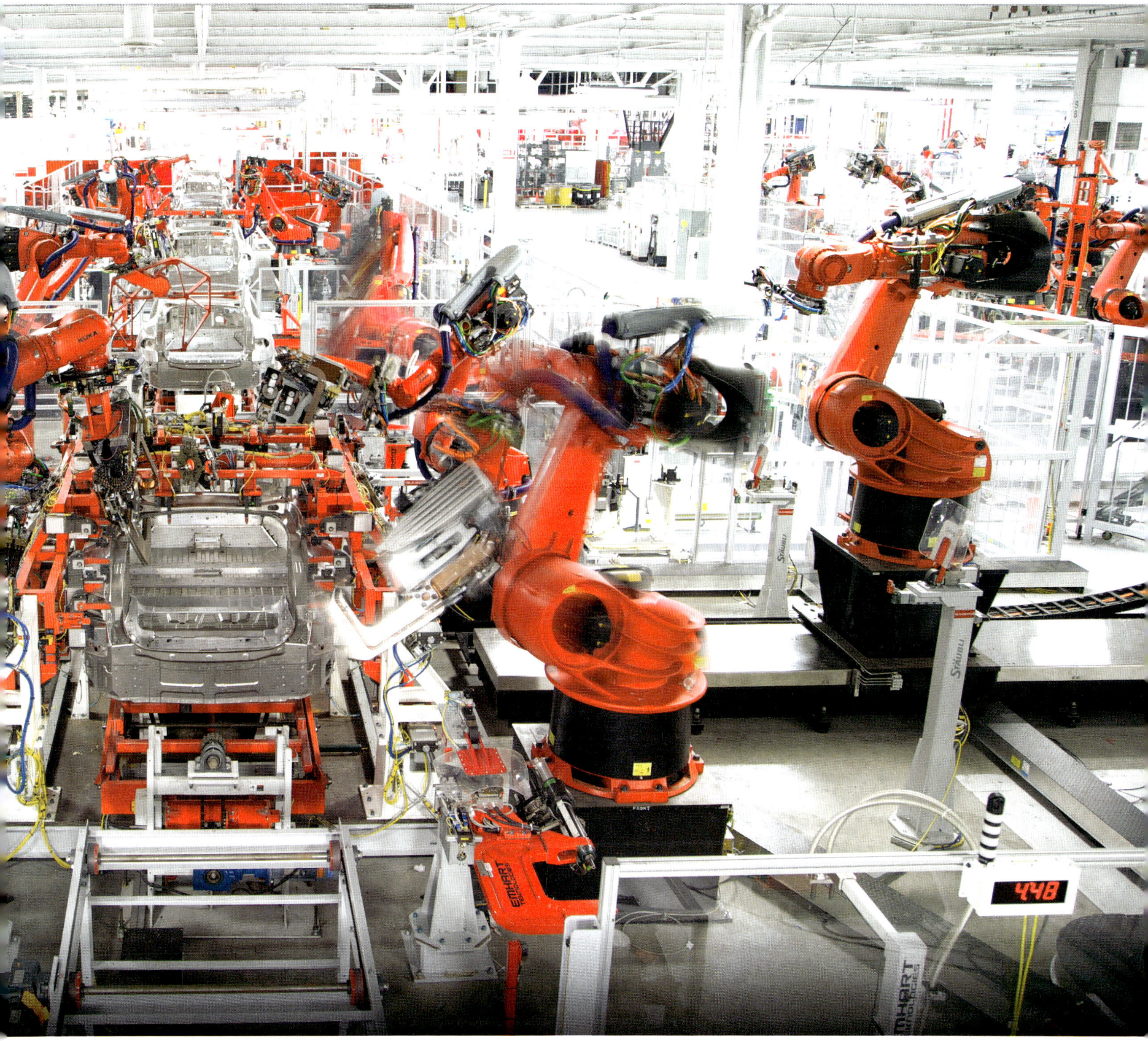

"Old assembly equipment was torn out and robots were installed"

4 Paint
This is a four-step process that involves preparation and three layers of paint. The car then travels on a belt to a 176°C (350°F) oven to cure the paint.

5 Final assembly
The painted doors and lids are removed for further work, while carpet, air bags and the main console are installed inside the car. The entire sub-assembly containing the motor, transaxle, inverter and rear suspension is bolted to the body of the car.

6 Quality testing
Tests include a rolling road and checking for leaks, as well as a visual examination at an inspection station within the factory.

7 Delivery
The car is now ready to be delivered and is shipped to various Tesla showrooms all over the world.

[redacted]

AUTOMATED FEATURES

How the Model S can switch lanes and park by itself

Although not quite a driverless car, the Model S does boast an array of automated features including autopilot, lane change assist and automated parking. The most revolutionary of these, autopilot, works by utilising a forward radar, 12 long-range ultrasonic sensors positioned around the car, a forward-facing camera and a digitally-controlled electric braking system.

The camera reads road signs and checks for objects in front of the Model S' projected line, while the radar and ultrasonic sensors constantly sense five metres (16 feet) around the car to check for objects such as cars in traffic. The data is fed to the car's engine control unit (ECU), which determines what lane or path the Model S needs to take. The idea is to take the strain out of situations such as congestion, offering increased comfort for the driver.

Similarly, the software and hardware is able to steer to keep the Model S within a designated lane, or even change lanes with just a tap of a turn signal, all while managing speed by reading road signs. Automatic parking is also possible under the same technology. The car will notify the driver when it detects an available parking space and be capable of smoothy manoeuvring into it.

Autopilot explained

Find out how this futuristic feature helps drivers to keep a safe distance

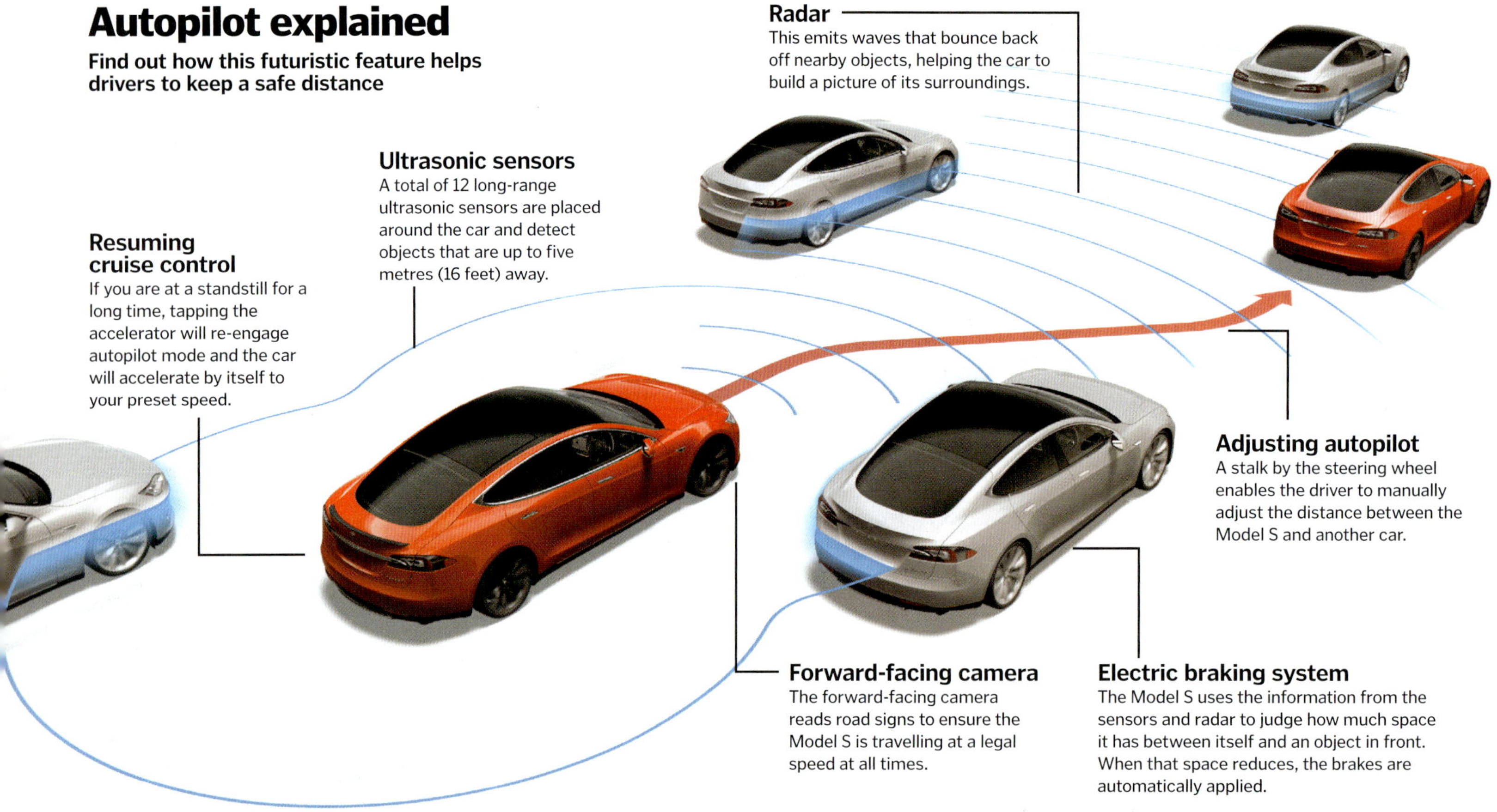

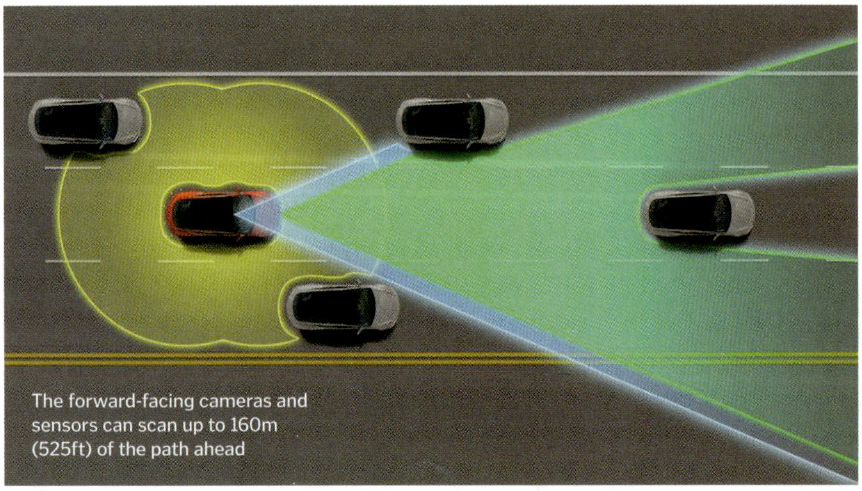

The forward-facing cameras and sensors can scan up to 160m (525ft) of the path ahead

The Speed Assist function makes sure that the Model S keeps within the speed limit of the road

DID YOU KNOW? Tesla CEO Elon Musk is also the founder of advanced spacecraft and rocket manufacturer SpaceX

IN THE DRIVER'S SEAT

It may look like a conventional car from the outside, but the interior is laden with next-gen tech

Aside from there being no transmission tunnel running through the middle of the car (or even a gear stick for that matter) offering up more space, the interior is akin to that of a conventional vehicle. There are two seats up front, a rear bench in the back, and even an extra two rear-facing child seats in the boot space, should you wish to pay the optional £2,500 (nearly $4,000). However, the genius of the Model S lies with the huge 43-centimetre (17-inch) touchscreen in the centre of its dashboard. This interface is the main control hub for the entire car: the driver operates the touchscreen to access a variety of menus and settings, which control everything from opening the sunroof to providing satellite navigation.

On purchase of a vehicle, an owner is encouraged to download the Tesla Model S app, which lets you precondition the car's climate ready for your arrival, as well as flash the headlights or honk the horn – useful if your Tesla is parked in a busy multi-storey car park. The app also provides a live location of the car's whereabouts via a satellite view powered by Google, ideal in the event of the car being stolen. Added to this, the app remotely notifies the owner when the Model S has finished charging, aiding the efficiency of the car in fitting in with the driver's day-to-day lifestyle.

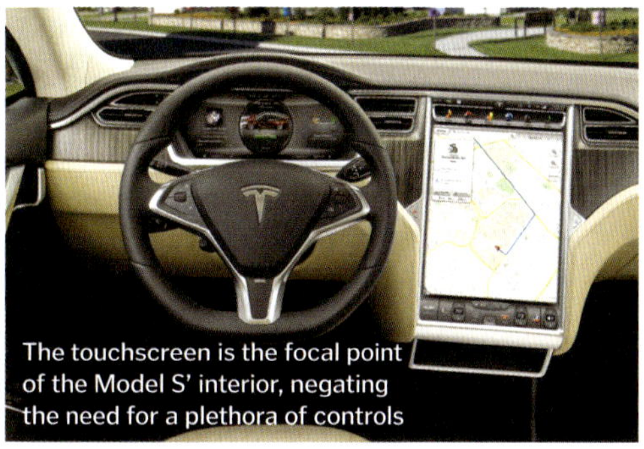

The touchscreen is the focal point of the Model S' interior, negating the need for a plethora of controls

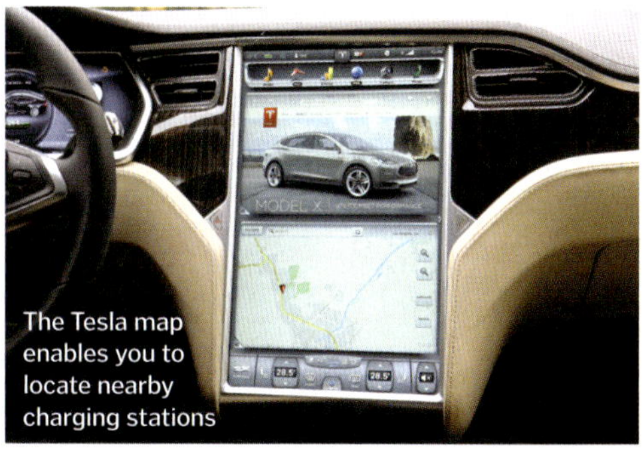

The Tesla map enables you to locate nearby charging stations

Q&A with Tesla UK's Georg Ell, country director

What do you think is the biggest advantage of owning a Tesla right at this moment?

It's the opportunity to be part of something that is shaping the future of motoring. It's future-proof, fun, exciting and safe at the same time. In 200 years from now, people will say Tesla was the [point] where we, as a planet, decided to turn our back on internal combustion engines that poison our air and damage the atmosphere. The quality of air is so bad that 50,000 people die per year due to poor air quality. Tesla is leading the change: people will soon look at motoring today much in the same way as when they think back to a time when smoking on aeroplanes and in pubs was permitted. It's a slice of the future, today.

How will you ensure a Model S is still on the road in ten years' time?

Because there are so few elements to a Tesla. It's more viable than a conventional car as the system is simpler: all that's left on our car when stripped back is a single moving part – the motor. This makes it far more easier to maintain financially than a conventional internal combustion-engined vehicle.

Lithium-ion batteries are known to deteriorate after a number of charges. What is Tesla doing to combat this?

Tesla currently gives an eight-year, unlimited mileage warranty on the battery and drivetrain. We're also developing a drivetrain that can achieve a million miles! Batteries will have an element of degradation, about one per cent per 10,000 miles, but our battery capacity is improving year-on-year by five per cent. We are also working on a system where Tesla owners can pay to upgrade their battery in future, should they wish. We also guarantee to buy a customer's car back from them in three years' time, and that's at a minimum of 50 per cent of the value of the car.

What are the greatest challenges for Tesla over the next five years?

A lot of it comes down to our own execution of following the plan and doing a good job. We're doing a lot with consumers, government and the wider industry to show our cars are more viable and better than a conventional car. The increase in consumer acceptance will grow competition and we welcome that. We are a drop in the ocean in terms of our size as an automotive company, but the pie will get bigger. National government is very excited about electric cars, we just need to ensure [that] local governments are equally [as] excited, helping us put more chargers in the street to ensure more people can feasibly drive our cars.

How to stop a speeding car

Police use the precision immobilisation technique

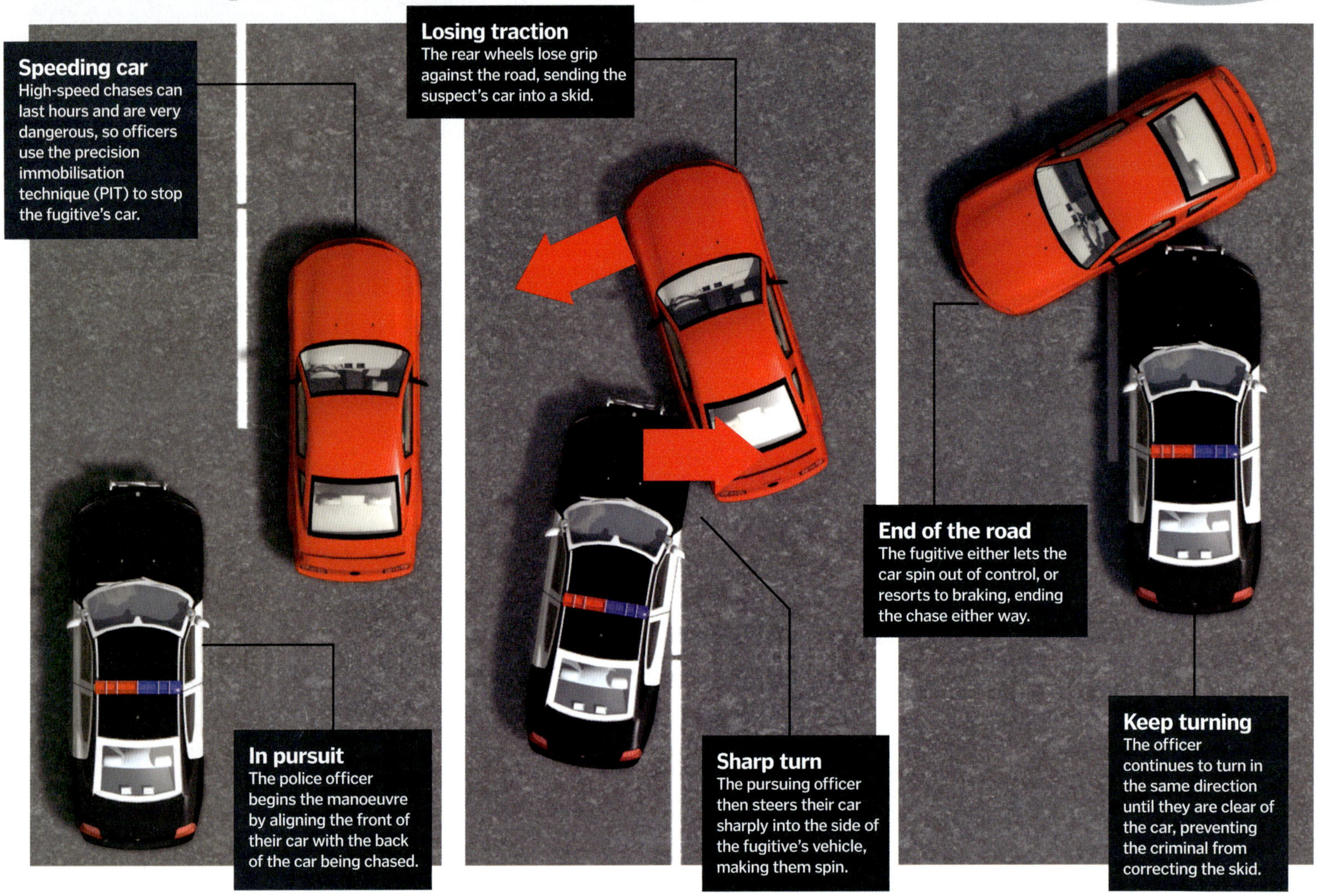

GHOST ships

The next-gen stealth ship that flies through the waves

Minimising drag is an important consideration when designing ships, as friction between the vessel and water greatly reduces efficiency. Juliet Marine Systems (JMS) Inc has tackled this problem by incorporating innovative technology into its demonstration ship called GHOST.

This twin-hull ship is similar to a catamaran, with two wing-like struts attached to the main cabin. The end of each strut features a submerged tubular hull containing the propulsion system. Instead of being pushed along, front-mounted propellers on each hull pull GHOST through the water. Whereas a conventional propeller vessel leaves a trail of foam in its wake, GHOST's unique design redirects the bubbles to surround the twin hulls with pockets of gas. This effect is known as supercavitation, allowing the boat to glide through air rather than water, which JMS claims can reduce drag by a factor of 900.

GHOST's wings can also be repositioned to lift the main cabin above the water. Rising above the bumpy waves ensures a smooth ride, protecting the crew from impact injuries and sea sickness, while also improving the stability and accuracy of onboard sensors and weapon targeting.

GHOST is designed for military use, but can be adapted for commercial and recreational purposes

The mechanics of mountain bikes

The incredible tech powering your off-road adventures

Bicycles are remarkably efficient modes of transport. Just look at a typical car, which converts petrol into motion via combustion: only around 20 to 25 per cent of that fuel will be transformed into useful kinetic energy, while the rest ends up as waste heat and pollutants. Compare that to the 90 per cent efficiency that a typical bike derives from the driving force of your legs. But just like motorised vehicles, a bike specialised for a Tour De France-style road race or cruising along a flat promenade, will be very different from those designed for a rough, off-road track.

The rigours of off-roading – which include uneven terrain, wet and slippery mud and wild inclines – mean that mountain bikes need to be much more robust than other types of bike. It's easy to spot the differences when a mountain bike and a road bike, for example, are side by side. Mountain bikes will have much wider tyres – three or four times the width of a road bike – with a more pronounced grip. The bike will feature front and sometimes rear suspension, often twice the number of gears, a thicker frame and a disc brake system. Even a bad cyclist on a road bike could outpace a person riding a mountain bike on flat, even terrain because road bikes are so much lighter and their tyres are smoother. But in unforgiving, off-road conditions, a mountain bike is in its element.

Gear up to go

The pace at which you can turn the pedals will be dictated by the incline your bike is on. Obviously, this is going to be a lot more difficult cycling uphill than on a flat surface, so mountain bikes incorporate a number of different-sized sprockets – or cogs – to produce a gear ratio that will allow you to ride more comfortably. A 27-speed gearing system, for example, will incorporate three chainrings at the front and nine sprockets at the back. Changing the gear ratio will allow you to cover more or less ground while maintaining the same pace, so tackling a steep incline or taking advantage of a downhill is never out of the question.

Mountain bikes typically have 21, 24 or 27 gears, compared to the 11 of a road bike

Built for punishment

These components allow a mountain bike to go where no other bike dares

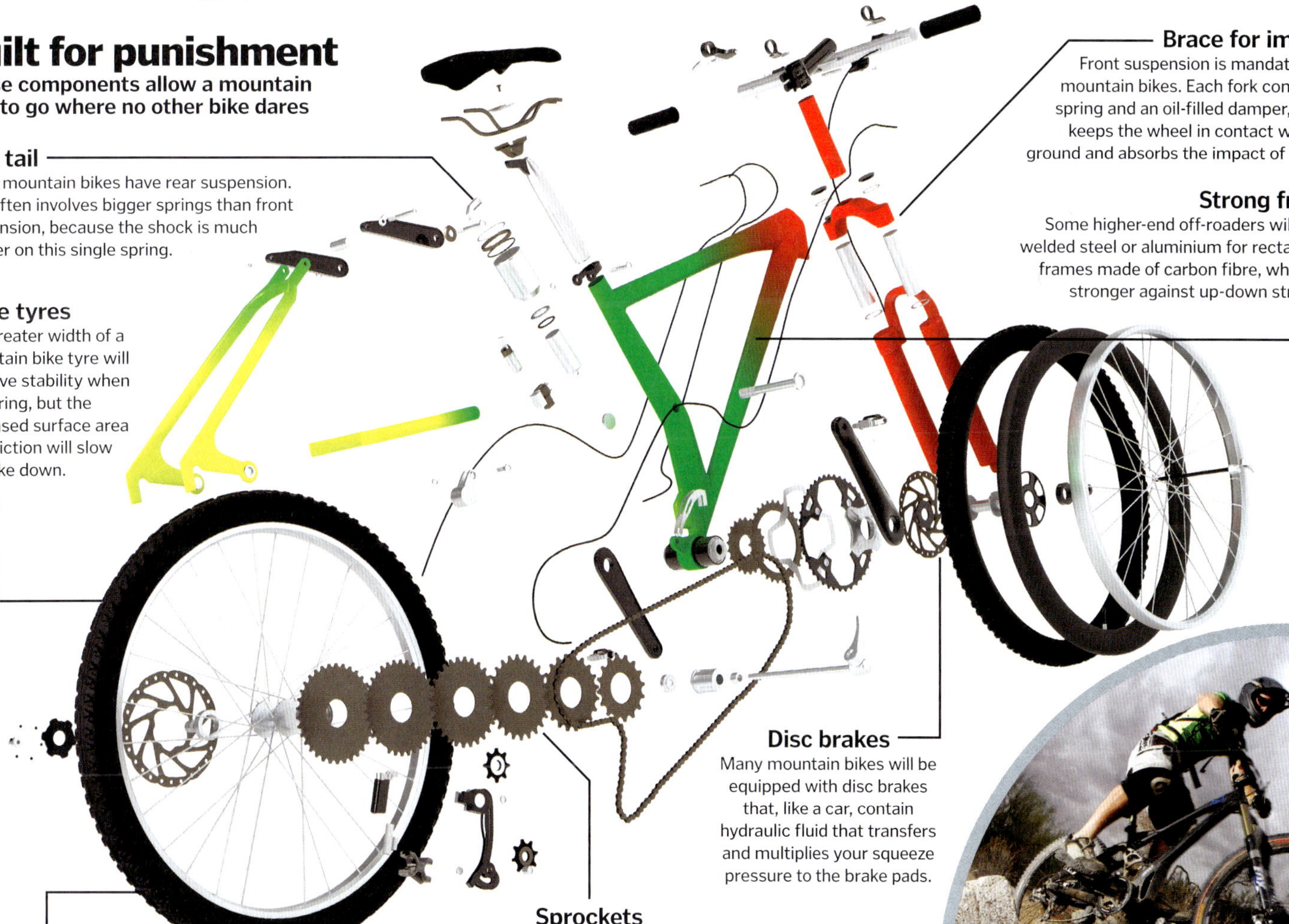

Soft tail
Some mountain bikes have rear suspension. This often involves bigger springs than front suspension, because the shock is much greater on this single spring.

Wide tyres
The greater width of a mountain bike tyre will improve stability when cornering, but the increased surface area and friction will slow the bike down.

Brace for impact
Front suspension is mandatory for mountain bikes. Each fork contains a spring and an oil-filled damper, which keeps the wheel in contact with the ground and absorbs the impact of jumps.

Strong frame
Some higher-end off-roaders will forgo welded steel or aluminium for rectangular frames made of carbon fibre, which are stronger against up-down stresses.

Disc brakes
Many mountain bikes will be equipped with disc brakes that, like a car, contain hydraulic fluid that transfers and multiplies your squeeze pressure to the brake pads.

Sprockets
The number of cogs, or sprockets, determines the number of gears a bike has and thus, the variety of terrain it can tackle.

Lugging weight
The knobs on a tyre, or 'lugs', dig into loose dirt and mud to provide extra grip.

Mountain bikes with full suspension are ideal for rough terrain, as they help to absorb impact

SEEK & DESTROY SUPER SUBMARINES

THE INCREDIBLE TECH POWERING THE WAR BENEATH THE WAVES

Lurking in the depths, hundreds of submarines are currently patrolling the world's oceans, performing a range of very important, and often covert, missions. These stealthy vessels were first widely used during World War I, with Germany's U-boats responsible for destroying several British supply ships during the conflict, and have since changed the face of naval warfare forever.

Always referred to as boats rather than ships, as a matter of naval tradition, submarines have come a long way since the human-powered vessels of the past. Most modern submarines use either diesel-electric propulsion or nuclear reactors to keep them running. The former are equipped with diesel engines to drive the submarine's propellers and charge its batteries while on the surface. Then, when submerged, those batteries power electric motors that spin the propellers to move it through the water.

The need to recharge the batteries and replenish fuel for the engines gives these submarines a limited range, so many navies prefer nuclear-powered vessels instead. These

The unmanned Boeing Echo Voyager

boats can stay underwater for weeks at a time, using nuclear fission to release energy in the form of heat, which in turn generates steam to drive a turbine and spin the propellers.

Now crucial tools for navies large and small, submarines transport crews all over the world; sneaking up on enemy ships, launching missiles, and gathering information while remaining hidden in dark, murky waters. They can generally be divided into two categories: attack submarines, which are designed to seek and destroy enemy ships, and ballistic missile submarines, which attack land-based targets. The US Navy currently has 72 submarines in active service, 54 of which are attack vessels.

It's not just the military that uses these clever underwater crafts, though. With scientists knowing more about outer space than they do about the world's oceans, submarines are incredibly useful for studying marine environments, at depths too great for human divers to reach alone.

In recent years, new unmanned underwater vehicles (UUVs) have begun appearing in the water, capable of conducting dangerous missions, while human crews remain safely on the shore or a nearby ship. These vehicles are small with a limited range, but in the future they could replace the submarines we know today.

> "The US Navy currently has 72 submarines in active service"

HMS Astute firing a cruise missile

Submarines: in depth

Major milestones in the development of underwater vessels

Drebbel I
The first submarine was invented by Dutch engineer Cornelius Drebbel. It was an enclosed wooden rowing boat covered with watertight greased leather, and had air tubes protruding to the surface to supply oxygen.

Turtle
The first recorded submarine attack was during the American War of Independence by the Turtle. It was used in an attempt to blow up the HMS Eagle, but the pilot was unable to attach the bomb to the ship's hull.

Nautilus
American inventor Robert Fulton's submarine was driven by a hand-cranked propeller, but a collapsible mast and sail provided the propulsion. The sub was commissioned by Napoleon to use against the British.

Plongeur
Powered by engines running on compressed air, the French Navy's Plongeur was the first submarine to not rely on human propulsion. It had a ram and torpedo, but engine problems meant the boat never passed the trial stage.

USS Holland
Irish engineer John Philip Holland was the first to use electric motors and an internal combustion engine to power an underwater vessel. His creation was purchased by the US Navy and influenced many designs.

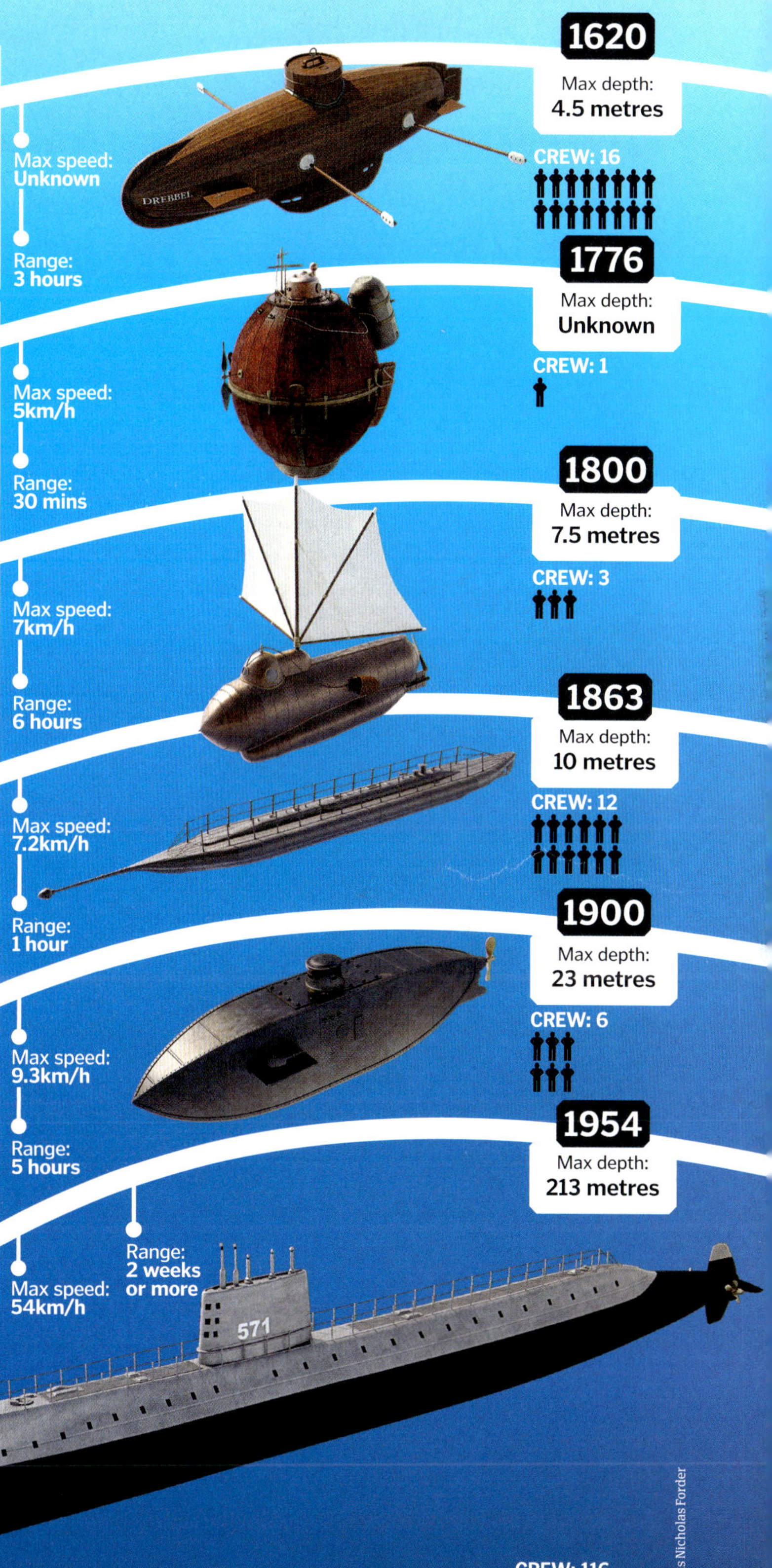

CREW: 116

USS Nautilus
The first nuclear-powered submarine combined stealth and speed in order to revolutionise naval warfare. Constructed under the direction of US Navy Captain Hyman G Rickover, the 97-metre long USS Nautilus accomplished the first voyage under the geographic North Pole, and had a career spanning 25 years.

LIFE ON BOARD A SUBMARINE

How crews survive hundreds of metres beneath the sea

The job of a submariner is physically, mentally and emotionally demanding, as they can spend months at a time living in cramped conditions, with only the other members of their 100-plus crew for company. In the past, they had no means of communication with the outside world for the entire length of their mission, but today email can be used to keep in touch with loved ones at home.

Of course, the human body isn't built for life below the waves, so keeping a crew alive requires some clever technology and engineering. To protect them from the crushing water pressure, the submarine features a strong inner hull in addition to the outer hull that gives the vessel its streamlined shape.

Oxygen is supplied via pressurised tanks, or can be created on board by splitting seawater into hydrogen and oxygen using an electric current. The carbon dioxide the crew breathes out is then removed using scrubbers – devices that trap the CO_2 in soda lime using a chemical reaction. Fresh water is also created on board, as seawater can be heated to remove the salt, and then the water vapour can be cooled and condensed into a drinkable liquid.

Crewmembers of the USS Augusta (now decommissioned) moor their sub to the pier

Deep-sea rescue

If a submarine is damaged, perhaps due to a collision or an onboard explosion, then the crew will radio a distress call and launch a buoy that will signal their location. Rescue will come in the form of a Deep-Submergence Rescue Vehicle (DSRV), a mini-submarine that can be transported by truck, aircraft, ship or another submarine. Once it is near to the damaged vessel, the DSRV can dive down, search for it using sonar, and then latch on to its hatch. When an airtight seal has formed, the hatch is opened and the crew can load on to the DSRV in groups of 24.

The US Navy's Deep-Submergence Rescue Vehicle, Mystic, attached to the USS La Jolla attack submarine

How a nuclear submarine works

Take a tour of a modern deep-sea vessel to discover how it powers through the depths

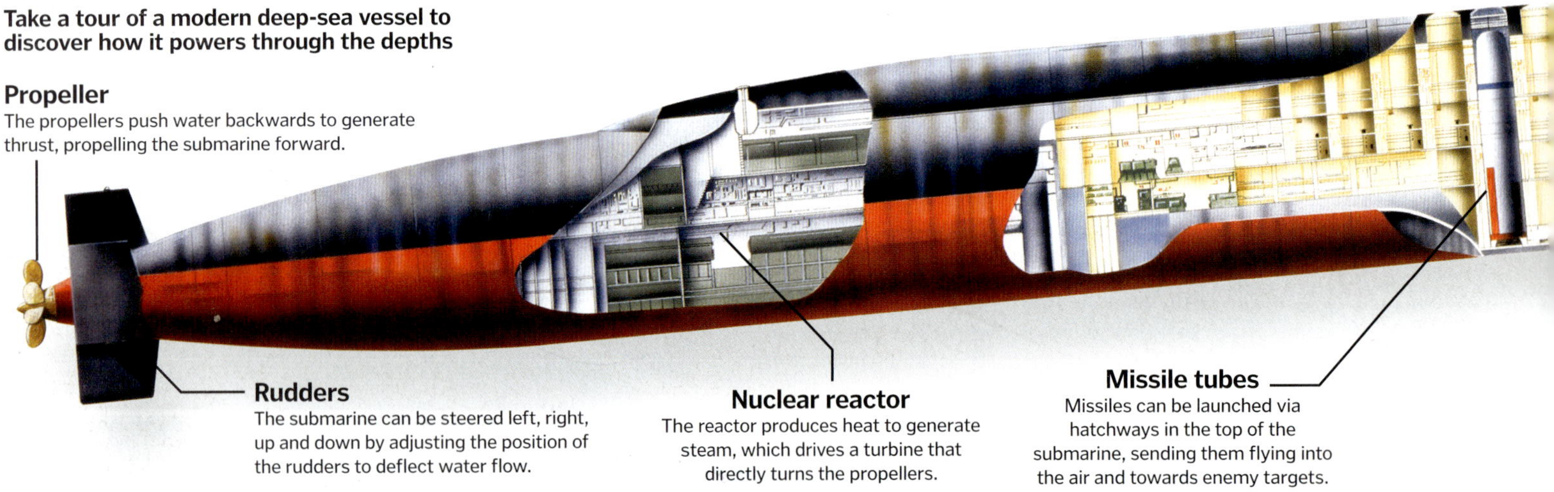

How do submarines dive?

Normally, a boat floats because the volume of water it displaces weighs the same as the boat itself. In order to sink, a submarine must weigh more than the water it displaces, creating a negative buoyancy. This is achieved by flooding ballast tanks, located between the sub's inner and outer hulls. To maintain a set depth, there needs to be a precise balance of air and water in the ballast tanks so that the sub's density is equal to that of the surrounding water.

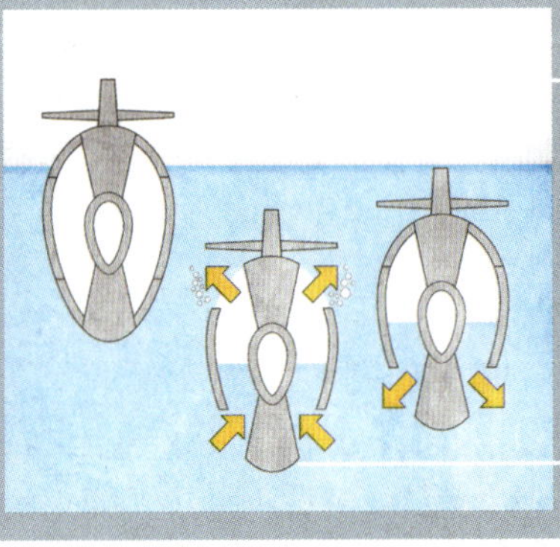

Surfacing
The water inside the ballast tanks is pumped out and replaced with air stored in tanks, making the submarine lighter and able to surface.

Diving
Hatches are opened to fill the ballast tanks with water, making the submarine heavier than the water it has displaced, and causing it to sink.

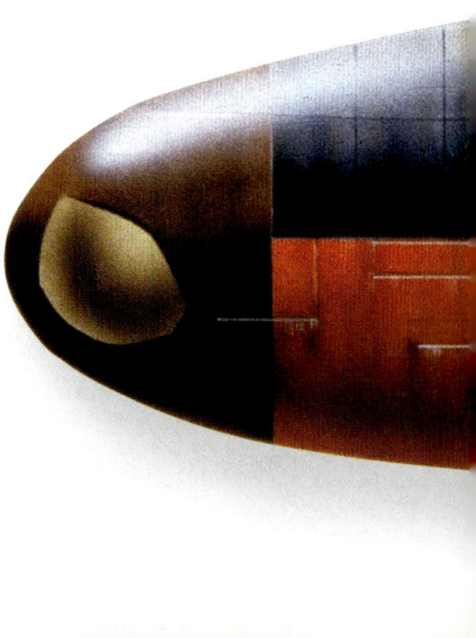

HMS Ambush returning to its home port, HMNB Clyde

"Keeping a crew alive requires some clever technology and engineering"

Underwater navigation

Little light is able to penetrate 200 metres below the ocean surface, so submarine crews use other methods to find their way. Inertial guidance systems can help to keep track of the sub's journey from a fixed starting point, using gyroscopes and accelerometers to measure changes in motion, but must be regularly realigned to ensure the vessel remains on course. On the surface, this can be done using GPS, radio and radar satellite navigation systems, but underwater, sound navigation and ranging (sonar) are used. This helps to identify ocean-floor features, allowing the crew to plot the sub's location.

Sound waves

The sonar sphere emits pulses of sound waves that travel through the water.

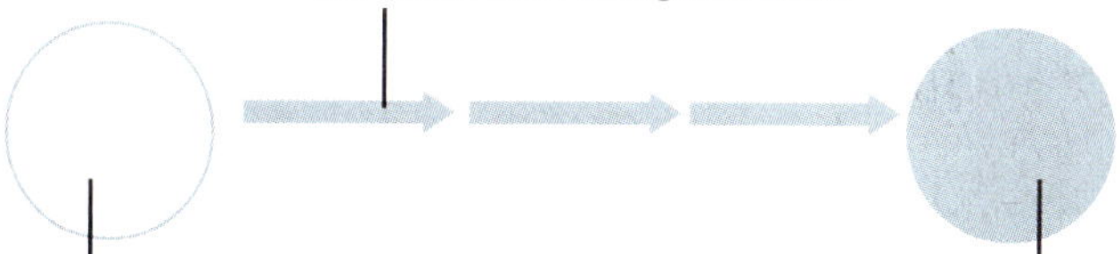

Calculating distance

By measuring the time that it takes for the sound wave to get back to the sphere, the distance between the sub and the object can be calculated.

Bounce back

When the sound waves hit an object, they reflect back towards the sonar sphere.

Snorkel

When surfaced, air enters the sub through a snorkel, but when submerged, oxygen is generated on board the boat.

Antenna

Underwater communications are carried out using low-frequency radio waves, which are able to penetrate the water.

Ballast tanks

This compartment is used as a ballast to provide stability for the submarine, and works by controlling the boat's buoyancy.

Periscope

Objects above the surface can be observed via a series of mirrors that reflect light down to the viewer's eye.

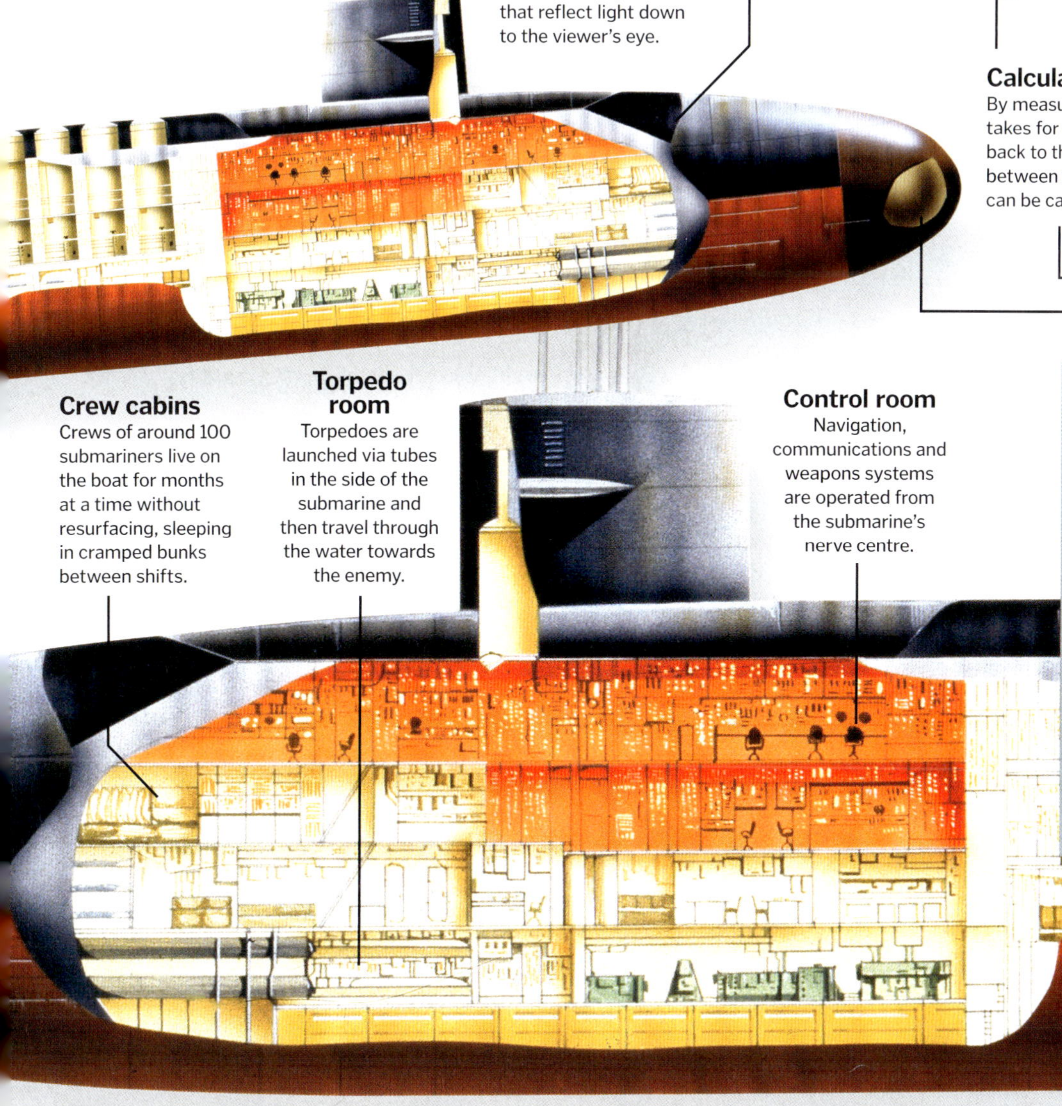

Crew cabins

Crews of around 100 submariners live on the boat for months at a time without resurfacing, sleeping in cramped bunks between shifts.

Torpedo room

Torpedoes are launched via tubes in the side of the submarine and then travel through the water towards the enemy.

Control room

Navigation, communications and weapons systems are operated from the submarine's nerve centre.

New recruits learning the ropes at the US Navy's Basic Enlisted Submarine School in Connecticut

SUPERSONIC SUBS

This underwater craft could circumnavigate the globe in just half a day

Moving at speed through water is very difficult, as liquid creates more drag than air. This means that you need a lot of energy to push through water at high speeds, and most modern submarines are only powerful enough to travel at around 75 kilometres per hour. However, researchers at the Harbin Institute of Technology in China are developing technology that could allow submarines to travel at the speed of sound, so around 5,400 kilometres per hour in seawater.

Their method is based on supercavitation, which was first developed by the Soviets in the 1960s to create high-speed torpedoes during the Cold War. It works by creating a supercavity of air around the vessel, reducing drag and allowing it to reach much faster speeds. The Soviets successfully achieved this with their Shkval torpedo, which could reach speeds up to 370 kilometres per hour, but it could only travel for a few kilometres, and couldn't be steered.

Steering is a problem because rudders, the typical method of navigation underwater, require water to create drag, and so will not work in a bubble of air. To overcome this, the Chinese scientists have created a liquid membrane that can be sprayed over the submarine, reducing drag on one side so that it can be steered in the other direction. So far, however, a method of underwater propulsion for long-range supersonic travel has yet to be developed, so their dreams of travelling from Shanghai to San Francisco in 100 minutes are still a long way off.

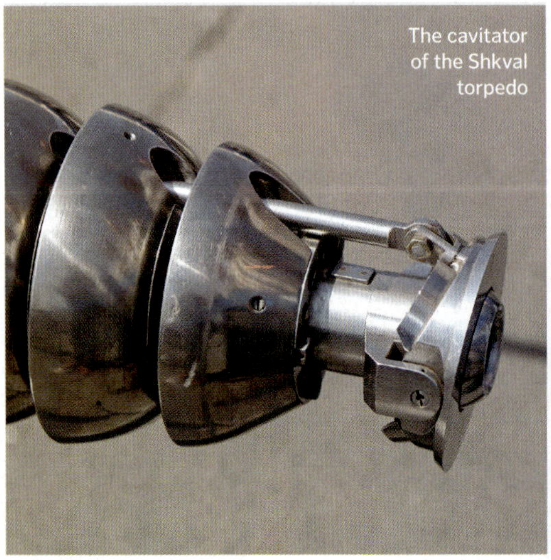

The cavitator of the Shkval torpedo

Speeding through the water

How would a supersonic submarine reach the speed of sound?

Ordinary submarine

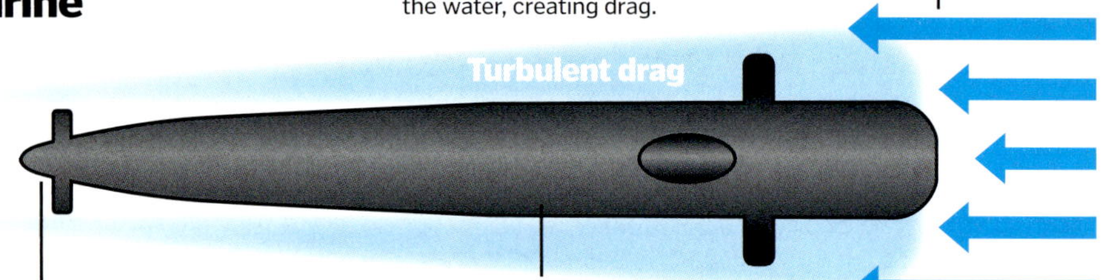

Drag
Friction between the water and submarine resists its motion through the water, creating drag.

Thrust
The submarine's propellers generate thrust, which pushes the submarine through the water.

Speed limit
To reach high velocity, lots of energy is needed to generate an amount of thrust much greater than the drag.

Supercavitating submarine

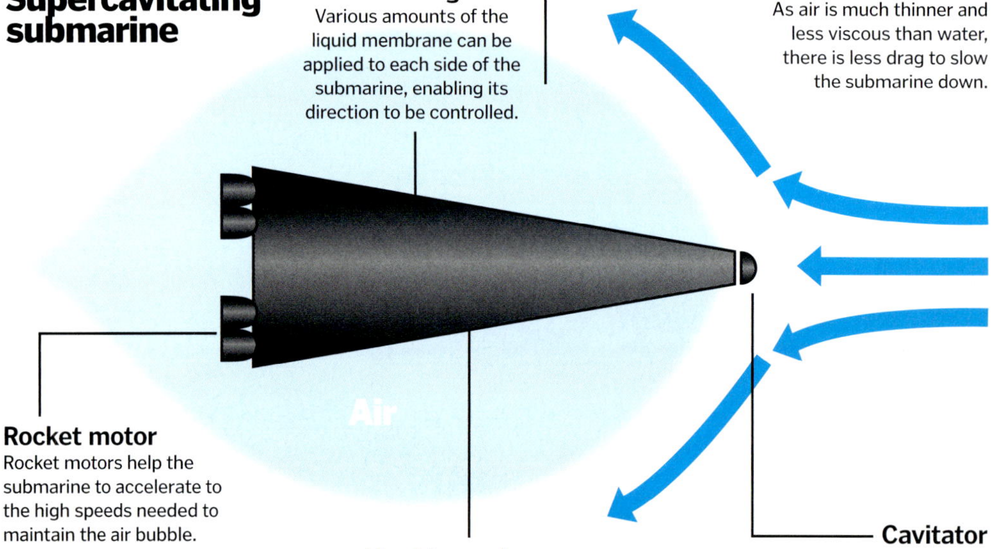

Steering
Various amounts of the liquid membrane can be applied to each side of the submarine, enabling its direction to be controlled.

Less drag
As air is much thinner and less viscous than water, there is less drag to slow the submarine down.

Rocket motor
Rocket motors help the submarine to accelerate to the high speeds needed to maintain the air bubble.

Liquid membrane
When first launched, a special liquid is sprayed over the submarine to reduce drag and get the vessel up to speed.

Cavitator
Once the submarine is travelling fast enough, the cavitator ejects gas from the nose with enough force to create a bubble around the vessel.

Inside the USS Bowfin torpedo room. This sub has since been decommissioned

SUBMARINE DRONES

The autonomous underwater vehicles that render crews unnecessary

Keeping crews safe and alive at sea is a risky and costly business, so it's no wonder that the world's navies are already developing unmanned underwater vehicles (UUVs) to do the dangerous work for them. One particular area where these underwater drones are useful is mine hunting, as they can search for and even destroy underwater explosives while keeping the crews of nearby ships out of harm's way. The US Navy currently uses the Woods Hole Oceanographic Institution's (WHOI) Remote Environmental Monitoring UnitS (REMUS) vehicles for this very purpose, as each one is capable of doing the work of 12 human divers.

It's not just the military that these UUVs can help, as the ability to fit them with a variety of cameras and sensors also makes them useful for conducting scientific research. Underwater drones can survey and monitor places that are incredibly difficult for humans to reach, and gather information about marine wildlife in their natural environment. For example, WHOI's SharkCam drone has enabled scientists to observe the underwater hunting behaviour of great white sharks for the first time, showing that they use the darkness at great depths to avoid detection before ambushing their prey.

Ocean robots

Discover the important roles of unmanned vehicles

1

Sub hunting
The US Navy's Sea Hunter is the world's largest unmanned ship. It can sail on its own for up to three months at a time, using its short-range radar to detect diesel-electric submarines.

Unmanned surface vehicles

2

Deep diving
Built by Boeing, the ECHO Ranger can dive to depths of 3,000 metres, and was developed to capture high-res images of the ocean floor for the oil and gas industry. It is now also being used for underwater intelligence, surveillance and reconnaissance missions.

3

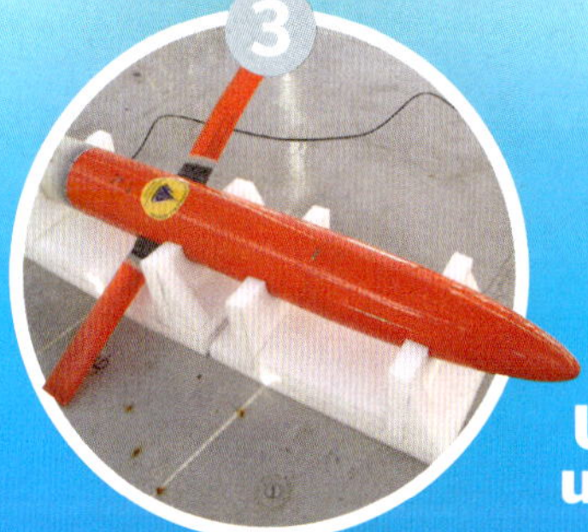

Long-distance gliding
WHOI's Spray Glider uses small changes in its buoyancy, combined with lift from its wings, to propel itself through the water. This means it uses little power, so can travel for 3,600 kilometres at a time, taking scientific measurements from its surroundings over long periods.

Unmanned underwater vehicles

4

Hull inspections
The US Navy's Hovering Autonomous Underwater Vehicle inspects the hulls of ships for explosive devices or damage. Data is gathered by the high-res imaging sonar, then sent to operators on board the ship in real time via a fibre-optic tether.

5

Cargo delivery
The dual-use Proteus submersible can operate autonomously or manned, as it can transport divers or deliver payloads over hundreds of kilometres without human intervention. There's space for up to six people inside, and it has a top speed of 18 kilometres per hour.

6

Harbour protection
Inspired by a tuna fish, the BIOSwimmer drone is being developed for the US Department of Homeland Security to patrol harbours and inspect ships. It has a flexible back section and fins to help it manoeuvre through the water, even in harsh environments.

7

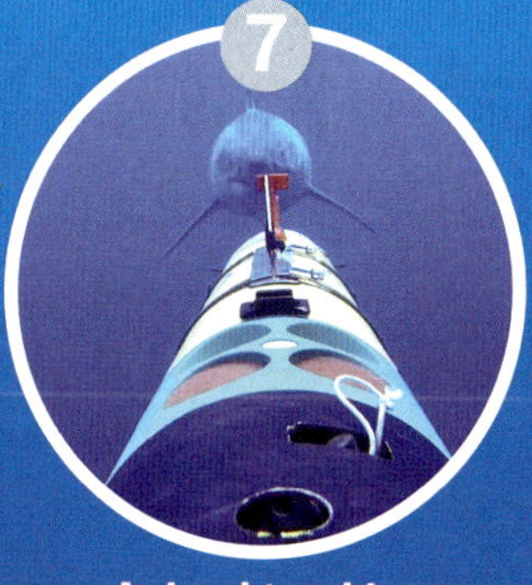

Animal tracking
WHOI has outfitted one of its REMUS UUVs with instruments that enable it to locate, track and film marine animals. The SharkCam is pre-programmed to home in on a signal from a transponder beacon that is attached to an animal such as a great white shark.

Unmanned underwater vehicles

8

Amphibious missions
Capable of flying in the air and swimming underwater, the Naviator is the first amphibious drone. It has to stay tethered to its operator for continuous communications, but should help the military detect and map mines, and assist with search and rescue operations at sea.

9

Mine hunting
Designed to swim ahead of a ship, Saab's Double Eagle SAROV can detect, classify and dispose of mines in the vicinity. It can be remotely operated or function autonomously. Once a mine has been detected, it deploys a smaller mine sniper vehicle to destroy it.

THE FUTURE OF SUBMARINES

What will underwater crafts look like in years to come?

With technology advancing at speed, it will not be long before we find out whether the future of submarines is supersonic, unmanned or something else entirely. In fact, the latter is being explored by defence and security company Saab, and it is currently constructing two new super-stealthy Type A26 submarines for the Swedish Navy. With intelligence gathering and surveillance along coastlines becoming increasingly important, these high-tech submarines will be able to operate in shallow waters, and also feature Genuine HOlistic STealth (GHOST) technology, making them virtually silent and almost impossible to detect.

Per Neilson, program manager for the A26, says: "It will be much quieter, the sensors will be more advanced – detecting and documenting everything that goes on in the sea – and there will be a number of new capabilities such as the multi-mission portal in the bow that allows for the hosting of divers and small manned or unmanned vehicles. It will be a first-class intelligence-gathering platform." The A26 sub will dive to depths of 200 metres and carry a crew of 26. It is due to be completed by 2022.

The A26 submarine will be 62 metres long and weigh around 1,800 tons

GHOST sub

The Swedish Navy's new high-tech submarine that will be invisible in the water

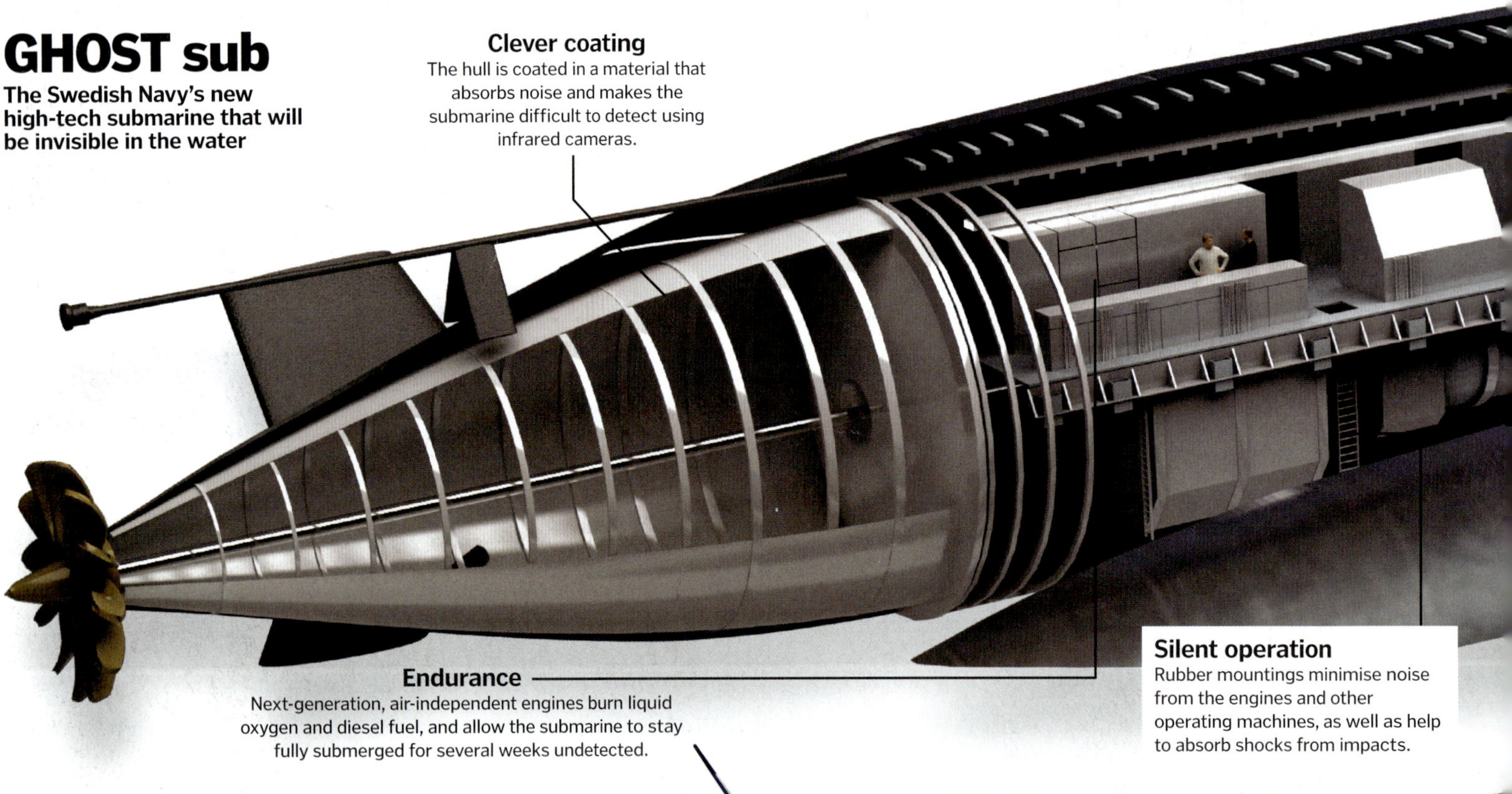

How you can explore the ocean

High-tech submarines aren't just reserved for the world's navies and scientists; DeepFlight has created a personal underwater craft that just about anyone can use to explore the oceans. The Super Falcon Mark II is an electric craft that can be operated with minimal training, and dives to a maximum depth of 120 metres. It can carry two people, a pilot and a passenger, and is small enough to fit on a standard yacht, so you can take it for a dive wherever you are in the world. The submarine is safe to use around marine wildlife, and if you do encounter any trouble, whether it's shark-related or not, it will automatically return to the surface.

The Super Falcon Mark II is the underwater equivalent of an airplane, able to fly through the ocean

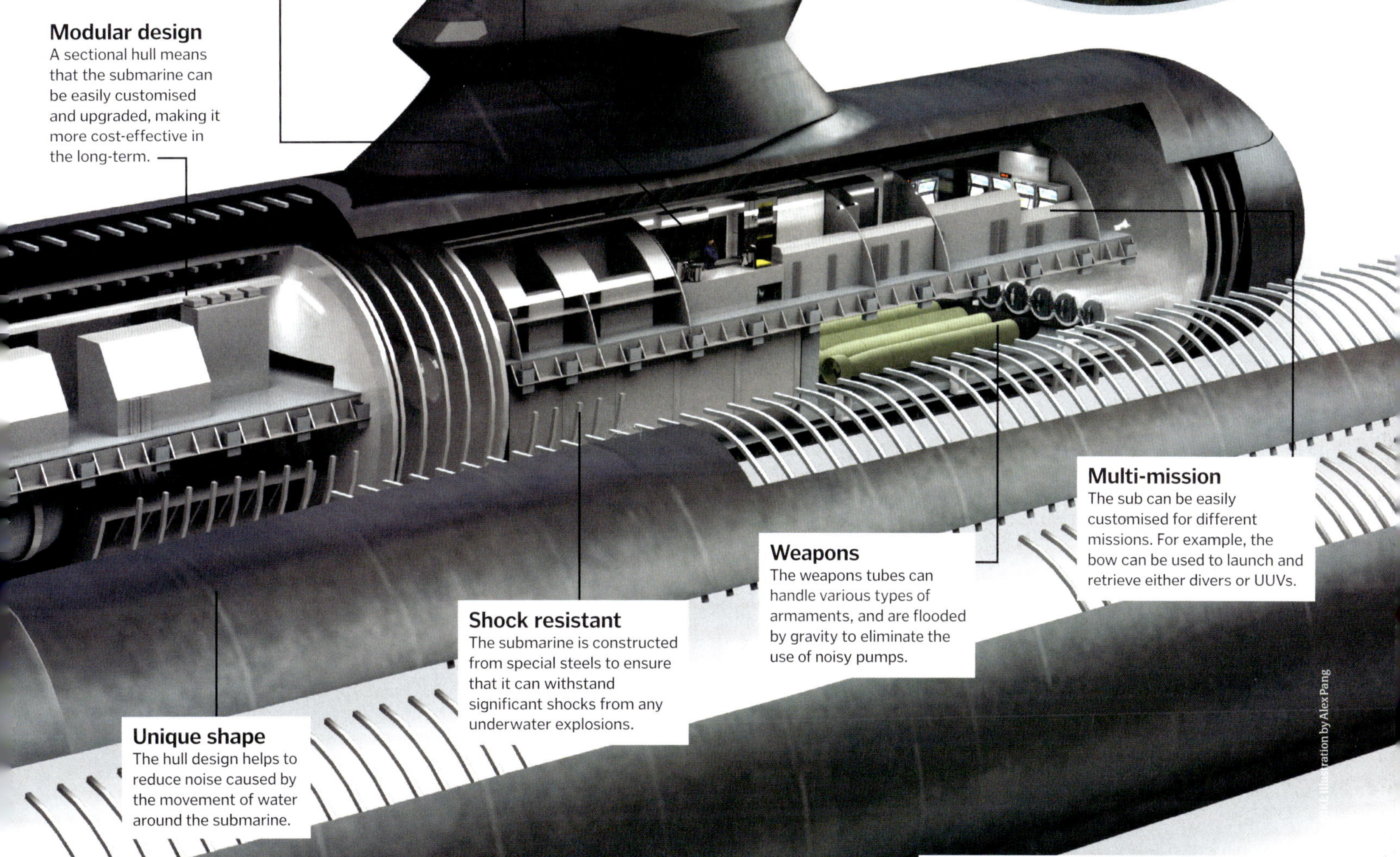

Illustration by Alex Pang

The A26 has a maximum speed of 22 kilometres per hour, and can stay at sea for 45 days at a time

The A26 will be able to withstand temperatures down to -2°C

Divers can be deployed from the sub's bow for stealth missions

TECHNOLOGY

058
Vacations of tomorrow

048
The science of football

047
Inside a wind turbine

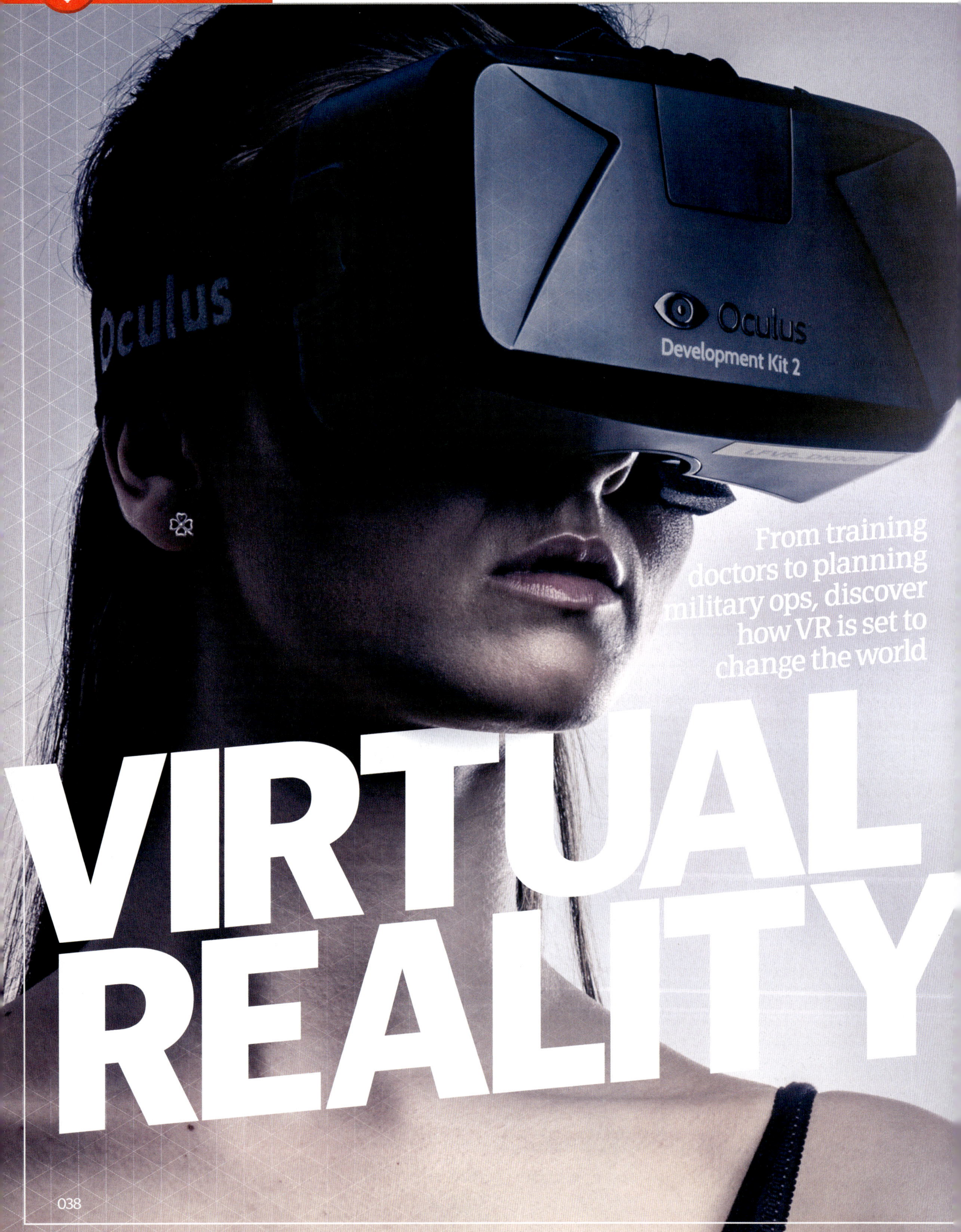

From training doctors to planning military ops, discover how VR is set to change the world

VIRTUAL REALITY

DID YOU KNOW? Jack White has an app that plays a 360-degree video of one of his gigs when viewed using Google Cardboard

This is the year when virtual reality changes life as we know it. That's according to research from Deloitte, which predicts sales to reach $1 billion (£700 million) in 2016 when the Oculus Rift and headsets from Sony, HTC and PlayStation are finally released.

"Head-mounted displays are going to be like toasters," says Dr Albert 'Skip' Rizzo, Director of Medical Virtual Reality at the University of Southern California's Institute for Creative Technologies. "You might not use it every day but everybody's going to have one." Whether you want to step inside the video games you play, or explore far-flung places from the comfort of your sofa, VR is set to usher in an entirely new era of home entertainment.

For some people though, VR is already drastically changing day-to-day life, as the technology has a wide range of uses that extend far beyond gaming. From performing remote surgeries and treating medical conditions, to training soldiers and planning military operations, hundreds of groundbreaking applications are currently being explored.

But while this tech is getting most of us excited, there are some that are left feeling cybersick. The symptoms are similar to motion sickness and it's caused by a mismatch of sensory inputs. The brain expects things to be in sync, but in a simulated scenario, you observe movement – like the rickety track of a rollercoaster – but you don't feel it. It's the opposite of traditional motion sickness, which occurs when you feel movement in your inner ear, but you don't see it. The result is the same though, and it's a big obstacle to making virtual the new reality.

> "Hundreds of groundbreaking applications for VR are currently being explored"

Receiving feedback other than visuals and sound is another issue, as it is difficult to recreate a sense of touch that enables you to fully interact with the world around you. On top of this, virtual reality is currently a solitary experience, as others cannot share what you're viewing through the headset. However, with developers already working on ingenious solutions, such as haptic feedback gloves, wireless tracking technology and programmes that can create avatars of your friends, the virtual future is set to be one of endless possibilities.

Predicted uses of VR by the year 2025

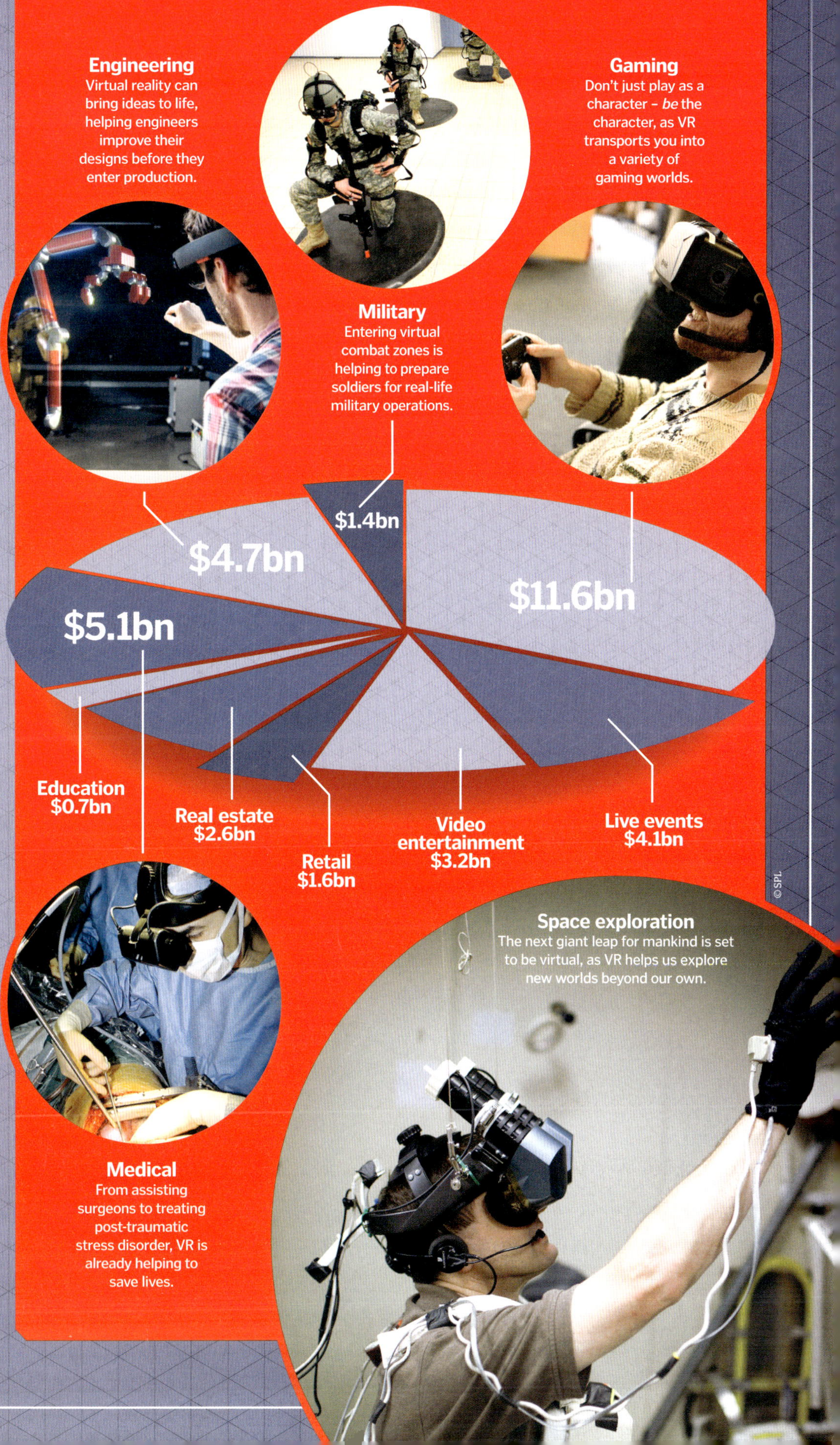

HOW DOES VR WORK?

The kit that transports you into virtual worlds

Several mobile headsets that require your smartphone to work are already available, but it is the high-end connected kits that will really show off what VR can do. The Oculus Rift and HTC Vive are the current front-runners, with the former already available to pre-order for around $600 (£425) and expected to start shipping in March. These headsets feature built-in displays, are powered via a cable and require external sensor systems to track your movements.

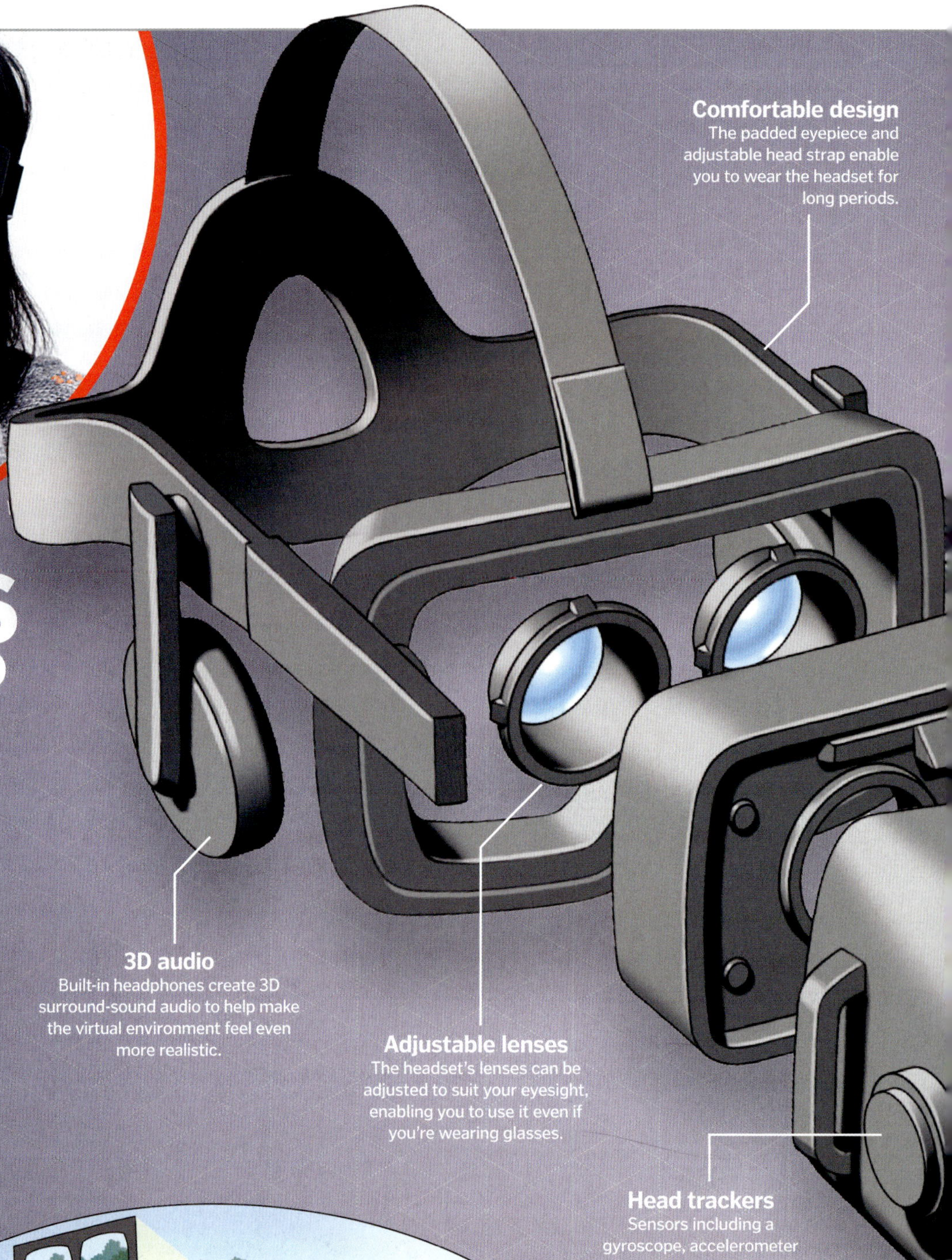

Tricking the brain

How do VR headsets fool you into thinking virtual worlds are real?

Opening the Rift

How does the Oculus headset put you inside the game?

Virtual versus augmented reality

Microsoft's HoloLens may look like a VR headset, but it is in fact an augmented reality device. Rather then cutting you off from the real world to immerse you in a virtual one, the translucent screens that sit in front of your eyes overlay virtual elements onto what you already see.

Forward-facing cameras and sensors on the headset analyse your surroundings so that the 3D holograms can be superimposed onto the objects in front of you. For example, you can transform your living room into a *Minecraft* universe, or project video chat conversations onto your bedroom wall. What's more, the HoloLens is completely wireless, as all of the computing power is built into the headset. This means they you can wear them like a regular pair of glasses as you walk around.

Microsoft's HoloLens is much more than a virtual reality headset

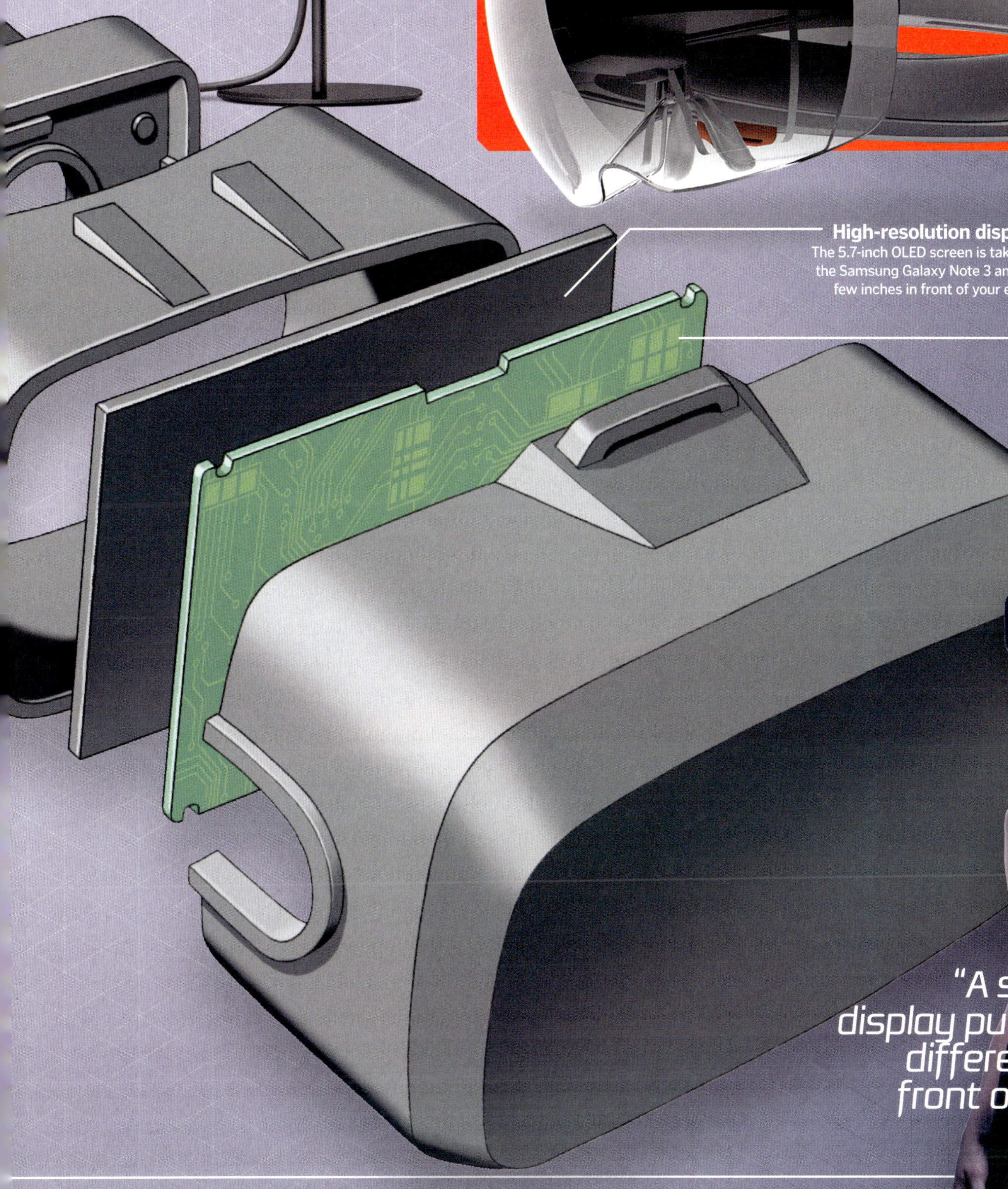

"A split-screen display puts a slightly different image in front of each eye"

NEXT-LEVEL GAMING

Get ready to redefine the meaning of fun

Gaming and other forms of entertainment have been the main driving force fuelling the development of this technology. It's predicted to be the main function for VR in the coming years, and already a wide range of accessories have been designed to enhance the experience. The Virtuix Omni is a motion platform that enables you to walk or run to control your avatar in a virtual world, as opposed to just staying seated and turning your head while you tap at an Xbox controller. Then there's Oculus Touch, a pair of wireless controllers that let you feel as though your virtual hands are your own, meaning you can reach out and interact with objects in the game.

Step into the game

How the Virtuix Omni treadmill lets you take a virtual stroll

Virtual hands

The tech that gives you the power to reach into the game

> "Gaming is predicted to be the main function for VR"

VR coasters and virtual cinemas

You can already ride virtual rollercoasters using a VR headset – so long as you can stomach the slightly nauseous feelings – but one of the UK's biggest theme parks is now taking things a loop further. The new Galactica rollercoaster at Alton Towers requires each rider to pop on a VR headset, making them feel as though they are flying through space while they are in fact hurtling along a track at 75 kilometres per hour.

For the adrenaline averse, there's virtual cinema – apps that recreate the traditional movie theatre experience. Already available for the Oculus and Google Cardboard, they allow you to choose a seat and then enjoy the film without any annoying distractions from popcorn munchers. That's not all though, as film directors such as Ridley Scott are already producing VR content that will enable you to step into the films themselves.

Galactica is the world's first rollercoaster entirely customised for the full virtual reality experience

BATTLEFIELD VR

Forget Call Of Duty – how can virtual reality revolutionise real-life military operations?

Military organisations are often among the first to adopt the latest technological innovations and virtual reality is no exception. There are many potential applications for VR in combat, but British engineers from BAE Systems are working on some truly groundbreaking concepts. They are planning to create a 'mixed reality', using headsets to overlay virtual images, video feeds, objects and avatars onto footage of the operator's actual surroundings, which are recorded by a front-facing camera.

One use for this is in developing a portable command centre that can be transported in a briefcase and set up anywhere. The user would simply put on a headset and interactive gloves, and be able to monitor situations anywhere in the world. This would enable them to direct troops and even bring in artificially intelligent avatars to provide updates and advice. Another use for mixed reality is the 'wearable cockpit', a headset that overlays virtual displays onto the pilot's real-time view, enabling them to customise controls based on their own preferences and mission objectives.

As well as assisting soldiers when they are in battle, VR can also be used to train them before they get there. Headsets can be used to simulate a real-life combat zone, which can be experienced from a safe, controlled environment, keeping the soldier out of harm's way.

Of course, staying stationary during training isn't ideal, so a variety of devices have been designed to give soldiers complete freedom of movement in virtual environments. The Virtusphere is a hollow ball on wheels, which rotates in any direction as the person moves inside. Sensors communicate the user's movements to their VR headset, so their view can be updated accordingly. Alternatively, the Cybersphere is another human-sized hamster-ball, which doesn't even need a headset to create a virtual battlefield.

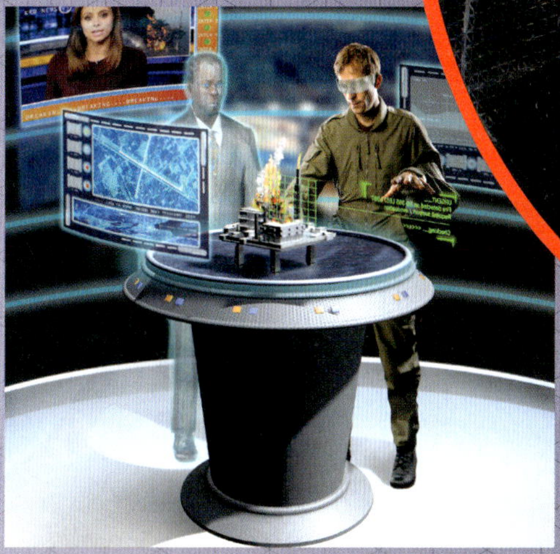

A portable command centre would let military personnel manage emergencies from anywhere in the world

The Virtusphere lets soldiers move freely in a virtual battlefield environment

BAE Systems' wearable cockpit overlays the pilot's view with useful graphics

Step into the Cybersphere

The hamster ball for humans trains soldiers for battle

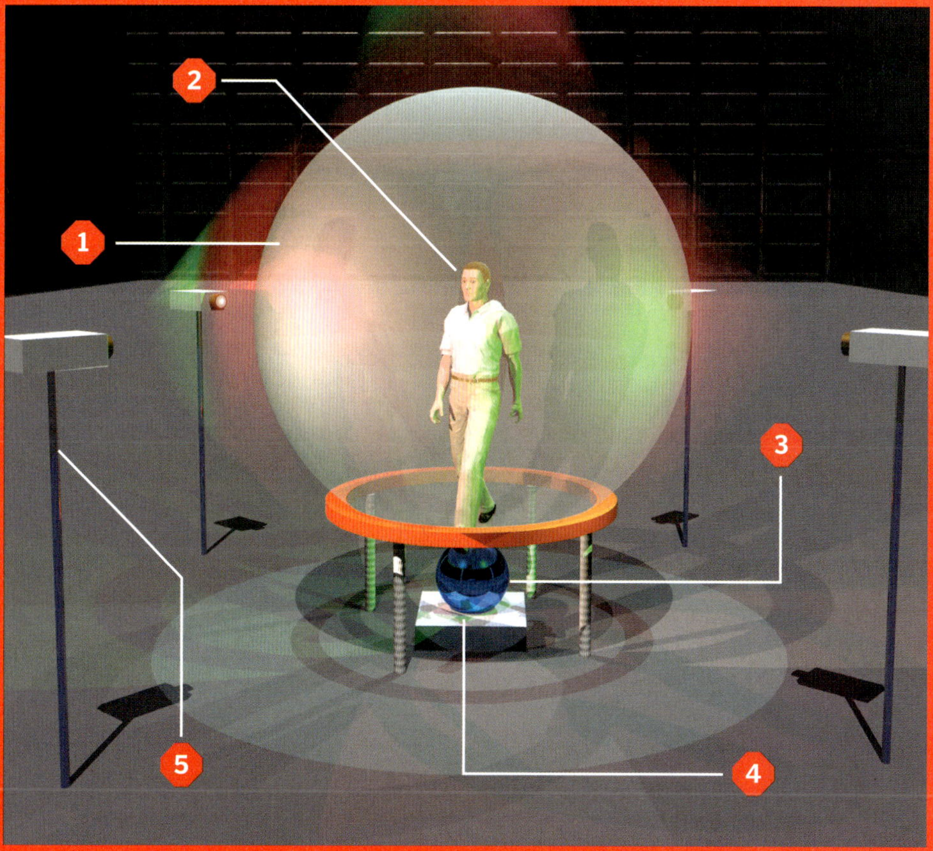

1 Freedom of movement A hollow, translucent sphere measuring 3.5 metres in diameter sits on a cushion of air, which allows it to rotate freely.

2 Rolling around As the user walks, runs or crawls, they cause the sphere to rotate, although the structure itself remains stationary.

3 A second sphere The movement of the large sphere is transferred to a smaller sphere; spring-loaded supports connect the two parts.

4 Motion tracking Rotation sensors record the movements of the smaller sphere to update the images that are then seen by the user.

5 Wrap-around view Images of a virtual world are projected onto the interior walls of the sphere, so the user inside does not need to wear a headset.

GOOD FOR YOUR HEALTH?

The groundbreaking applications in healthcare

In a recent report about the growth of virtual and augmented reality, investment banking firm Goldman Sachs estimates that the industry will be worth $80 billion by the year 2025. It also predicts that, aside from video games, healthcare will be one of the biggest applications for the technology.

Already, VR is being used to train surgeons, allowing them to practise complex procedures on a virtual patient before they get to the real thing, and it can even be used to conduct robotic surgeries too. Wearing a head-mounted display, the surgeon can control a robotic arm that is capable of making smaller, more delicate movements than human hands could ever manage, plus it enables them to operate on a patient remotely from an entirely separate location.

There is also a wide range of applications for which virtual reality can be used to treat patients directly. For example, VR can enable people with phobias and post-traumatic stress disorder to face their fears in a virtual world, in order to help combat them in the real one.

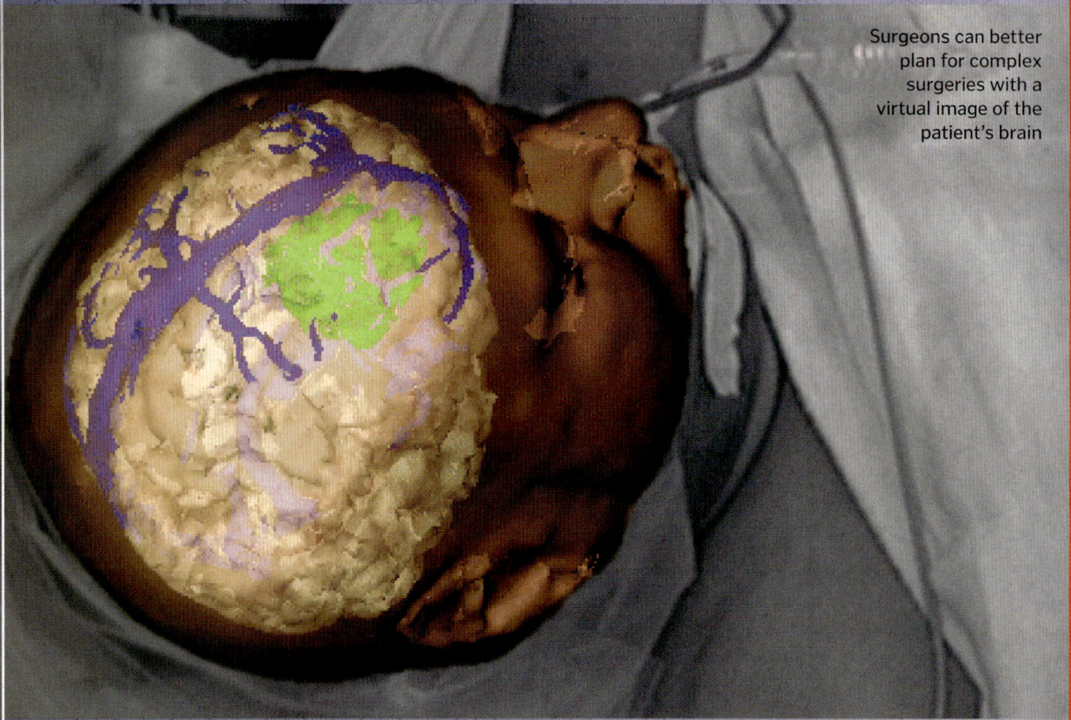

Surgeons can better plan for complex surgeries with a virtual image of the patient's brain

EDUCATION

Discover how VR can really bring lessons to life

Imagine being able to visit outer space or walk with dinosaurs instead of just reading about them in a textbook. Virtual reality could transform the way subjects are taught in the classroom, and one company is already developing a library of experiences that can educate students of all ages.

"Virtual reality offers a new way to view the world," says David Whelan, CEO of Immersive VR Education. "For the first time in humanity we can walk a mile in other people's shoes." The Apollo 11 experience, for example, lets you step onto the Moon as Neil Armstrong. "This is much more powerful than reading about the moon landing in a book," he adds. "Virtual reality has the potential to revolutionise education in the same way that reading and writing did thousands of years ago."

Virtual reality can enable students to experience events from history and impossible-to-visit places

Virtual treatments

At the University of Southern California's Institute for Creative Technologies, Dr Albert 'Skip' Rizzo and his team are using virtual reality for a number of game-changing clinical purposes. We spoke to him about their amazing work...

How are you using VR to treat post-traumatic stress disorder (PTSD)?
One of the typical treatments for PTSD is prolonged exposure therapy. You ask the person to close their eyes and imagine the trauma that they went through as if it's happening right then and get them to describe it to you. By doing that repetitively in a safe and supportive environment, eventually the anxiety that it provokes in them diminishes. It sounds kind of counterintuitive at first but there's actually quite a lot of research to support this. What we do with VR is simply to deliver this previous imagination-only approach in an immersive virtual reality simulation.

We have developed 14 different virtual worlds that represent a diverse range of experiences, and the clinician is able to adjust them in real-time, for example to change the time of day or introduce sound effects. The patient does exactly what they would do in traditional exposure therapy, but the clinician then tries to mimic their experience in the simulation to enhance the effects.

What other clinical VR projects are you working on?
One project is building a job interview training system for people with high-functioning autism – people that are very bright but have a difficult time with social interaction. We've built a simulation that has six different job interviewers, that can be set at three different levels, from a soft touch, nice interviewer to a more hostile interviewer that puts you ill-at-ease, giving them the opportunity to practise. We've also made virtual patients that give clinicians an opportunity to essentially mess up with a digital character before they get to a live one.

Are there limitations of the tech in this field?
The limitations right now have really diminished. I started in this game back in the early 90s, when it required a $200,000 computer, and you had bulky head-mounted displays with low resolution, limited field of view, poor tracking and primitive graphics. There was a network of people that wanted to do this work, but it was challenging because the technology really sucked.

But now the technology has finally caught up with the vision. Computing power has consistently gotten better and faster, which is needed for good rendering, and of course the games industry has driven advances in graphic development that are phenomenal. So the limits right now are the limits of our imagination and the funding to evolve these applications and test them in a consistent way.

Dr Rizzo uses virtual reality simulations to treat post-traumatic stress disorder

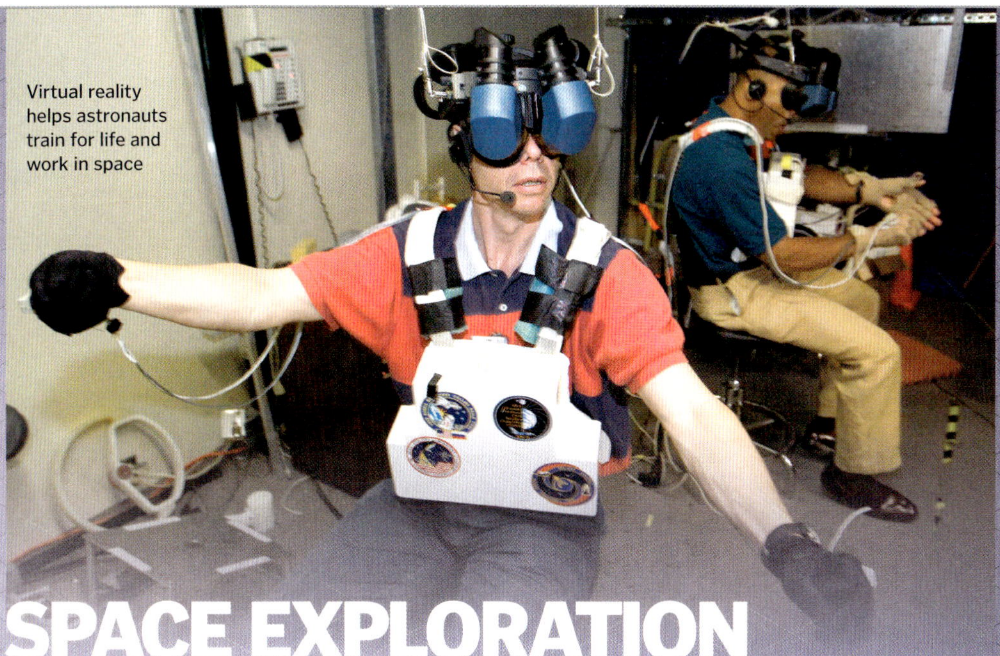

Virtual reality helps astronauts train for life and work in space

SPACE EXPLORATION

A new way to work in space and tour the Solar System

Virtual reality has already become a crucial part of astronaut training, enabling them to practise spacewalks in a virtual environment before doing them for real, and is even being used once they get into space. A Microsoft HoloLens onboard the International Space Station enables ground operators to see through the eyes of the astronauts and provide real-time guidance, as well as project helpful holographic illustrations onto their view.

For tasks that astronauts are not able to do themselves, a head-mounted display enables operators on the ground to see through the eyes of NASA's Robonaut instead, which can then mimic its operator's movements to perform tasks just like a human. Virtual reality also makes it possible to explore other planets from the safety of Earth, as NASA scientists now have the ability to step into images taken by the Curiosity Rover to walk on Mars for the first time.

> "Ground operators can see through the eyes of astronauts and give real-time guidance"

DESIGNING

VR can help visualise engineering designs

When designing a new product, it's difficult to get a sense of what the finished item will be like from 2D illustrations. With virtual reality, designers and engineers can use 3D modelling to create virtual prototypes of ideas, and use a head-mounted display to examine them from all angles. For example, car manufacturers can sit inside the design of a new vehicle to make sure it looks and feels right before they build the real thing. Any tweaks can easily be made in the 3D design, rather than creating a new prototype from scratch.

Microsoft HoloLens will enable engineers to view and interact with their designs in 3D

Virtual world

Stereoscopic tech will touch almost every industry

Archaeology

VR headsets enable archaeologists to walk around places as they would have appeared in the past, giving them a better understanding of what life was really like there. They also make it possible to see ancient sites that are otherwise too remote, dangerous or fragile to visit in person.

Crime solving

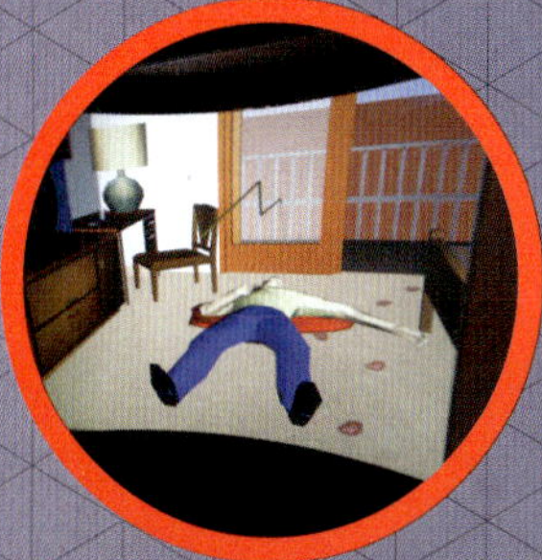

Based on factual data and photographs, 3D reconstructions of crime scenes can be created and explored using head-mounted displays. This enables investigators and even juries to examine the scene in great detail without contaminating any evidence, helping them to deduce what may have happened.

Sport

As well as creating a more immersive way to watch sporting events at home, virtual reality can also be used to improve the athletes' performance. While training in a virtual simulation, their body movements can be monitored in real-time, providing useful feedback to improve their game and help them avoid injury.

Tourism

Before you book your next holiday, your travel agent may be able to give you a taster of your destination using virtual reality. Popping on a headset will transport you to far away places, and even let you visit locations it's not possible, or too expensive, to travel to in real life.

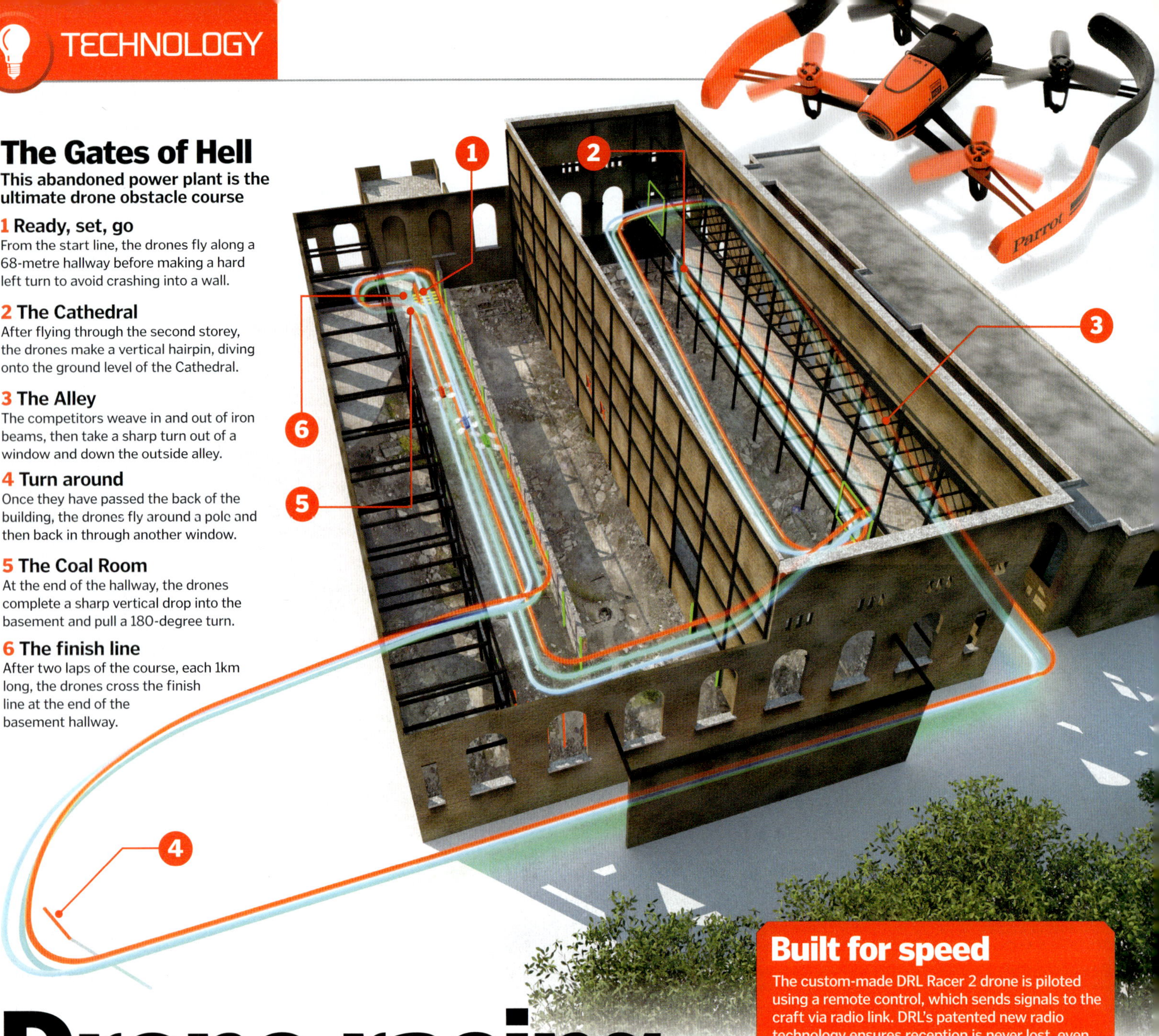

The Gates of Hell

This abandoned power plant is the ultimate drone obstacle course

1 Ready, set, go
From the start line, the drones fly along a 68-metre hallway before making a hard left turn to avoid crashing into a wall.

2 The Cathedral
After flying through the second storey, the drones make a vertical hairpin, diving onto the ground level of the Cathedral.

3 The Alley
The competitors weave in and out of iron beams, then take a sharp turn out of a window and down the outside alley.

4 Turn around
Once they have passed the back of the building, the drones fly around a pole and then back in through another window.

5 The Coal Room
At the end of the hallway, the drones complete a sharp vertical drop into the basement and pull a 180-degree turn.

6 The finish line
After two laps of the course, each 1km long, the drones cross the finish line at the end of the basement hallway.

Drone racing

The new high-octane sport putting quadcopter pilots to the test

Swooping through the air at 130 kilometres per hour, flying through narrow hallways and veering around tight corners, this isn't your average quadcopter flight. In the world of professional drone racing, pilots' skills are pushed to the limits as they manoeuvre their flying machines around some of the toughest obstacle courses on Earth.

One of the biggest tournaments of this kind is the Drone Racing League (DRL), a global competition that sees the world's top drone pilots compete for prize money and, more importantly, world champion status. This Formula 1 for drones features a series of races held in enormous sports stadiums and derelict buildings around the world. All of the competing pilots fly the same model of drone, the DRL Racer 2, in order to test their skills on a level playing field. In each race, they score points by passing checkpoints and finishing the course within the allotted time, and at the end of the heats the pilot with the most points is crowned the winner.

The 2016 season is already underway, with the first race held in New York at a course nicknamed 'The Gates of Hell'. Lit by neon lights and featuring multiple floors, this three-dimensional racetrack is a true test of aerobatic skill as the pilots must fly their drones right, left, up and down at great speed. There are plenty of daring manoeuvres and spectacular crashes to keep the audience entertained and inspire the next generation of master pilots.

Built for speed

The custom-made DRL Racer 2 drone is piloted using a remote control, which sends signals to the craft via radio link. DRL's patented new radio technology ensures reception is never lost, even when the drone flies out of sight through hallways and underground, so the pilot is always in control. HD cameras mounted on the drone transmit a live video feed, also via radio link, to goggles worn by the pilot, enabling them to get a drone's-eye view of the course as if they were in the cockpit.

The drones themselves are made from lightweight carbon fibre, so they only weigh around 800 grams, and can reach top speeds of 130 kilometres per hour. 100 colour LEDs make each quadcopter easily identifiable and are bright enough for the audience to see the action from hundreds of metres away. After every lap, each pilot's drone is replaced with a new fully-charged model, ensuring they can go the distance.

All DRL pilots have a fleet of DRL Racer 2 drones to use for each race

DID YOU KNOW? *The University of Virginia is designing a mega-turbine, with each of its blades wider than two Airbus A380 planes*

Inside a wind turbine

The process of generating clean electricity from the power of the wind

Wind turbines are a familiar sight on hilltops and coastlines, their huge blades turning high above the ground. They're tall for a reason – as wind flows over the land and around buildings, it's broken into uneven packets of air that are too slow to turn a turbine's enormous blades. To capture the smoothest, fastest wind, the blades need to be far off the ground.

Each of the turbine's blades shares its shape with bird and airplane wings – they are rounded on one surface and flat on the other. This design is called an aerofoil and gives the blade lift as it turns, so it can use the energy from wind more effectively. Inside the wind turbine's cabin, the rotating blades are connected to an electric generator via a heavy-duty gearbox. Essentially, it acts like a set of bike gears; every time the blades complete one rotation, a shaft on the other side of the gearbox rotates 30 times. The generator's job then is to turn all of this kinetic – or moving – energy into electrical energy.

For this it uses electromagnetic induction, where a moving wire in a magnetic field produces electricity. In a wind turbine's generator, a huge magnet surrounds a loop of wire connected to the gearbox's shaft. Thanks to the wind, the blades rotate, spinning this wire up to 1,800 times every minute, and generating a stream of electricity in the process.

Wind turbines are usually found near the coast or on hilltops

What can we use wind energy for?

In countries like Denmark, wind turbines produce enough electricity to power millions of homes, and it makes its way to them via the grid – a nation-wide network of cables and pylons. However, the amount of electricity they produce is tricky to manage, because wind turbines produce electricity intermittently (only when the wind blows). Often, much of the electricity they produce is wasted, but the German city of Mainz has a found a clever way to harvest this surplus electricity. By using it to split water (H_2O) into hydrogen and oxygen, it can produce hydrogen gas, which is perfect for use in emission-free fuel cell cars.

Behind the blades

Hidden inside the sleek structure is a complex system that turns wind into electricity

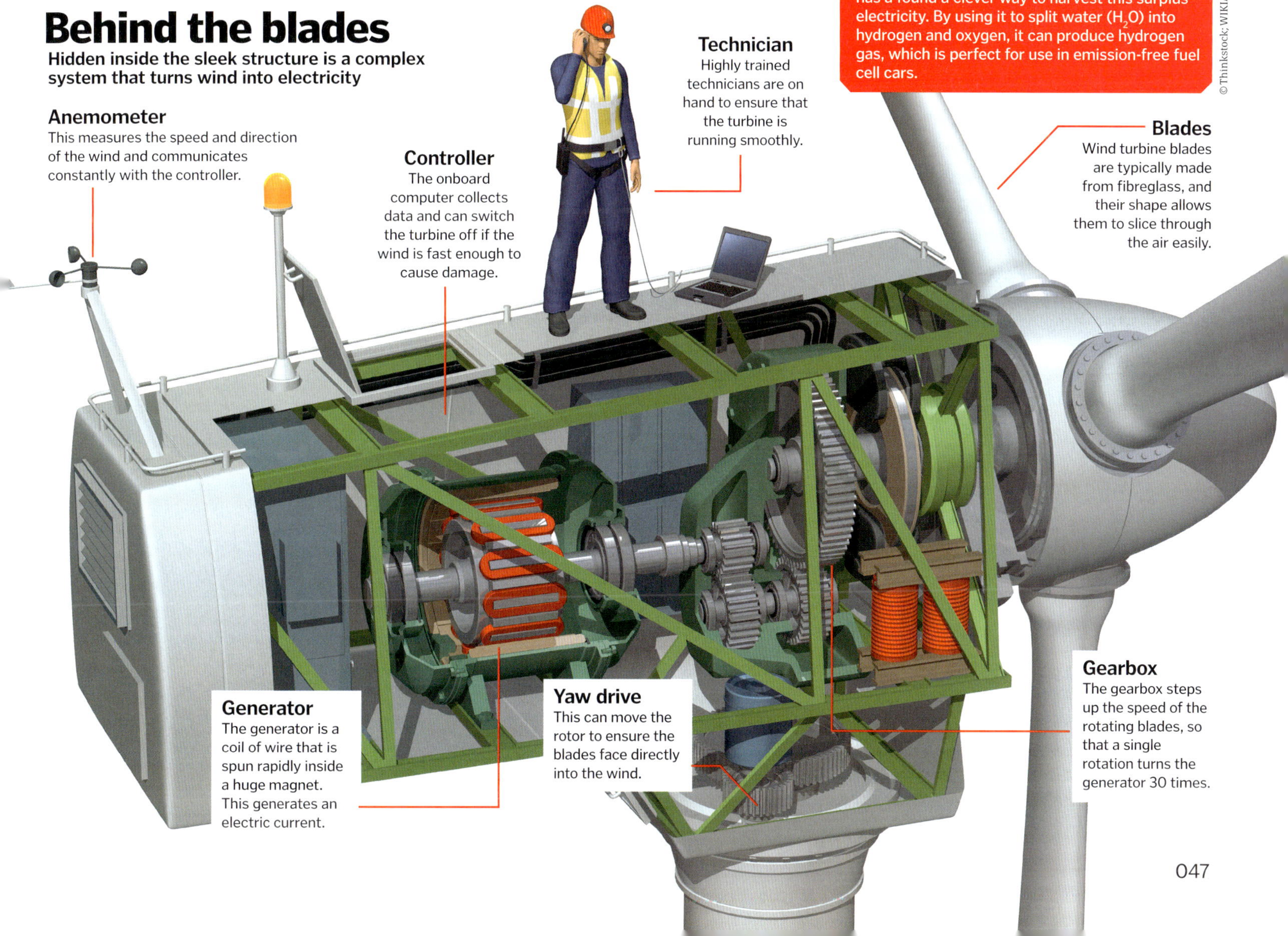

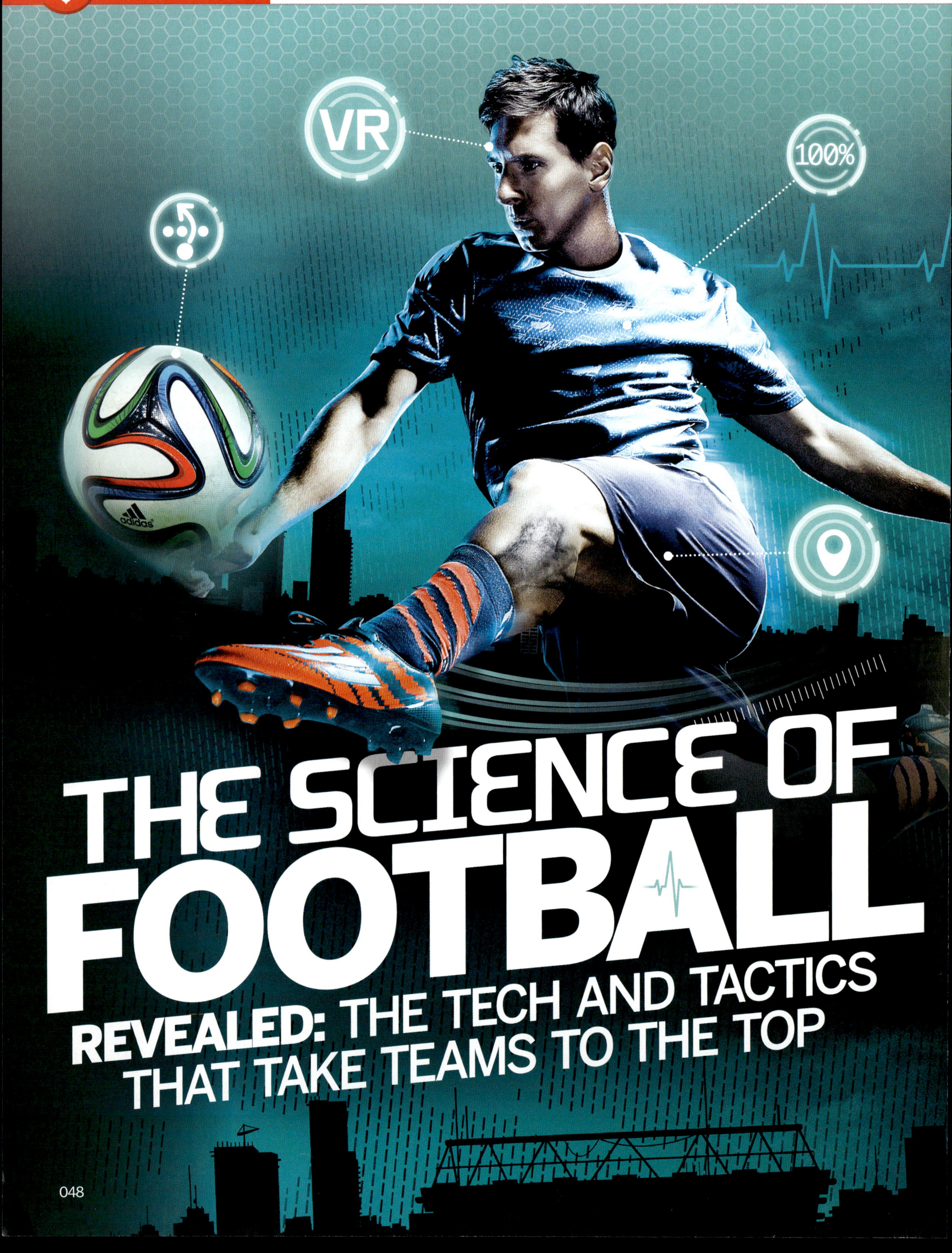

THE SCIENCE OF FOOTBALL

REVEALED: THE TECH AND TACTICS THAT TAKE TEAMS TO THE TOP

> "We can predict what a football match of the future may be like based on current tech"

Picture it now: it's the 2050 World Cup final. Three-time winners China are facing off against Germany in the newly renovated Wembley Stadium. Around the world, millions of fans sit in their homes wearing virtual reality (VR) headsets; they all have the best seat in the house, right on the half-way line for kick-off. As the first goal is scored, the VR viewpoint switches to that of the player and suddenly millions of people are seeing the goal as the striker saw it, then as the goalkeeper, then from behind the goal. Those that couldn't get to their VR headsets watch the replay projected as a 3D hologram by their smartphones, and as the players run to the corner to celebrate with their fans, biometric sensors built into their kits, or even their skin, give the team managers minute-by-minute readouts of their fitness levels.

It might sound far-fetched, but when you think back to football matches just 20 or 30 years ago, it's astonishing how far the game has come in such a short time. Some of the things we take for granted in the modern game still weren't even part of the rules back then – did you know, for example, that shin pads weren't even made compulsory by FIFA until 1990? When you consider what has changed, the concepts above don't seem so unlikely.

Recent advancements in tech like VR, camera systems and even kit design have meant that the latest competitions have been the most sophisticated yet. And, with more and more technology being introduced at each tournament, the future of the beautiful game is likely to be one that is as reliant on computers and smartphones as it is on players at the top of their game.

The exciting thing is that we can predict what a football match of the future may be like based on the technology that has been added to the game in recent years, and advancements that are being developed right now. Whether it's simple things, like the disappearing spray now carried by referees, or more cutting-edge tech like cameras that allow for 3D replays, read on to discover how football matches will evolve even further in the next few years.

World Cup tech

The gadgets and gizmos that made the 2014 World Cup the most advanced yet

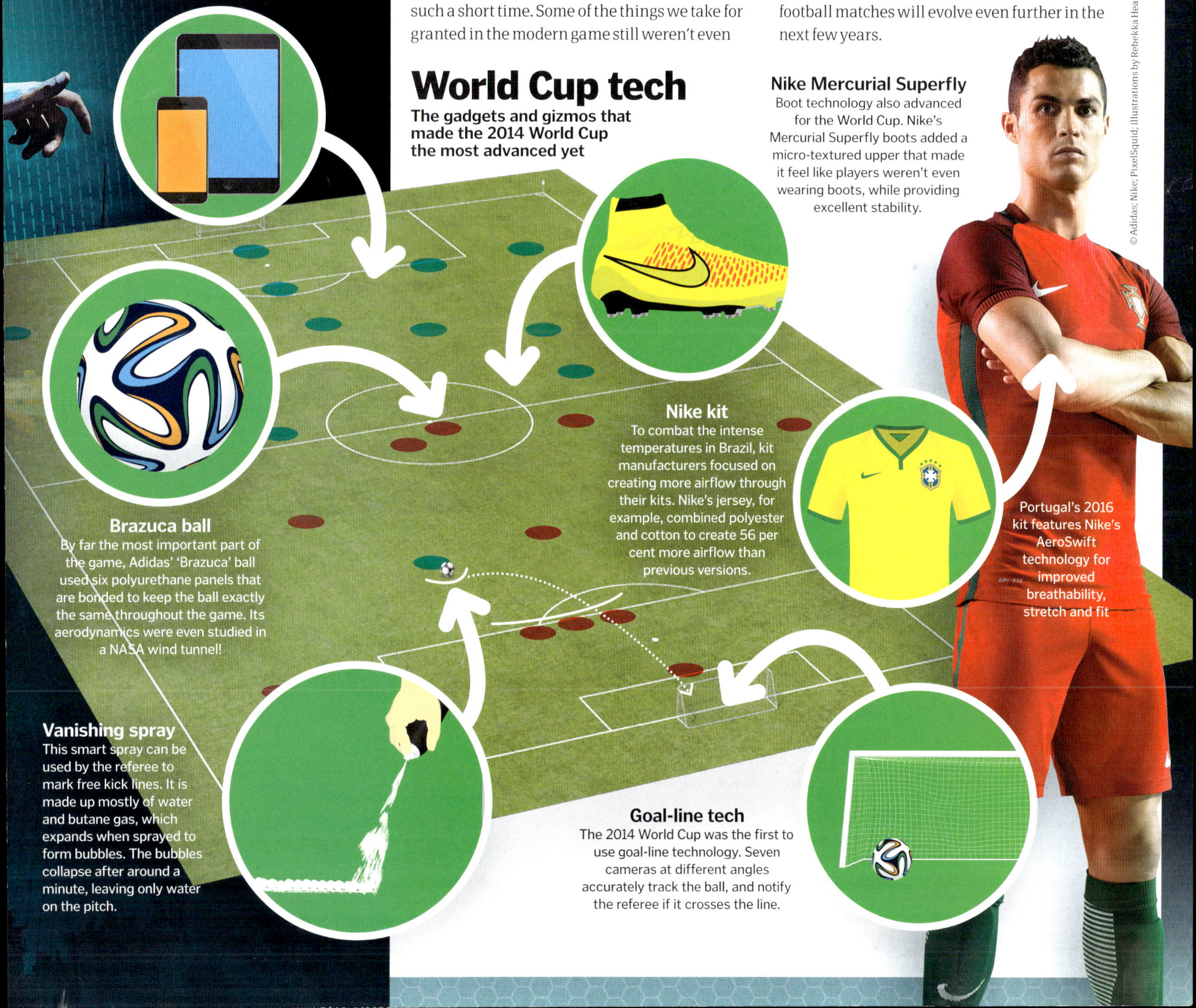

Individual aspects of a player's game can be closely analysed

TRAINING TEAMS OF THE FUTURE

The techniques that will take footballers to the next level

While many of the advancements in the sport over the next few years will certainly be in the stadium, on the pitch and in the homes of fans, some of the biggest changes will actually occur away from the cameras. Training sessions are being transformed as coaches learn more about how athletes' bodies work, as are the ways in which players prepare for their next big match.

New technology, like the Adidas MiCoach smart ball, now allows training sessions to be tracked more closely, and individual aspects of a footballer's game to be closely analysed on the training field. Sensors built into the ball present data about each kick – for example, you can see how hard a shot was struck, follow the flight trajectory, and reveal impact points to help give more insight into how the player is performing. The information feeds straight into a smartphone app via Bluetooth, so players and coaches can instantly see how to get more curl on a free kick, generate more kicking power, or take better penalties.

Virtual reality training

Players are using VR systems to improve without even having to move a muscle

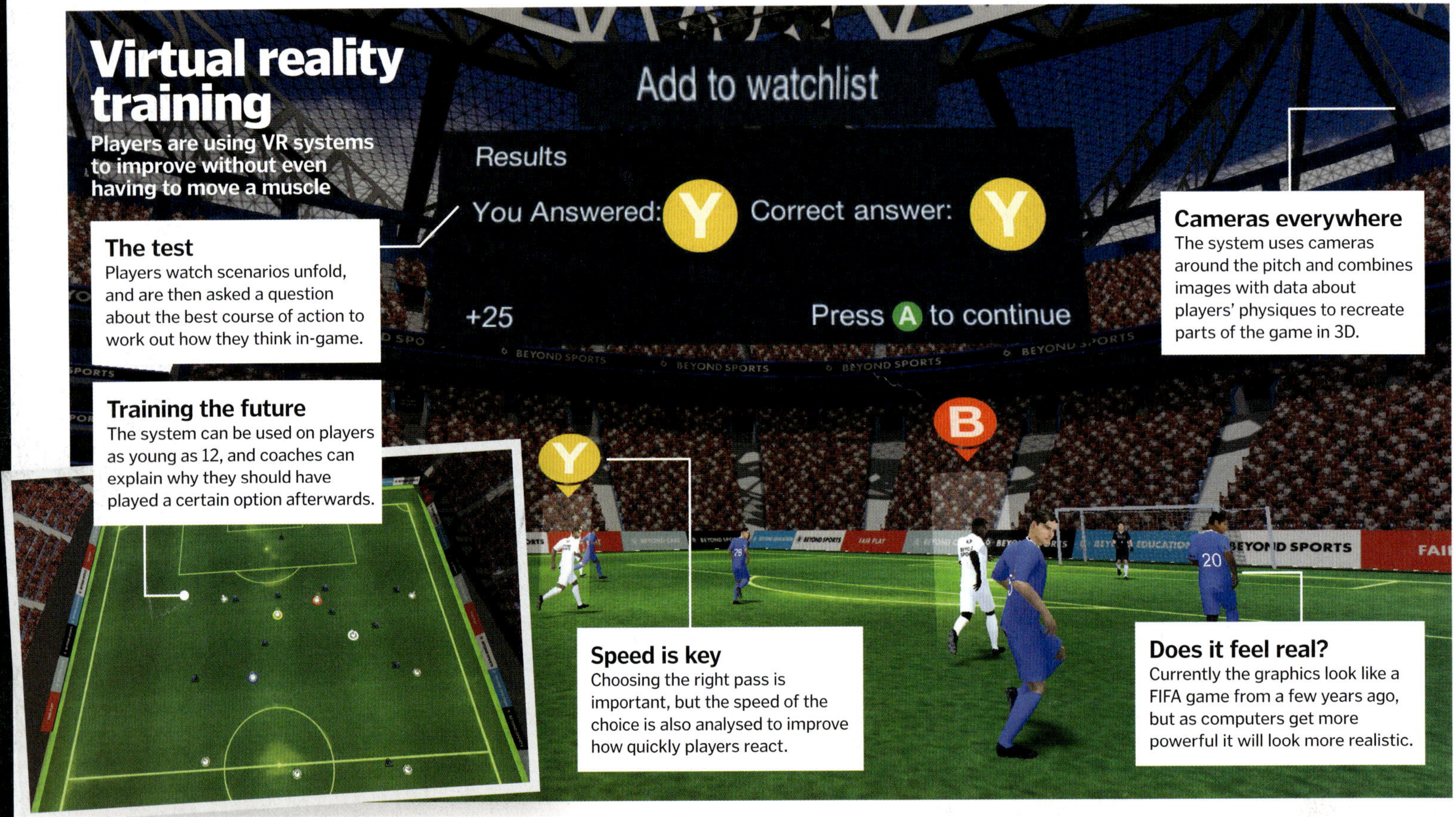

The test
Players watch scenarios unfold, and are then asked a question about the best course of action to work out how they think in-game.

Training the future
The system can be used on players as young as 12, and coaches can explain why they should have played a certain option afterwards.

Speed is key
Choosing the right pass is important, but the speed of the choice is also analysed to improve how quickly players react.

Cameras everywhere
The system uses cameras around the pitch and combines images with data about players' physiques to recreate parts of the game in 3D.

Does it feel real?
Currently the graphics look like a FIFA game from a few years ago, but as computers get more powerful it will look more realistic.

Q&A Professor David Sumpter reveals the maths behind the match

What are the similarities and differences between maths and football?
At first sight they look very different. One is a game where you kick the ball about and the other is a mental activity. But when you dig a bit deeper, there are real similarities. Maths is not as abstract as we sometimes paint it. Solving applied maths problems involves lots of the spatial thinking and problem solving that confronts footballers. There is also a lot of theory, in terms of formations and tactics, in football and this requires logical thinking very similar to mathematics.

Do footballers actually use maths when training and on the pitch?
They do, and they have done for a long time! I was speaking with ex-Chelsea and Everton player Pat Nevin about this recently. He told me that when he played for Scotland in the 1980s they would plan attacking triangles. So, long before the current interest in data in football, coaches would use mathematical concepts to describe how they wanted their teams to play. What I have found in my research is that a lot of the patterns of play we see on the pitch are mathematically optimised. The positioning of the players uses space efficiently and maximises the chance of a pass being successful.

How can maths help a team win a penalty shootout?
The secret of a good penalty is unpredictability. Of course the striker needs to hit the ball hard and a long way from the keeper, but choosing the side is the difficult part. If you always kick to a random side then

DID YOU KNOW? *Patents filed by major tech companies like Apple show ideas for smartwatch bands that analyse sweat*

Coaches are also focusing on how to get more from the players physically, and modern tech is helping to prolong the fitness of top professionals. In the 2014 World Cup, for example, the England team had coolers filled with drinks, each one tailored to a specific player's needs. Exercise scientists, coaches and nutritionists worked together with experts from a university to create drinks customised for each player, with different electrolytes depending on the amount of fluid that each player lost during the match. In future, kits will likely include sensors that can accurately track a player's physical state, from their temperature to their pulse, and tailored drinks could be made up by machines on the side of the pitch to give them what they need to perform.

Training sessions are no longer just a place to work on your own game, but to study the opponents' too. Tablet computers are regularly provided to players, which contain notes and videos on specific members of the opposition team. In the future, VR systems may allow players to relive moments in virtual environments to study the movements of opposition players. Technology will, undoubtedly, improve the quality of football in the next few years, as well as the way we watch.

Tracking the action

Technology that tracks a player's status might sound like something we can expect 20 years from now, but thanks to the Viper Pod, it's already here. The device weighs less than 50 grams and is just eight centimetres tall, slipping into the pocket of a custom-made base layer. A built-in GPS module allows the player's position to be tracked without the use of cameras, and the accelerometer and gyroscope can measure acceleration, collisions and more. There's even a heart-rate monitor that reads a player's pulse. The data is sent to a computer, so coaches can see these real-time stats, as well as analyse it later. It's currently used by Manchester United, Barcelona, Juventus and many other teams for training, with more being added to the list all the time. Soon, we may know if that big-name player really is giving 110 per cent!

© PixelSquid

There are multiple sensors built into the Viper Pod to track a player's movement and body status

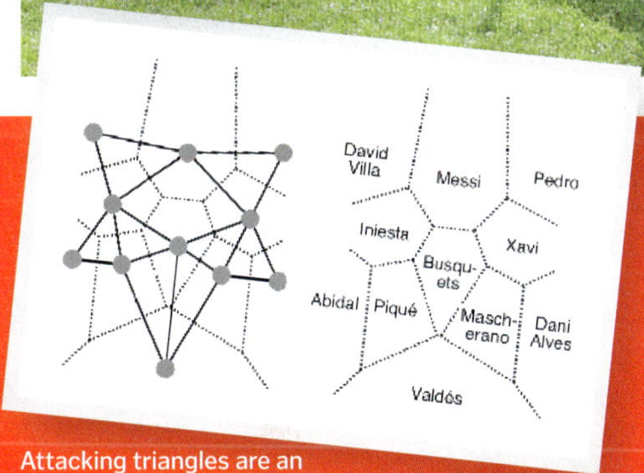

Attacking triangles are an example of maths in football

the keeper has no way of predicting which way the ball will go.

How can maths be used to train footballers?

I think it is an important part of training. Football players are typically intelligent people and it is important to explain to them 'why' some things work on the pitch and why others don't. It is here that maths comes in. It shouldn't be explained so much in equations but in concepts like angle, spin and passing networks.

What's your favourite example of football maths?

It's hard to choose! The book is full of them. Here are a few:

- Understanding how the technical staff create half-time maps of the opposition's playing style to identify weaknesses.
- Making player forecasts, comparing how Andrea Pirlo stands in the eye of a storm and how Bastian Schweinsteiger creates a whirlwind.
- Learning about what player stats do and don't tell us, and how teams use them on the transfer market.
- Listening to chants spread through the ground and understanding why songs grow exponentially.

Soccermatics by David Sumpter is out now, published by Bloomsbury

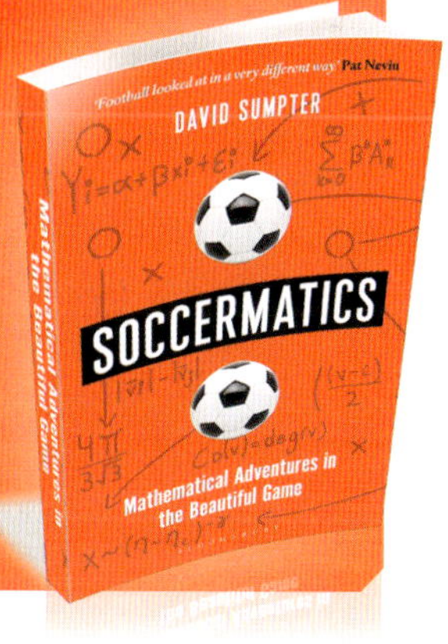

The next-gen stadium

What new tech will soon be packed into the pitch and stands?

Lighting made smarter

LEDs now make lighting more efficient, but balloons carrying special coloured bulbs could create a more ambient natural light that would make evening games more comfortable to watch.

GETTING A DRONE'S-EYE VIEW

As drone technology gets smaller and cheaper, we may well see them buzzing over the pitch. The important thing here is for the drones to be so small and light that, if the ball struck them, they wouldn't change its trajectory or deflect it towards the goal, for example.

Tiny drones could even be piloted by fans wanting to watch on their phones

Personalised ads

If augmented reality becomes more commonplace, fans could start seeing personalised advertising while they watch the game, showing products they are actually interested in.

Flying cameras

While drones are currently large and easily damaged, soon the technology will be so small that tiny cameras could fly above the game, following players without disrupting the match.

"LET'S SEE THAT AGAIN… IN 3D"

The FreeD system currently used in NBA uses a series of cameras to capture a moment from every angle. Software combines these viewpoints and creates '3D pixels' to draw a view of the event in 3D space. The footage plays, then pauses – allowing the camera to spin around the subject and create a 3D picture of the scene – before the action completes.

The camera system freezes the action and spins around it, giving a 3D view

Player-worn cameras

As technology advances, it will be easier for cameras to be included in kits, so fans can relive goals from the point of view of the scorer.

THE TECH-DRIVEN FAN EXPERIENCE

How new advancements will change the way we watch the game

For the moment, there really isn't anything like sitting in the stands with tens of thousands of fans as you cheer for your favourite team. However, in the future, things could be very different. While currently fans pay a premium to watch a game, soon they may be accessible to everyone via the power of VR. Special camera set-ups can now film a full, 360-degree view that records video for VR playback. Soon, these may be used to broadcast games live to VR devices around the world, which would allow you to slip on a headset and watch the game as if you were sitting in the stadium.

Combine these visuals with a specially designed seat that vibrates alongside the chanting, cheering or foot-stamping of the crowd, and a surround-sound headset that records the sound from inside the stadium, and you'd be experiencing something close to what the fans with tickets see and hear.

Even better, with multiple camera rigs around the stadium you could change your seat throughout the game, so you're always behind the goal when your team scores. This

DID YOU KNOW? *The smallest camera-carrying drone measures less than four centimetres across and can stream 420p video*

Smart camera systems
Much like the goal-line system, cameras may be positioned around the stadium to help referees make decisions about penalties and other key moments in the match.

Maintaining the surface
Sensors will soon be built into pitches to monitor the hardness and wetness of the surface, as well as the player and ball position.

Live data
The big screens in stadia currently show replays of goals and display team information, but this could be taken further with live stats or other facts about the game.

THE MAGIC SPRAY
You may have seen physios charging onto the pitch to fix a player with a 'magic spray'. Of course, this concoction is actually just a mix of chemicals that reduce pain and swelling, increase blood flow to aid tissue repair, or dissipate heat around the site of the injury.

The 'magic spray' rapidly relieves pain so players can get back to the game

Pitch-level cameras
There may soon be cameras that rise out of the pitch to track the action from ground level. Sensors would allow them to retract automatically if players are nearby.

Augmented reality
VR might help fans at home to feel like they're in the stadium, but augmented reality could also allow fans watching live to see stats and replays on special glasses while watching the game.

experience may be a few years away, but it's an exciting prospect. Something that will likely happen a little sooner, though, is the addition of detailed player stats for fans, both at home and in the stadium. As sensors like the Viper Pod become smaller and more common, fans can compare the performances of their favourite stars and cheer on the players who are reaching exhaustion, as well as make suggestions for how to change formations or make substitutions based on performance.

Sofa fans will soon get the same experience as those inside the stadium

> "As body sensors become more commonplace, data can be broadcast to fans"

THE FUTURE OF FOOTBALL

How much will the beautiful game have changed by 2050?

While much of the tech mentioned in this feature is already being developed, or is available right now, we couldn't blow the final whistle without looking a little further into the future of football. By 2050, technological advances will have changed the game that we know and love so that it goes far beyond virtual reality and goal-line sensors.

By then, technology like 'active skin' will allow computers to link to the nervous systems of players. At first, this will be used to track players' physiological data in real-time, but as the technology advances it will become more expansive. When training, a player's movements will be tracked in real-time, and neural stimulation will help players tweak their technique to bring it close to what the computer would consider 'perfect'.

Spectators might be able to watch miniature 3D recreations of games at home on their coffee tables, and they could be in control of the camera angle. But why stop there? Beyond 2050, we could see fans actually controlling the players on the pitch via an android! Excited? You only have 35-50 years to wait...

The footballer of 2050

Preview the gadgets players could be sporting

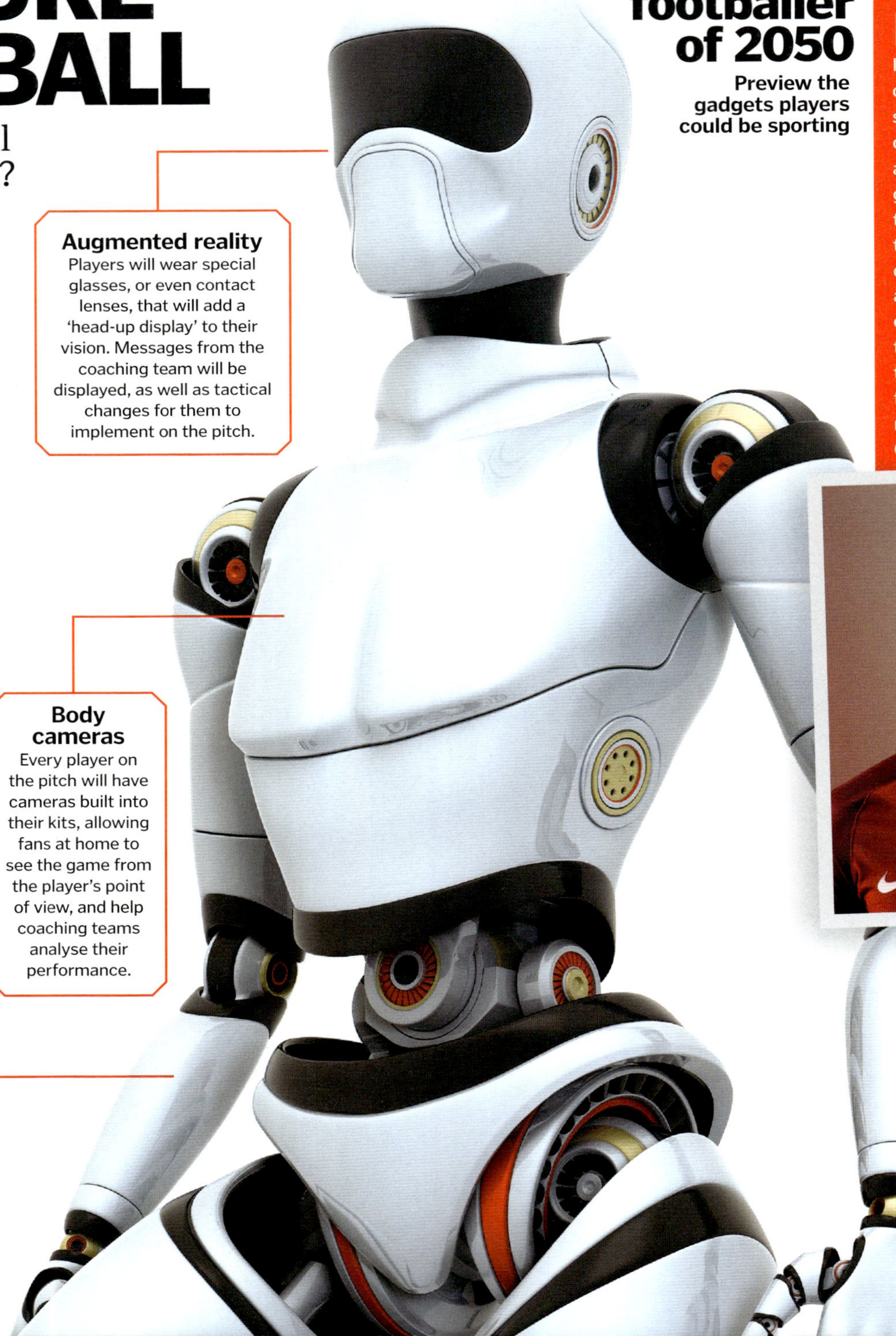

Augmented reality
Players will wear special glasses, or even contact lenses, that will add a 'head-up display' to their vision. Messages from the coaching team will be displayed, as well as tactical changes for them to implement on the pitch.

Body cameras
Every player on the pitch will have cameras built into their kits, allowing fans at home to see the game from the player's point of view, and help coaching teams analyse their performance.

Biometrics
Each player's biometric data will be analysed by sensors either sewn into their kits or embedded in their skin, giving fans and coaches extensive access to stats and player information.

Building the perfect player

If you've ever watched clips from the RoboCup championships – with teams of Nao robots shuffling towards a ball and frequently falling over – you wouldn't think that android football has any hope of taking the place of the real deal. The goal of RoboCup is to develop an autonomous team of droids capable of beating the top human team by 2050, but the project is still in its early days. With continued advancements in robotics and artificial intelligence, these androids could even be capable of learning from footage of today's legends. A robot that combines Ronaldo's trademark free-kicks with Neymar's unbelievable flicks and Messi's close control could well be named humanoid of the match in the 2050 World Cup final.

RONALDO

NEYMAR

MESSI

Future football tech

Robot cameras, holographic replays and more

2020s

- Retractable cameras in turf
- Active contact lenses
- Referee augmented reality tools

2030s

- Tiny drone cameras follow players
- 'Active skin' used for health monitoring
- Pitch condition data sensors

2040s

- Real-time player data available
- Audio links to coach allowed
- 3D holographic smartphone replays

2050s

- Sensory simulation – fans 'feel' the game
- Online players compete in 'real' games
- Robot football starts becoming commonplace

2060s

- Fans control android players
- Smart ads based on the fans' physiological data
- Full android leagues set up

"By 2050, 'active skin' will allow computers to link to the nervous systems of players"

The ultimate ball
The football of 2050 will be far more than a bag of air. It will be packed with impact sensors to track shot power, as well as GPS sensors to give specific location data for decisions like penalties.

Sensory gloves
Sensors built into a goalkeeper's gloves could link to sensors built into a fan's skin, simulating the feel of the ball as they make a save. Combined with VR this would be an incredible experience.

Android players
Fed up of your team losing every week and wish you could control players? That could become reality in 2050 – leagues of human-controlled robots may be ready for kick-off.

Powered-up boots
Accelerometers built into shoes will be commonplace, with live data combining with that captured by the ball to analyse every kick a player makes, both live and after the game.

The next-gen football will be packed with cool tech like impact sensors

3D without glasses

Throw away those tired old specs and immerse yourself in a 3D movie at home

With more and more 3D content heading our way, 3D TVs are the latest must-have in home entertainment. However, there's one big disadvantage; most people don't want to wear a pair of chunky 3D glasses while sitting in their living room. Unfortunately, without the glasses, the picture is just a blur, as they are needed to filter the light that reaches the viewer's eyes so that each one sees a different image.

Now though, TV manufacturers are experimenting with glasses-free 3D, which uses a technique known as autostereoscopy. A parallax barrier is placed in front of the screen to direct a different image to each of the viewer's eyes. For 2D content, the barrier can be deactivated, but at the touch of a button the picture can be made to jump out at you on the sofa. Normally for this to work, the viewer would need to sit in a 'sweet spot' directly in front of the screen, but software can be used to form strips of images, creating additional viewing points, so multiple people can enjoy the 3D action together.

2D viewing

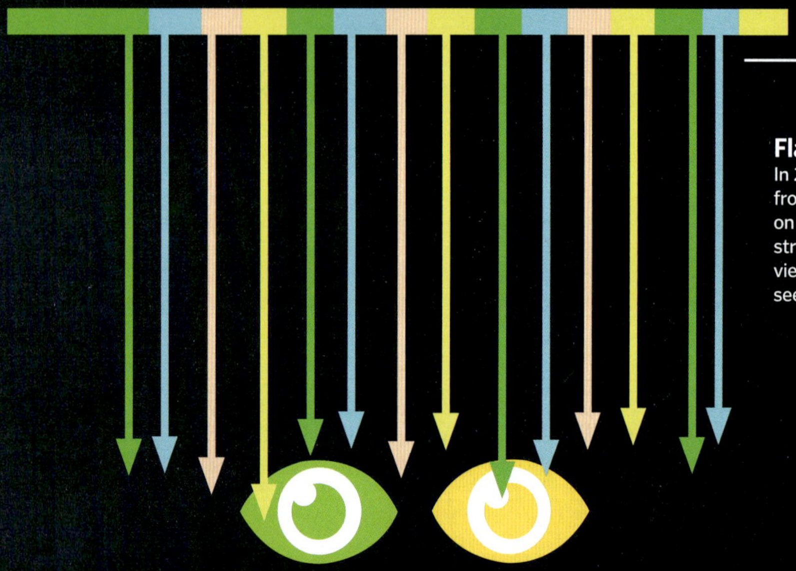

Flat image
In 2D mode, light from all of the pixels on the screen travel straight to the viewer, so each eye sees the same view.

3D viewing

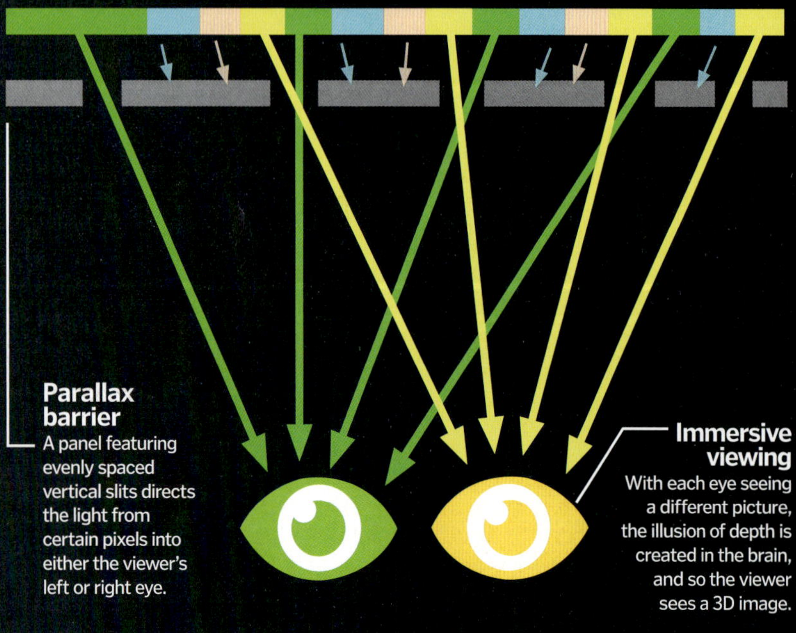

Parallax barrier
A panel featuring evenly spaced vertical slits directs the light from certain pixels into either the viewer's left or right eye.

Immersive viewing
With each eye seeing a different picture, the illusion of depth is created in the brain, and so the viewer sees a 3D image.

How juicers work

The machines that can turn the contents of your fruit bowl into a refreshing drink

There are a few different types of juicer you can buy for your kitchen. Some use a corkscrew-like device to squeeze the juice from the fruit, but the most common are centrifugal juicers, which work through spinning.

When the fruit is pushed through the feed tube at the top, it falls into a basket, which acts as a centrifuge. A centrifuge is any machine that spins its contents in one continuous direction, and the ones found in juicers can spin at over 97 kilometres per hour. An electric motor spins the basket, which has a grater at the bottom to chop the fruit into smaller pieces.

As the fruit spins, inertia and centrifugal force push it up against the basket wall, which features lots of tiny little holes. The spinning motion forces the liquid from the fruit though these holes, and it collects in the juice container, ready to drink. Meanwhile, the remaining pulp is forced up and over the edges of the basket, where it falls into a waste container, ready to be thrown away.

Centrifugal juicers spin fruit at high speeds to extract the liquid goodness

Harnessing the Sun

How vast solar power towers generate electricity

The Sun's rays are focused onto the power tower

When light hits a solar panel, it generates an electrical current by nudging electrons away from their atoms, but solar power towers are different. These harness the heat of the Sun.

Power towers sit at the centre of rings of angled mirrors, or 'heliostats', which track the Sun as it passes across the sky. They reflect the light, focusing it all onto the tower. Inside, fluid (originally water, but now more often molten nitrate salt), heats up under the intense light. The heated liquid is used to generate steam, which in turn is used to drive a turbine.

This ingenious way of collecting solar energy allows heat to be stored even when the Sun goes down, providing a supply of electricity that can be used overnight and on cloudy days. Solar power towers aren't without their problems, though. The mirrors concentrate the Sun's energy to such intensities that wildlife entering the ring is in serious danger. Crescent Dunes Solar Energy Project in Nevada reportedly vaporised over 100 birds in just six hours. However, when compared to the environmental damage caused by coal-fired power plants, these towers still come out on top.

Inside a power tower

The key to harnessing the Sun's power lies inside a network of pipes

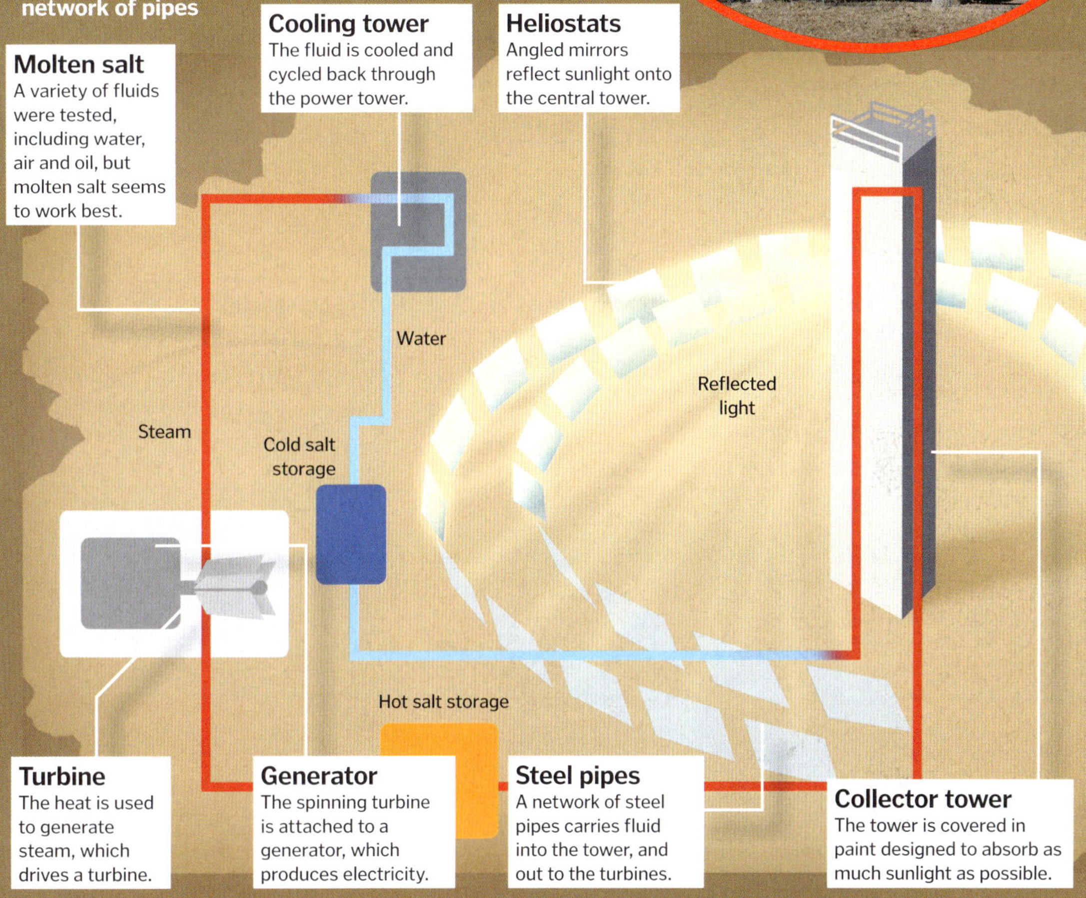

Shrink-wrap seals

How does plastic cling so tightly to products?

Shrink-wrap contracts when heat is applied, forming a secure seal around food products as they travel to and from our supermarkets. The secret behind the stick is polymers – long molecules made up of smaller units joined together. Before the wrap has been shrunk, these molecules are stretched out, forming neat, parallel bundles. When heat is applied, they curl up, knotting together and shrinking down by up to 50 per cent.

The most common material for shrink-wrap used to be polyvinyl chloride (PVC), but it is quite sensitive to changes in temperature. When it gets hot, it hardens. The newer plastic, polyolefin, is much more stable. Shrink-wrapping machines coat products in plastic, before running them through a heated tunnel to shrink the covering down to size.

Shrink-wrap clings tightly to cans and bottles from factory to supermarket

The packaging process

Sealing food packets in plastic is surprisingly simple

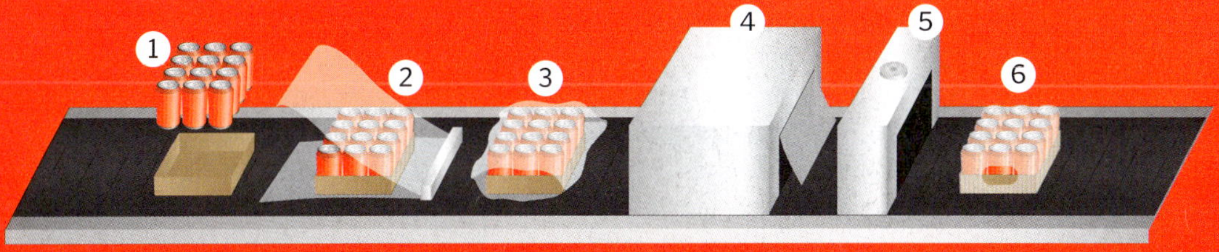

1 Products Food products are transported on either boards or trays.

2 Wrapping The products are encased in plastic wrap, covering the top and bottom edges.

3 Sealing At this stage, the plastic is sealed, although it is still loose.

4 Shrink tunnel Inside the shrink tunnel, the plastic is heated and polymer chains curl up.

5 Cooling fan The plastic is then cooled by fans, which sets the chains into their new positions.

6 Finished product The shrunken plastic fits snugly around the product, ready for shipping.

HOLIDAY 2050

YOUR TICKET TO THE HIGH-TECH VACATION OF THE FUTURE

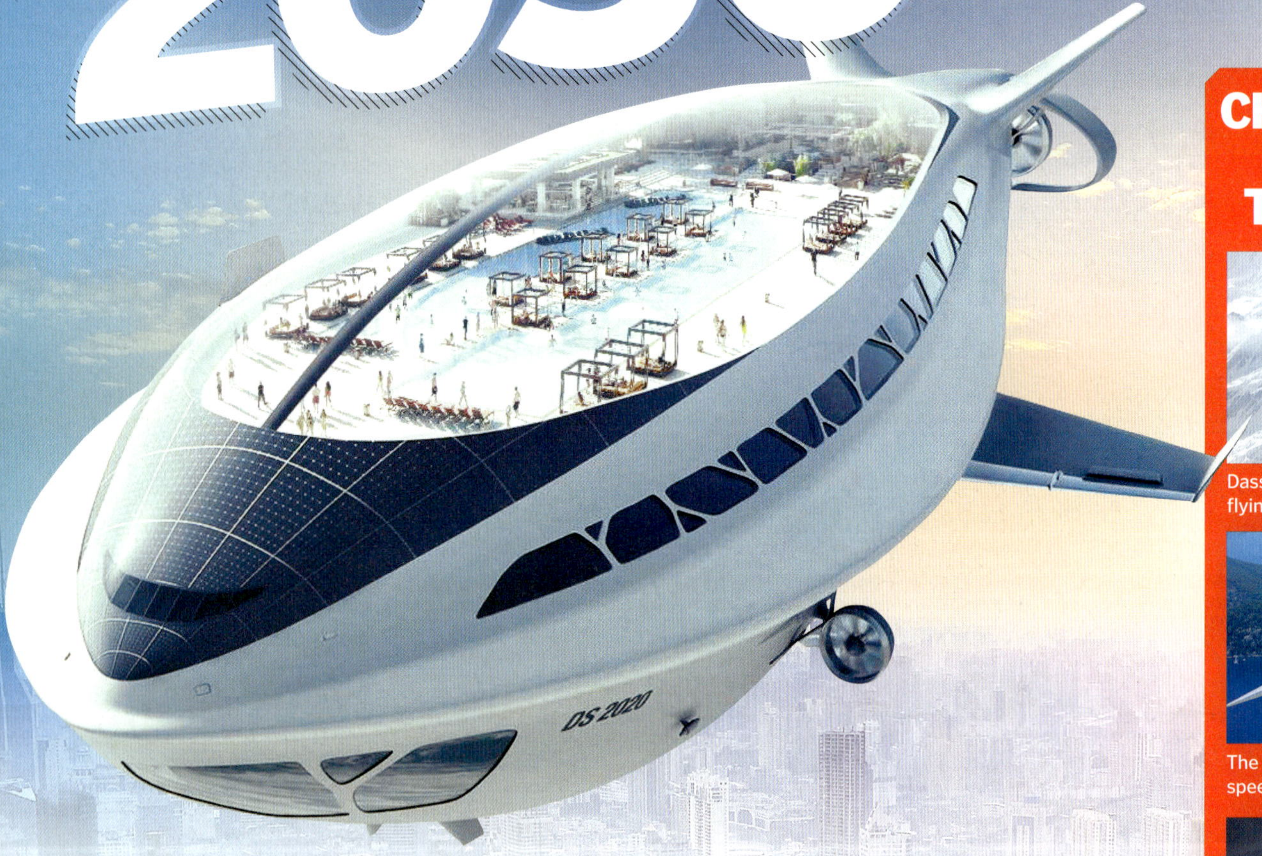

It's 2050 and taking a vacation is easier than ever, thanks to the latest technological breakthroughs. Over the next few pages, we'll guide you through every step of your trip, from planning and booking, to travelling and making the most of your stay.

Some of the tech involved might seem unbelievable, but all of it was in fact already real, or in development, in the year 2016. Take the process of booking your trip, for example. You may have been using websites to find the best deals, but now you don't need to enter your information, as online travel agents already know your preferences. Gareth Williams, CEO and co-founder of travel company Skyscanner, said: "Travel search and booking will be as easy as buying a book on Amazon."

There's no longer any guesswork involved in picking your destination either, as Nik Gupter, Skyscanner's director of hotels, predicted back in 2016: "In ten years' time a traveller will be able to take a virtual reality walk through the hotel he is planning to book in real-time."

The stress of travelling is long gone and getting to your destination is almost as enjoyable as the holiday itself. In 2016, Melissa Weigel from design studio Moment Factory said: "In the near future, airports will be an intrinsic part of the holiday experience." Since then, automated check-in and speedy security scanning has made boarding your flight a breeze.

Holiday destinations have also changed a great deal, as futurist Daniel Burrus predicted: "Relatively affordable trips in low Earth orbit that enable you to experience a few minutes of weightlessness will happen very soon." With spaceflight commonplace, we've now got our sights on the Moon and Mars.

CHOOSE YOUR MODE OF TRANSPORT

Dassault Systèmes' concept for a flying cruise liner

The Spike S-512 jet will mirror the speed of Concorde

Avoid the airport altogether by taking your TF-X flying car

The 90-metre luxury JAZZ yacht features an indoor pool

BOOKING YOUR HOLIDAY

Get the VIP treatment from the off

Choose a destination

Social media and online retailers use members' profiles to monitor activity and alter the content they see. Travel brands now operate in a similar way, logging your likes and dislikes, while facial coding algorithms, as developed by Affectiva, enable search engines to read human expressions and gauge how happy you are with the results.

IN DEVELOPMENT

Use an e-agent

You can rent an artificially intelligent e-agent from your local travel company to help plan your trip. The tech is similar to JIBO – the personal assistant released in 2015 that uses two hi-res cameras to recognise faces and algorithms to learn your preferences and adapt.

IN DEVELOPMENT

EXISTS

Take a virtual vacation

VR headsets enable you to try before you buy. By using dual lenses with a slightly different image in front of each eye, it recreates your normal stereoscopic vision and fools your brain into thinking virtual worlds are real. Disney's Revel system, developed in 2012, uses electrical signals to create the feeling of touch.

IN DEVELOPMENT

Book with ease

While apps like Expedia enabled 2016 holidaymakers to arrange most aspects of their trip, 2050 takes the tech a step further. You can use a one-stop app to book your flights, hotel and holiday activities with a couple of taps of your smartwatch. Even transport to the airport will be taken care of.

AT THE AIRPORT

How tech will take the stress out of travelling

IN DEVELOPMENT

Smart tags

As you drop off your bags, they're fitted with tags containing Near Field Communication (NFC) chips. When they come into close contact with another NFC chip inside the scanner, your personal and flight data is transferred wirelessly. You can then track each scan via an app.

IN DEVELOPMENT

Biometric scans

Instead of a passport, a biometric data card is used to identify you. Images of your eye, taken with a camera that records visible and infrared light, capture the exact position of the iris' unique patterns and features. As you board the plane, your eyes are scanned and matched.

EXISTS

Speedy checks

The Picosecond Programmable Laser is a scanner that vibrates the molecules in your body and possessions to identify different substances, from traces of gunpowder to the contents of your stomach. It's 10 million times faster than a conventional scanner.

ON THE PLANE

Your journey will fly by as you explore the onboard entertainment options

Instead of waiting around at the gate, you are free to explore the airport's rooftop gardens, art exhibitions and shops at your leisure, safe in the knowledge that a 3D holographic assistant will appear to tell you when the plane is boarding.

Holograms have been around since the development of lasers in the 1960s, but recent advancements in technology mean they're now much more impressive. They used to be created by splitting a laser beam in two and directing each beam towards an object using mirrors. The beams were then reflected off the object and at the point where they recombined, a still hologram of the original object formed. In recent years, we've mastered moving holographic images, resulting in ultra-realistic 3D content for entertainment and practical uses.

When it's time to stroll onto the plane, you'll find that the Airbus Concept Cabin has become reality, and you're no longer confined to your own seat. First class and economy have been replaced with zones tailored to your different needs, whether you want to relax, mingle with other passengers or play some games.

Sit back, relax and fly

CONCEPT

Skyscanner's personalised aircraft seat concept will provide ultimate comfort on your journey

Smart lighting
Red wavelengths of light stimulate the brain's production of the sleep hormone melatonin, helping you drift off and fight jetlag.

Constant connection
Next-gen 5G mobile internet and advanced satellite broadband are available throughout the flight.

Sonic disrupters
Devices embedded in the seat rest prevent other passengers from hearing your private conversations.

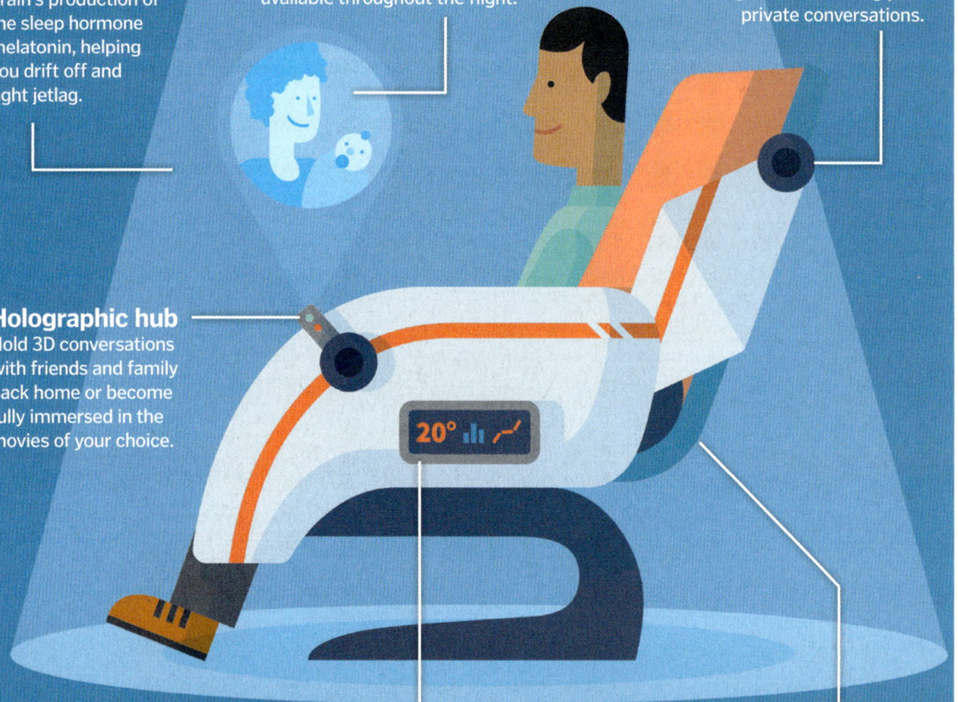

Holographic hub
Hold 3D conversations with friends and family back home or become fully immersed in the movies of your choice.

Climate control
Built-in climate control lets you monitor and adjust heating and cooling systems for your individual seat.

Memory-foam seat
The roomy aircraft seat moulds to your body shape, providing comfortable support that minimises back pain.

CONCEPT

Modular aircraft

A cabin design with zones for work, rest and play

Relaxing atmosphere
Soft aromas and gentle sounds fill the cabin to help ease you into a deep sleep.

Private pods
Pop-up rooms allow you to hold business meetings, have a romantic meal or read the kids a bedtime story on the flight.

Immersive entertainment
Practise your tennis or golf at the virtual gaming wall or put on a VR headset to be transported to a cinematic world.

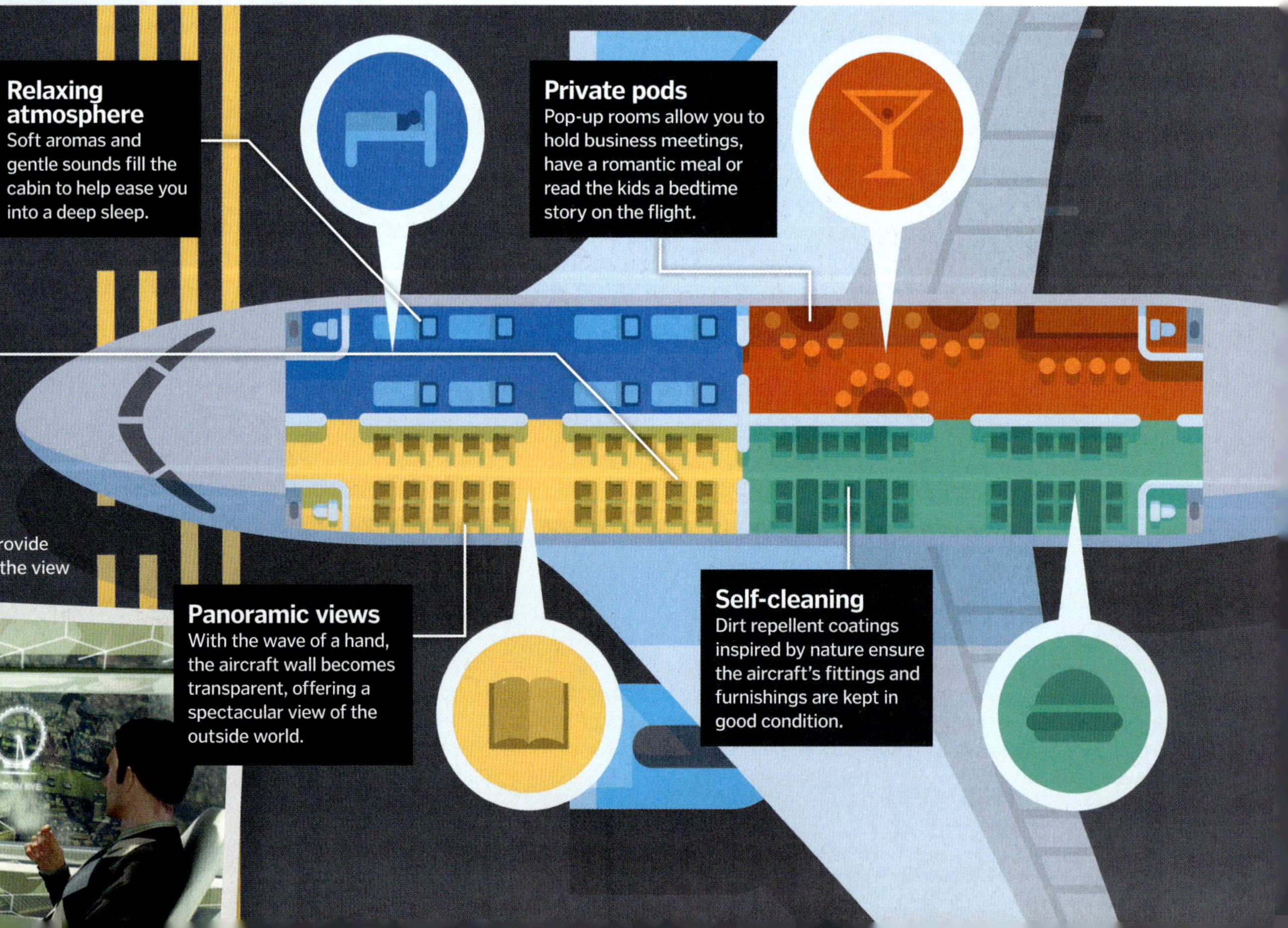

Panoramic views
With the wave of a hand, the aircraft wall becomes transparent, offering a spectacular view of the outside world.

Self-cleaning
Dirt repellent coatings inspired by nature ensure the aircraft's fittings and furnishings are kept in good condition.

Interactive window displays provide interesting information about the view

YOU HAVE REACHED YOUR DESTINATION

The smart hotel room will ensure the stress-free experience continues

Once you've stepped off the plane and swiftly passed through immigration with your biometric card, you will find another driverless taxi waiting to take you to your hotel. Instead of having to pick up your room key at the check-in desk, you can proceed straight to your room and unlock it using your smartphone, a system that was adopted early by Hilton and Marriott hotel chains.

Your bags are delivered to your door by a robot butler, such as Botlr, the droid employed by Aloft Hotels at their Californian establishments. He can be summoned via an app to bring you any toiletries you may have forgotten to pack, or deliver a tasty snack to help you refuel after your long journey.

Just as everything in your own home is connected to the internet, all of your hotel room's appliances are smart and intuitive too. You can even upload your home temperature preferences to the room's Nest thermostat, and display family photos on the digital wall displays, to help you feel really at home.

A good night's rest is guaranteed as the Sleep Number x12 bed features sensors that monitor your sleep, ensuring the alarm clock gently wakes you at the optimum time, and can tilt the pillows to stop your partner snoring. All of this tech already existed as of 2016, but has since been adopted by hotels throughout the world.

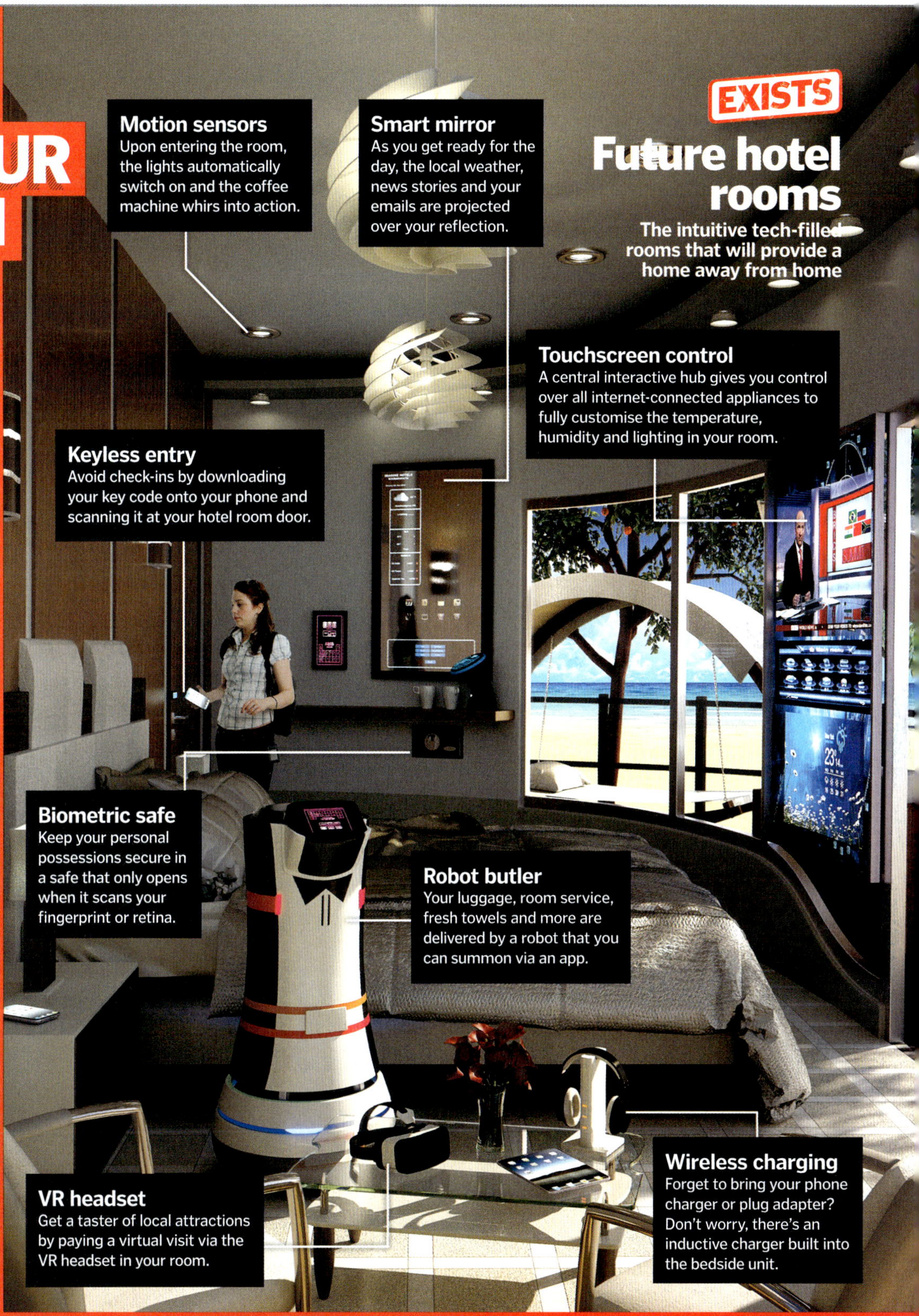

WEIRD HOTELS THAT ACTUALLY EXIST

©ICEHOTEL/Paulina Holmgren

The frozen hotel

Made entirely from 'snice' – a mixture of snow and ice – the Icehotel in Sweden melts in the summer and is rebuilt every winter, with construction taking just six weeks. Temperatures inside the hotel are between -5 and -7 degrees Celsius.

The salt palace

Located on the edge of the world's largest salt flats in Bolivia, the Palacio de Sal has been built using one million blocks of salt and features 16 rooms, a spa and a golf course. Everything from the walls to the beds is made entirely from salt.

The jumbo experience

If you haven't had enough of airplanes by the time you leave the airport, then Jumbo Stay will let you dwell in one too. The converted 747-200 jumbo jet is grounded near Arlanda Airport in Sweden and features over 30 rooms.

At the spaceport IN DEVELOPMENT

Catch a space plane into orbit from your local spaceflight hub

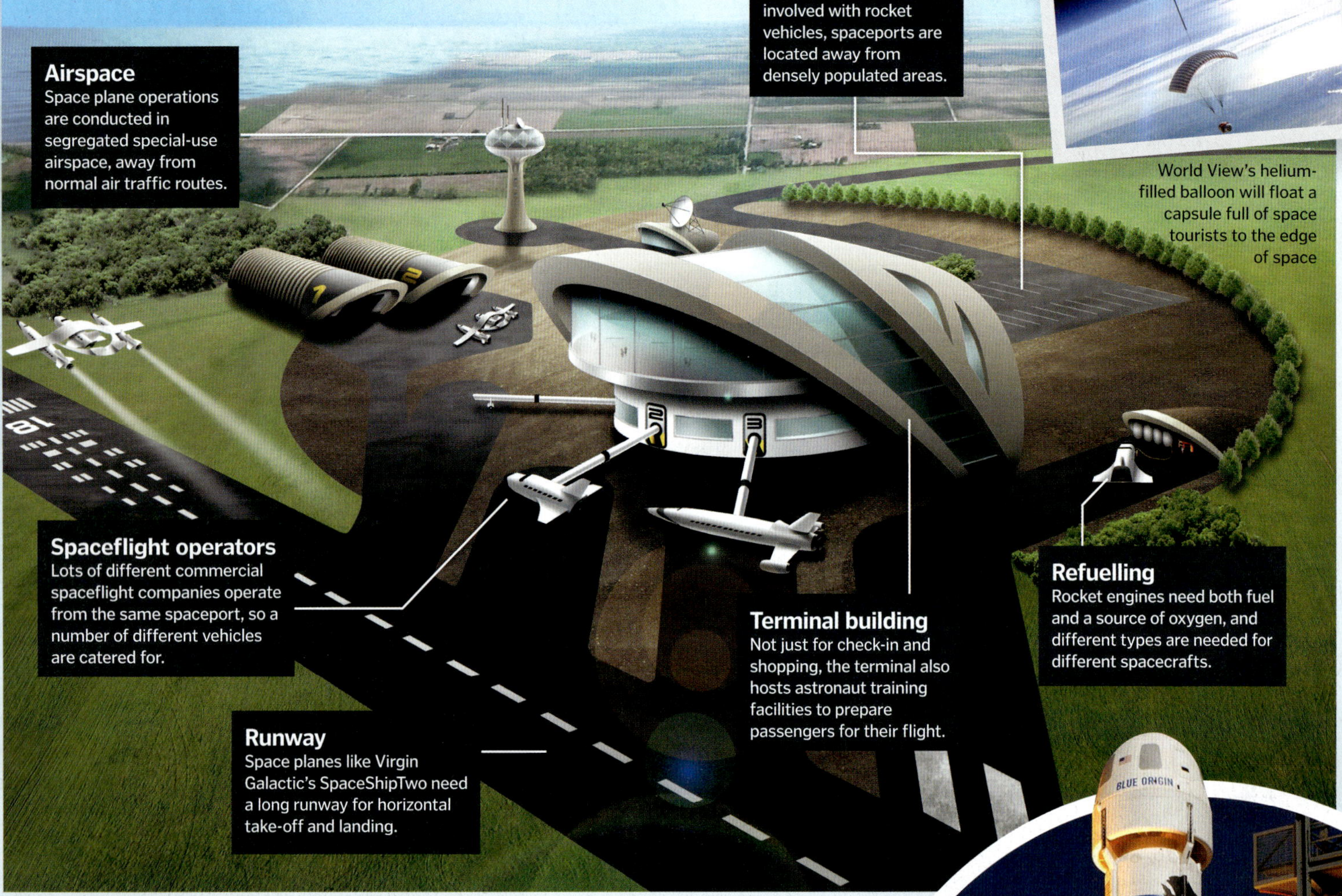

World View's helium-filled balloon will float a capsule full of space tourists to the edge of space

SPACE TOURISM

Take a trip that's literally out of this world

If you really want to escape from it all, then how about leaving the planet altogether? Space tourism is a billion dollar market in 2050 and there are several companies offering trips. Blue Origin, the company set up by Amazon founder Jeff Bezos, can offer you breathtaking views from its New Shepard spacecraft as you soar over 100 kilometres above Earth.

You'll need to arrive at the desert launch site in West Texas two days before your flight so you can begin your astronaut training. You'll receive mission and vehicle overviews, in-depth safety briefings and instructions on how to move in a weightless environment. When the morning of your flight arrives, it's time to scale the steps of the launch tower and climb through the hatch of the capsule, which sits on top of an 18-metre tall rocket.

Once you're strapped in and have received final clearance for launch, the countdown to lift-off will begin. The extreme acceleration will force you back into your seat and you'll experience over 3 g for 150 seconds and then the booster engine will cut off as you glide into space. The capsule will separate from the booster, and from the serene silence will come the signal to release your harness.

As you float out of your seat and marvel at the weightless freedom, you'll forget that you're travelling faster than Mach 3 – three times the speed of sound – and stare back at Earth out of the capsule window. Before descent, you will return to your seat to strap in for re-entry. Forces of over 5 g will push against you before the parachutes deploy and thrusters fire, reducing your speed as you gently float back to Earth. Once you've landed, just miles from where you launched, you can go and collect the complimentary souvenirs of your thrilling trip. That's right; novelty keyrings still exist in 2050.

Blue Origin first vertically landed a booster in 2015, paving the way for reusable rockets

XCOR Aerospace is planning to launch its Lynx spaceplane from its Curaçao spaceport

UNDERWATER HOTELS

Sleep, eat and relax with the fishes

Back in 2016, the closest thing to an underwater suite was the five-star Atlantis, The Palm, in Dubai. The floor-to-ceiling views of a colossal aquarium created such a spectacular illusion that celebs like Kim Kardashian were willing to splash the cash to stay there.

But while a fully-fledged underwater haven like the Water Discus Hotel was just a concept in 2016, its doors are open in Dubai in 2050. Once you arrive by boat or helicopter from the shore, you can relax in your room and watch the marine critters swim by, or sign up for a diving course to get even closer to the action. You don't even need to go back up to the surface in order to get in the water, as there's sea access direct from the underwater disc.

Underwater suites at The Palm, Dubai, offer views of 65,000 marine animals

CONCEPT

The Water Discus

Get up close with marine life in Dubai's ocean hotel

ENVIRONMENT

076
Nature's top predators

066
How the world could end

086
Canada's Spotted Lake

IT IS ESTIMATED THAT 99.9 PER CENT OF ALL SPECIES THAT HAVE EVER INHABITED EARTH ARE EXTINCT. ARE HUMANS NEXT?

HOW THE WORLD COULD END

FROM SUPERVOLCANOES TO NUCLEAR WINTERS, THE SCIENTIFIC THEORIES IN DANGER OF BECOMING REALITY

Illustration by Tobias Roetsch

A SUPERVOLCANO BLOWS

A cataclysmic eruption plunges the planet into a brutal volcanic winter

Supervolcanoes are the leviathans of volcanism. Defined by their ability to blast more than 1,000 cubic kilometres (240 cubic miles) of material into the air, they are a thousand times larger than the 1980 Mount Saint Helens eruption – the most destructive volcanic eruption in recorded US history.

Geologists have never witnessed a supervolcanic eruption, but by looking at remnants of previous cataclysms, they can piece together alarming details. These eruptions rain debris and fiery destruction on a geographical region as large as Europe, but it's the gases they inject into the stratosphere that could spell disaster for humanity.

During a super-eruption, a scalding plume of gas would belch almost to the edge of space. Levelling off, it would spread out around the globe, forming a veil of sulphate aerosols that would persist for several years and trigger a volcanic winter.

The veil would reflect and absorb incoming solar radiation, warming the upper atmosphere and preventing heat from reaching the surface. The result would be extreme instability in the climate system. Surface temperatures would tumble rapidly, leading to agricultural collapse and famine. Some even speculate that these conditions could lead to the onset of an ice age.

Such catastrophic super-eruptions are rare; the last we know of occurred 27,000 years ago in New Zealand. But they are inevitable. Critically, we have no idea when the next one will strike and absolutely no way to prevent it.

Volcanic winter

Global climate in the aftermath of a supervolcanic eruption

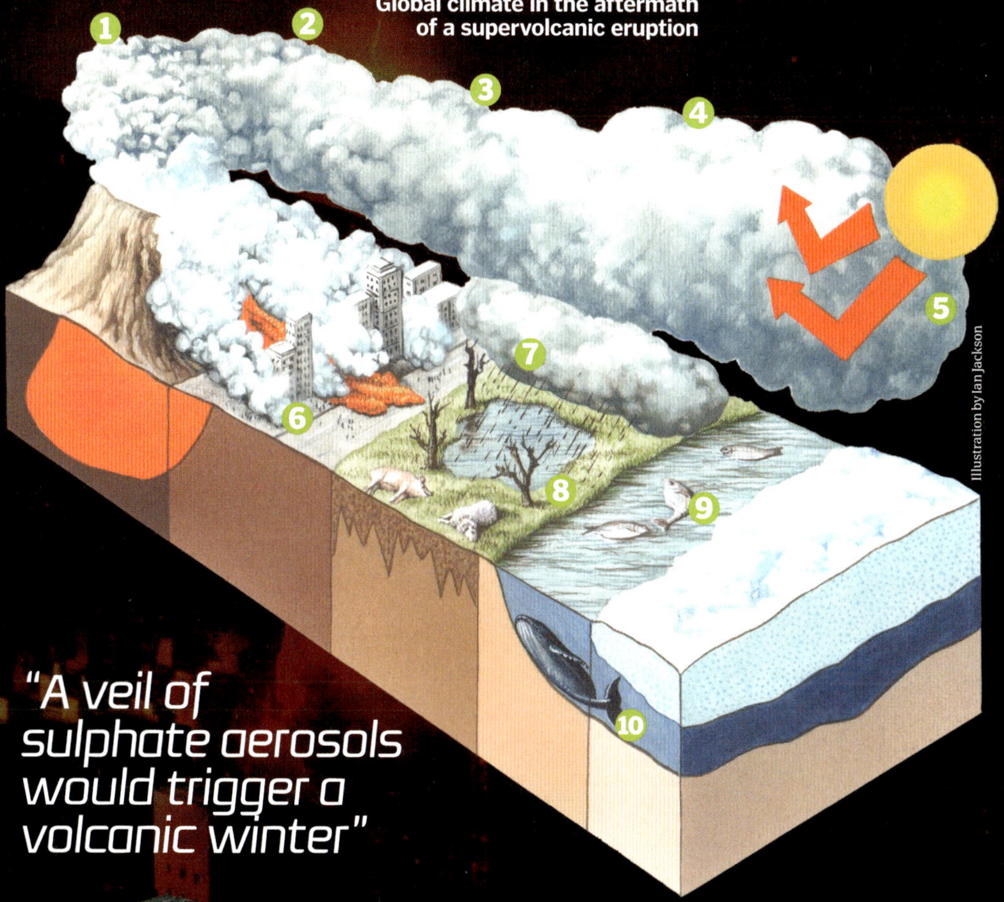

1 Ash cloud
Suspended ash blocks the Sun for several weeks and all air traffic - including aid to the region - is disrupted.

2 Increased cloud formation
Sulphate aerosols also act as cloud condensation nuclei, encouraging thicker cloud formation and further blocking of sunlight.

3 Stratospheric warming
Incoming sunlight is reflected and absorbed, warming the upper atmosphere and affecting air circulation and weather patterns.

4 Ozone depletion
Chlorine, bromine and other aerosols interfere with atmospheric chemistry, encouraging depletion of the ozone layer.

5 Aerosol veil
Sulphate particles disperse widely, blocking sunlight for years and causing surface temperatures to plummet.

6 Fallout
Ash and rubble buries homes, roads, power grids, sanitation systems and agricultural land; famine and disease rage.

7 Acid rain
Sulphate aerosols combine with water and fall as acid rain, stripping vegetation and poisoning soils, acidifying lakes, damaging structures and causing respiratory irritation.

8 Vegetation dies
Buried by ash, ravaged by acid rain, or strangled by freezing summer temperatures, crops fail, livestock dies, causing widespread famine.

9 Oceanic circulation chaos
Reduced sea surface temperatures scramble normal oceanic circulation, altering global weather patterns in unpredictable ways.

10 Marine biology collapse
Disturbed circulation and reduced deep-water upwelling hampers nutrient flow, threatening the entire oceanic food chain.

> "A veil of sulphate aerosols would trigger a volcanic winter"

Mount Tambora's colossal caldera is 6km (3.7mi) wide and 1.1km (0.7mi) deep

Mount Tambora and the year without summer

In 1815, Mount Tambora on the Indonesian island of Sumbawa erupted, ejecting 50 cubic kilometres (12 cubic miles) of material skywards in one of the most powerful eruptions in recorded history.

Tambora claimed an estimated 70,000 lives in the region, and caused climate mayhem across the Northern Hemisphere. Dubbed "the year without a summer", 1816 saw June snowfall in New York and widespread crop failure, famine, disease and riots, bringing the death toll to several hundred thousand. Despite its far-reaching consequences, Tambora was at least ten times smaller than a supervolcano.

NUCLEAR WINTER

The smouldering aftermath of nuclear conflict blacks out the Sun

With the power to demolish entire cities in seconds, nuclear bombs are the most devastating weapons on the planet. In many ways, those annihilated in the first moments of a blast could be considered the lucky ones.

In the 1980s, prominent scientists including Carl Sagan warned that a nuclear war between the US and the Soviet Union could drive the globe into a catastrophic nuclear winter. Incinerated cities and forests would send heaving clouds of Sun-blocking ash into the stratosphere – it could take years for particles to be rained out.

In a worst-case scenario, it is theorised that 99 per cent of the Sun's light would be blocked for several months, resulting in noontime twilight and the halting of photosynthesis. Surface temperatures could plummet tens of degrees below normal levels for years or even decades, bringing crippling arctic conditions to the entire globe. Plants, animals and humans would perish in the darkness.

Nuclear winter

How nuclear conflict could wreak havoc on global climate and the environment

The mushroom cloud of the 'Fat Man' bomb after it detonated in Nagasaki, Japan, instantly killing around 80,000 people

How many nukes would destroy Earth?

How the world's most famous nuclear bombs stack up

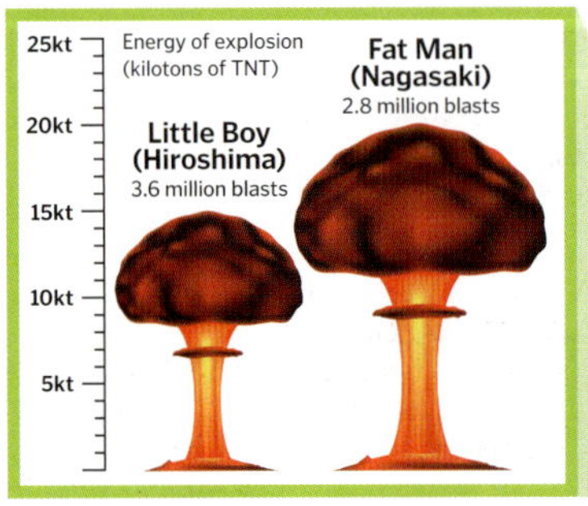

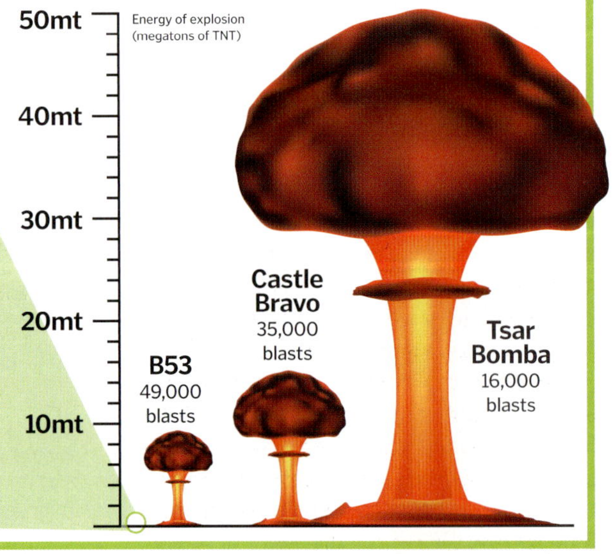

ASTEROID IMPACT

A celestial wrecking ball smashes into Earth

Asteroids are hunks of rocky space debris, left over from the creation of the planets, which whizz around our Solar System, orbiting the Sun. From time to time they cross paths with us and, while impacts on the scale of the infamous ten-kilometre (6.2-mile) dinosaur-destroyer are rare, an asteroid a fifth the size could spell disaster for civilisation.

With energy greater than 10 million Hiroshima bombs, the impact shock would flatten everything within a 300-kilometre (186-mile) radius. Dust and debris would cause an 'impact winter' and most living things would perish. An ocean strike would trigger monumental tsunamis, obliterate entire coastlines, and inject seawater into the atmosphere – destroying huge swathes of the ozone layer and exposing survivors to devastating levels of UV radiation.

Five ways to head off an asteroid

Given enough forewarning, there are a few tricks that might successfully avert a collision

1 Pull it
Position a 'gravity tractor' 250m (820ft) from the surface; the spacecraft's gravitational pull would gradually tease the asteroid onto a new path.

2 Slam into it
Smash a fast-moving spaceship into it, altering its velocity by a sliver and eventually creating a significant path drift.

3 Push it
Land an ion-drive rocket engine on the surface, and build up enough thrust to nudge it off course.

4 Nuke it
Detonate a nuclear bomb nearby; vaporising surface material would deflect the asteroid's course.

5 Blow it up
Bury a thermonuclear bomb deep beneath its surface, detonate, and hope none of the fragments head our way.

Did an asteroid cause the K/T extinction?

Famous for the demise of the dinosaurs (and 80 per cent of all animal species), the K/T extinction event occurred about 66 million years ago. Scientists' theories that a gigantic space rock was to blame are strongly supported by the existence of a 180-kilometre (112-mile) impact crater – dated as 66 million years old – at Chicxulub in Mexico.

RUNAWAY GREENHOUSE EFFECT

Human activities set in motion an unstoppable warming of the planet

The greenhouse effect is essential to life as we know it. Just like a glass greenhouse lets in light but traps heat, insulating gases in our atmosphere protect us from the deathly cold of space.

But since the Industrial Revolution, humans have upset the delicate balance of the atmosphere. Concentrations of carbon dioxide (CO_2), released when fossil fuels are burned, and other 'greenhouse gases', have risen at an alarming rate, forming a thick blanket around Earth, trapping excess heat and nudging global temperatures upwards.

While warmer weather might be welcome in some places, 'feedback loops' complicate the effects of higher temperatures. Increased evaporation will cause denser cloud cover, exacerbating the warming effect because clouds themselves are strong insulators. Longstanding carbon 'sinks' – rocks and oceans that pull CO_2 out of the atmosphere – will become unstable and release their stores, accelerating the problem still further.

Scientists warn of a tipping point – a temperature beyond which the problem can no longer be dialled back. If we reach this point, a runaway greenhouse effect would cause temperatures to soar to several hundred degrees Celsius, boiling the oceans and making life on Earth impossible.

Absorption
Greenhouse gases absorb outgoing infrared and reradiate some of it back towards Earth, trapping heat in the lower atmosphere and causing an overall warming.

Outgoing infrared
Some of the outgoing infrared energy is absorbed by the atmosphere and reflected back down towards the surface, while the rest is radiated into space.

Reflection
About 30 per cent of incoming radiation is scattered by the atmosphere or reflected by clouds back out to space.

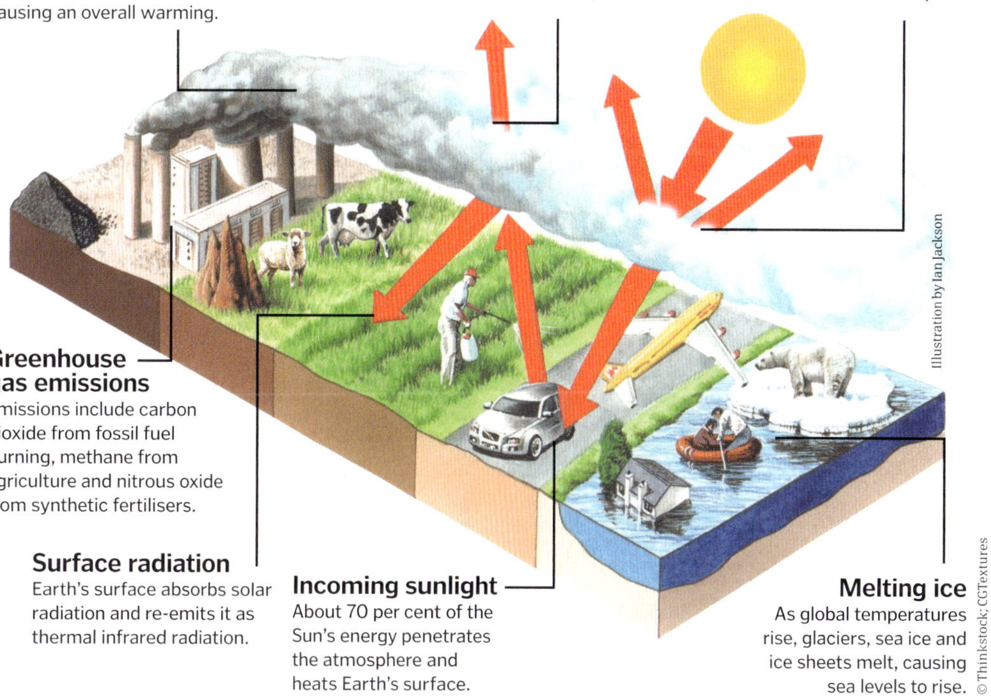

Greenhouse gas emissions
Emissions include carbon dioxide from fossil fuel burning, methane from agriculture and nitrous oxide from synthetic fertilisers.

Surface radiation
Earth's surface absorbs solar radiation and re-emits it as thermal infrared radiation.

Incoming sunlight
About 70 per cent of the Sun's energy penetrates the atmosphere and heats Earth's surface.

Melting ice
As global temperatures rise, glaciers, sea ice and ice sheets melt, causing sea levels to rise.

Illustration by Ian Jackson

THE SUN DIES

In its twilight years, our local star turns on us

The Sun supplies the energy for almost all of life on Earth, but all good things come to an end. When the Sun's time comes and it starts to run out of fuel, its core will collapse as the outward force – due to fusion – can no longer balance the strong inward force of gravity. At the same time, its outer envelope will inflate, expanding the star into a red giant, and engulfing the orbits of Mercury, Venus, and – potentially – Earth.

Eventually, the dying Sun will transform into a dense white dwarf surrounded by a dazzling planetary nebula. Humans won't be around to see this; the Sun's fuel supply will start to run low about five billion years from now, but Earth will be inhospitable long before.

Planet-gobbling star caught in the act

In 2012, astronomers stumbled upon a planet murder in progress. They found that red giant star BD+48 740 currently contains unexpected levels of lithium. This rare element is easily destroyed in stars, indicating that it has recently digested something with the mass and composition of a planet.

A swallowed planet is vaporised and its material blends into the star

Red giant Sun

The view from Earth as the Sun grows old

Plants disappear
As the climate warms, carbonate rock formation – which sucks CO_2 from the atmosphere – speeds up. Although this temporarily stunts overall warming, eventually there is no longer enough CO_2 for plants to photosynthesise. All animal life is doomed.

Temperature rises
As it ploughs through its fuel reserves, the Sun gets about ten per cent brighter – and therefore hotter – every billion years. The increase makes Earth inhospitable to all life in under a billion years.

Red giant approaches
Billions of years after Earthly life is obliterated, the Sun will begin its red giant phase, swallowing Mercury and Venus and bearing down on our now barren rock.

Earth's fiery demise
Although some experts suggest that the Sun's reducing gravitational pull will allow Earth's orbit to spiral outwards to safety, most agree that it will be devoured and vaporised.

Oceans evaporate
Soaring temperatures cause the oceans to boil. The atmosphere fills with water vapour and the surface turns into a desert. Without water, all but the hardiest microbes die off.

Today: the Sun is at a distance of one astronomical unit (1 AU) – 150mn km (93mn mi) – from Earth

"The dying Sun will swallow Mercury, Venus, and – potentially – Earth"

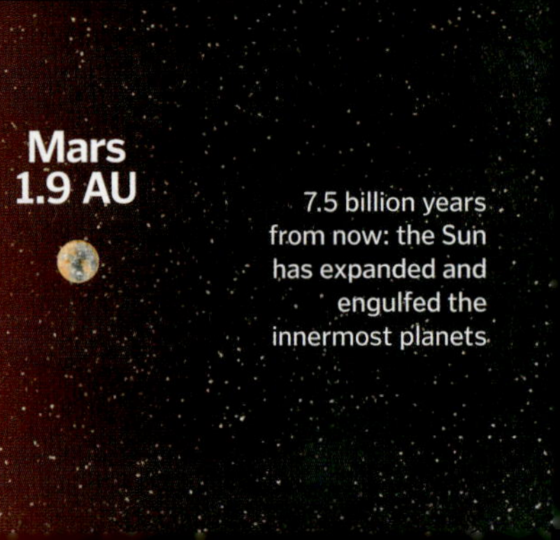

7.5 billion years from now: the Sun has expanded and engulfed the innermost planets

GAMMA-RAY BURST

An explosion hundreds of thousands of light years away annihilates the ozone layer

Gamma-ray bursts (GRBs) are the brightest events in the universe. Produced by the explosion of massive stars, they emit focussed beams of intense gamma radiation. They can last anywhere from a fraction of a second to several hours, and can release as much energy in ten seconds as the Sun will produce in its entire lifetime.

If the Earth were unlucky enough to get caught in a GRB's almighty death beam, the effects would be catastrophic. It would trigger atmospheric chemistry that would destroy the ozone layer – leaving life on the surface exposed to deadly ultraviolet radiation.

Earth in the firing line

According to astronomers, GRBs are triggered close enough to affect life on Earth about once every five million years. Evidence in the tree ring record suggests our latest hit was nearly 1,250 years ago. Tree rings from all over the world show 20 times the normal level of carbon-14 in the year 774, an effect that scientists calculate could have been caused by a GRB about 13,000 light years from Earth.

Some scientists believe that GRBs may also have been responsible for some of the major extinction events that have happened throughout Earth's history, including the Ordovician-Silurian event approximately 440 million years ago, where 60 per cent of marine invertebrate life perished.

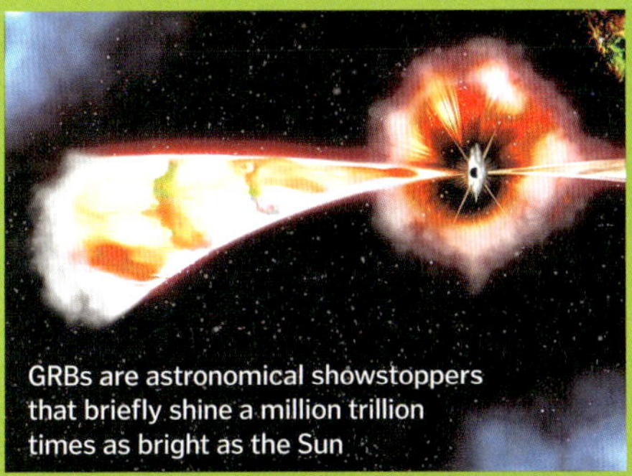

GRBs are astronomical showstoppers that briefly shine a million trillion times as bright as the Sun

Anatomy of a long GRB

Step-by-step guide to the brightest electromagnetic events in the universe

1 Star death
When a massive star's energy dwindles and it nears the end of its life, it swells to become a red giant. When its fuel supply finally runs out, the star collapses under its own gravity, crushing its core into a black hole.

2 Supernova
The heat created by the collapse (around 100bn°C/180bn°F) forces particles violently outwards from the core. As these slam into the star's collapsing outer layers, a shock front forms and blasts the layers away in a supernova explosion that lasts days, weeks or months.

3 Expulsion
Matter falls into the rapidly spinning black hole. As it is devoured, narrow jets of intense radiation blast out along the black hole's axis of rotation, producing an intense flash of high-energy gamma rays.

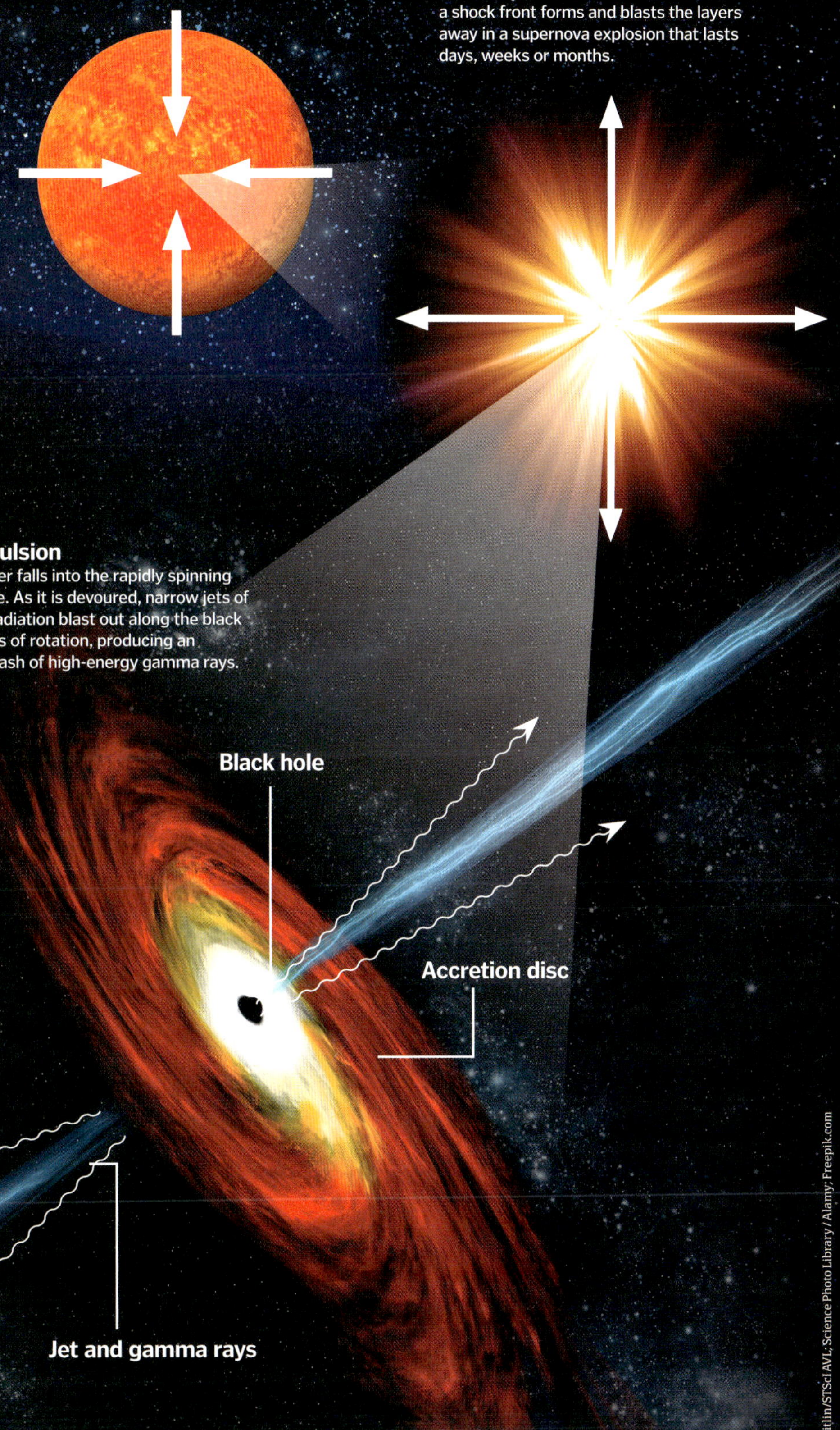

GLOBAL PANDEMIC

Infectious disease sweeps the planet, eradicating the entire human race

A pandemic is an outbreak of infectious disease that spreads throughout much of the globe. Human history is punctuated by debilitating pandemics and, despite medical advances, it's only a matter of time before we see another.

Today's standards of sanitation and medical research help us stay one step ahead of most infectious agents, but widespread international travel and increased population densities make it much easier for a global pandemic to threaten us all.

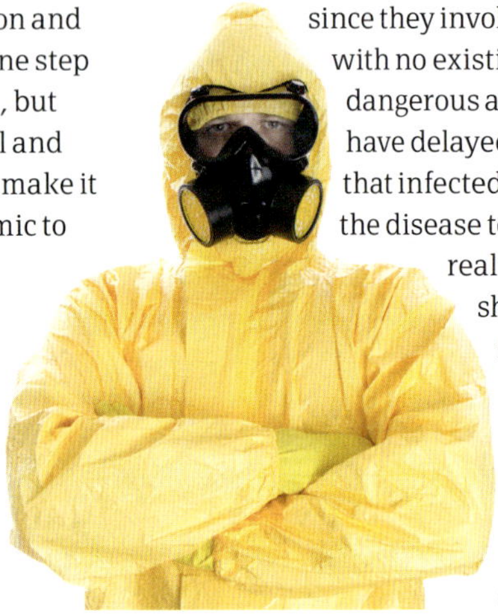

In 2003, SARS (severe acute respiratory syndrome) – a serious form of pneumonia – spread to six of the world's seven continents within months, infecting an estimated 8,000 people and killing 750. More recently, Ebola – a grisly disease ravaging West Africa with a death toll over 11,000 – threatened to go pandemic in late 2014 after cases popped up in travellers arriving back in North America and Europe.

Emerging diseases pose the biggest problem, since they involve unknown pathogens with no existing vaccinations. The most dangerous are highly contagious but have delayed symptom onset, meaning that infected people unwittingly spread the disease to many others before realising they are sick. Shape-shifting diseases that mutate fast are almost impossible to vaccinate against. In today's hyper-mobile, city-dominated world, a deadly disease combining these three features could spell doom for the human race.

The Black Death

One of the deadliest pandemics in human history, the Black Death was the second plague pandemic. Originating in China in the 1330s, it spread along the Silk Road trade routes to Europe, where it claimed the lives of an estimated 60 per cent of the population. Victims developed high fevers, vomited blood, and usually perished within a week.

Medieval doctors did not know what caused the Black Death, and were unable to stop it spreading

Outbreak

The deadliest pandemics in human history

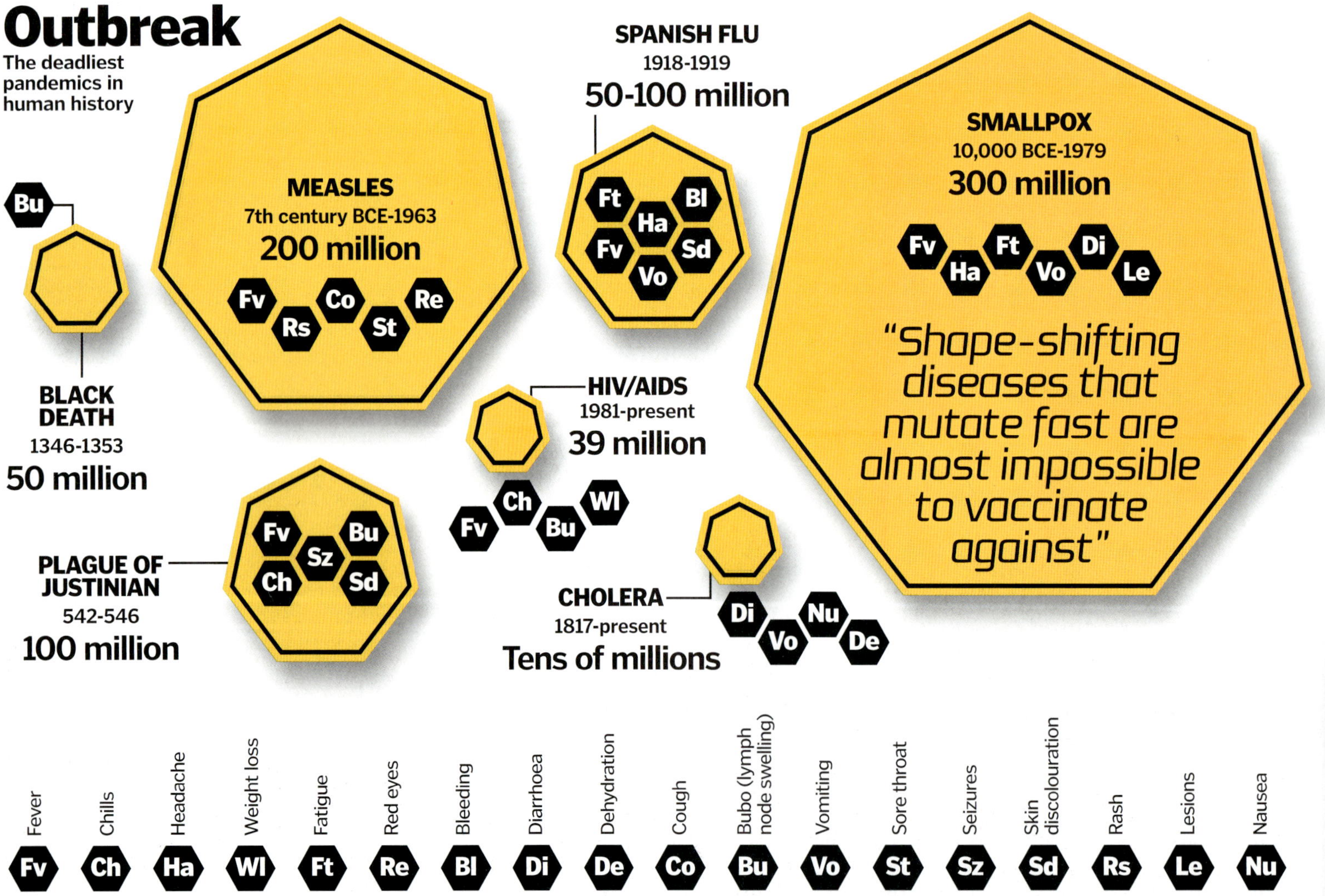

DID YOU KNOW? Engineers have already managed to design a machine that can autonomously create a better version of itself

ROBOT TAKEOVER

Artificial intelligence transcends human intelligence and turns on its creators

I, Robot, *2001: A Space Odyssey*, the *Terminator* movies; we all know how this goes down. But some computer scientists believe that we're fast approaching a moment known as 'the singularity' – a tipping point where self-aware machines surpass the capabilities of the most intelligent human mind.

Beyond this point, it's impossible to predict how things will pan out. An unchecked superhuman intelligence would be so incomprehensible to us that we would no longer be able to control it, and if it decided to terminate the human race, we would be powerless to stop it.

AI could supersede the human race if appropriate controls aren't built in

Experts weigh in

You may dismiss public fears about artificial intelligence (AI) as the result of too much sci-fi entertainment. But when prominent thinkers and technologists start expressing concern, it's time to take notice.

Some of the leading minds of our time – including physicist Stephen Hawking, Microsoft co-founder Bill Gates, and engineer and entrepreneur Elon Musk – have spoken out publicly over the last year, warning that the majority of people don't appreciate the speed with which AI technology is advancing and the very real threat it could pose.

Musk and Hawking were also among thousands of AI scientists and tech-savvy thought leaders to sign an open letter calling for a ban on offensive autonomous weapons.

CHOOSE YOUR OWN APOCALYPSE

Which of these doomsday scenarios will become a world-ending reality?

Optimists would assure you that humanity will avoid foolish nuclear wars, begin to behave responsibly in response to climate change, get serious about controlling AI, and stay one step ahead of emerging diseases. These things, at least, are feasibly within our control. Beyond that, we are at the mercy of the laws of physics.

Statistically, a supervolcano is most likely to hit first. A devastating super-eruption is thought to occur about once every 100,000 years, whereas world-threatening GRBs and asteroids rear their heads perhaps only once in every 500,000.

In truth, it's likely that a combination of catastrophic events – and a chaotic human response to them – will secure our demise. If they don't – the Sun will be hot on our heels in a billion years' time.

China's rainbow mountains

The vivid colours of the Zhangye Danxia rock formations are a mineral marvel

China's Gansu Province, in the central north of the country, is home to a truly spectacular view. The striated colours of the Zhangye Danxia National Geological Park rise up from gullies and canyons in the rocks, and perfect stripes of earthy reds, oranges, whites and browns form craggy peaks that cover over 500 square kilometres.

The stripes in the rocks were originally horizontal, as layers of sandstone and other minerals built up over millions of years. Each layer was created as particles of rock were deposited through wind or water to form sediments. As new sediment layers gathered over time, their weight compacted the layers beneath until they cemented together to form rock.

We are able to see all of these cemented layers in the rock at Zhangye Danxia because tectonic activity has crumpled the Earth's crust and forced the rock upwards, exposing the different sediment sections in stunning rainbow stripes.

Some 50 million years ago, the Indian Plate smashed into the Eurasian Plate, causing the tectonic event that formed (and is still forming) the Himalaya mountain range. This caused a geological ripple effect, uplifting mountains and buckling the ground in different areas. In the case of the Zhangye Danxia Geological Park, the layers of sedimentary rock were exposed.

After the rainbow rocks were uplifted, other physical properties were then immediately at work, eroding and sculpting the landscape as it appears today. Sandstone is typically rather soft, and so forces of dust-laden wind, rushing water and the freezing and thawing of ice have all helped to mould the landforms.

The last piece of the rainbow mountain puzzle lies within the sediment layers themselves. Various minerals were deposited in the layers alongside the grains of sand and rock, and as these have been exposed to the elements as the ground uplifted, they have begun to oxidise and stain the sandstone layers. For example, one of the most prevalent colours in the landscape is a burnt copper hue. This occurs as elemental iron reacts with oxygen in the air – the same way that metal rusts – staining the landscape a dusky red.

"Tectonic activity forced layers of rock upwards, exposing stunning rainbow stripes"
© Getty

NATURAL BORN KILLERS

Revealed: The deadly tactics of the world's greatest hunters

DID YOU KNOW? *Wolves have astounding endurance capabilities and will track and chase their prey all day if they have to*

Whether it's a lion taking down a wildebeest, or a spider devouring a wasp, the predator–prey relationship is a constant carousel of eat or be eaten. It's survival of the fittest. Unfortunately, it's very often the little guy that pays the price for the never-ending march of life. That's because Mother Nature has gifted many of the predators of the animal kingdom with incredible adaptations to lighten the load and simplify their task, no matter how high up they are in the food chain.

There's no stronger hunting force than that of a pack. It has the benefit of teamwork, the use of varied skills, as well as safety in numbers. The drawback for animals hunting in groups is that there has to be enough food to go around, but that's remedied by the fact that many hands, or paws, make light work.

Wolves are a key example of pack hunters, where the relationships between the animals are so intricate that they are able to communicate effectively and work as one ruthless unit. Each individual animal will have a specific role to play, often based on age, gender and social standing.

A similar structure applies to many other animals. For example, an African community of chimps have been hunting together so efficiently that they have decimated the population of their prey, the red colobus monkey. Dolphins, too, will maximise their prey intake by working together to trap fish. Living in close familial units, dolphins communicate in a conversation of complex clicks and whistles for efficient fishing.

Dolphins' cetacean cousins, killer whales, also employ this technique. These highly intelligent ocean giants have been frequently witnessed swimming in formation to create a giant bow wave, washing the seals perched atop ice floats into their waiting jaws. Killer whales have been known to spend hours and hours chasing down their prey, relying on their stamina to keep up the pursuit until their prey tires.

This type of persistence hunting is employed by many other group predators as well as lone rangers, usually those with athletic builds and ravenous appetites. Wolves and wild dogs use the combined strength of the pack to pursue the prey until they collapse with exhaustion.

A successful predator is not a fussy eater; take the hyena, for example. These animals are known for being first-class scavengers, able to sniff out carrion from over four kilometres away, but they're also skilled hunters. Prone to marauding in pairs, one hyena will distract a mother

> "Wolves are able to communicate effectively and work as one ruthless unit"

Hunting with the wolf pack

Strength and wit are used to take down prey

1 When the pack is on the prowl, they're searching for signs of food and assessing favourable factors such as the weather and terrain.

2 Once the prey is spotted, the pack approaches. They may herd the prey into an advantageous area, or track them to cause panic and fatigue.

3 When the prey (often a herd of deer, or other hoofed animals) is panicked and running, the wolves will come in from different sides to lunge at the group.

4 Smaller and slower individuals of the herd, such as the very young, weak or elderly are the easiest for the individual wolves to pick off.

5 Once a wolf has taken down a victim, the chase will stop. The wolves will bite to restrain and dispatch the prey before tucking in.

wildebeest and the other will move in for the calf. In larger groups, it's possible to take down even larger animals for a more profitable kill. Hyena too use the endurance hunting method; they can sprint at 60 kilometres per hour, and can sustain a speed of 40 to 50 kilometres per hour over a distance of five kilometres, snapping at the hooves of their quarry until the panicked beast gives up the ghost.

Lone hunters don't have the combined strength of a pack or a pod to rely on, and so will often have some amazing adaptations to help them in their quest for nutrition. One such critter is the red fox. These brush-tailed foragers pick up low frequency sounds and are able to hear small rodents as they scamper under nearly a metre snow. Without even seeing the target, a fox can launch an accurate pounce, leap into the air and then land to pin its prey down. Scientists believe that foxes actually align themselves with Earth's magnetic field to pinpoint the exact location of their prey, preferring a northeasterly attack for an incredible 73 per cent success rate.

Snakes also use super senses to hunt. They detect a cocktail of visual and chemosensory cues to track down a suitable victim, and are also capable of seeing endothermic heat signatures. Once they have singled out a tasty morsel, constrictor species will deploy the death squeeze. Studies have shown that snakes can match the strength and duration of the constriction to the heartbeat of their prey, making for a scarily efficient dispatch.

Burly brown bears, on the other hand, have the advantage of being at the very top of the food chain. They are solitary and omnivorous and will nibble on nuts and berries or use their sheer bulk to take down deer and even moose.

Yet for many lone hunters, the element of surprise is crucial for success, and that is where the ambush hunter thrives. Setting traps and lying in wait is a very energy-efficient way of hunting. On land, one of the largest ambush hunters is the tiger, which relies on its rich camouflage of stripes for concealment until the opportune moment to strike. Tigers are also excellent swimmers and have been known to attack from the water.

Red foxes use the Earth's magnetic field to line up an accurate pounce on prey

As well as camouflage, the use of tools to hide in plain sight is a feat of magnificence in the animal kingdom. Devious species of both crocodiles and alligators are known to place twigs and sticks across their noses, then lie in wait for unsuspecting birds. Thinking that they're plucking up some prime nesting material from the water, the bird is then quickly snapped up – the first ever evidence of tool usage in reptiles.

> "A predator's environment can govern how it interacts with its prey"

BEARS AND THE SALMON RUN

How brown bears fish out the tastiest mouthful

At the peak of the salmon run, a dominant male can catch up to 30 fish per day

POD TACTICS

Dolphins have an array of clever tricks for catching their prey

PREDATOR STATISTICS

The rate of hunting success can vary. Polar bears only have a ten per cent success rate, but just one 55-kilogram seal has enough blubber and energy to sustain a bear for around eight days. Here are some more killer statistics to show just how hard predators have to work to survive.

The predatory sleuth of the marine world is the octopus. Hunting crabs and crustaceans, these cephalopods are able to disguise both their colour and texture to avoid detection. Once close enough to its victim, the octopus will then swoop down to envelop the morsel in its arms, delivering a bite laced with a potent neurotoxin capable of turning crab innards to mush.

The animal kingdom also hosts opportunistic predators who sit back and wait until an ideal situation happens upon them. The lemon shark is one such beast. It positions itself in the middle of a large shoal of fish, but doesn't make its move until another predator enters the fray. As the other encroaching hunter launches an attack and panics the shoal, the lemon sharks are free to take their fill of fish from the chaos, a fine meal served with minimum effort.

A predator's environment can govern how it interacts with its prey, and how it is adapted to suit its place in the food chain. In water, predators must be quick and agile, hydro-dynamically shaped and capable of instant bursts of speed. The bluefin tuna is an excellent example of this. Unlike most fish it is warm-blooded, which helps its muscles work faster and more efficiently for nifty prey-snatching sprints though the water. Great white sharks are also well adapted. Their huge rows of pointed, serrated teeth are the best possible tool for tearing through skin and blubber, sawing up and devouring the prize before any scavengers get a look in.

On land, the cheetah is an excellent example of an animal perfectly suited to its hunting environment. On the open grassland plains of Africa, there is nowhere to hide, so the cheetah must be stealthy to get close to its hoofed prey. Once in position, the big cat can reach 100

A HYENA PACK ON THE PROWL

The ultimate scavengers are also skilled and speedy hunters

> *"One hyena distracts the mother, while the other moves in for the calf"*

kilometres per hour during an incredible sprint, catching its prey unawares. The cheetah's long tail aids balance and its claws don't retract to provide traction on the dry soil.

Where larger animals have the advantage of size and power, smaller critters have to develop more cunning ways of taking down prey. Being toxic is a helpful trait, as in the case of the black widow spider. The venom used by this infamous arachnid paralyses its prey, which can include small mammals and reptiles.

Similarly, the box jellyfish is shockingly toxic. Jellies are at the mercy of ocean currents and don't really look predatory, yet the sting of this gelatinous hunter can kill a human in seconds. It delivers a potent neurotoxin via stinging cells called nematocysts. The fish or shrimp is killed at the touch of a tentacle, and the jelly can get to work on digestion.

The common view of a predator is one that charges in with tooth and claw, and there are plenty of those on Earth. But the natural world is constantly showing us ingenious methods that animals use to secure their next meal. The electric eel for example, is capable of discharging thousands of tiny, battery-like cells to produce shocks of 600 volts. These fish stun their prey and tuck in.

The marine cone snail has another curious strategy. At night, it sneaks up on a resting fish, then quickly extends a proboscis, a nose-like organ shaped like a harpoon. It swiftly injects the fish with toxins to paralyse it and then swallows it whole.

One of the most ingenious predation methods belongs to the archerfish, the small Asian species that uses a water pistol to gun down its insect dinner. The fish compresses its gills to shoot a jet of water from its mouth and accurately knock prey into the water. It even adapts its firing angle to compensate for the refraction of light in water.

Whether it's speed, claws or deception that makes these predators so deadly, they all have one thing in common: the motivation to survive. Killer instincts and cunning skills have been honed over generations to produce a natural world full of elite hunters.

Changing colour and texture helps the octopus to sneak up on its victim

PREDATOR STATISTICS

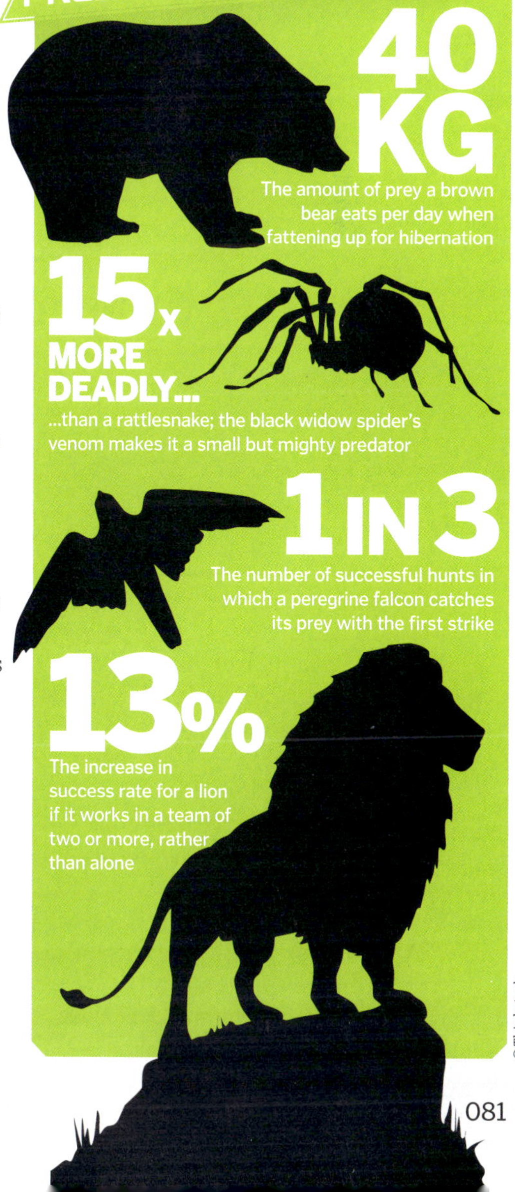

40 KG
The amount of prey a brown bear eats per day when fattening up for hibernation

15x MORE DEADLY...
...than a rattlesnake; the black widow spider's venom makes it a small but mighty predator

1 IN 3
The number of successful hunts in which a peregrine falcon catches its prey with the first strike

13%
The increase in success rate for a lion if it works in a team of two or more, rather than alone

CATS VS DOGS

It's time to settle this rivalry once and for all. Which pet comes out on top?

It's no surprise that dogs and cats have the majority vote as domestic pets. Humans are a tactile bunch, and nothing gets the pleasure centres in our brains firing more than petting an adorable animal. Nearly half of all UK households have pets, with 24 per cent having a dog and 17 per cent owning a cat.

We are hard-wired to take care of things we find cute and helpless like our own offspring, so we can't help but coo over little puppies as if they *were* our own. This relationship is enhanced by the almost intuitive way that our pets respond to us, and when you realise that dogs and humans have evolved together, it's not hard to comprehend how the mutts have been branded as 'man's best friend'.

Recent studies have proven that dogs can recognise emotion on faces, display jealousy and they're even able to coherently watch TV (when there are animals involved). They learn in the same way that children do, are susceptible to emotional contagion (try yawning next to your pup and see if he yawns too) and have a distinct awareness of time.

Although cats, as solitary creatures, aren't fussed about joining in every aspect of our lives, they've been proven to pay more attention than we often assume. Cats can recognise our moods and react accordingly, they can get us to help them without us even noticing and even replicate sounds that subliminally galvanise us into action. Cats also see humans as their surrogate family – has your kitty ever brought you back a live-or-dead gift? She's actually trying to impart her hunting knowledge. Kittens are raised by their mothers, who will begin to teach them by bringing back dead prey. If Tibbles is delivering you large, live prey to dispatch yourself, then congratulations – you're ready to accompany her on the hunt.

Felines are the natural survivors of the pet world and although we love caring for them, cats could survive just fine without our help. Interestingly, evolutionary research has shown that cats have been involved in the extinction of over 40 dog species by outcompeting them for food.

Whether you're a cat person or a dog person, read on to find out the amazing attributes of both species, and you might just switch your side.

ROUND 1: PHYSICAL ABILITY

Cats are the gymnasts of the pet world – they are light, nimble and have an amazing 'righting' reflex that means they always land on their paws. They also have impressive night vision, acute hearing and two ways to sense smells. Ever seen your cat lifting his lips in a snarl? That's him using his Jacobson's organ to home in on a scent.

So in the battle of the senses, the kitties seem to win by a whisker – apart from in the nose category. Dogs 'see' the world through scent, and can sniff out some odours in parts per trillion – the equivalent of detecting one teaspoon of sugar in a million gallons of water! A study has also shown that dogs favour using different nostrils, depending on how the smell makes them feel.

When it comes to physical strength and stamina, the moggies put up an excellent fight, but the hounds have the edge. There's a breed for every task, and dogs are capable of going to extremes. Cats can run fast, with a top speed of 48 kilometres per hour, but dogs can run fast for a very long time. Cats can jump high, but dogs can jump far, time and time again. Greyhounds can hit 68 kilometres per hour, huskies can brave sub-zero temperatures, collies are super agile, and there are even Newfoundland dogs that jump into water from helicopters to save human lives.

Vision
A dog sees the world like human red-green colour-blindness, and their field of view stretches 240 degrees - wider than a cat.

Hearing
18 muscles help to move a dog's ears into perfect position, and they can hear up to 45 kHz.

Smell
A dog's nasal cavity is lined with at least 125 million sensory receptors, compared with our 5 to 10 million.

Teeth
Adult dogs have 42 permanent teeth with large canines and incredibly strong jaws.

Strength
Each breed of dog has different strengths, but most have incredible stamina - able to run for three kilometres or more at high speed.

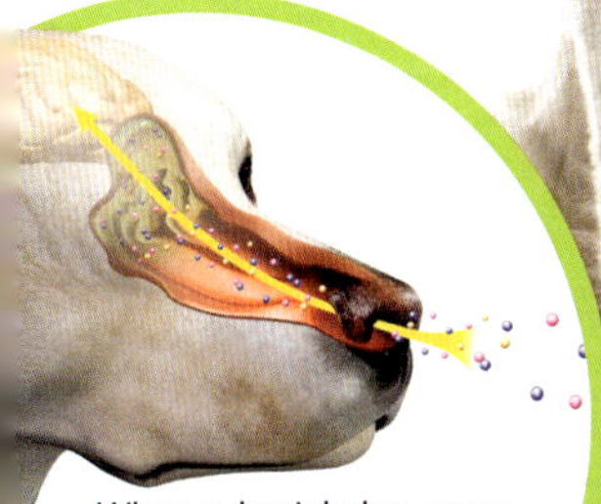

When a dog inhales, some of the air is respired and the rest is dedicated to scent identification

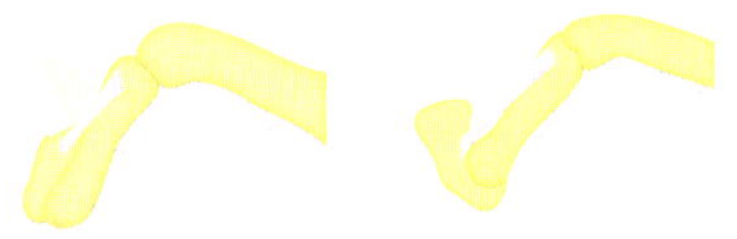

Cat claws are part of a cat's 'toe' bone, extending and retracting with flexing muscles

Your cat's rough tongue has many tiny backwards-facing barbs (papillae) for rasping meat and grooming

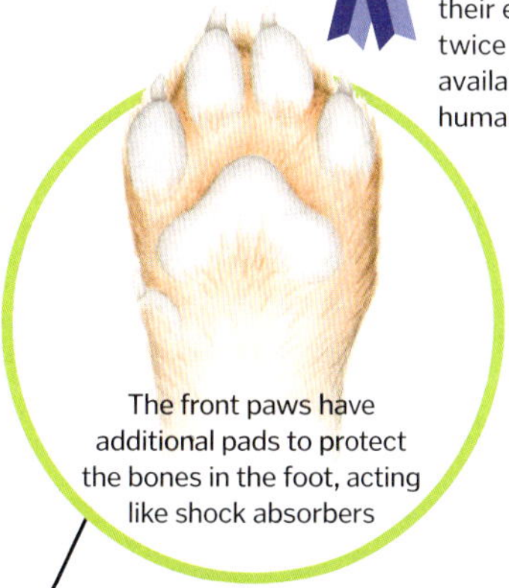

The front paws have additional pads to protect the bones in the foot, acting like shock absorbers

Hearing
Their large, pointed ears swivel to hear frequencies up to 80kHz, while humans can only hear 20kHz.

Vision
With light-reflective layers in their eyes, cats use twice as much available light as humans to see.

Smell
As well as using their nose, cats have a Jacobson's organ in the roof of their mouth, which they also use for scent.

Tail
Tails help with balance, communication and act as a rudder to steer the body when running at full speed.

Skeleton
The feline's super-flexible spine and lack of collarbone helps it to twist the body and fit through tiny gaps.

Evolutionary advantages

Dogs have been domesticated for a very long time. Last year, a genetic study suggested the process began over 30,000 years ago, and that modern-day domestic dogs are descended from various regional wolf populations.

It's thought that wolf domestication happened as opportunistic animals followed nomadic humans, benefitting from their scraps. The aggressive wolves would likely have been eradicated as humans would not have tolerated toothy predators. In time, the gentler wolves would have been selectively bred.

In contrast, domestic cats first appeared around 9,500 years ago, probably in the Middle East. Their ancestors are wildcats, which still roam various wildernesses across the world today and whose lineage can be traced back 130,000 years. It's thought that domestication occurred as plentiful rodent populations attracted wildcats to live near human settlements, and then they may have been fed and homed in order to keep rat numbers down.

The first domesticated dogs descended from grey wolves, most likely from China

All domestic cats are thought to descend from the European wildcat

ROUND 2: COMMUNICATION

Dogs and cats spend a huge amount of time with us. We cuddle them, stroke them and let them into every part of our daily lives – so it's not surprising that our furry friends have developed intuitive ways to communicate with us.

Vocalisations play a large part. Dogs have a hugely flexible range, including whimpering, yipping, growling and barking. Adult wolves don't bark (although juveniles do), so barking has been developed through human-dog evolution specifically as a language for us to understand. Dogs will also use eye contact to connect with us and even follow our gaze in order to figure out what we're looking at. This is a purely domestic habit, as wolves in the wild don't make eye contact with humans.

Cat meows have an even more ingenious hook than a dog's woof, however. From living alongside humans for so long, cat noises have evolved to contain acoustic patterns that connect with us on a subliminal level. A cat's 'solicitation purr' – a mix of purr and loud meow that no one can resist – uses the same frequency as a baby's cry and kick-starts our instinctual desire to protect and care.

Body language plays an even larger part in pet communication. This is how animals show their emotions. A happy cat that wants to be stroked will arch his back under your hand and purr, but if a cat shrinks away, he's not interested. Flattened ears can mean they're worried or anxious, and hissing and spitting means they're ready to fight. Conversely, when your cat does that curious 'slow-blink' at you, this is a relaxed gesture that means all is well with the cat's world.

Dogs also use body language in many different ways. When Fido's ears are perked up, his head high and tail wagging, he's a happy boy. But if he's hiding, with ears down or flattened with his tail between his legs, this is a sign of a dog that's worried or frightened. A truly content dog will lie on his back, exposing his neck and tummy to the world. When a dog strikes this pose, scratch away – he'll love it. Yet when a cat does it, you might just get a scratch yourself, as this generally isn't an invitation.

Science shows us that pets can calm us down and make us happy

Stress relievers

Both cats and dogs are winners when it comes to helping us relax. Studies have shown that petting a furry friend lowers the heart rate and blood pressure, reduces the stress hormone cortisol and promotes the release of feel-good hormones serotonin and oxytocin. Cats and dogs provide unconditional love, and can relieve loneliness and help with depression. Both types of pets can work as therapy animals, where they make visits to hospitals and care homes to cheer up those in need.

Emotions and our pets

It's no secret that our pets seem to be in tune with our emotions, but how much do they actually know? One recent study presented dogs with pictures and sounds showing both positive and negative emotions in humans. They found that the animals spent more time focusing on the image when it matched the sound of the associated emotion. Instead of being a learned response as previously thought, this highlights that dogs can distinguish moods.

Another recent study was able to show that cats exhibit – albeit modestly – different behaviours by taking cues from their owners. For example, if the owner was happy, the cat was more likely to purr and want to be close to them. It's possible that cats associate their owner's good mood with rewards, in turn making the cat happy. The fact that dogs show stronger reactions could be because they have had longer to adjust to life with humans.

Reactions to our moods

Happy

- ☐ Mouth open
- ☐ Tail wagging
- ☐ Energetic and bouncy

- ☐ Purring
- ☐ Closeness
- ☐ Slow blinking

Angry

- ☐ Tail between legs
- ☐ Ears back
- ☐ Cowering, hiding

- ☐ Avoidance
- ☐ Waving tail
- ☐ Jumping up high

ROUND 3: INTELLIGENCE

The average dog has the intelligence of a two-year-old child, and they also have a larger brain in comparison to their body size than cats. However, cats have a larger cerebral cortex than dogs, which is the area of the brain responsible for cognitive information processing.

As these animals are different species with wildly different histories and lifestyles, it's difficult to compare them to decide who is the beast with the biggest IQ (as opposed to comparing dog breeds for intelligence – the border collie wins, in case you were wondering) but each species has intelligent attributes in its own right.

One thing to consider is training. Dogs are very easy to train because they love to work for a reward. They also learn in the same way that human children do. But it's not widely known for cats to perform so well. This is because they're fiercely independent animals, but don't be fooled; although it's difficult, they *can* be trained, just not in the specific way that dogs can (although there are some cases that claim otherwise). If your cat wakes you up in the night and you get up to feed him, you've unintentionally trained him to do this again and again.

Cats are very perceptive, and will use your actions and reactions to govern their behaviour as it benefits them. Some might say that this is an even more intelligent attribute than a dog's ability to do a handstand on demand!

Numeracy

Recent studies have shown dogs can identify higher numbers of dots when faced with a selection of images. This is likely to be because dogs are pack animals, and in the wild, wolves need to know numbers of their own as well as rival groups. Dogs can also detect simple additions and subtractions.

But how do cats fare? A numeracy test isn't really a fair game, because as solitary creatures it's more important for them to be able to perceive size rather than numbers. This is the outcome of a few tests on moggies, but it's also notoriously difficult to hold their interest in these kinds of tests, making it hard to gain a clear comparison!

Dogs can perceive numbers somewhat better than cats, who aren't really interested in being tested!

Do our pets listen?

The doggy brain interprets voices rather like ours do. MRI scans of dogs and people showed that similar regions of the brain responded to human voices – the first time this has been witnessed in non-primates. Dogs also respond to the emotion conveyed in the voice, explaining why vocal communication between humans and dogs is so successful.

With cats it's a slightly different story; although they can recognise their owners' voice over that of a stranger, studies show that compared to dogs, they don't place as much significance on this and easily ignore us. It's thought that this is because cats weren't actively domesticated by humans in the same way as dogs.

By placing dogs in an MRI scanner, researchers found their brains react to voices in the same way as human brains

Dogs with jobs

German shepherds are bold, athletic and brainy, making them ideal dogs for police work

Canines are keen to please and love nothing better than to complete tasks for a reward – whether that's a tasty treat or a quick tug of war. This trainability coupled with their amazing senses can be honed for a huge array of jobs for human benefit. Service dogs such as guide dogs, therapy dogs and medical detection dogs make everyday lives easier. Search and rescue dogs, police dogs, sniffer dogs and military dogs work hard to keep us safe. They can also be trained for other manual work, such as herding, sledding, retrieval and even pulling carts.

Venus flytrap

Insects don't stand a chance when they land on this killer plant

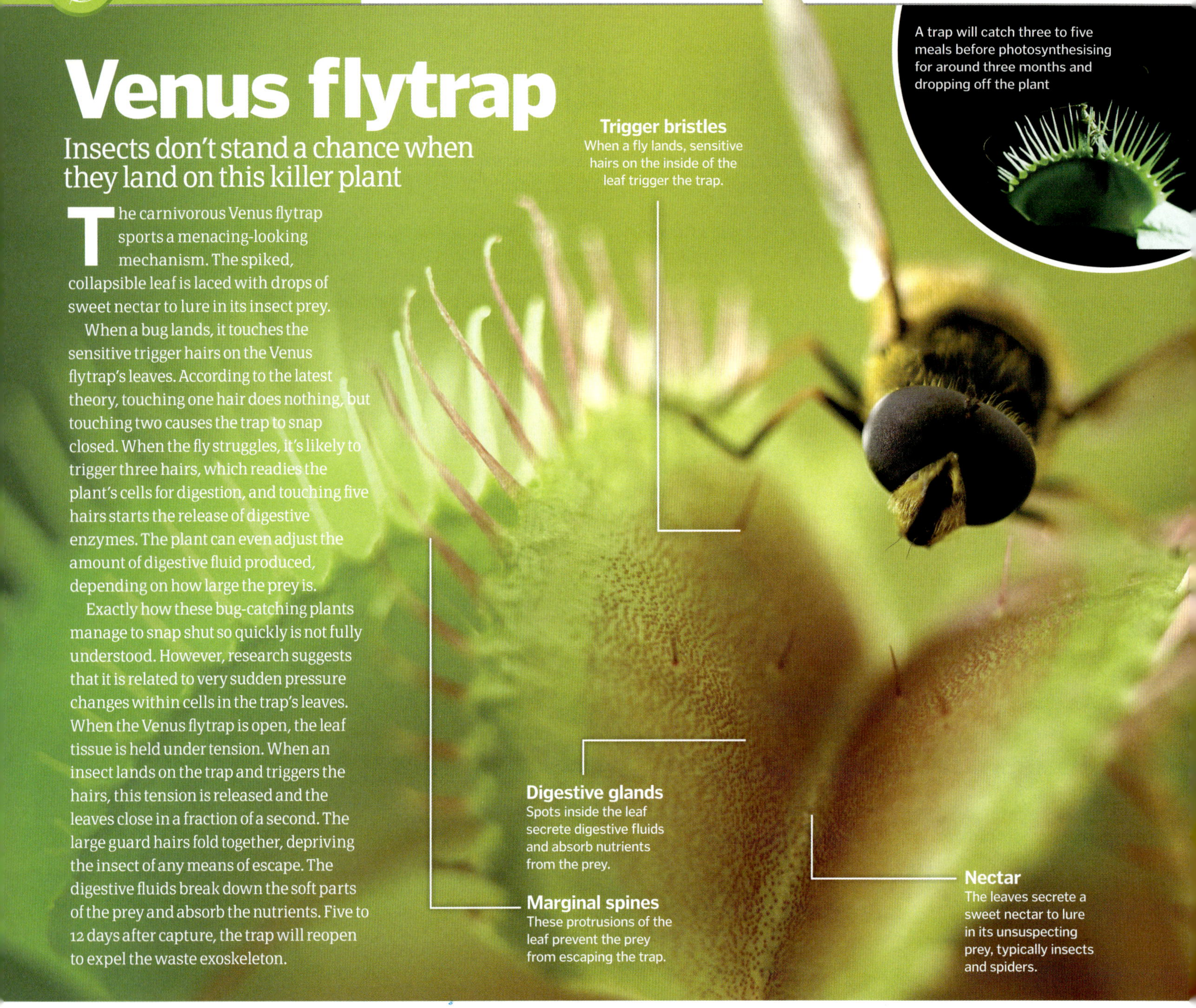

The carnivorous Venus flytrap sports a menacing-looking mechanism. The spiked, collapsible leaf is laced with drops of sweet nectar to lure in its insect prey.

When a bug lands, it touches the sensitive trigger hairs on the Venus flytrap's leaves. According to the latest theory, touching one hair does nothing, but touching two causes the trap to snap closed. When the fly struggles, it's likely to trigger three hairs, which readies the plant's cells for digestion, and touching five hairs starts the release of digestive enzymes. The plant can even adjust the amount of digestive fluid produced, depending on how large the prey is.

Exactly how these bug-catching plants manage to snap shut so quickly is not fully understood. However, research suggests that it is related to very sudden pressure changes within cells in the trap's leaves. When the Venus flytrap is open, the leaf tissue is held under tension. When an insect lands on the trap and triggers the hairs, this tension is released and the leaves close in a fraction of a second. The large guard hairs fold together, depriving the insect of any means of escape. The digestive fluids break down the soft parts of the prey and absorb the nutrients. Five to 12 days after capture, the trap will reopen to expel the waste exoskeleton.

Canada's Spotted Lake

Nestled in a mountainous, forested landscape is a masterpiece of nature

Near the town of Osoyoos, in Canada's British Columbia, lies a lake covered in large, round patches that look as if they have been drawn on by hand. This amazing natural phenomenon appears every summer when scorching temperatures cause the shallow water of the lake to evaporate.

Covering an area of around 16 hectares, the patches that give Spotted Lake its name are actually pools of rich minerals, including calcium, sodium sulphates and magnesium sulphate, as well as traces of silver and titanium. Hues of green and blue decorate the landscape, and throughout the summer the spots change colour and shape as the minerals adapt to further evaporation. When the fresh water disappears, the bed of the lake is exposed, providing natural walkways through the mineral-rich pools.

However, walking through the Spotted Lake pools isn't a possibility for visitors, as it's owned by the Okanagan Nation. To the native community of the Okanagan Valley, the lake is known as 'Kliluk' and holds special spiritual and historical significance. It was bought back from a private owner in 2001 so that it could be protected from development.

There are 365 circles in Spotted Lake, one for every day of the year!

Life cycle of a frog

Discover how a cluster of cells transforms into a hopping, croaking amphibian

The cycle begins when frogs mate. The male holds the female in a position known as amplexus and fertilises her eggs as they are laid. A female frog can lay a clutch of around 3,000 to 6,000 eggs.

Within each jelly-like sphere is a black dot – the developing tadpole. The embryos feed off the surrounding jelly as they grow, and then once they have developed rudimentary gills and a tail after about a week or a month (depending on the species), tadpoles hatch. The hatchlings feed on the rest of the frogspawn jelly mass, as well as any algae that has grown on it.

Throughout the next few weeks the tadpoles undergo a fast metamorphosis. First their external gills disappear, replaced by internal gills, which in turn are replaced as lungs develop. The tadpoles also grow legs while they turn into froglets – strange round critters that resemble their adult form, while still retaining their powerful tail. The front legs are the last to develop, and the tadpole's tail is shortened as it is reabsorbed into the body.

The little frog is now a miniature version of its parents at just one centimetre in length. After around 16 weeks of development it can leave the water, breathe air and feed on bugs and insects.

1 Amplexus
The male positions himself behind his mate and holds her firmly with his front legs.

2 Spawning
During spawning the female lays her eggs, which are then fertilised by the male.

3 Eggs
Frogspawn is buoyant, and large clumps of the gelatinous egg mass can be seen floating on a pond's surface.

4 Tadpole
After a few weeks, the small tadpoles hatch with external gills and long tails.

5 Froglets
As the tadpole grows, it develops a strong tail as well as powerful back legs.

6 Metamorphosis
In several stages, the tadpole grows adult eyes and front legs and loses its tail.

7 Adult frogs
The young frog continues growing once it leaves the water. After around three years it is ready to reproduce.

Tadpoles are often seen in large groups, sometimes called 'clouds'

The Galapagos Islands

Nestled on the equator in the Eastern Pacific are islands so special, they changed our natural history forever

Found far off the coast of continental Ecuador is an archipelago of 13 main islands, along with many other rocks and islets that form one of the most extraordinary ecosystems on Earth. Famous for spurring on Charles Darwin to develop his game-changing theories of evolution and natural selection, the rocky ocean outcrops of the Galapagos Islands were first discovered in 1535 by the Bishop of Panama. He was on his way to Peru when his ship was carried to the islands by currents. There started a long history of the islands' use by pirates, whalers and sailors alike, before Darwin made his famous visit on the HMS Beagle in 1835. Today, the main islands support around 25,000 people in communities on Santa Cruz, San Cristobal, Isabela and Floreana.

Much like Hawaii, the Galapagos Islands were formed by volcanic activity. Situated above a tectonic hotspot, giant plumes of molten rock from the Earth's core forced their way to the surface, sputtering upwards and solidifying in layers through the water. Over time, the new rock finally broke the surface, and so the Galapagos Islands were born. And they aren't finished forming yet, as volcanoes on the youngest island still erupt. The most recent was in 2009, when La Cumbre Volcano on Isla Fernandina blew on April 11, releasing pahoehoe lava flows and giant swathes of volcanic ash.

Beneath the sea, the volcanic island chain continues for hundreds of miles, where the underwater islands that failed to break the surface provide shelter for countless marine species. The exact location of this archipelago in the Pacific means that the Galapagos benefits from the confluence of three major ocean currents: the warm Panama current, the deep-sea Cromwell current and the cold Humboldt current. Where deep-sea currents collide, there are areas of nutrient upwelling, which produces a fertile boom of life and forms the base of the entire island food chain. This happens in abundance around the Galapagos, bringing oceanic visitors from far and wide to enjoy the bountiful buffet delivered by the currents. And where the oceans are teeming with unique species, life on land follows suit.

One of the most fascinating things about these islands is the astounding array of plants and animals that live there. Unique species call the islands home – creatures that cannot be found anywhere else in the world. Giant tortoises, marine iguanas and flightless cormorants are all local favourites, not to mention the Galapagos penguins – the only

On the map

The animals of the Galapagos are surprisingly tame, having never needed to fear humans

penguins to be found north of the equator. What is more amazing is that each island has its own completely separate subspecies of many of these creatures. The region has one of the highest levels of endemism in the world, making the islands incredibly fascinating for scientists to study.

But how does an island chain so extremely isolated in the middle of the Pacific, 966 kilometres (600 miles) from continental Ecuador, bloom into an oasis of life? The answer, once again, lies in the sea. The archipelago is found along the equator; couple this with the presence of the cool Humboldt and Cromwell ocean currents and this allows the islands to display both tropical and temperate climates, a property that is mirrored by the array of animals living on the islands.

Yet although the wildlife is bountiful, it's also rather unevenly balanced. There are lots of reptiles such as marine and land iguanas, but no amphibians; plenty of birds including the blue-footed booby and waved albatross, but few mammals save for a handful of species including the Galapagos sea lions. There are also lots of grasses and ferns, but a distinct shortage of flowering or seeding plants.

This is a direct reflection of how Galapagos was populated by life. Plants and animals had to find their way there by chance, which can happen two ways: by air or by sea. Grasses and ferns have much lighter seeds that can be blown in the wind, and seabirds simply fly there (bringing hitch-hikers with them on feathers or in their guts)! Those that arrived by sea are hypothesised to have travelled on makeshift craft – such as rats on rafts of floating debris – bringing in hardy, salt-tolerant seeds from coastal plants on the mainland.

Because of these incredible creatures, the Galapagos Islands became an Ecuadorian national park in 1959 and was declared a UNESCO World Heritage Site in 1978. Due to the amazing marine life that lives in and visits the surrounding waters of the archipelago, the area was declared a biological marine reserve in 1986, and in 1990 the Galapagos waters also became a whale sanctuary.

Galapagos habitats

The distinct environmental factors of this archipelago provide plenty of complex habitat variations

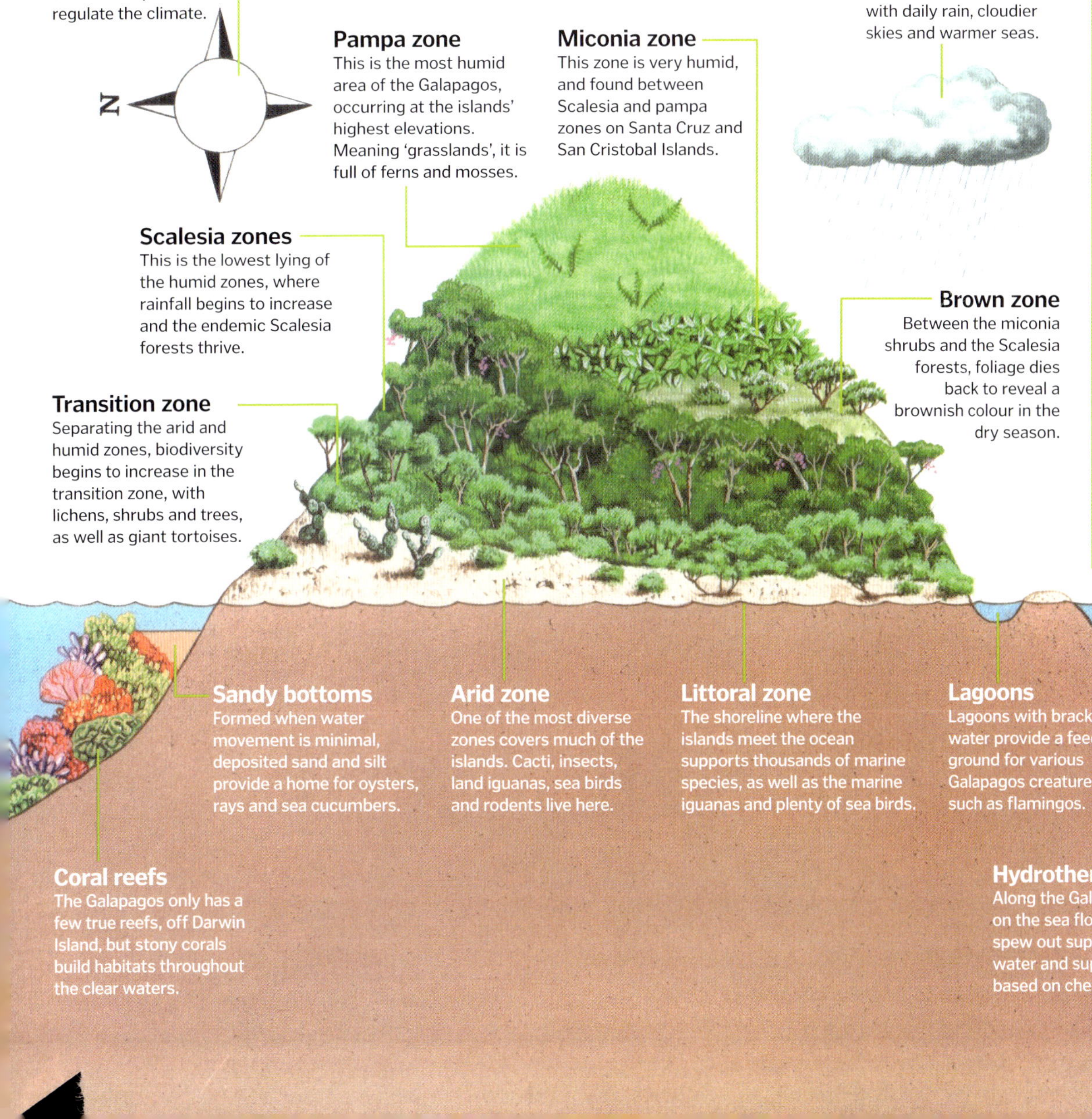
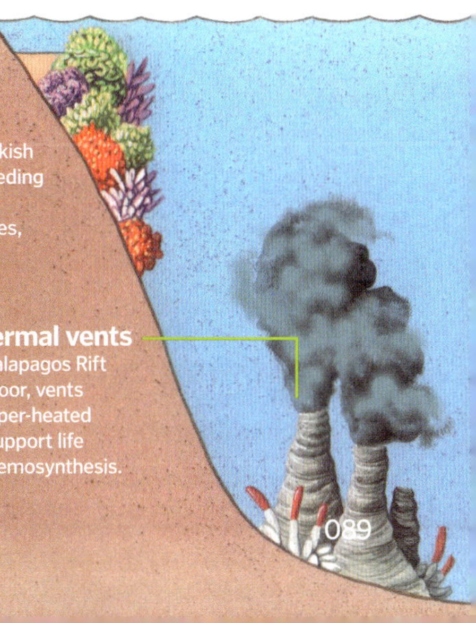

The islands and Charles Darwin

The Galapagos Islands are famously linked to Charles Darwin, and his groundbreaking theory of evolution. Darwin visited the chain of islands in 1835 on the second voyage of the HMS Beagle, where he explored numerous islands and was captivated by the extraordinary biodiversity. Although he took a great many notes, it wasn't until he returned to Britain that he came to thinking about how the species on each island had developed. He compiled his journals and sketches alongside those of his fellow travellers and then two years after the Beagle's return he began to develop his theories of evolution and natural selection. His monumental book *On The Origin Of Species* was published in 1859.

Darwin speculated that Galapagos finches evolved from a common ancestor and adapted to their habitats

FLORA AND FAUNA

The plants and animals of this unique archipelago are like no others on the planet

The Galapagos is an ecosystem populated by incredible living things. Probably the most well-known creatures that call these islands home are the giant Galapagos tortoises – huge reptiles that can reach up to 1.5 metres (five feet) in length and live for over 100 years!

Each island is home to a distinct giant tortoise species, and there are approximately 14 known members of their genus. Their populations suffered after being hunted by whalers, pirates and sailors, and the introduction of new animals to the islands led to increased predation and competition for food. Perhaps one of the most famous Galapagos inhabitants was Lonesome George – the last Pinto Island tortoise – who died in 2012, marking the extinction of his species.

Another of the Galapagos' superstar species is the marine iguana, also exclusive to this island chain. Despite their fearsome appearance, the iguanas are herbivorous. They are the only kind of iguana to use their long, flattened tails to propel them through the saltwater to feed on algae and seaweed beneath the waves.

The islands have been designated as a national park and conservation area to protect their incredible species diversity; approximately 80 per cent of land birds and 97 per cent of reptiles and land mammals found there are endemic. The waters around the islands are also a protected marine reserve, and the list of unique species doesn't stop on land. The reserve protects over 50 species of fish that are only found in that location. It's a haven for sea turtles and even a whale sanctuary to protect the larger ocean visitors.

Sir David Attenborough was thrilled to be the first to film the Galapagos pink iguana

New species spotted

It seems that the Galapagos Islands are still surprising scientists in the 21st century, with new species being unearthed at a surprisingly high rate. An ocean survey in 2009 revealed coral species new to both the Galapagos and to science, as well as some thought to be extinct. In 2012, a new deep-sea catshark species was discovered, and even the third species of land iguana remained unstudied until the turn of the millennium. The huge pink iguana is found only on the slopes of Wolf Volcano on Isabela Island.

Threats & conservation

The delicate Galapagos ecosystem has been vulnerable to numerous threats in the past, such as invasive species arriving and outcompeting the natives for food and space (goats and fire ants are particularly destructive), illegal fishing and human overpopulation. To tackle these issues, the various charities and foundations that look after the islands, such as the Galapagos National Park and the Charles Darwin Foundation have laid out plans for ecosystem management as well as education, to allow communities of the Galapagos to be involved in the protection of their island home.

Populations of waved albatrosses are closely monitored

SCIENCE

106
Your guide to the elements

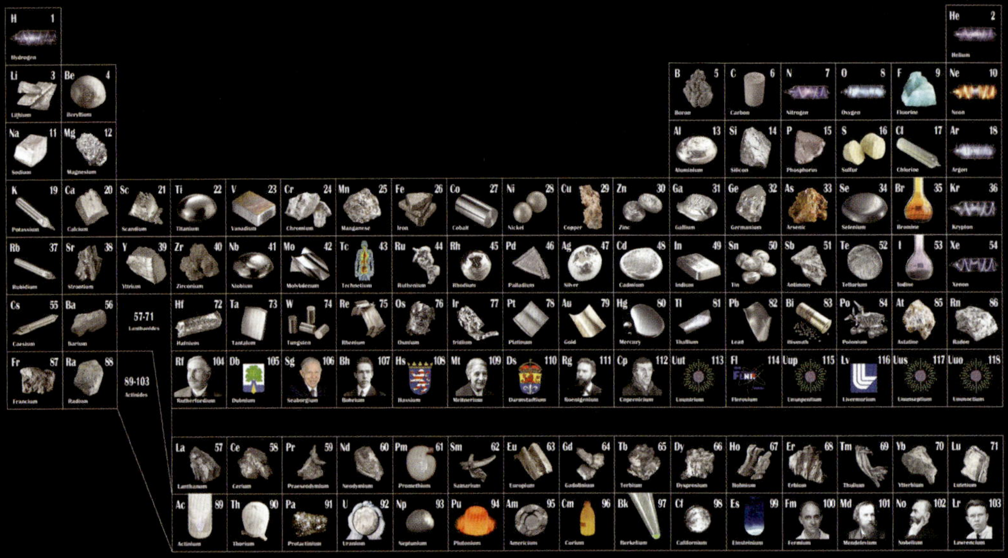

104
The quietest place on Earth

104
The physics of dance

"Modern medicine can already seem miraculous, but the advancements on the horizon are even more incredible"

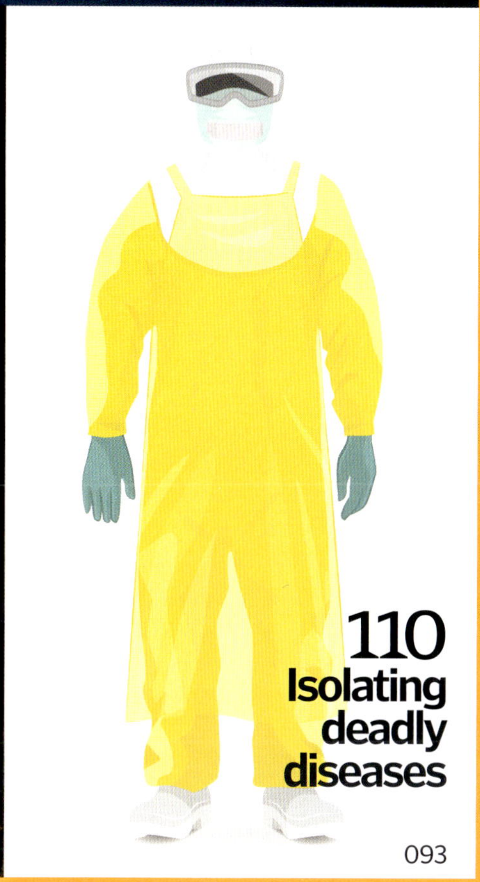

AMAZING NEW MEDICAL TECH!

MIRACLE SCIENCE

REVEALED: THE BREAKTHROUGHS THAT WILL SAVE YOUR LIFE

Modern medicine would seem miraculous to people living less than 100 years ago, but the advancements on the horizon are even more incredible. Scientists and engineers from a wide range of different specialisms are bringing the latest developments together to create an array of new medical technologies that could completely transform the way we diagnose, treat and even cure disease.

Nanotechnology is taking medical treatment down to the molecular scale, focusing on the minute machinery that keeps the body ticking over, while stem cells could provide a renewable source of replacements for every cell in the human body. Personalised medicine promises to tailor treatments to each patient's individual genetic profile, and advances in neuroscience, computing, robotics and electronics are allowing advanced prosthetics to respond directly to commands sent by the brain. Vaccinations could one day be delivered painlessly by thousands of microscopic projections, while custom combinations of vitamins or drugs could be printed into convenient daily pills.

We can't be sure which of today's cutting-edge techniques will make it to the medical clinics of the future, but with technology moving this rapidly, there are certain to be more medical 'miracles' just around the corner.

NANOMEDICINE

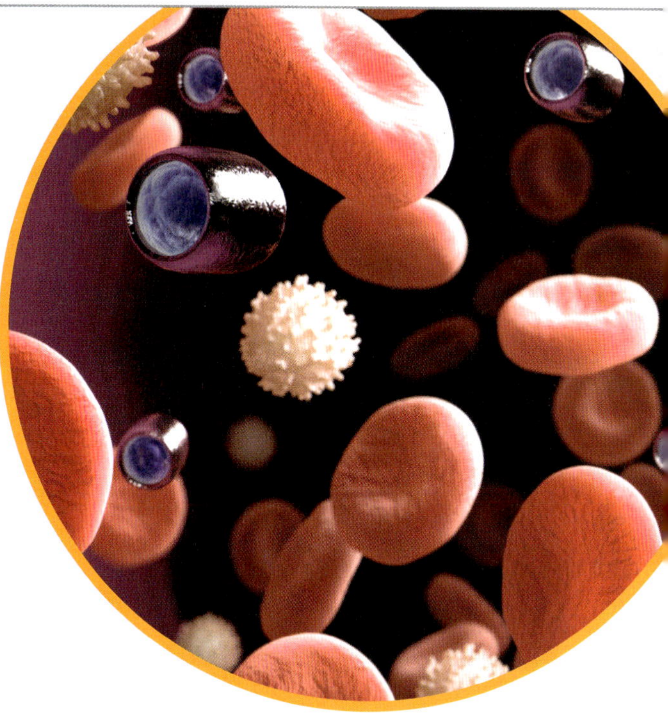

The molecular machinery that keeps the human body running is built on a nanometre scale. Haemoglobin molecules (the proteins that carry oxygen in your blood) are roughly 5 to 7 nanometres in diameter – that's about 10,000 times smaller than the width of a human hair!

Nanomedicine attempts to interact with this miniature world using materials that measure less than 1,000 nanometres across. Down at this tiny scale, scientists hope to develop high-precision nanotechnology that could repair or replace damaged cell components.

Nanomaterials have already entered the clinic, where they are being used to make capsules that carry tiny packages of drugs into the body. Some capsules help to protect the drug from being broken down as it travels to the right part of the body, and others assist with targeting, ensuring that the treatment gets to the right place.

Nanomedicine in action

Nanoparticles made from fatty molecules can help to guide drugs to the right part of the body, such as a tumour

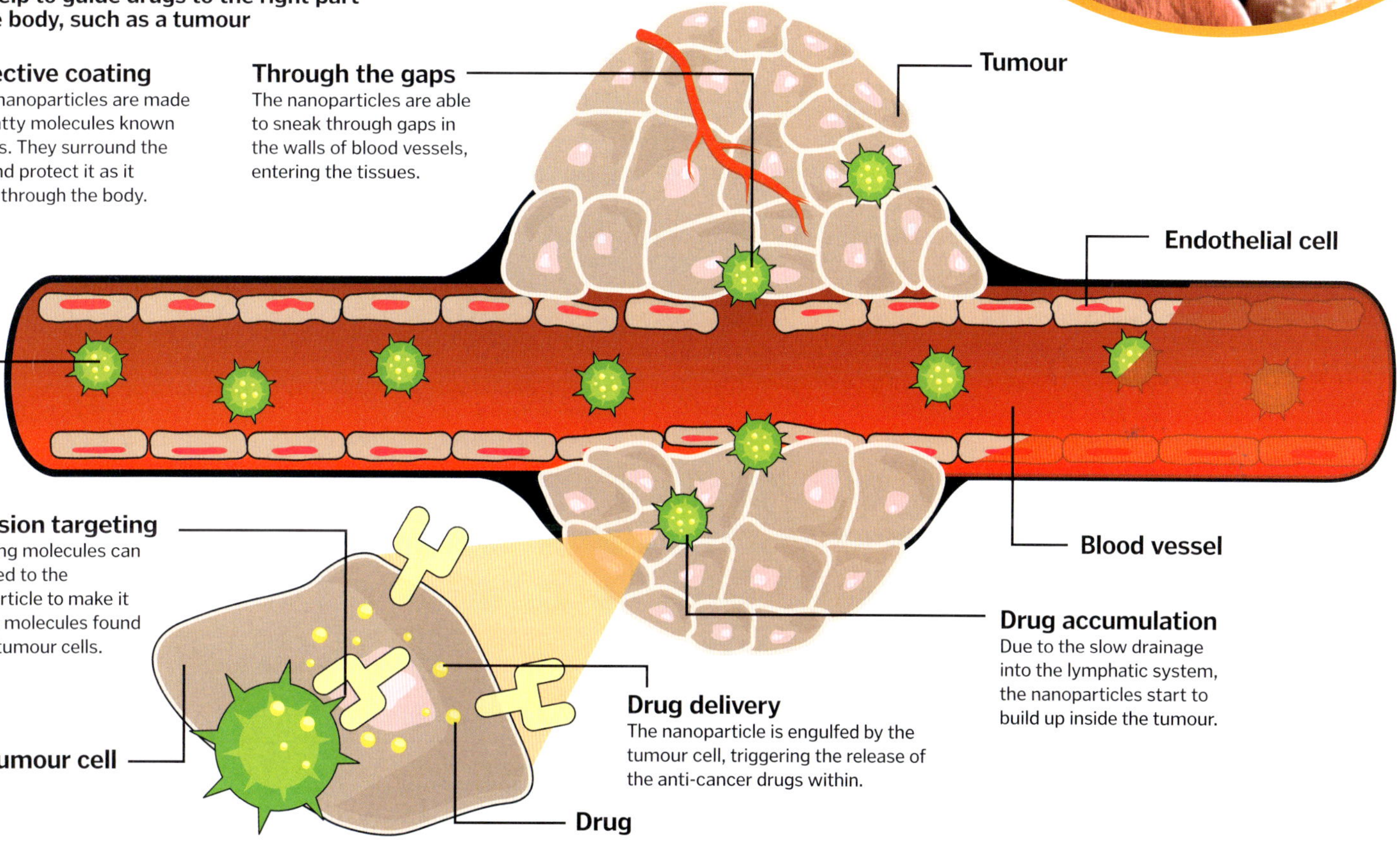

Detecting diseases

Inspired by the Star Trek Tricorder, the Qualcomm Tricorder XPRIZE offers $10 million (over £6.5 million) to a team able to design a portable medical analyser. The aim is to be able to detect 16 common diseases, such as anaemia, diabetes and tuberculosis, and to monitor five vital signs, including blood pressure, heart rate and oxygen saturation. Technology like this could make diagnosis much simpler, potentially even allowing people to monitor their own health at home.

The competition has been running since 2012, and the winner is due to be announced in 2016. Finalists include the Scanadu Scout, which can monitor vital signs like pulse and blood pressure when held next to the head, and the rHEALTH sensor, which can detect pneumonia or even Ebola from a tiny drop of blood.

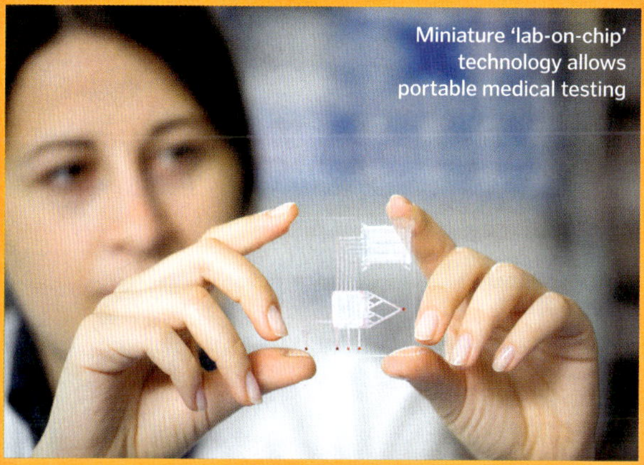

Miniature 'lab-on-chip' technology allows portable medical testing

Teixobactin stops bacteria making the cell walls that they need to protect themselves

REGENERATING DAMAGED TISSUE

With incredible capacity for regeneration, stem cells have the potential to replace every cell in the body

Most of the cells in your body are highly specialised; each is dedicated to its individual role, and once it has committed to becoming a certain cell type, the decision is permanent. Stem cells, however, have not yet chosen a specialism. Instead, they support growth and repair, and are able to carry on making copies of themselves long after most other adult cells would have stopped dividing. Each of those copies can rest, make more copies, or begin the process of transforming into a specialist cell.

The specialism that the stem cell chooses varies based on the signals that it receives, and depending on the type of stem cell that it is – an embryonic stem cell, or one of the many different kinds of adult stem cell. Embryonic stem cells are by far the most powerful; they are found in the developing embryo and, with the right signals, can transform into any type of cell in the human body.

Given these properties, it is no wonder that stem cells are receiving a lot of attention. Doctors already perform stem cell transplants to replace lost bone marrow, and stem cells are used to create skin grafts. In the future, it is hoped they will be used to repair damaged tissues inside the body, or even to rebuild entire organs.

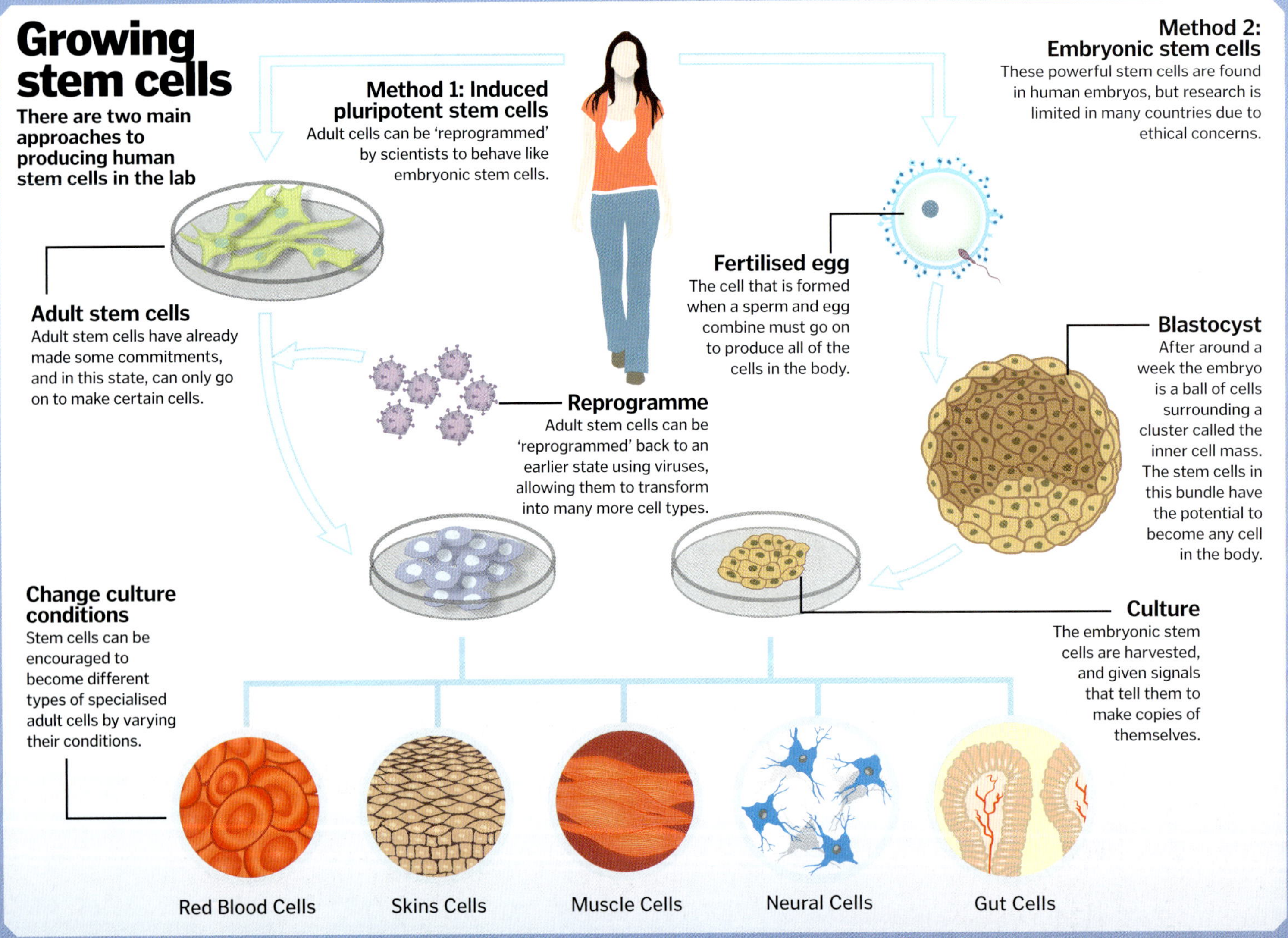

IS STEM CELL THERAPY A GOOD IDEA?

There are arguments for and against using stem cells for medicine

Advantages

- ✔ Stem cells could be used to repair tissues.
- ✔ They could help to build entire organs for transplant.
- ✔ Your own stem cells would be a perfect genetic match.

Disadvantages

- ✘ The long-term effects of using stem cells are not yet known.
- ✘ There are ethical concerns surrounding the use of human embryos.
- ✘ There are many diseases that stem cells cannot treat.

DID YOU KNOW? *It is predicted that 700,000 people in the United Kingdom will be living with late-stage AMD by 2020*

CURING THE BLIND

Could stem cells be used to restore sight?

The London Project to Cure Blindness is a collaboration between Moorfields Eye Hospital, University College London, the University of Sheffield, the British Government, and pharmaceutical company Pfizer. It aims to tackle a disease called 'wet age-related macular degeneration' (wet AMD), which causes rapid loss of central vision.

The team are using stem cells to grow sheets of retinal pigment epithelium (RPE) cells. These cells form a brown-coloured layer on the back of the eye that helps to absorb scattered light, aiding with vision, and help to nourish and protect the rods and cones that detect light entering the eye. The RPE cell layer can become damaged in wet AMD, so the team have used stem cells to grow a patch of new RPE cells to replace them.

The new cells behave just like the real thing in the lab, so in 2015, the first patient received the new treatment as part of a clinical trial. The initial results of the two hour operation will not be known until December 2015, and after that, a further nine patients will be tested to find out whether this pioneering treatment is safe, and crucially, whether it works. In the future, the team hope to be able to use stem cells to grow new rod and cone cells, repairing damage to the light-sensing machinery of the eye.

What is age-related macular degeneration?

Age-related macular degeneration (AMD) is the leading cause of sight loss in adults the UK, affecting more than half a million people. The most common type is 'dry' AMD, caused by the breakdown of light-sensitive cells at the back of the eye, but people can also have more aggressive 'wet' AMD, caused by abnormal blood vessel formation. Both types lead to a loss of central vision.

AMD doesn't cause complete blindness, but affects the central vision, leaving only the edges intact

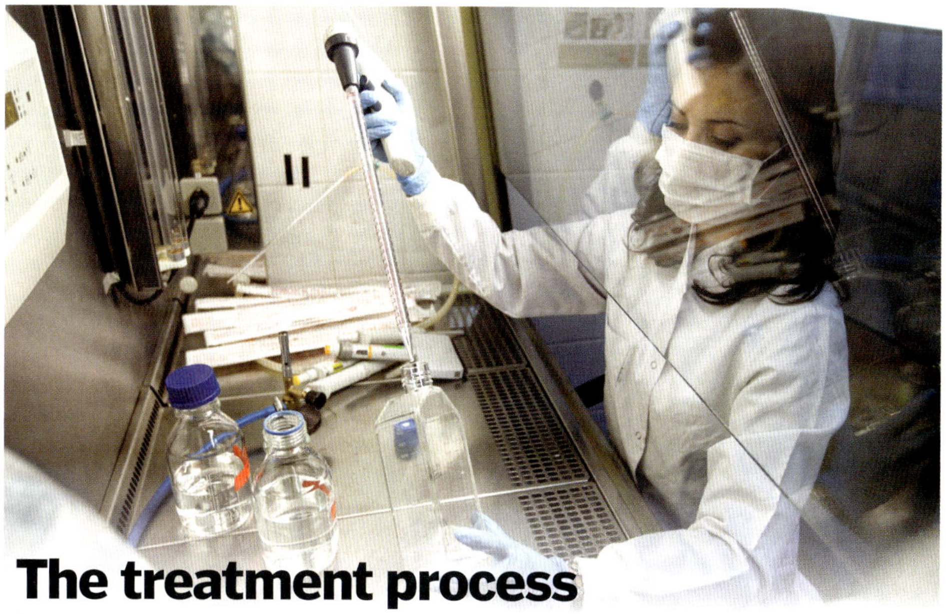

The treatment process

How stem cells can be transformed into specialised eye cells in the lab

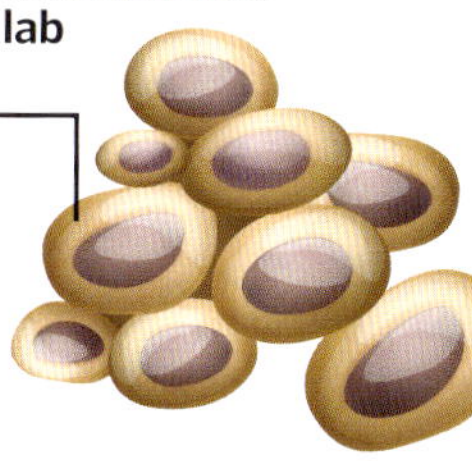

1 Collect stem cells
Stem cells are able to make copies of themselves indefinitely, and are capable of transforming into any cell in the human body, making them the perfect tool for repairing damaged tissues.

2 Add growth factors
The stem cells are given chemicals called growth factors, which encourage them to divide over and over to produce hundreds of identical clones.

3 Add differentiation factors
Researchers can control what type of cell the stem cells will become by using different combinations of chemicals. This process is known as differentiation.

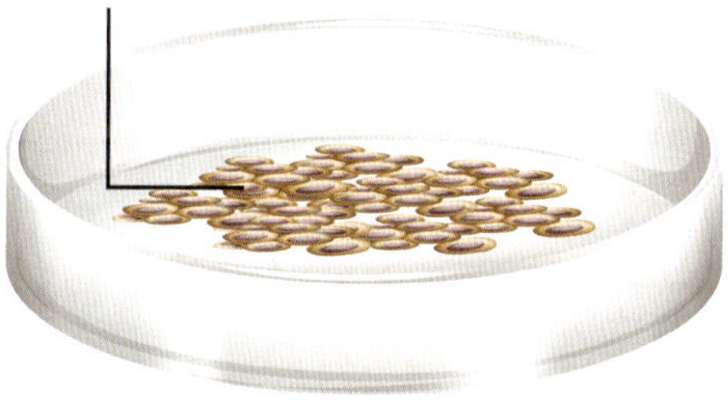

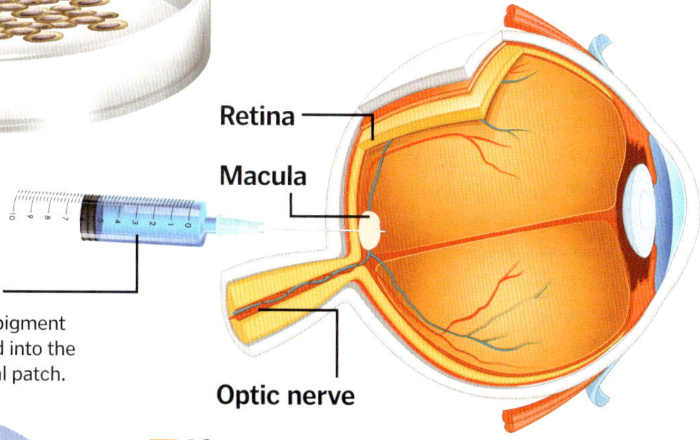

4 Implant the cells
The layer of new retinal pigment epithelium cells are implanted into the back of the eye using a special patch.

5 After treatment
It is hoped that this treatment will help to restore some central vision to patients with age-related macular degeneration.

"The specialism that the stem cell chooses varies based on the signals it receives"

DEFEATING SUPERBUGS

If we are going to survive future infections, we need to tackle antibiotic resistance

Just like humans, bacteria have variations in their genes that give them slightly different characteristics. This means that some bacteria will succumb to antibiotics faster than others. If the more hardy bacteria survive until the course of antibiotics has finished, they can then go on to create an entire colony with the same genetic advantages. The antibiotic you took before will no longer be effective in treating the infection. The more antibiotics are used, the more this cycle repeats, and there are now several strains of bacteria that are able to resist the effects of some of our most powerful drugs. Even more worryingly, antibiotic resistance genes can be passed from one bacterium to the next, and even between species.

Antibiotic resistance

How do bacteria manage to survive high doses of our most powerful medications?

1 Different genes
Like us, individual bacteria from the same species can have slightly different genetic profiles.

2 Antibiotics
Antibiotics kill bacteria or stop them dividing, and they can affect both 'good' and 'bad' bacteria.

3 Some survivors
Some bacteria have genetic traits that help them to survive antibiotic treatment, so they can continue dividing.

4 Sharing genes
Resistant bacteria can sometimes pass their genes on to neighbouring bacteria, giving them resistance too.

How it spreads

Overuse of antibiotics in people and animals is driving antibiotic resistance

Teixobactin

The first new antibiotic discovered in 30 years!

In 2015, scientists unveiled Teixobactin – a new antibiotic that has the potential to combat fatal infections such as pneumonia and tuberculosis. This latest discovery was found in the same source of many other antibiotics – soil – where it is produced naturally by other bacteria. It marks a huge step in the bid to control drug-resistant strains of superbugs.

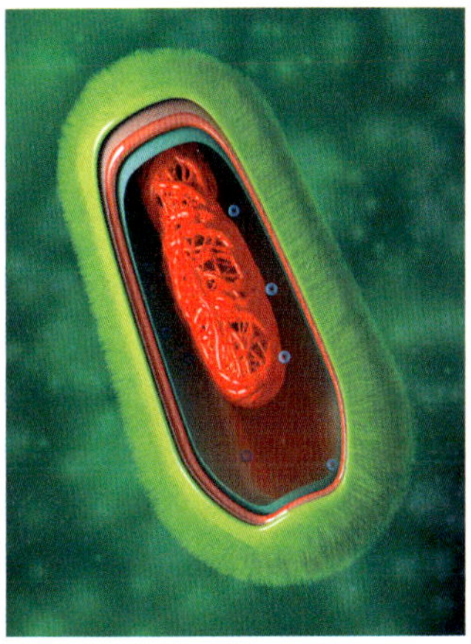

Teixobactin stops bacteria making the cell walls that they need to protect themselves

£10 million prize to solve antibiotic resistance

The 2014 Longitude Prize encourages both amateur and professional scientists to develop a test that can be used to help doctors choose the right antibiotic quickly and cheaply. Ensuring that we only take antibiotics when we need them, and that we are only given ones that will work on our specific infection, is crucial if we want to slow antibiotic resistance.

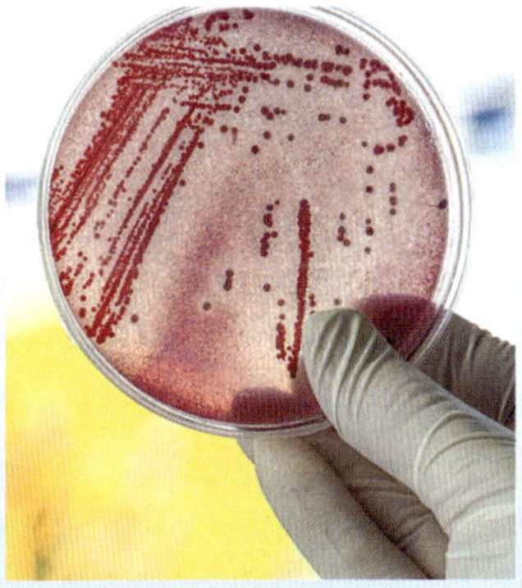

The Longitude Committee will judge entries every four months until the end of 2019

PERSONALISED MEDS

In the future, treatments will be designed for your unique genetic characteristics

The genetic differences that make us all unique also affect how we respond to medical treatment, and the genetic makeup of bacteria and viruses directly impacts their reaction to different drugs. Armed with an understanding of the genetics driving these different responses, we are moving toward a time when treatments could be personally matched to each patient. Steps are already being made with this kind of precision medicine in the treatment of cancer, where genetic differences in the tumour cells play a huge role in whether or not different treatments will work.

Matching medicines to genetics

People have different genes, so they respond differently to the same drugs

Patients awaiting treatment
These people all have the same cancer, but their genes are subtly different.

Different responses
Genetic differences affect how long it takes to clear the drug from the body.

Tailored dosage
The patient can be given a dosage that matches their genetic makeup.

Normal drug clearance
Most patients can clear the drug quickly from their bodies.

Gene version one
A blood test identifies the patients as having the gene for normal clearance.

Normal dose
The patients that will clear the drug quickly are given a normal dose.

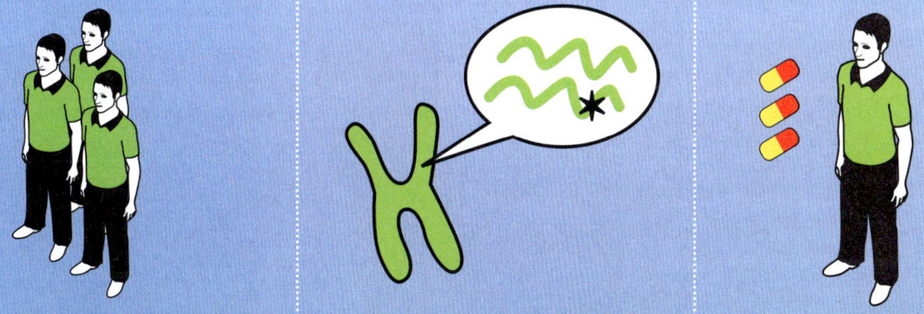

Slower drug clearance
If the drug is cleared slowly, it can build up in the body, increasing side effects.

Gene version two
The blood test reveals a different gene, that gives a slower drug clearance.

Medium dose
The patients that clear the drug more slowly are given a lower dose.

Poor drug clearance
A few patients clear the drug so slowly that normal doses become dangerous.

Gene version three
The gene identified in these patients means the drug will clear very slowly.

Low dose
The patients that struggle to clear the drug are given a small dose.

PRINTING BODY PARTS

The future holds custom-printed drugs and prosthetics, and even replacement body parts

Plastic 3D printers are a natural fit for creating prosthetics, but some of the most exciting medical 3D printers use a different kind of 'ink'. Using precision techniques, scientists are working on combining different medicines into one compact pill. Different ingredients could be included in the printer to control when each drug is released, and custom pills could be printed for each patient. This goal is still decades away, but printers could be used to make vitamin supplements much sooner.

3D printers can also be used to create custom surgical implants, from plates, to replacement joints, to scaffolds used to encourage cells to grow into new tissues. These printed structures can either be long-lasting or soluble. However, 3D printers don't just produce artificial body parts; they are also able to recreate the real thing. Some 3D printers are designed to print with living human cells, forming sheets of tissue that could be used as grafts to repair damage. Researchers at the Wake Forest Institute for Regenerative Medicine, North Carolina, are also working on printing cells directly on to the body to repair wounds. Printing entire organs is the ultimate goal, but whether it is actually possible is a topic of debate among scientists.

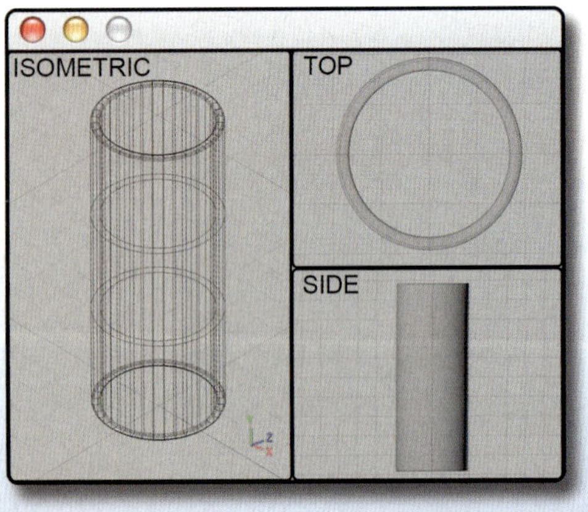

1 Computer control
The shape of the final printed structure is first mapped out on a computer, providing a template that can be used by the printer to construct the real thing.

3D medicine
Printed medical supplies are on their way, and some are already available

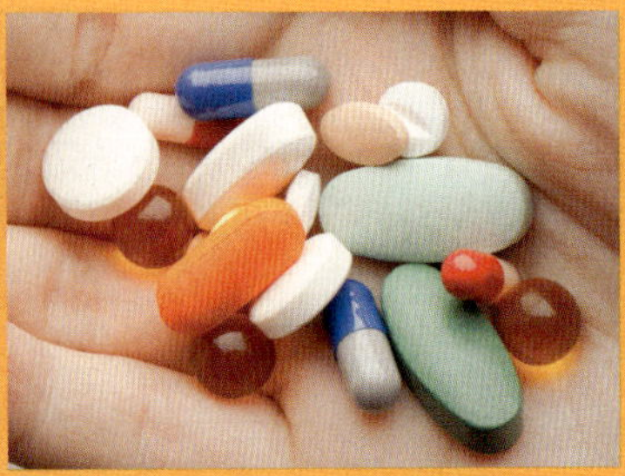
3D printed drugs

Replacement organs

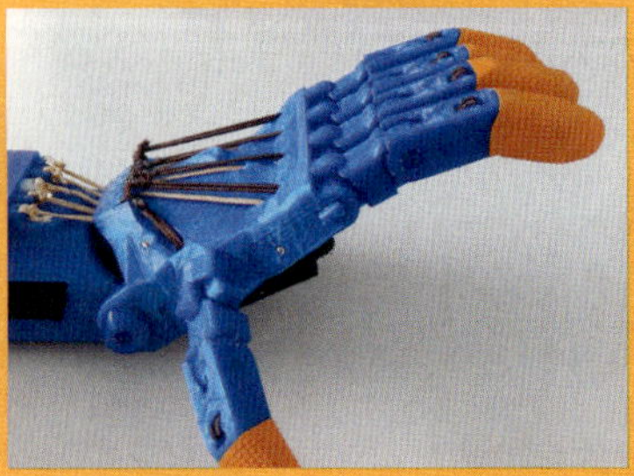
Prosthetics

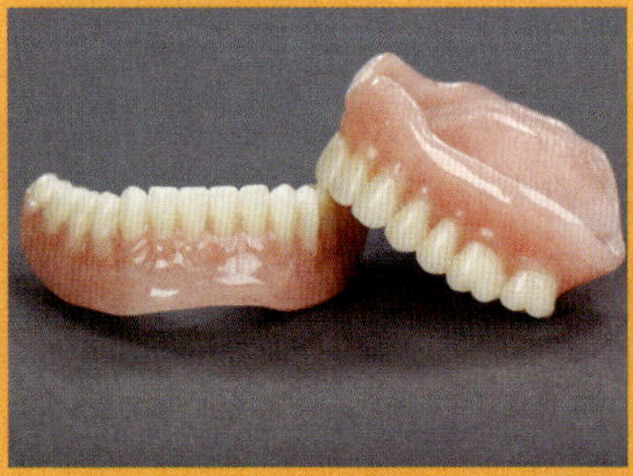
Dentures

Illustration by Nicholas Forder

HELPING PEOPLE WALK AGAIN

The future of medicine is not just about biological advancements – robotics, prosthetics and complex electronics are set to play an increasingly important role in health care. Existing medical prosthetics are able to respond to nerve impulses or muscle movements in the body of the wearer, and now research teams are plugging medical aids into the brain.

Brain-to-tech interfaces read the electrical patterns of the brain. These can be recorded across the scalp using an electroencephalogram (EEG), and the patterns can be decoded by a sophisticated computer algorithm. A team at the University of California, Irvine, have developed a system that monitors signals from the brain, and transforms them into a series of electrical pulses. The pulses travel down wires attached to the muscles in the legs – effectively doing the job of the spinal cord.

The technology is still in development, but in early tests it enabled a man with a spinal cord injury to walk for the first time in seven years. Similar interfaces are also being trialled for use with prosthetics, and scientists are even working on sensors that can recreate the sensation of touch.

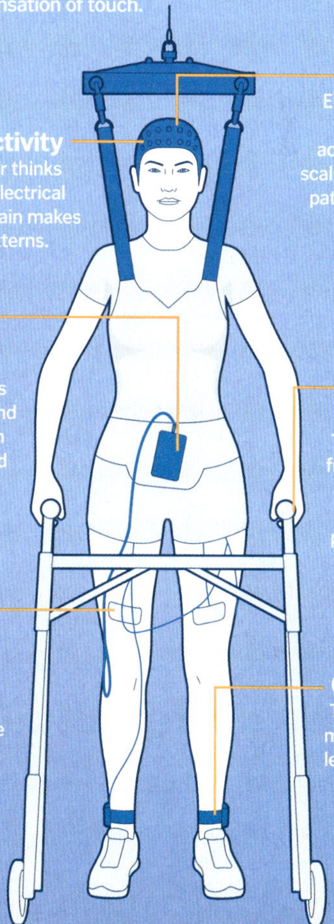

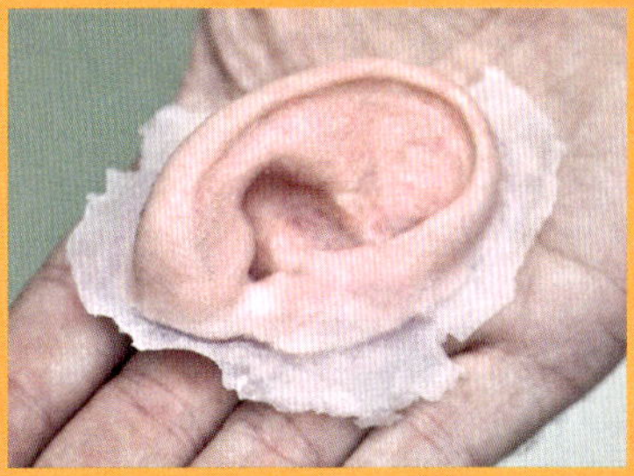
Skin grafts

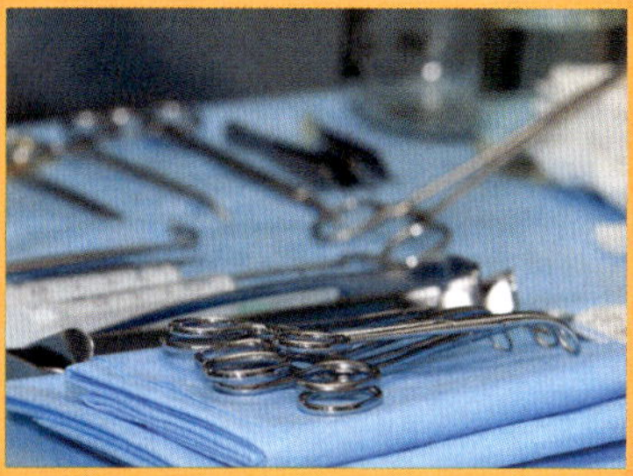
Medical equipment

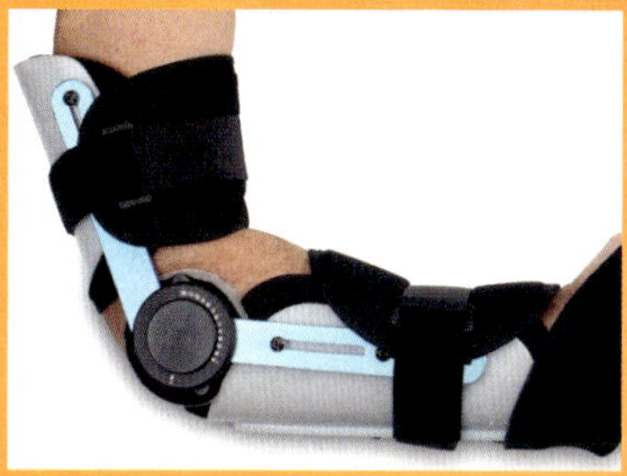
Splints, casts and braces

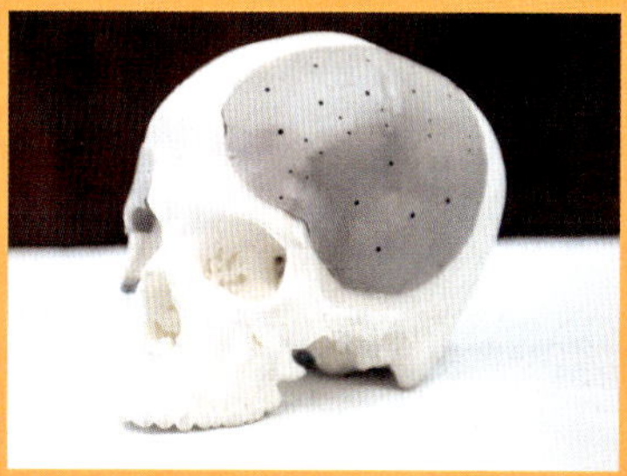
Bone implants

© Alamy; Rex Features

FUTURE VACCINES

The immune system fights infections much more efficiently if it has encountered them before

Most vaccines are made from a weakened or inactivated form of the pathogen, or even just some of its parts. These are injected into the body along with chemicals known as 'adjuvants', which help to get the immune system moving. The infection never takes hold, but as the immune system works to clear the vaccine, it develops highly targeted weaponry that can be used to fight the real thing.

These types of vaccinations have changed the world. Smallpox was eradicated in 1980 after a vaccination programme, and vaccines keep dozens of other infectious diseases at bay, but new techniques are being developed to take this protection even further. 'Recombinant viral vector' vaccines hijack viruses and use them as vehicles. Viruses inject their genetic information into cells, but using genetic engineering scientists can delete the genes that make them dangerous and replace them with something useful. Using this technique, harmless viruses are being created to carry training materials into the body to teach the immune system how to fight infections, or even non-infectious diseases like cancer.

A similar technique, known as DNA vaccination, directly injects genetic information into the muscle (usually attached to something like microscopic gold beads). These genes carry the instructions to make molecules found on infections, allowing the immune system a sneak peek before it has to encounter the real thing.

Painful needles could be replaced with harmless silicon patches in the future

Painless injections

The Vaxxas Nanopatch is one square centimetre (0.2 square inch) of silicone, coated in around 20,000 microscopic projections. These spikes are too small to see, but the end of each one is coated in vaccine.

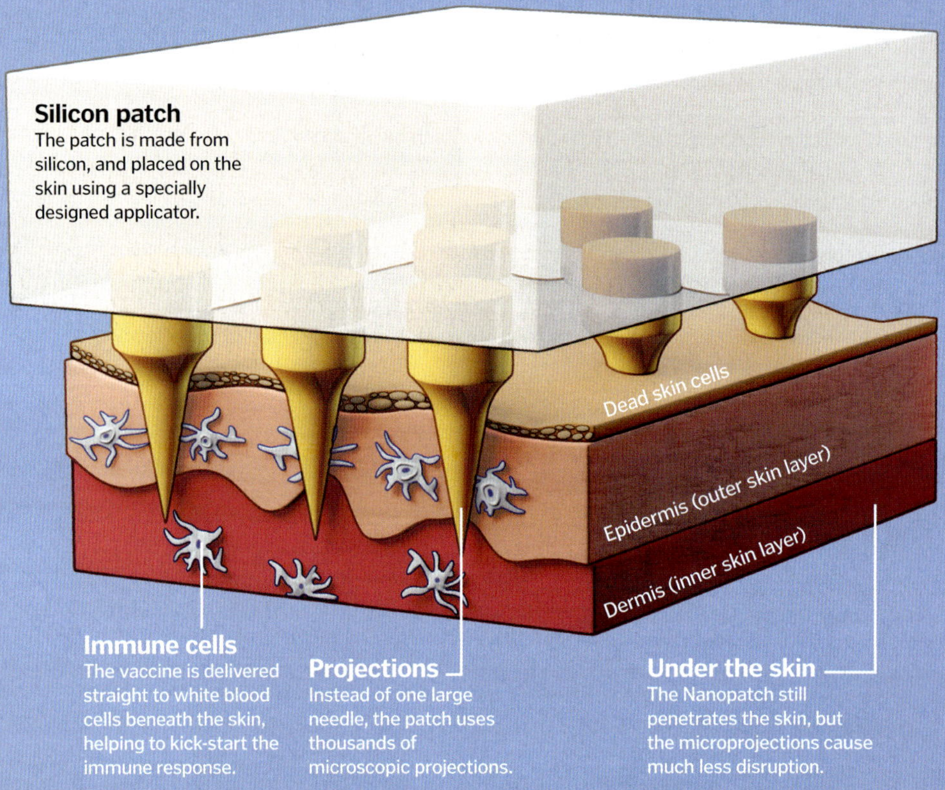

Illustration by Nicholas Forder

A vaccine for HIV?

Scientists at the Scripps Research Institute in Florida are designing a vaccine that could help to prevent HIV infection. Their new treatment blocks the virus when it tries to stick to human cells, and has stopped HIV taking hold in animals

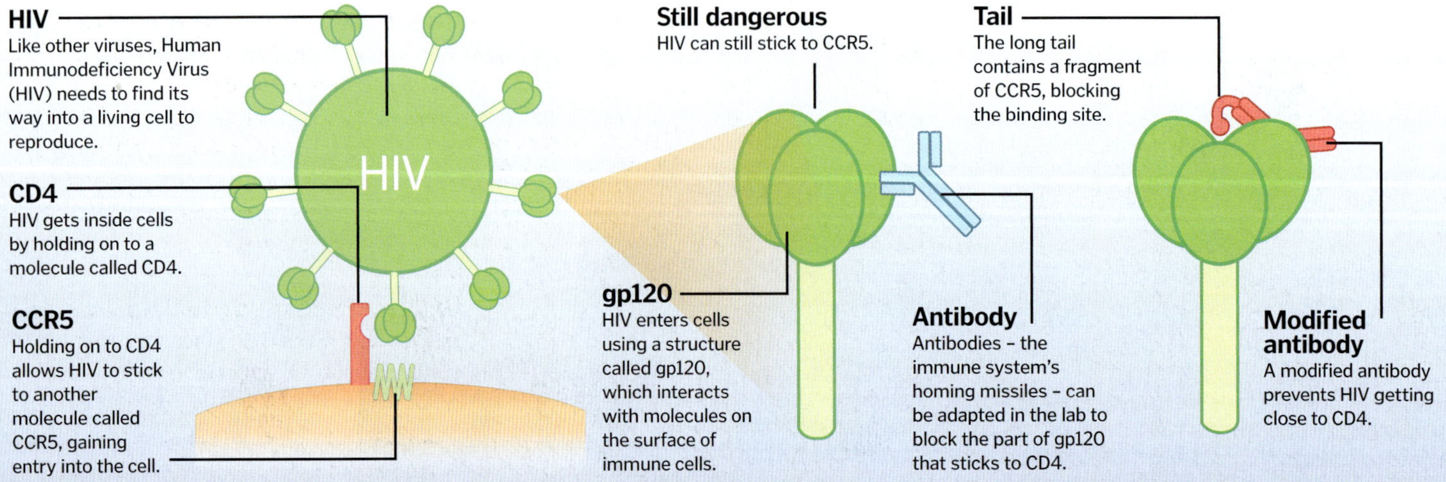

NEEDLE-FREE EBOLA CURE

How a nasal spray could protect against one of the world's most deadly diseases

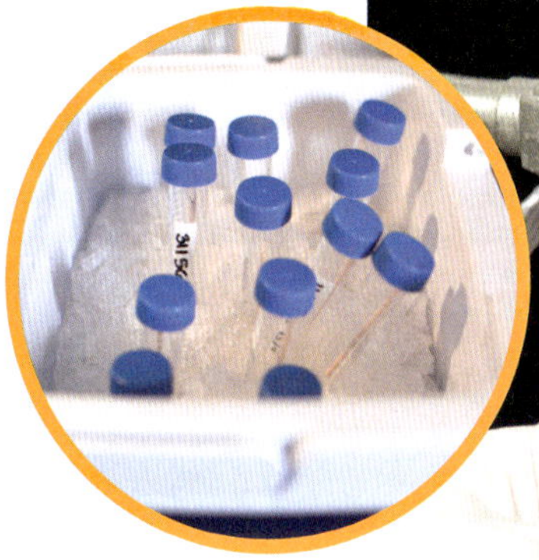

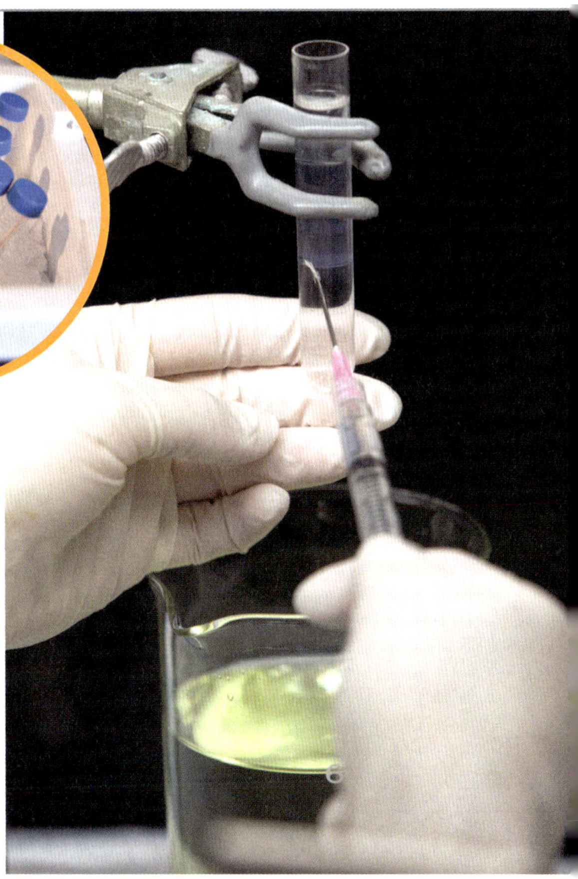

The current Ebola outbreak in West Africa has taken the lives of over 10,000 people so far, but finally a cure is on the horizon. For the past seven years, Dr Maria Croyle and her team at the University of Texas have been working on a vaccine that offers long-term protection against the deadly virus, and their latest tests show that it has a 100 per cent success rate in primates.

The vaccine, which is inhaled through the nose instead of injected, could enable fast control of future outbreaks and revolutionise the way life-saving drugs are produced. It's just one of the incredible discoveries explored in National Geographic's new series, *Breakthrough*. We spoke to Dr Croyle to find out more about her work and what the future holds for vaccines.

How did you develop the Ebola vaccine?

I was contacted by two scientists who were First Responders to many of the Ebola outbreaks and very interested in my project to develop a needle-free vaccine. I spent two months in their laboratory, where they had the genetic material for Ebola, and we developed the vaccine, which is essentially a cold virus called the adenovirus.

We took out the DNA from the cold virus that allowed it to replicate and make us sick, and replaced it with the sequence of the protein that covers the outside of the Ebola virus. We figured if we could get an immune response against that protein, the virus is pretty much dead in the water and can't make someone sick.

Why does it take so long to develop a vaccine?

It's great to rush something out to the people that need it, but if there is any chance that it may not be safe, that could completely destroy a vaccine that may otherwise be very good. So that's why there is something called the 'three animal rule'. Essentially you have to test the vaccine in three animal models that reflect the human disease. Throughout the whole process, not only did we look for the fact that there's a good immune response, we also looked for toxicities that could cause a problem.

What are the most important benefits of a needle-free vaccine?

A lot of places affected by the Ebola outbreak are very isolated villages where they are not used to people that aren't part of their culture. It isn't acceptable for someone outside of that to go after them with a needle. Plus, the nasal spray alerts the immune system to the areas where one would be exposed to Ebola – through cuts or abrasions in the skin – much faster than an injection does.

The needle-free Ebola vaccine is inhaled through the nose instead of injected

What stage is the vaccine at right now?

It's ready to go. We're currently in the process of talking with two major companies that have the resources to produce it on a large scale and can really help to get it to the people who need it most. We really hope within the next year it will be available.

How do you think the process of producing vaccines will change in the future?

The way we stabilise the vaccine is unique and we think it will change the way certain vaccines that need refrigeration are produced. In our studies with mice and guinea pigs, we found that if we placed the vaccine under the tongue, it seemed to work really well. So we stabilised the vaccine in this thin, flexible film that almost looks like a fruit rollup. This way, we found that we could store it at room temperature for at least three years. We could then simply put it in an envelope, ship it to where it was needed and once it got there, add water to the sheet of vaccine and in minutes it could be used as a nasal spray.

Breakthrough is the ground-breaking series about some of the world's leading scientists and how their cutting-edge innovations and advancements will change our lives in the immediate future and beyond. It is currently airing on Sundays at 10pm on the National Geographic Channel.

The physics of dance

Ballet dancers perform a precise balancing act every time they take to the stage

Gravity pulls ballet dancers downwards, while the floor pushes up, counteracting and balancing the force. But balanced forces don't necessarily mean a balanced dancer. Mass is the overall amount of matter that the dancer has inside their body, and to stay on their feet, they need to ensure that the centre point of that mass remains right above the spot where their feet touch the floor.

If the dancer were spherical, their centre of mass would be smack in the middle, making balancing easy. But they have a head, arms and legs, and each time they move, their centre of mass moves too. This makes balancing more challenging, but by using their limbs as counterweights, dancers can stay upright in the most incredible poses.

The dancer's feet in contact with the floor also generate another force: friction. This stops them slipping as they move, and it can also be used to generate torque, or spin. During spins, arms and legs can be used to stunning effect. Thanks to the law of conservation of angular momentum, if a dancer brings their arms and legs inwards during a spin, they will spin faster. Bringing them out again can slow the dancer down to a gentle stop.

Ballet forces

Dancers work hard to keep their centre of mass in line with the floor

The quietest place on Earth

The extraordinary rooms that make it possible to hear your own heartbeat

You haven't truly experienced silence until you've been in an anechoic chamber. These rooms are made from heavy concrete with rubber-sealed doors to prevent any sound at all from getting in. Inside, the walls are covered in foam wedges to absorb internal noise, and the floor is a suspended mesh to eliminate the sound of footsteps. Every inch is designed to absorb reflections of sound waves, so you hear absolutely nothing.

These chambers are mainly used to test the performance of speakers, microphones and other products, but they also help astronauts to prepare for the eerie silence of space. The longest anyone has been able to bear the quiet for is 45 minutes.

Orfield Laboratories, which is in the US, currently holds the Guinness World Record for the quietest place on Earth, as the walls can absorb 99.9 per cent of sound.

In this environment, all a person can hear is the thumping of their heart, which can quickly drive them crazy, and with no perceptual cues to help them balance, it's also incredibly disorientating and difficult to stand or move. So next time you wish for a bit of peace and quiet, think again.

Anechoic chambers absorb all sound so there are no echoes

Gravity maps

The Earth might look round, but our gravity is lumpy

If Earth were smooth like a ball, its gravitational field would be equally smooth, but you only have to look out of the window to see that our planet has lumps and bumps. It is uneven both inside and out, and this affects our gravitational pull.

Albert Einstein explained that gravity occurs because mass distorts space and time. Stars, planets, and even humans create dips in the fabric of the universe, and objects that come close will fall in to these. The more mass in a given space, the more of a dip is created, and the stronger the gravitational field.

It makes sense then, that Earth's gravity is not uniform. The planet is covered with mountain ranges, valleys and seas, and is made up of chemical elements with different atomic weights and densities. Even the movement of water in the oceans or the melting of glaciers can have an impact. All of these inconsistencies across our planet create an ever-changing map of so called 'gravity anomalies'.

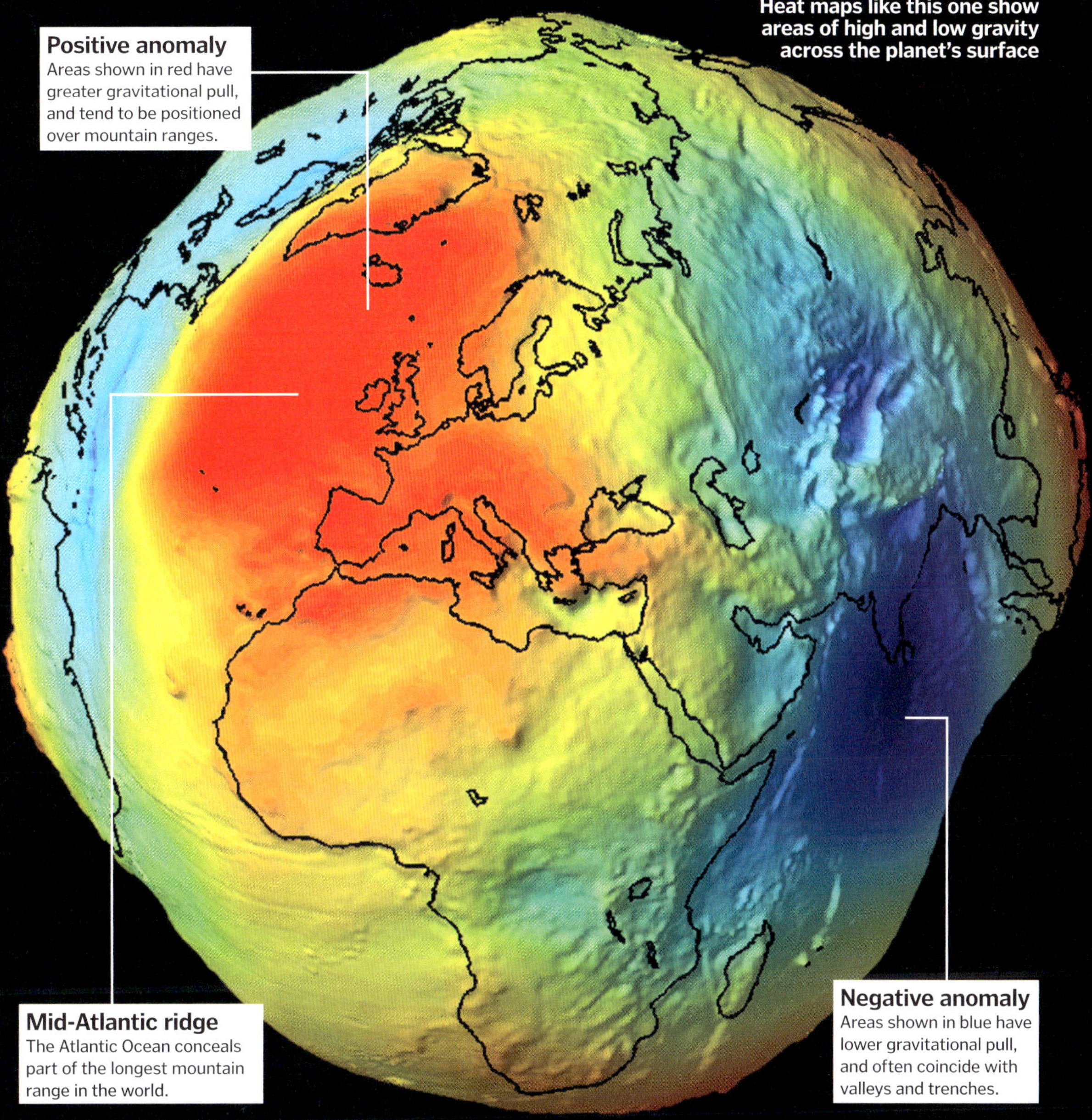

Earth's gravity
Heat maps like this one show areas of high and low gravity across the planet's surface

Positive anomaly
Areas shown in red have greater gravitational pull, and tend to be positioned over mountain ranges.

Mid-Atlantic ridge
The Atlantic Ocean conceals part of the longest mountain range in the world.

Negative anomaly
Areas shown in blue have lower gravitational pull, and often coincide with valleys and trenches.

Tooth whitening

How do you get that perfect Hollywood smile?

The hard enamel outer surface of each tooth is coated in a layer called the pellicle. It is made mainly from proteins found in the saliva, but can also contain trapped particles from food, drink, and cigarette smoke. Over time, these can cause discolouration. The film can be removed by brushing, or by scraping, sonication, or chemical treatments, but if the compounds sit on the teeth for too long, the underlying enamel can also become stained. This doesn't tend to cause any harm, but it can't be removed by cleaning alone.

Dentists offer two main forms of tooth whitening: carbamide and hydrogen peroxide. They both act as bleaching agents and work to lighten the stains. The chemicals are most often applied as gels inside a specially made gum shield that is moulded to the shape of your teeth, and laser light can also be used to speed up the process. At-home treatments are also available, but the NHS advises against their use. The kits might not be strong enough to have the desired effect, and if the gum-shield doesn't fit properly, the chemicals could leak and cause gum damage.

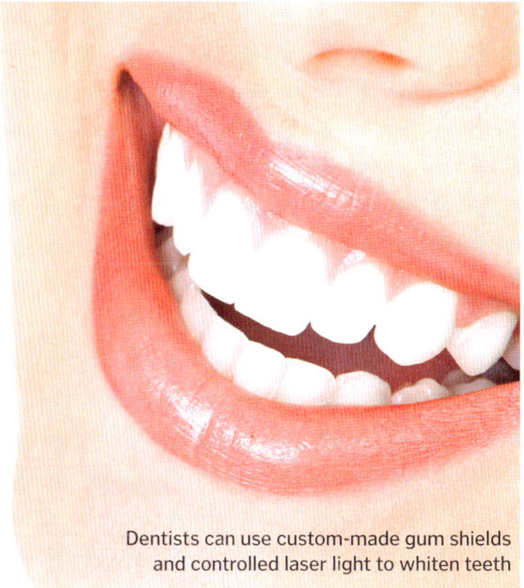

Dentists can use custom-made gum shields and controlled laser light to whiten teeth

YOUR GUIDE TO

How these chemical building blocks make up life, the universe and everything

All of the 118 elements in the periodic table are made from the same three key ingredients – protons, neutrons and electrons. The protons and neutrons make up the nucleus at the centre of each atom, while the electrons whizz around the outside and make chemical bonds with other atoms. The identity of each atom is determined by the number of protons in its nucleus, known as the atomic number. Hydrogen has one, helium has two, lithium three, and so on. The periodic table lists the elements in this order.

Protons are positively charged, while electrons are negatively charged; an atom will have an equal number of each. The electrons are arranged in 'shells' around the nucleus. Each row of the periodic table represents a new layer of electron shells, and each column represents how full the outer shell is. For example, elements in the first column of the periodic table – including lithium and sodium – have just one electron in their outer shell, while those in the second column – such as beryllium and magnesium – have two.

The number of electrons in the outer shell affects how the element behaves, so those in the same column have similar properties. Atoms like to have a full outer shell of electrons, so those with one or two extras are keen to give them away, and those with gaps want to fill them up. If you drop any of the elements from the first column into water, they will fizz, flame or even explode as they race to share their spare electron with other atoms, but if you did the same with the elements in the last column, nothing would happen. These elements have a full outer shell, so don't need to share their electrons with other atoms.

Most of the elements in the periodic table occur naturally on Earth, but any element heavier than lead (number 82) is unstable and gradually undergoes radioactive decay. Elements heavier than uranium (number 92) have to be made artificially. Join us as we explore the periodic table, and delve into the elements that shape our everyday lives.

How to read the periodic table

There are three key pieces of information about each element to look out for

Atomic number
The atomic number tells you how many protons each atom has. This is different for every element.

Chemical symbol
Each element has a one or two letter symbol. It is often based on Latin, and may not relate to the English name.

Atomic mass
Some tables also give the atomic mass, which corresponds to the total number of protons and neutrons in the atom.

6
C
Carbon
12.011

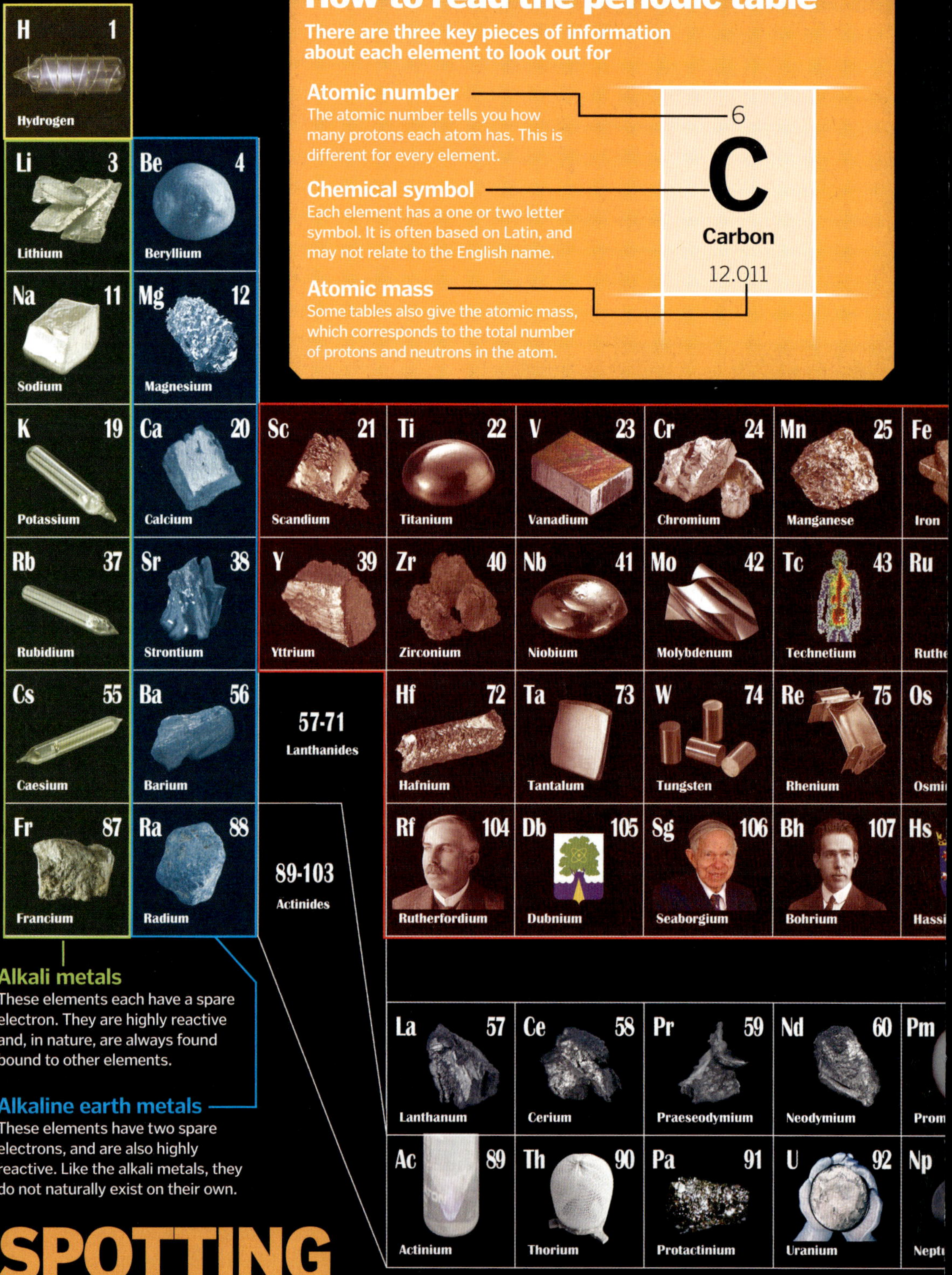

Alkali metals
These elements each have a spare electron. They are highly reactive and, in nature, are always found bound to other elements.

Alkaline earth metals
These elements have two spare electrons, and are also highly reactive. Like the alkali metals, they do not naturally exist on their own.

SPOTTING PATTERNS

The chemical elements have more in common than you might think

THE ELEMENTS

Filling in the gaps

In the 1800s, just 63 of the 90 naturally occurring elements had been discovered, and many scientists tried and failed to come up with a system of organising them. The puzzle was finally solved by Russian chemist Dmitri Mendeleev in 1869. He arranged the elements in order of their atomic mass, and noticed how elements with similar properties grouped together periodically. While others had tried to order them strictly according to atomic mass, he wasn't afraid to move elements around, leaving gaps where he thought that undiscovered elements should sit.

Non-metals
The elements in the top right corner of the periodic table are the non-metals. Most are gases or solids at room temperature.

Halogens
The halogens are missing one electron from their outer shell, and will react violently with the alkali metals to form salts.

Noble gases
These elements have a complete outer shell of electrons and do not react with other elements.

Transition metals
The elements in this block have more than one partially filled electron shell, giving them interesting chemical properties.

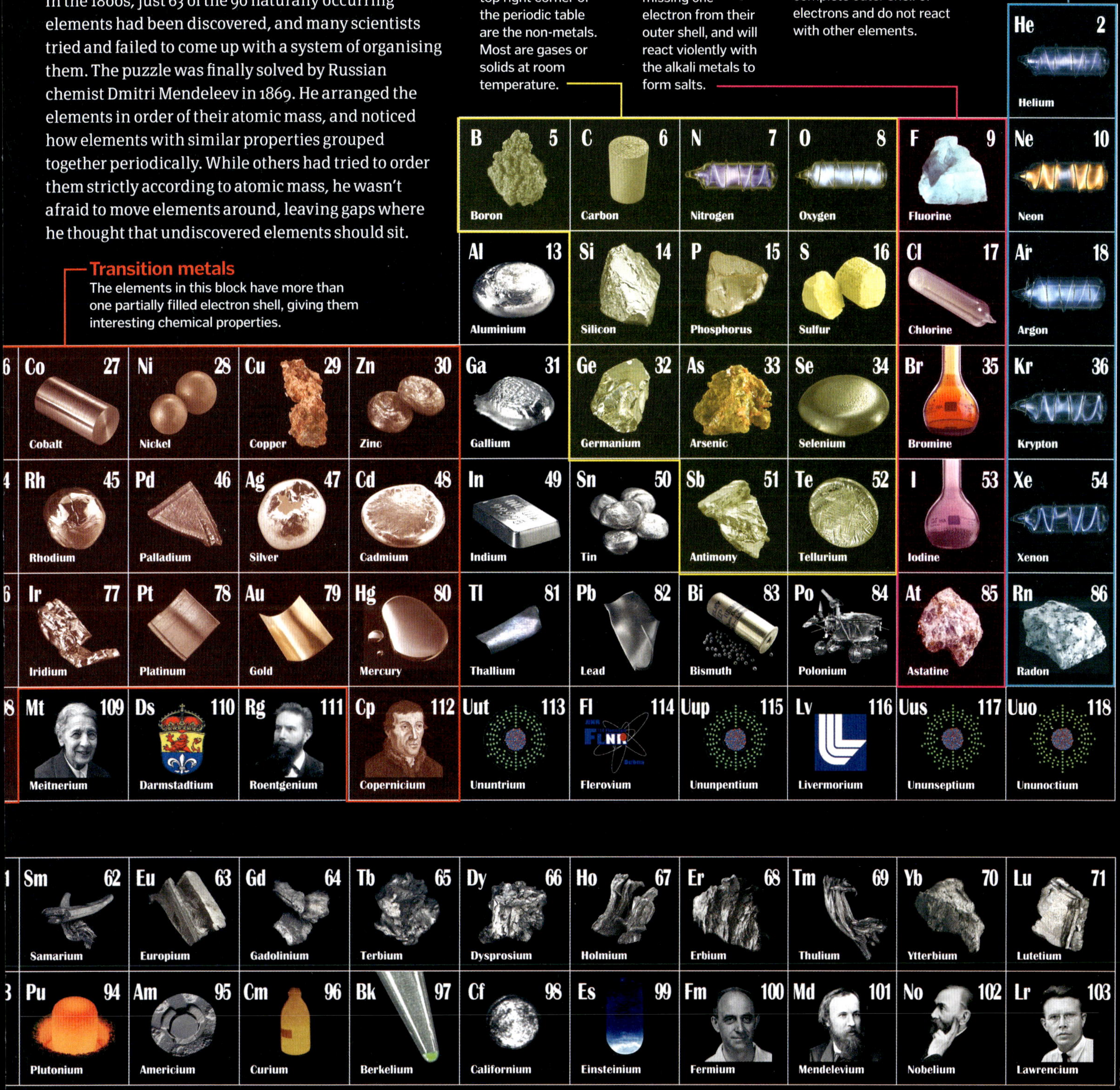

"The puzzle was finally solved

EVERYDAY ELEMENTS

Look around and you'll discover dozens of different elements

Gas-discharge lamps

These lamps typically contain neon, argon, krypton, or xenon, which are noble gases. When an electric current is passed through the gases, they become excited, and when they drop back down to a normal energy level, they release photons of visible light.

Heat resistant glass

Borosilicate glass, which is found in the kitchen and in the lab, contains at least five per cent boron oxide. Boron has a high melting point, which helps the glass to resist thermal shock, going from hot to cold and back again without shattering.

Coins

In the UK, 1p and 2p coins are made from copper-plated steel (iron and carbon), 5p and 10p coins are nickel-plated steel, 20p and 50p coins are cupro-nickel (copper and nickel), and £1 and £2 coins are nickel-brass (copper, nickel and zinc). These elements are cheaper than gold or silver, and durable too.

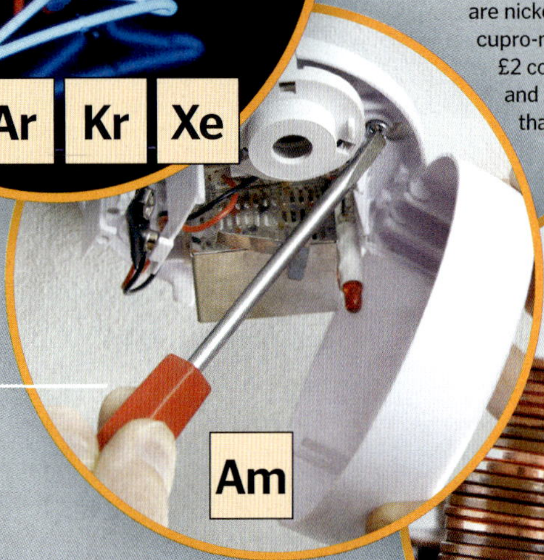

Smoke detectors

Many smoke detectors contain small amounts of americium. This radioactive element releases alpha particles, which 'knock' electrons away from gases in the air and towards a positively charged plate in the smoke detector, generating a current. When smoke gets in the way, the current stops and the alarm sounds.

Fireworks

The colours of fireworks are produced using various combinations of elements, which burn with different coloured flames. Strontium and lithium salts burn red and calcium salts burn orange, while sodium salts burn yellow, barium salts green, and copper salts blue. Purple can be made by mixing strontium and copper.

Phone ingredients

The shiny metal, glass and plastic exteriors of smartphones can contain lots of different elements, including aluminium, magnesium, carbon, and oxygen, but this is just the tip of the iceberg; the circuitry, battery, cameras and speakers contain dozens more. Silicon chips coated with antimony and arsenic sit beside batteries containing lithium and cobalt, and the features that we take for granted, like colour screens, are made possible by rare Earth metals like terbium and europium. Finding uses for all of these elements is a real achievement, but as demand for electronics soars, our limited resources could start to run out.

In | Sn | O

Indium tin oxide film
Three elements – indium, tin and oxygen – make up the conductive film inside touch screens.

Al | Si | O | K

Aluminosilicate glass
This tough glass is made from a mixture of aluminium, silicon, oxygen and potassium.

Li | Co | O

Lithium ion battery
The positive electrode contains lithium, cobalt and oxygen, and the negative electrode is made from carbon.

La | Gd | Dy

Rare earth circuitry
Smartphone circuitry contains rare earth metals like lanthanum, gadolinium and dysprosium.

Cu | Ag | Au | Ta

Precious metal wiring
Copper, silver, gold and tantalum are used in micro-electrical components and wiring.

YOU ARE MADE OF STARDUST

The elements that make up our bodies were forged inside ancient stars

Hydrogen is the smallest element, and formed in vast quantities after the Big Bang, along with a less plentiful supply of helium, and even smaller amounts of lithium and beryllium. But making the heavier elements required more energy. Hydrogen and helium gas clumped together to form clouds, and these clouds collapsed to form stars with enough heat and pressure to trigger nuclear fusion; inside the stars, the nuclei of hydrogen atoms slammed together, fusing to form helium.

As the stars aged, the helium atoms started to create even heavier elements, including carbon, nitrogen and oxygen. Depending on the mass of the star, this process sometimes continued, producing the nuclei of most of the elements up to number 26, iron. After this critical point, fusion reactions stop releasing energy. When stars run out of useable fuel, they collapse, kicking layers of gas and heavy elements out into space.

For the most massive stars, this process involves a powerful explosion called a supernova, which provides enough energy to make the elements that are heavier than iron. The remnants of these old exploded stars mix with yet more hydrogen gas and go on to make more star systems, like our own Sun and planets, providing us with the range of elements we have on Earth today.

"The remnants of old exploded stars go on to make more star systems"

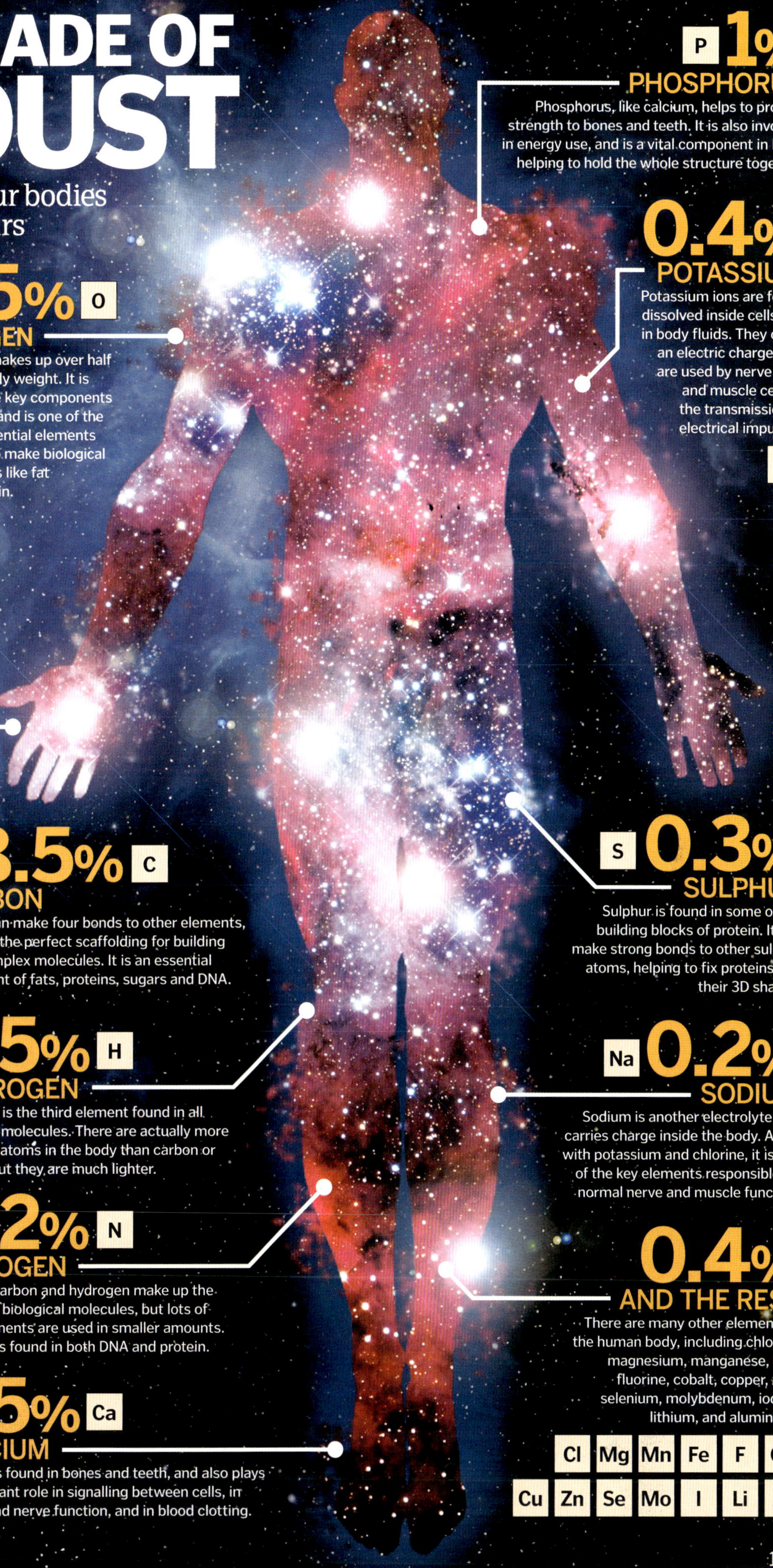

65% O OXYGEN
Oxygen makes up over half of our body weight. It is one of the key components of water, and is one of the three essential elements needed to make biological molecules like fat and protein.

18.5% C CARBON
Carbon can make four bonds to other elements, making it the perfect scaffolding for building large, complex molecules. It is an essential component of fats, proteins, sugars and DNA.

9.5% H HYDROGEN
Hydrogen is the third element found in all biological molecules. There are actually more hydrogen atoms in the body than carbon or oxygen, but they are much lighter.

3.2% N NITROGEN
Oxygen, carbon and hydrogen make up the core of all biological molecules, but lots of other elements are used in smaller amounts. Nitrogen is found in both DNA and protein.

1.5% Ca CALCIUM
Calcium is found in bones and teeth, and also plays an important role in signalling between cells, in muscle and nerve function, and in blood clotting.

P 1% PHOSPHORUS
Phosphorus, like calcium, helps to provide strength to bones and teeth. It is also involved in energy use, and is a vital component in DNA, helping to hold the whole structure together.

0.4% POTASSIUM K
Potassium ions are found dissolved inside cells and in body fluids. They carry an electric charge, and are used by nerve cells and muscle cells in the transmission of electrical impulses.

S 0.3% SULPHUR
Sulphur is found in some of the building blocks of protein. It can make strong bonds to other sulphur atoms, helping to fix proteins into their 3D shapes.

Na 0.2% SODIUM
Sodium is another electrolyte that carries charge inside the body. Along with potassium and chlorine, it is one of the key elements responsible for normal nerve and muscle function.

0.4% AND THE REST
There are many other elements in the human body, including chlorine, magnesium, manganese, iron, fluorine, cobalt, copper, zinc, selenium, molybdenum, iodine, lithium, and aluminium.

Cl Mg Mn Fe F Co
Cu Zn Se Mo I Li Al

Isolating deadly diseases

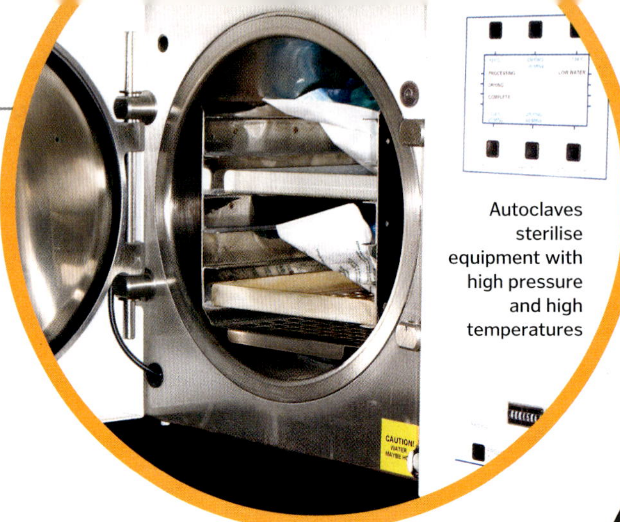

Autoclaves sterilise equipment with high pressure and high temperatures

When serious infection strikes, biocontainment units work to keep us safe

Hazard group 4 pathogens – such as smallpox, Lassa fever and Ebola – cause severe human disease. They are likely to spread, and there is usually no effective prevention or cure, so when infected patients come through the door, hospitals must act fast. The patients may be rushed to a separate facility known as a biocontainment unit. There are only a small number of these facilities worldwide, and every detail is geared towards infection control.

Biocontainment units are designed to be isolated from the main hospital, providing everything that the staff and patients might need in one safe, sealed space. The rooms have facilities for normal, high-dependency and emergency care; there are en-suite bathroom facilities, and staff can even perform minor surgery. Dedicated lab facilities allow tests to be performed immediately, without the need to transport dangerous samples.

To minimise the chance of airborne pathogens escaping into the hospital, these units have their own dedicated ventilation systems, and the pressure inside is kept slightly lower than the pressure outside. This means that air will have a natural tendency to move inwards, creating a constant breeze that helps to blow any infectious particles back inside.

All air leaving the facility is first passed through high-efficiency particulate air (HEPA) filters. These dense mats of glass fibres block, slow and stick to particles, filtering contaminants and preventing their escape. The filtered air is released high above the roof of the hospitals, dissipating into the atmosphere.

Inside the unit are clear divisions between the rooms. Staff members enter through designated areas to don their protective equipment, and exit through different areas to take it off again. The rooms are fitted with glass panels and intercom systems, and CCTV allows close patient monitoring, while minimising the risk of infection.

Nothing that goes in to the unit can come out until staff are sure it is clean. Items like suits, swabs and spoons are sterilised, either by searing steam or high-heat and high-pressure autoclaves. Disposable items are burnt.

Patient waste is bleached until nothing can survive, lab samples are dunked in sterilisation tanks before they are taken for testing, and some equipment is exposed to burning ultraviolet radiation. All of these measures help to ensure that the patients inside and outside the unit receive the best possible care, while minimising the risk of further infection.

Inside a biocontainment unit

The extreme measures that help to prevent outbreaks

Patient rooms
Rooms are equipped to deliver high-level patient care, with facilities for intensive treatment and even minor surgery.

En-suite facilities
Each patient has access to bathroom and shower facilities.

Keeping staff safe

No amount of bleach would protect against infectious disease without highly trained medical staff. The selection process to become a member of a biocontainment unit team is rigorous. On top of their medical expertise, dedicated unit staff are educated in microbiology, sterilisation, disinfection, emergency planning and laboratory maintenance.

The medical teams wear several layers of protection when interacting with patients inside the units. They are covered from head to toe, and staff are employed specifically to help the team get dressed and undressed for work. They wear full body suits that include respirators to clean the air they breathe, and their hands are protected by several pairs of gloves. All of this equipment needs to be put on and taken off in a specific order every time they enter or exit the unit, and there are specialist areas that allow this to be done safely.

DID YOU KNOW? *There are only four specialist biocontainment hospital units in the US and two in the UK*

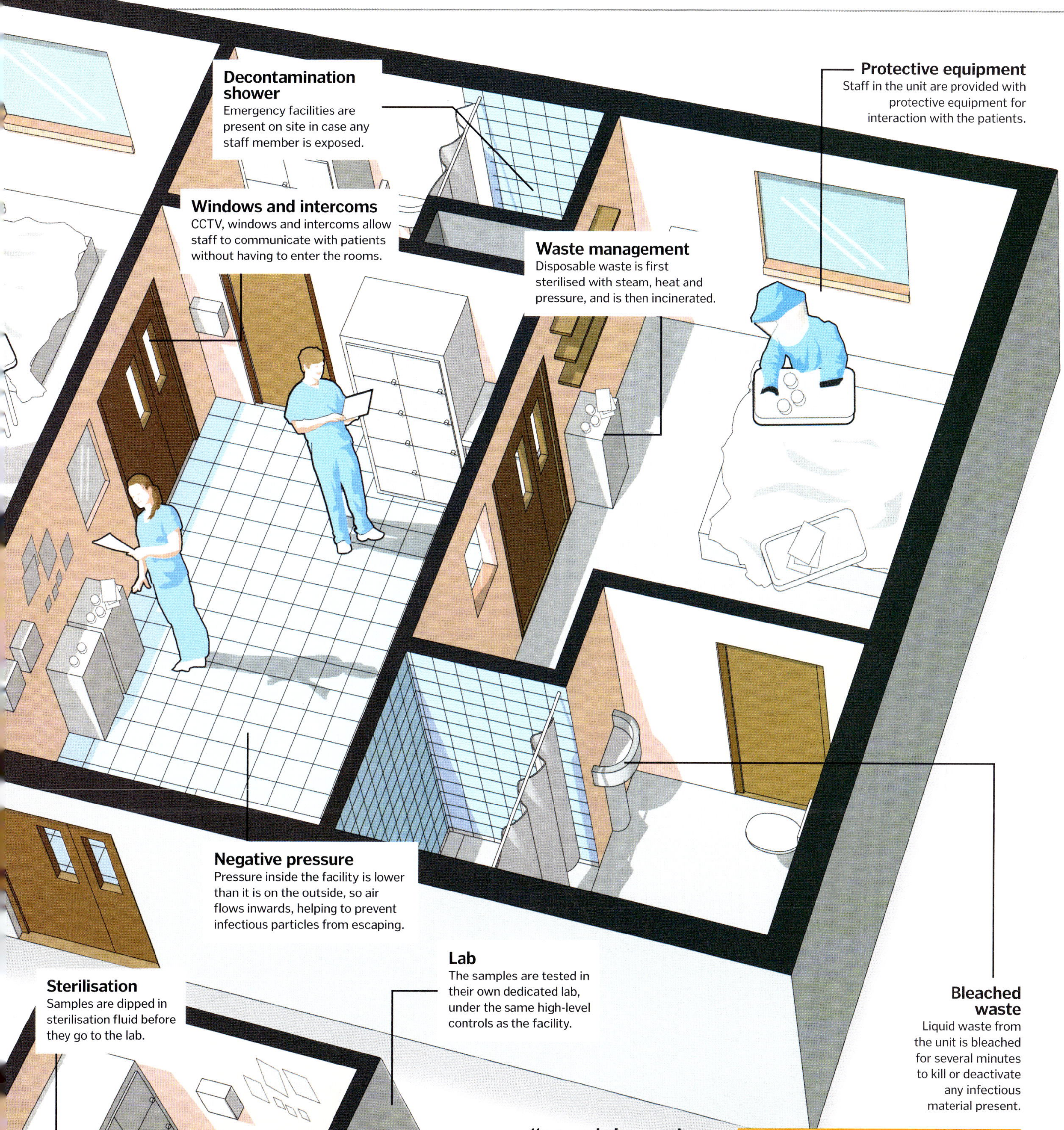

"Nothing that goes in to the unit can come out until staff are sure it is clean"

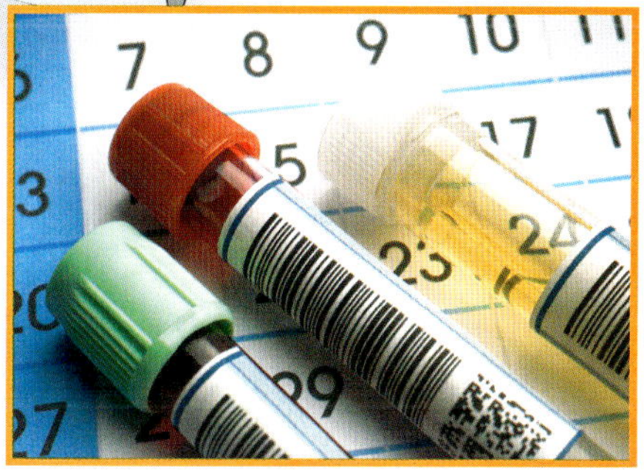

Sample tubes are dunked to sterilise the outside before they are sent for testing

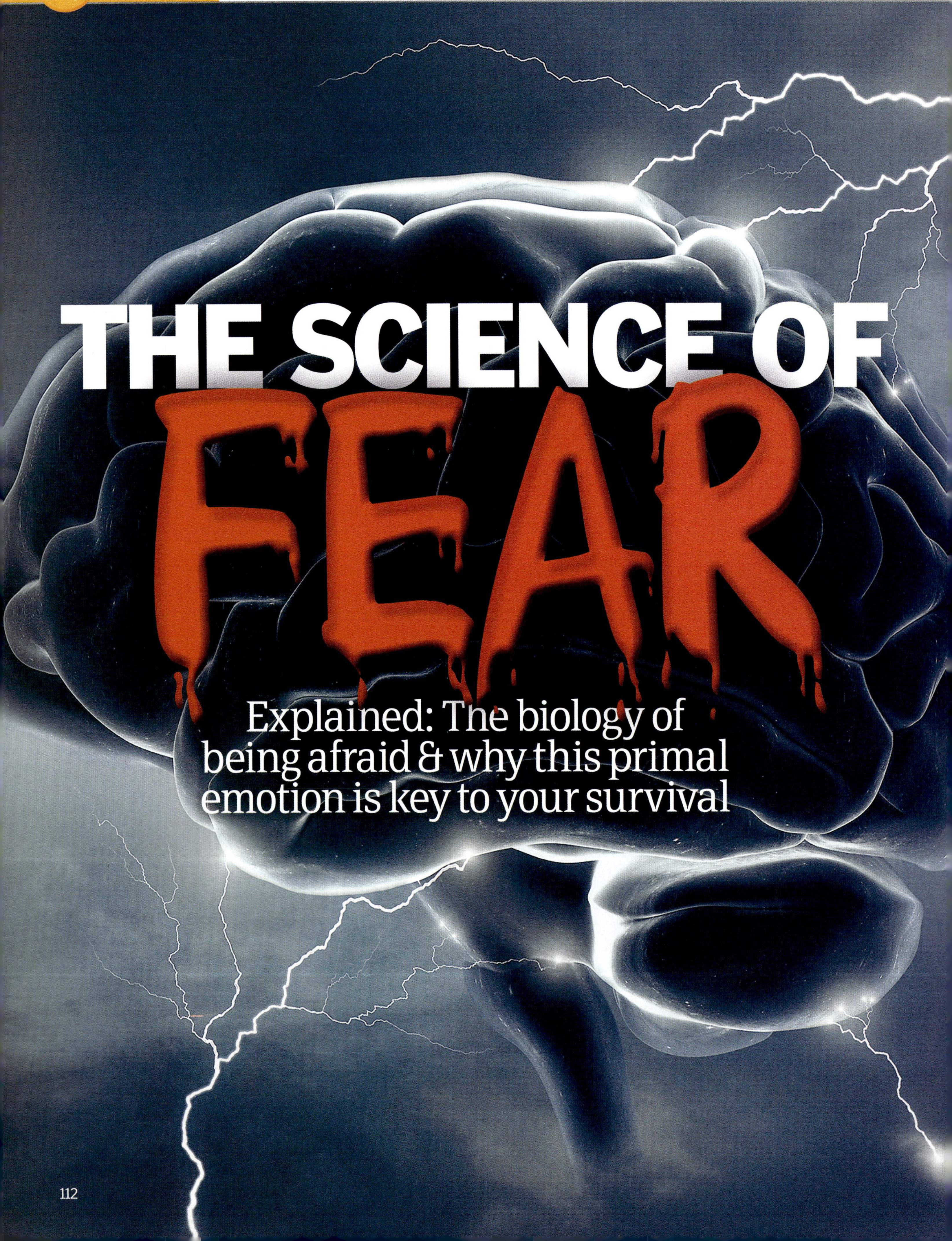

THE SCIENCE OF FEAR

Explained: The biology of being afraid & why this primal emotion is key to your survival

DID YOU KNOW? *Studies show that we identify images of snakes and spiders more quickly than non-threatening pictures*

Home alone at night, you hear a loud crash. In an instant your heart starts racing, your muscles tense and your breath quickens. You are immediately alert, primed to fight or flee the source of the sound, which turns out to be a pile of books falling off that shelf you've been meaning to fix. But in that moment, your brain and body reacted as if you were in mortal danger.

Fear is one of our strongest and most primal emotions. It's a big bad world out there, and being afraid of certain things protects us from potential danger to make sure we survive. Some evolutionary fears are hard-wired into our brains, but we can also develop new fears throughout our lives. As children we pick up on what makes our parents anxious, and we may also learn to fear certain things after negative experiences. Despite this, most of us are able to ignore our fears when it's clear we aren't in any immediate danger. We can enjoy the view from the top of a skyscraper rather than worry about falling, or turn out the lights safe in the knowledge that a predator won't devour us in the night.

However, people with phobias have an excessive fear response that causes both physical and psychological distress. These extreme fears are divided into three different groups: agoraphobia, social phobia and specific phobias. Agoraphobia is generally referred to as the fear of open spaces, but it applies to the dread of any situation that is difficult– to escape from, or where help would not be available if something went wrong. Social phobia is the intense fear of interacting with people or performing, while specific phobias are the fear of a particular situation, activity or thing.

These irrational fears can cause major disruptions to everyday life; somebody with acrophobia – an extreme fear of heights – may experience a panic attack simply trying to walk across a bridge. Depending on the trigger of their phobia, sufferers often go to great lengths to avoid situations that could affect them.

The cause of phobias is not always clear, but many cases are linked to experiencing or witnessing a traumatic event. For example, somebody may develop cynophobia – the fear of dogs – after being bitten. But whether the trigger is rational or irrational, as soon as the brain registers a scary stimulus, it activates the fight-or-flight response, thus preparing the body for action.

NATURAL FEARS

Some of our fears have developed as an evolutionary response to danger

"Even today, the majority of African lion attacks on humans occur after dark"

We are more afraid of what hides in the dark, rather than the darkness itself

Darkness

Sight is arguably our most important sense. When we are faced with pitch-darkness we are left vulnerable, unaware of what is around us. At night, our early ancestors were at risk of being attacked by nocturnal predators. A study from 2011 found that even today, the majority of African lion attacks on humans occur after dark, and are more likely when the Moon is below the horizon. Although being hunted while we sleep isn't a risk for most of us, we are instinctively more anxious when unable to see.

The fear of heights helps us avoid falls that could injure or kill us

Heights

A fear of heights is necessary to our survival, ensuring we are cautious in situations where we might injure ourselves. To study this, researchers set up a platform surrounded by a transparent material, giving the illusion of a cliff, and put young children on the platform to test their reaction. They found that most infants didn't try to move onto the transparent section, suggesting that they inherently avoided risking a drop. As our ancestors explored the world, this fear ensured they were wary of climbing to dangerous heights.

Although most snake and spider species aren't poisonous to us, we are innately cautious around them

Poisonous creatures

While we may not be terrified of them from birth, evidence suggests that we are predisposed to detect and recognise spiders and snakes quicker than non-threatening animals. One theory is that our early mammal ancestors, evolving in a world dominated by reptiles, needed to identify and react to snakes to avoid becoming dinner. Another hypothesis is that our ancestors evolving in Africa coexisted with a number of poisonous spider species for millions of years, so being able to spot and avoid them was a vital skill.

FIGHT OR FLIGHT

How your brain and body trigger this evolutionary survival instinct

A fear of flying is relatively common, and may have roots in the evolutionary fear of heights

Under normal circumstances, sensory information from your body is sent to the thalamus in the brain. The thalamus relays these signals to the cortex and the hippocampus for further processing, to provide a better understanding of what you're experiencing and put it into context. This analysis is forwarded to the amygdala, which triggers an appropriate emotional reaction to the situation.

When your brain receives signals that indicate some kind of danger, the course of action is slightly different. The process above still occurs, but this higher-level analysis takes precious time. The fraction of a second it takes to fully understand what's happening might be the difference between life and death. To make sure your body is instantly prepared to face a threat, the thalamus also sends the raw sensory information via a shortcut, directly to the amygdala.

As soon as the amygdala is alerted, it signals the hypothalamus. This part of the brain activates systems that release a cocktail of around 30 different hormones into the bloodstream. One hormone in particular, adrenaline, causes a variety of physiological reactions all around the body. For example, in the lungs it makes smooth muscle cells relax, expanding the air passages so more oxygen can reach the blood. It also stimulates cardiac cells so the heart beats faster, and makes muscles in the eyes contract to dilate the pupils. The physical changes produced by this sudden flood of hormones make up what is known as the fight-or-flight response. This instinctive reaction gets you ready to either take a stand and defend yourself, or escape to safety.

Not many of us experience life-threatening situations day-to-day, so more often than not our fight-or-flight response is triggered by a false alarm. The moment of panic you feel after hearing a loud bang, for example, is because neural signals from the shortcut reach the amygdala first. The fight-or-flight response automatically kicks in before the brain evaluates the situation, just in case. Once the amygdala receives more information and concludes you aren't in danger, it signals the thalamus to stop the fight-or-flight reaction, returning your body to normal.

The human brain is hard-wired to prepare for the worst; it may seem silly to treat every loud noise as a danger, but if the threat turns out to be real, this overreaction could save your life.

Fear on the brain

What happens when the brain goes into survival mode?

Thalamus
The thalamus is the first port of call for most sensory signals from the body. It relays this information to the relevant areas of the brain, like a switchboard.

Hypothalamus
The hypothalamus's primary role is to maintain homeostasis – keeping the body in a stable condition. It also regulates the secretion of hormones and initiates the fight-or-flight response.

Amygdala
The amygdala processes our emotional reactions and plays a role in decision-making and the formation of memories. It moderates our responses to events that affect our survival.

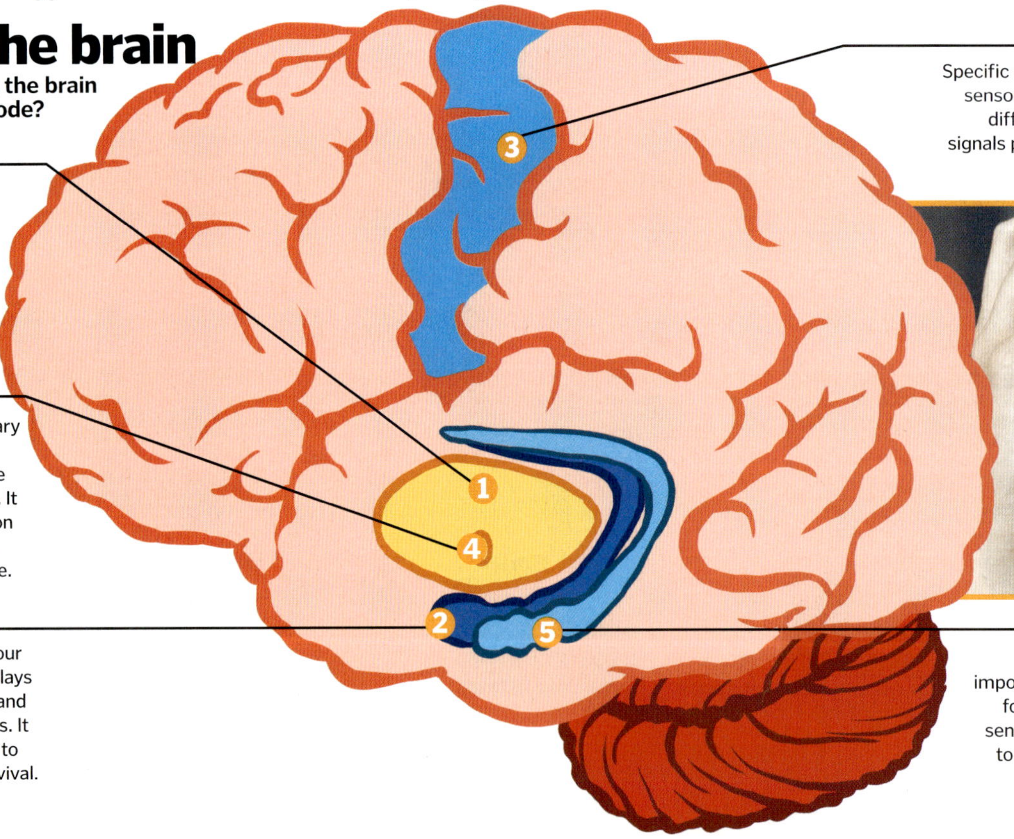

Sensory cortex
Specific regions of the brain analyse the sensory information from each of our different senses. They process the signals passed on from the thalamus to give them meaning.

Hippocampus
The hippocampus plays an important role in long-term memory formation. It compares incoming sensory information to past events to help establish a context for the situation you face.

1 Stimulus
When a potential threat is detected, the thalamus sends signals to the amygdala via two different pathways. One route is fast and direct, while the slower path analyses the situation and decides what should happen next.

2 Act first
The first pathway immediately assumes there's danger even if there is none – a safer option than vice versa. It goes directly to the amygdala, which sends signals to the hypothalamus to initiate the fight-or-flight response.

3 Analysis
The same information is sent along the more investigative route. Signals from the thalamus are sent to the sensory cortex, which interprets the data, followed by the hippocampus, to analyse the context of the situation.

4 Fight or flight?
The hypothalamus activates both the sympathetic nervous system and the adrenal-cortical system to trigger the fight-or-flight reaction. The impulses and hormones produced prepare the body for action.

5 Judgement
Once the situation has been analysed by the longer pathway, the hippocampus sends signals to the amygdala to either seize the fight-or-flight response if there is no danger, or to maintain it if there is.

DID YOU KNOW? *The 'Wilhelm scream' sound effect has been used in over 200 films, from Star Wars to Toy Story*

Anatomy of fear

The extreme reactions that occur when your body is put on high alert

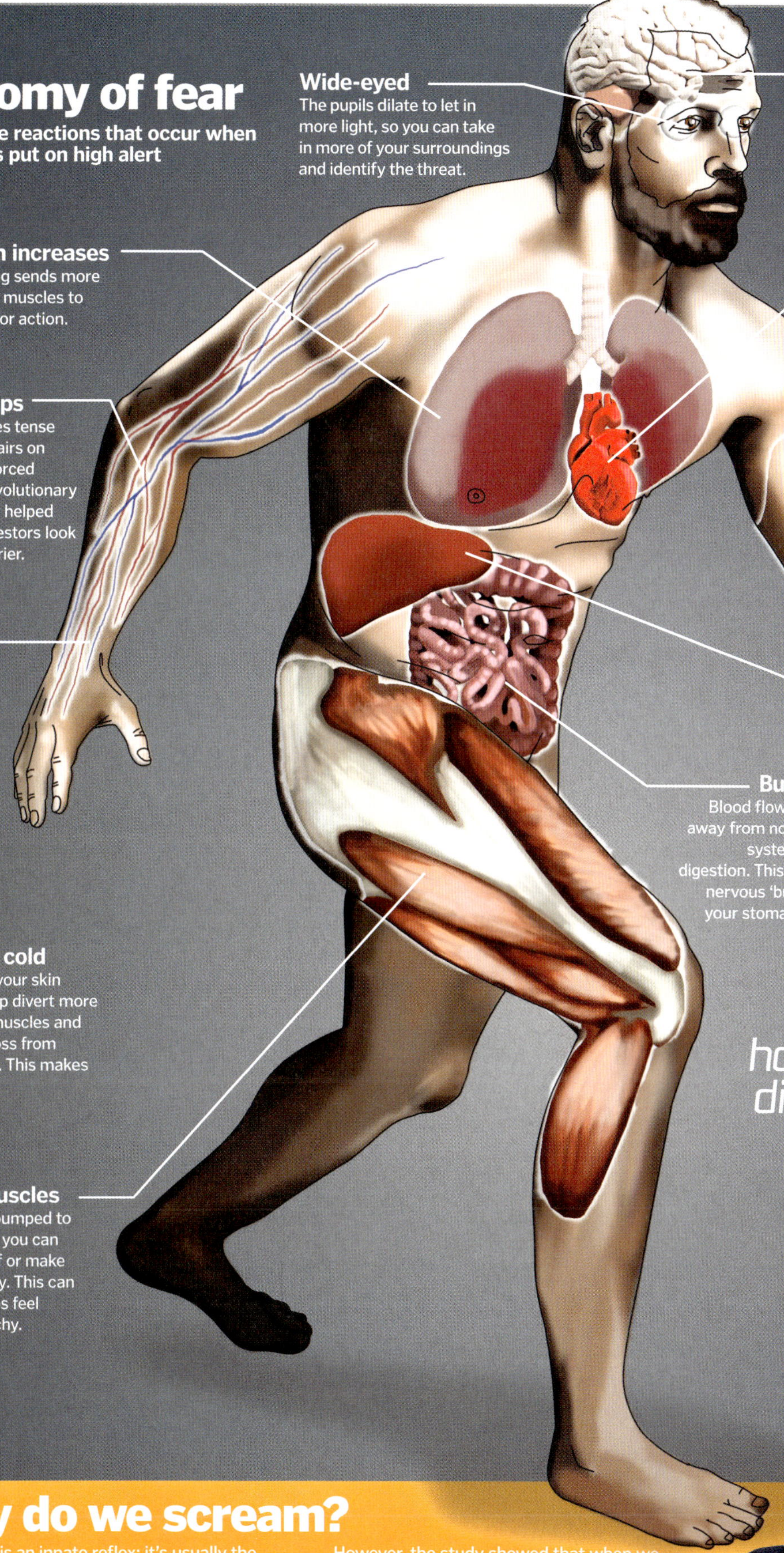

Wide-eyed
The pupils dilate to let in more light, so you can take in more of your surroundings and identify the threat.

Hormones
The activated sympathetic nervous system and adrenal-cortical system release dozens of hormones into the bloodstream to cause changes in the body.

Respiration increases
Faster breathing sends more oxygen to your muscles to prepare them for action.

Heart rate increases
The hormones adrenaline and noradrenaline are released to increase your heart rate, sending more blood to your muscles and brain.

Goosebumps
As your muscles tense up, the small hairs on your skin are forced upright. This evolutionary reflex probably helped our hairier ancestors look bigger and scarier.

Cold sweat
Your body anticipates immediate action, so you pre-emptively start to sweat in order to keep cool.

Butterflies
Blood flow is diverted away from non-essential systems such as digestion. This causes the nervous 'butterflies in your stomach' feeling.

Energy boost
Your liver starts breaking down glycogen into glucose, ready to supply the body with instant energy.

Blood runs cold
The vessels in your skin constrict to help divert more blood to your muscles and reduce blood loss from potential injury. This makes you feel cold.

"The time it takes to understand what's happening might be the difference between life and death"

Shaking muscles
More blood is pumped to the muscles so you can defend yourself or make a quick getaway. This can make your limbs feel tense and twitchy.

Why do we scream?

Screaming is an innate reflex; it's usually the first thing you do when you're born. Although we might also scream from excitement or pleasure, it is most often a cry of distress. Researchers from New York University conducted an experiment using brain scans to see how our minds react to screams. When we listen to normal speech, what we hear is sent to the auditory cortex for processing so we can make sense of the sounds.

However, the study showed that when we hear a scream, the signals are sent straight to the amygdala to activate the brain's fear response. The team also found that 'rougher' screams – those that change volume more quickly – were the most distressing. The results show that screams are a very effective method of communication in humans. They not only help convey danger, but also help make those who hear them more alert.

Screams are an example of a universal vocalisation; they are the same in every language

ARE FEARS GENETIC?

Your phobias could be passed down through generations in DNA

It was previously assumed that all irrational fears are learned through personal experience or taught to us by others. In cases where a person develops a phobia related to a traumatic event in their past, this is most likely the case. If somebody nearly drowns while swimming in the sea, for instance, it wouldn't be surprising if they develop aquaphobia, the fear of water. The brain makes a connection between the situation and the feeling of pain and panic, and commits it to memory.

However, it is now thought that some phobias have a genetic origin. Identical twins are more likely to share the same irrational fears than non-identical twins, even if they are raised apart from one another.

Experiments with mice have shown that fears they develop can be passed down to their children and even their grandchildren. The mice were conditioned to fear the scent of acetophenone – a sweet smelling chemical. Researchers found that the pups, and even the grand-pups, of the conditioned mice were startled by the scent too.

One explanation for this could be that parent mice communicate with their pups to effectively teach them what to fear. Studies have found that when mice are scared, they release pheromones that act as an alarm signal to other mice. However, in the acetophenone experiment, the pups proved to be sensitive to the scent from the very first time they encountered it. What's more, some pups of conditioned mice were fostered by non-conditioned mice. The non-conditioned foster parents were not afraid of the scent, but the pups were, suggesting the fear's origin was genetic rather than social.

It is not clear exactly how the conditioned fear is passed on to future generations of mice, but the current theory is that it is down to something called epigenetic inheritance. The original conditioning process leads to chemical modifications that change gene expression (which genes are switched on or off), without changing the DNA sequence itself. The researchers found that the conditioned mice and their offspring developed more scent receptors in their brains compared to non-conditioned mice. With more of these receptors, they can detect the presence of acetophenone at lower concentrations and so are alerted to it more easily.

Epigenetics is a relatively new area of research, but it stands to reason that fears and other memories may well be inherited this way in humans too.

Inheriting fears

A study with lab mice suggests that fear is a family affair

"Sets of identical twins often share the same irrational fears"

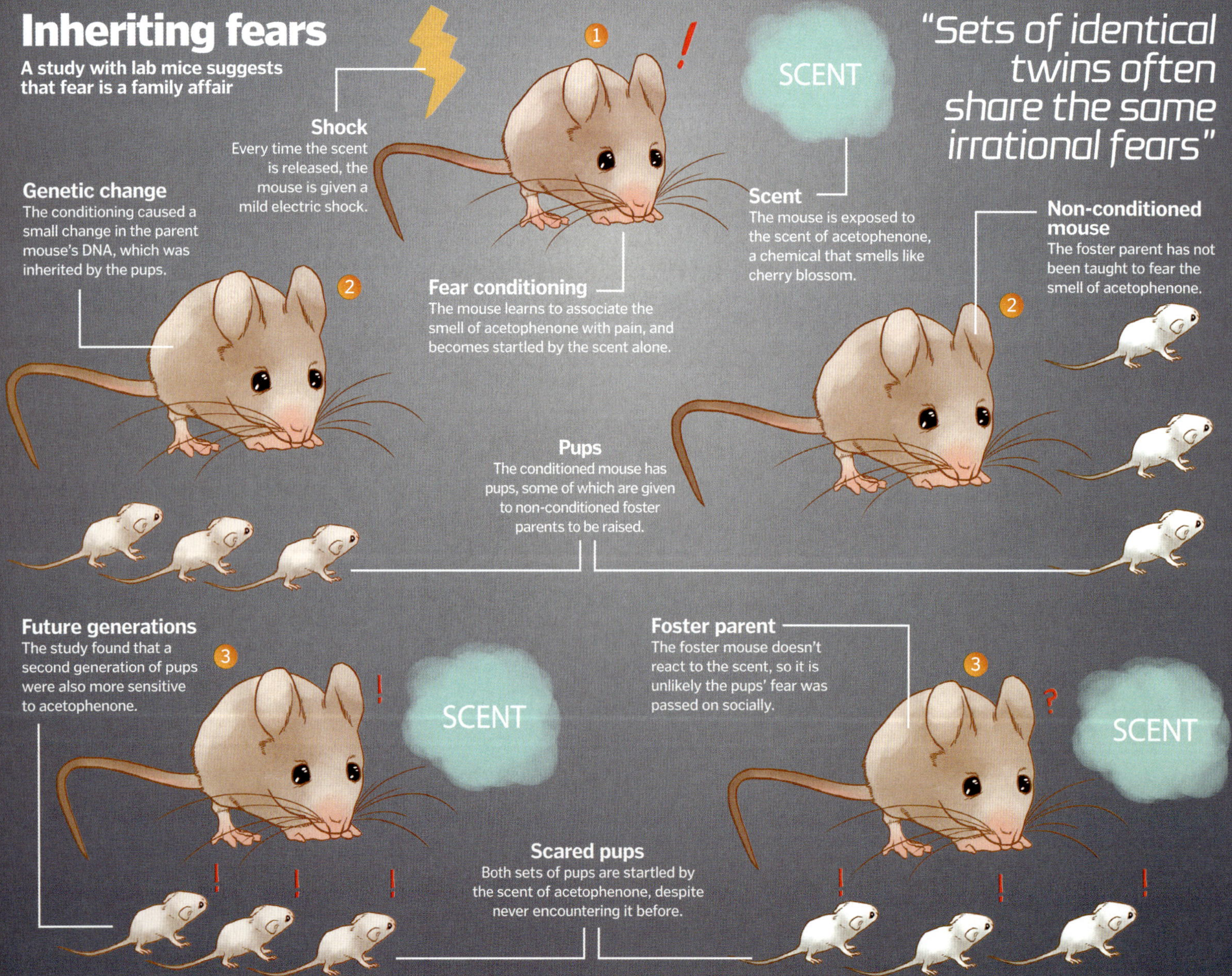

LIVING FEARLESSLY

Self-help gurus and motivational posters encourage us to be fearless, but in reality a life without fear would be incredibly dangerous. Studies have shown that when the region of the brain called the amygdala is damaged, people are more likely to take risks. Severe damage can even leave people with no sense of fear whatsoever – which can land them in some pretty scary situations!

For the past 25 years, scientists have been studying a patient (known as SM for anonymity) who lacks an amygdala. SM has experienced many traumatic events in her life – she has been held at both knife and gun-point, and was nearly killed during a domestic violence attack – but she did not react with any sense of desperation or urgency, even though her life was in danger.

Researchers took SM to an exotic pet store where, despite claiming she hated them, the snakes and spiders captivated her. Scientists noted her curiosity and compulsive desire to touch some of the more dangerous creatures, following repeated warnings from staff. The researchers concluded that SM's inability to detect or react appropriately to threats likely contributed to her disproportionate number of traumatic experiences.

By studying patients like SM, it is hoped that scientists can understand more about fear and discover new methods of helping people whose lives are plagued by it. For example, treatments that target the amygdala could benefit those who suffer from post-traumatic stress disorder.

People with damaged amygdalas are more complacent around potential threats

Sometimes it is just the thrill that makes people take unnecessary risks

SCARED TO DEATH

It's not just a figure of speech – it turns out you really can die of fright. The adrenaline released during the fight-or-flight response can be damaging in large amounts. This stress hormone encourages the heart muscle to contract, but if your body releases too much adrenaline, your heart is unable to relax again. Adrenaline can also interfere with the cells that regulate your heart rhythm, causing it to beat abnormally, which could be lethal.

While not directly deadly, prolonged anxiety can have a significant negative impact on your health. The fight-or-flight response suppresses the immune system, leaving you vulnerable to illness. Going into survival mode on a regular basis can lead to digestive disorders as this non-essential system is repressed. Long-term stress can also lead to weight issues by disrupting the metabolism; elevated levels of cortisol can make the body less sensitive to insulin. Muscles that are constantly tense and ready for action can cause headaches, stiffness and neck pain. The list doesn't end there; chronic anxiety has also been linked to cardiovascular problems, asthma and insomnia. Such a broad range of effects can be harmful to both physical and mental wellbeing.

Regularly activating the fight-or-flight response through anxiety or stress can cause serious health problems

Fear is an instinctive survival mechanism that helps protect us from danger

FACING YOUR FEARS

Can you retrain your brain to overcome a phobia?

Some phobia triggers are much easier to avoid than others. For example, people who suffer from a fear of bats (chiroptophobia) are highly unlikely to be plagued by these creatures day in, day out. Someone suffering from a social phobia, however, will struggle to lead a normal life.

There are a variety of different methods used to treat phobias. Among the most popular are talking treatments, such as cognitive behavioural therapy and exposure therapy, which work by retraining the brain to change how it responds to a phobia trigger. The approach is essentially the opposite of fear conditioning – the patient learns to associate their trigger with more rational, positive thoughts.

Another approach being investigated is tricking the brain into treating itself. Mentalist and illusionist Derren Brown conducted an experiment on his programme *Fear And Faith*, in which he gave people with different phobias a new wonder drug called Rumyodin. One subject, usually terrified of heights, was comfortably able to sit on the edge of a tall bridge. Another volunteer with a fear of performing in public was able to go to an audition. It was revealed that Rumyodin (an anagram of 'your mind') didn't exist, and the participants had simply been injected with saline solution and given sugar pills.

The incredible results are a demonstration of the placebo effect, a phenomenon in which a fake treatment has a very real result. Scientists are investigating how this effect can be exploited to treat both physical and psychological problems.

PHOBIA TREATMENT

Exposure therapy involves facing your fears one step at a time

"The patient learns to associate their phobia trigger with more rational, positive thoughts"

Exposure therapy

The aim of exposure therapy is to gradually desensitise the patient to the source of their phobia. The patient ranks situations from least to most terrifying. For example, an arachnophobe might place thinking about a spider at the bottom of their list, and having a spider crawl along their arm at the top. The patient works with a psychologist to systematically work their way through the list, using relaxation techniques or other coping mechanisms until they are comfortable with each stage. The patient's brain learns to relate each scary situation to being calm, reducing their anxiety.

Research suggests that CBT actually causes physical changes to the brain

Cognitive behavioural therapy

The aim of cognitive behavioural therapy (CBT) is to change how we think about certain situations. It is thought that irrational anxiety issues are caused by a patient's negative interpretation of events, rather than the events themselves. CBT is a talking therapy that helps patients assess their reactions to situations, replacing the worry cycle with more useful or realistic thoughts. Patients' brain scans indicate that CBT reduces the overactivity in the amygdala and hippocampus associated with phobias. Studies have also shown that CBT is as effective as medication in the treatment of many anxiety disorders.

Therapists can control the virtual scenario to suit the patient's progress

Virtual reality therapy

Exposure therapy isn't a viable option for all phobias, but modern technology offers an alternative. Advancements in virtual reality systems mean that patients can now face their fears through a headset rather than in the real world. This allows patients to face any number of situations relating to their phobia, while knowing they are in no physical danger. For example, somebody with a phobia of flying can take a course of sessions – in which they board a virtual plane and experience announcements, take-off, turbulence and landing – without having to buy a plane ticket each week.

TOP 10 STRANGEST PHOBIAS

The most common phobias stem from rational fears, but others are completely bizarre

SPACE

122
The search for alien life

130
Parallel universes

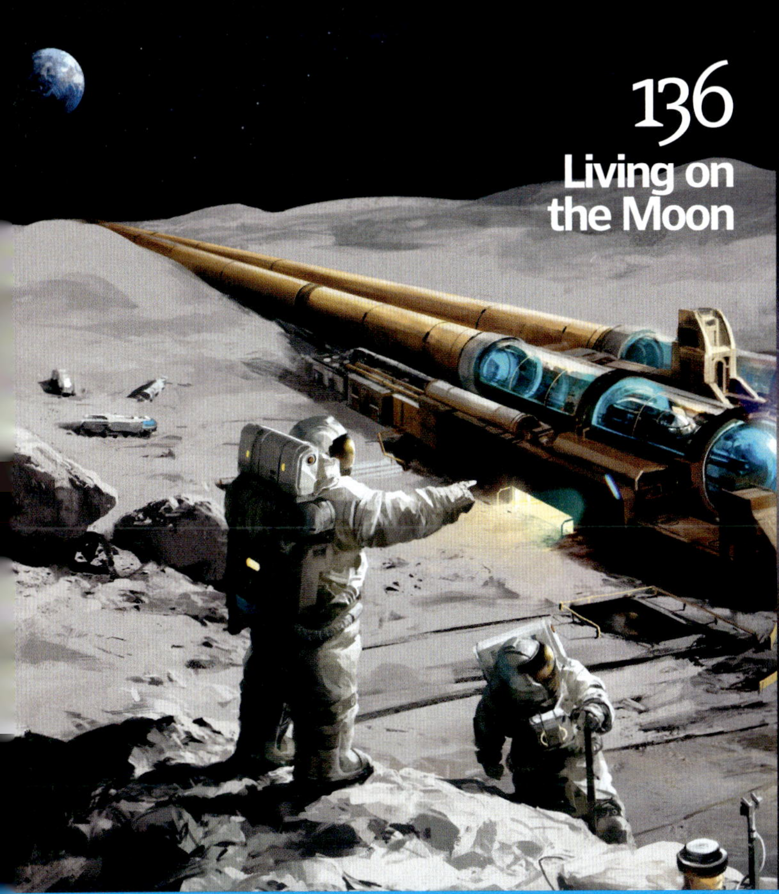

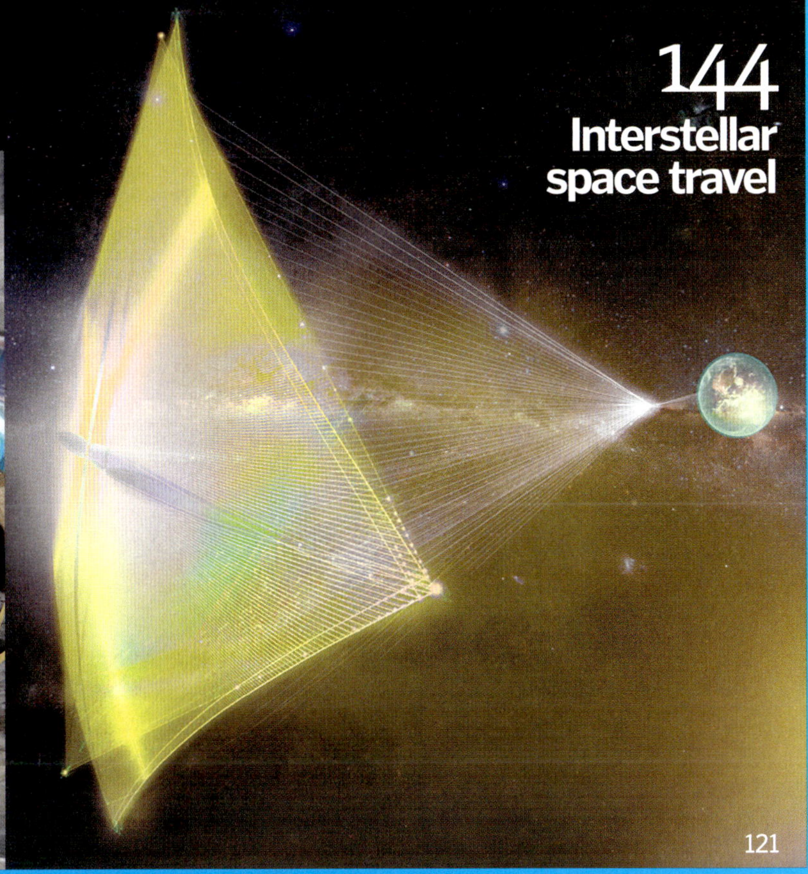

THE SEARCH FOR ALIEN LIFE

HOW THE GROUND-BREAKING SEARCH FOR LIFE COULD PROVE WE'RE NOT ALONE

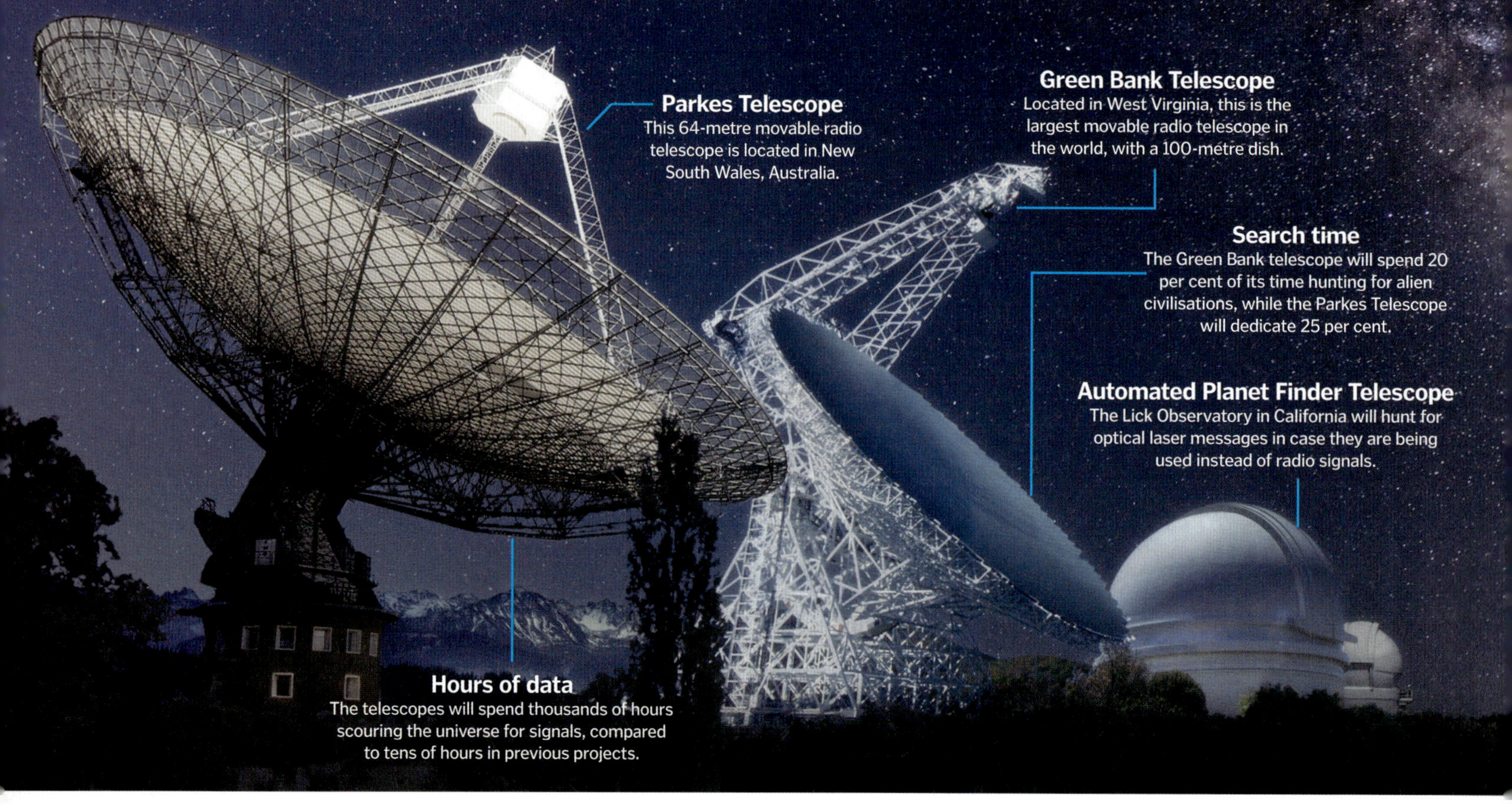

In this possibly infinite universe, could Earth truly be the only inhabited planet? Are we really that special, or is the universe actually teeming with life? Could there be advanced civilisations out there trying to make contact right now? In July 2015, Russian entrepreneur Yuri Milner and renowned physicist Stephen Hawking announced an ambitious new initiative to search for communications from advanced alien worlds. Breakthrough Listen is described by the National Radio Astronomy Observatory as "the most powerful, comprehensive, and intensive scientific search ever for signs of intelligent life in the universe".

The initiative has set aside $100 million (£66 million) over ten years to listen for signals from the nearest million stars in the Milky Way, and from the nearest hundred galaxies around us. Led by a team of internationally renowned experts that includes Astronomer Royal, Lord Martin Rees, the project will use some of the world's largest and most powerful telescopes. The search is based on the idea that among the hundreds of billions of stars in our close galactic neighbourhood, there are thousands of planets similar to our own. With the right environment and optimal chemistry, many scientists believe that life could evolve on some of these distant Earths.

If life exists on other planets, so too might intelligent life, who like us, could be interested in exploring the universe around them, and in making contact. This is not the first time that Search for Extraterrestrial Intelligence (SETI) experiments have been attempted. Dr Frank Drake, author of the Drake Equation and one of the scientific leads on the Breakthrough Listen project, was among the first to start scanning for extraterrestrial life back in 1960. The Breakthrough Initiative builds upon more than 50 years of experience, allowing the team to look further and wider than ever before.

So far, we have no proof that life has ever existed on any planet other than Earth, but if we can find just one example elsewhere, it will completely change the way that we view the universe. As Frank Drake said at the Breakthrough launch, "Right now there could be messages from the stars flying right through the room, through us all. That still sends a shiver down my spine. The search for intelligent life is a great adventure. And Breakthrough Listen is giving it a huge lift."

Scanning for alien transmissions

Breakthrough Listen will use three of the world's most powerful telescopes

> *"The search for intelligent life is a great adventure"*
> Dr Frank Drake

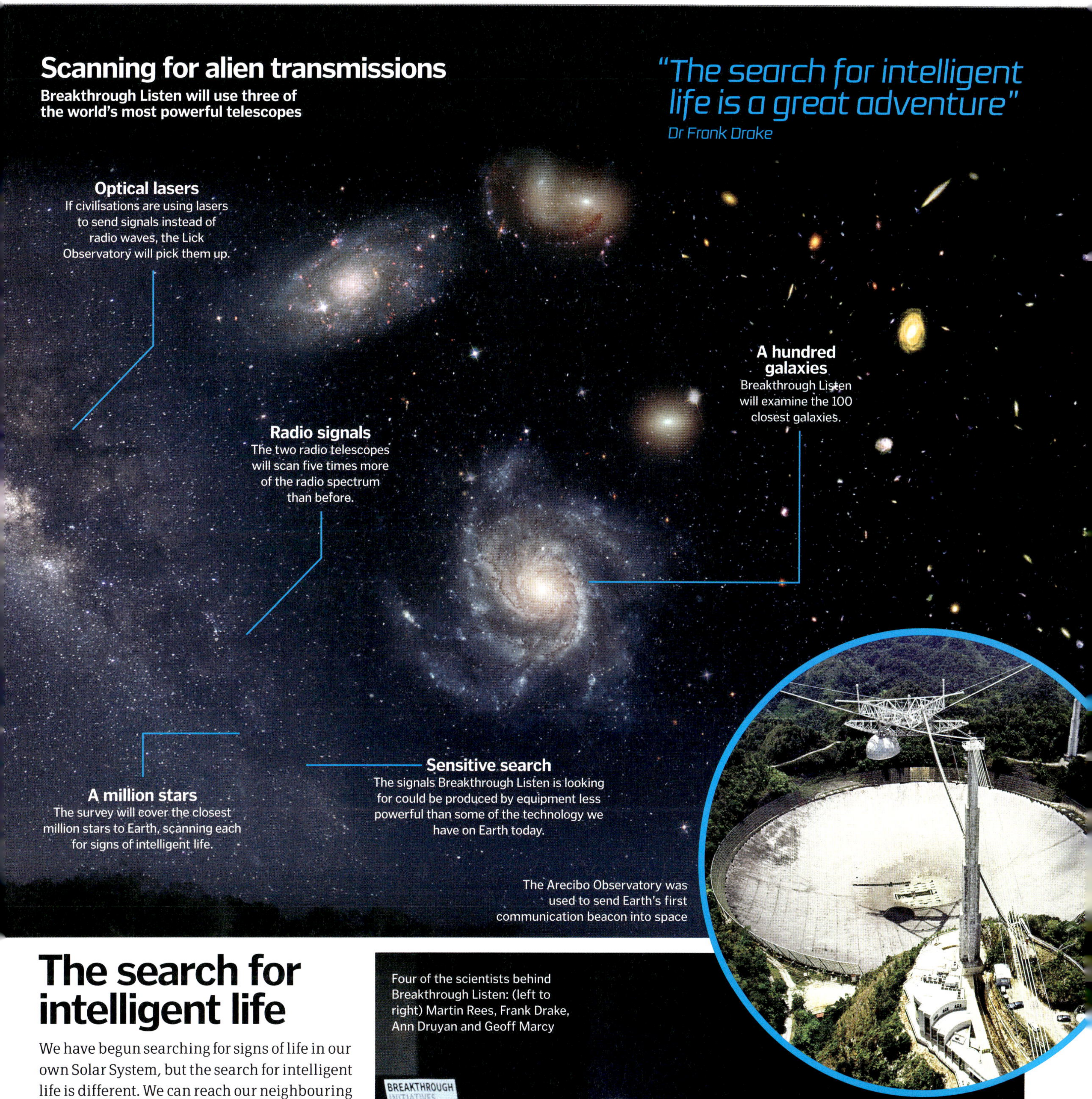

The Arecibo Observatory was used to send Earth's first communication beacon into space

The search for intelligent life

We have begun searching for signs of life in our own Solar System, but the search for intelligent life is different. We can reach our neighbouring planets and moons with probes and rovers, allowing us to sample the atmosphere and the soil directly to find even the tiniest traces of biological materials. But to find out whether there is life beyond the reaches of our spacecraft, scientists must take a different approach. We cannot yet tell whether primitive life exists on distant planets, but if advanced, intelligent civilisations have developed the technology to send messages out into space, we might be able to detect their signals.

Four of the scientists behind Breakthrough Listen: (left to right) Martin Rees, Frank Drake, Ann Druyan and Geoff Marcy

SIGNS OF LIFE

What do we actually look for when searching for aliens?

The search for intelligent life focuses less on what aliens might be made of, and more on how they might communicate. Distant planets in other star systems are too far away to see clearly, but we can pick up signals released into space. But how do we know what to listen for? We live in the same universe, so we share the same fundamental physics and chemistry. Communications have to reach over vast distances, travelling through the dust and gas of the universe without being lost or degraded, and scientists think that it is most likely that they would be sent using radio waves or powerful optical lasers.

Listening out for every single signal across the entire electromagnetic spectrum would be impossible, so to detect these communications, we need to try to think like aliens. This was first attempted in 1959 by two scientists from Cornell University; Giuseppe Cocconi and Philip Morrison suggested focusing in on a specific frequency, the 1,420 MHz 'hydrogen line'. Hydrogen is the smallest and most abundant element in the universe, and when its energy state changes it creates a characteristic spectral line, which is always at a frequency of 1,420 MHz. This falls into the microwave radio region of the electromagnetic spectrum, and is able to travel through dust and gas that block the path of visible light. Looking at the universe in this frequency allows us to see through dark clouds that normally block our view.

Cocconi and Morrison reasoned that civilisations more advanced than our own would also have used hydrogen line emissions to map the universe around them. If intelligent life forms also realise that other civilisations might be tuning in to this special frequency, they might use it to try and send a message. Frequencies either side of the hydrogen line are also monitored, in case alien life forms choose to reserve 1,420 MHz for scientific use, and some SETI experiments, including Breakthrough Listen, also monitor for pulses of laser light in case they are used instead of radio.

As the SETI Institute points out, "optical SETI requires that any extraterrestrial civilisation be deliberately signalling in the direction of our Solar System." This could happen by chance, but if aliens are signalling right at us, they might already know we are here.

We're over here!

The Arecibo Observatory greeted the universe in 1974

The Arecibo Message was a coded image sent out in the direction of 300,000 stars in the nearby M13 star cluster, over 40 years ago. It was constructed by shifting the frequency of the broadcast to spell out binary 0s and 1s. In less than three minutes, the message attempted to paint a picture of life on Earth for any intelligent life that might be watching.

> "Scientists are searching for planets and moons in the Goldilocks zone"

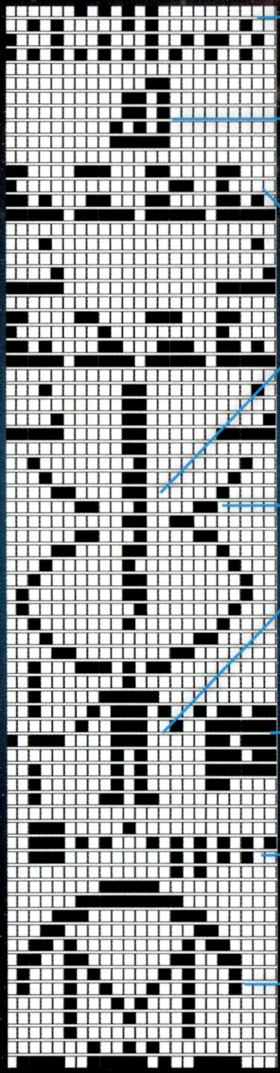

Extreme Earth life

Alien worlds needn't be exactly like ours; even on Earth, organisms survive in environments that are completely unsuitable for humans. Meet the Earth extremophiles.

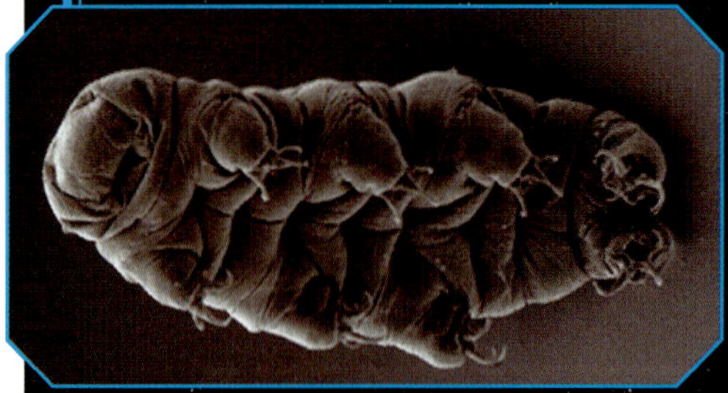

Tardigrades
Tardigrades can survive without water, in extreme cold, under high levels of pressure or radiation, and even in the vacuum of space.

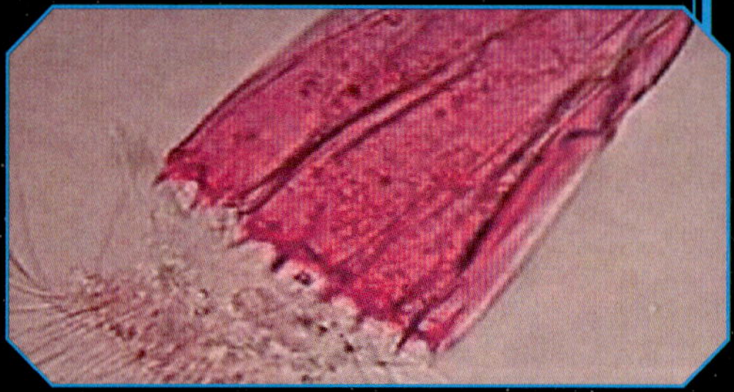

Animals that live without oxygen
In 2010, scientists reported three complex species living at the bottom of the sea, in an area known as a 'dead zone', where there is no oxygen.

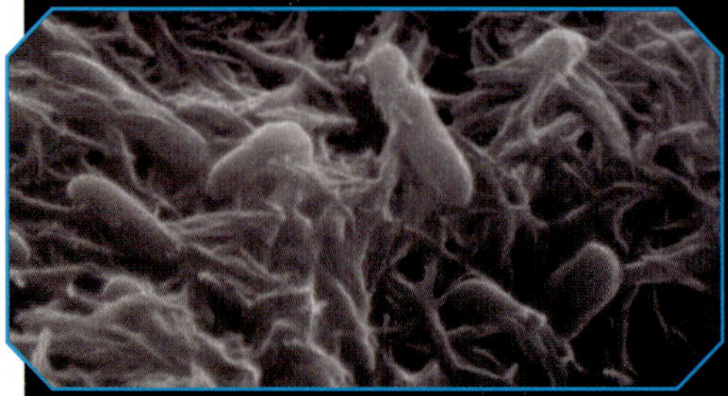

Electric bacteria
Shewanella bacteria can use metal ions and other compounds to release energy, instead of oxygen. This is not seen in any other organisms on Earth.

Extremophiles
Many other species thrive in extremes. For instance, thermophiles survive at high temperatures, and acidophiles withstand acidic conditions.

How to hunt for aliens

There are billions of stars in our galaxy alone, but which should we focus on?

The first step in the search for life is to define what life actually is. This is still a topic of debate, but it is generally agreed that living things are complex and organised. They use resources from their environment to generate energy, and build molecules for replication and growth. They react to their surroundings, adapt and reproduce, all of which requires complex chemistry.

The most abundant elements in the universe are hydrogen and helium, but helium does not form molecules with other elements, and hydrogen can't make complex molecules on its own. Oxygen and carbon are the next most plentiful, and together with hydrogen are the most abundant elements in Earth's organisms.

It might seem a bit egocentric to assume that life elsewhere in the universe will be based on the same components as life on Earth, but a closer look at the chemistry reveals why scientists are so focused on finding carbon and water. Carbon can make four bonds to other elements, providing the scaffold that allows complex molecules to be made. This property can be matched by silicon, but the chemistry is not quite the same. While we exhale carbon dioxide, a silicon-based equivalent might exhale sand.

Water provides a solvent in which these large, complex molecules can dissolve, enabling them to interact. Water is also good at maintaining stable temperatures, and the fact that ice floats means that lakes don't freeze solid. These properties are hard to match, although ammonia and hydrogen fluoride come close.

Given what we know about the chemistry and composition of the universe, scientists are searching for planets and moons in the so-called 'Goldilocks zone' or 'habitable zone', where liquid water might exist. If these conditions can support life on Earth, why not elsewhere?

Life in our Solar System

We might not have to look far to find aliens

Mars
NASA's rovers have shown that Mars was once home to vast pools and rivers, and in 2015, NASA confirmed that liquid water still flows on the Red Planet today.

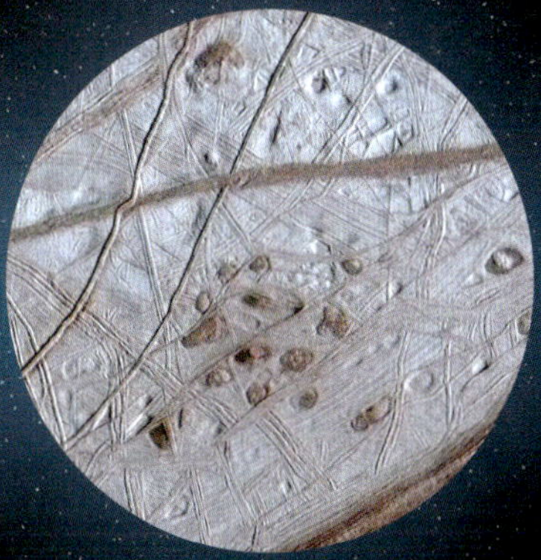

Europa
Jupiter's icy moon may have a salty ocean beneath its surface. NASA believes that it touches the moon's rocky core, providing chemical elements that could sustain life.

Enceladus
Saturn's moon Enceladus releases jets from its icy surface. Scientists believe that they could be carrying materials from a hidden liquid water ocean underneath.

Titan
Saturn's largest moon has an atmosphere of nitrogen and methane that intrigues scientists. Some suggest that methane-based life forms could inhabit Titan's seas.

Hunting for planets

Spotting distant planets is tricky, but new technology could help

To identify Earth-like planets elsewhere in the galaxy, scientists watch out for their shadows as they pass across their parent stars, but the closest stars are so bright that their planets are a real challenge to detect. The private aerospace and defence company Northrop Grumman are developing a screen known as the 'Starshade', which will fly in between orbiting telescopes and the stars they are trying to image. The petal shape should block out most of the star's light, letting only the reflected light from the planets pass through.

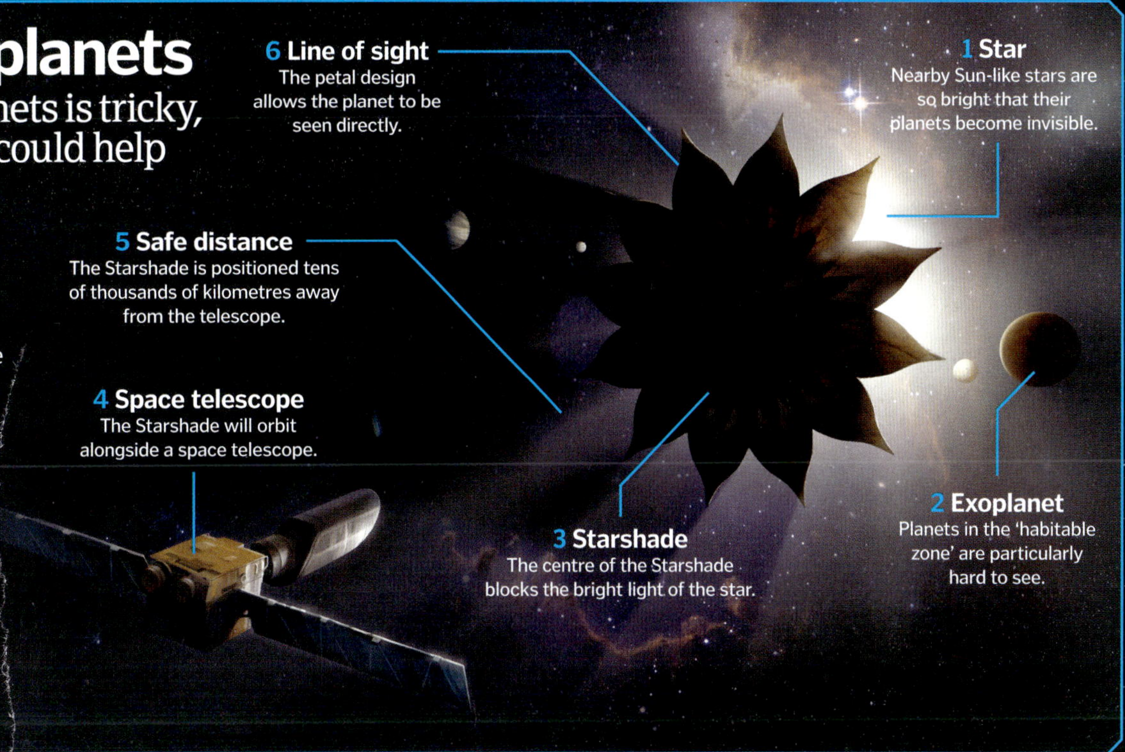

ARE WE ALONE IN THE UNIVERSE?

Top scientists think that Earth is just one of many inhabited planets

There are billions of stars in the universe, and some astronomers think it's likely that each one in the Milky Way galaxy has at least one planet. The director of the Space Telescope Institute in Baltimore, Matt Mountain, told NASA: "What we didn't know five years ago is that perhaps ten to 20 per cent of stars around us have Earth-size planets in the habitable zone." Being in the right zone is one thing, but being home to life is another. And being home to intelligent life with the technology to send signals out into space is something quite different again.

On Earth, moving from single-celled organisms like bacteria, to complex, multicellular organisms, like worms, fish, and humans took around 2.5 billion years, and it only happened once. As Professor Stephen Hawking pointed out in a lecture entitled Life in the Universe, "This is a good fraction of the total time available, before the Sun blows up." Assuming that life can get past this bottleneck, at least one species then needs to become intelligent enough to want to communicate with the universe. If this is possible, where is everybody? This question, known as the Fermi Paradox, was asked by Enrico Fermi in 1950. He argued that technologically advanced civilisations could colonise entire galaxies in just ten million years, fractions of the age of the Milky Way, so we really should have seen evidence of them by now.

It could be that there really are no other intelligent life forms in the galaxy, but there are dozens of other explanations. One of the most widely discussed is the idea that intelligent life might not survive long enough to make contact; it could be that asteroid impacts, supernova blasts, natural disasters and warfare wipe intelligent life forms out before they have a chance to explore. Ultimately, the lifespan of a civilisation is limited by the life of its parent star, unless of course, the life forms find a way to leave.

"Being in the habitable zone is one thing, but being home to life is another"

Have there always been Earth-like planets?

The universe is nearly 14 billion years old, but it hasn't always been able to sustain life. In the early days, as everything began to cool after the Big Bang, there were only two elements available: hydrogen and helium. These simple elements are not sufficient alone to build any kind of life. These gases formed the first stars and galaxies, and these new nuclear reactors smashed the small atoms together to make heavier elements like carbon and nitrogen. When these stars exploded, the new elements went on to form new stars. Our Solar System formed around 4.6 billion years ago, and star-forged elements like silicon and iron make up the planet that we live on. Until recently, scientists thought that the oldest stars wouldn't have Earth-like planets, but NASA's Kepler Space Telescope has found some that are orbiting stars more than twice the age of the Sun.

Kepler 452b orbits in the habitable zone around a star 1.5 billion years older than the Sun

How many worlds could send us signals?

Dr Frank Drake is a pioneer of SETI, and his equation uses probability to estimate the number of inhabited planets in the Milky Way that may be trying to make contact. It takes the rate of star formation in the galaxy and asks, how many of those stars have planets? Then how many of those planets are habitable, and how many of those are inhabited? Then how many have intelligent inhabitants? Finally, how many intelligent civilisations are actually sending signals? And for how long?

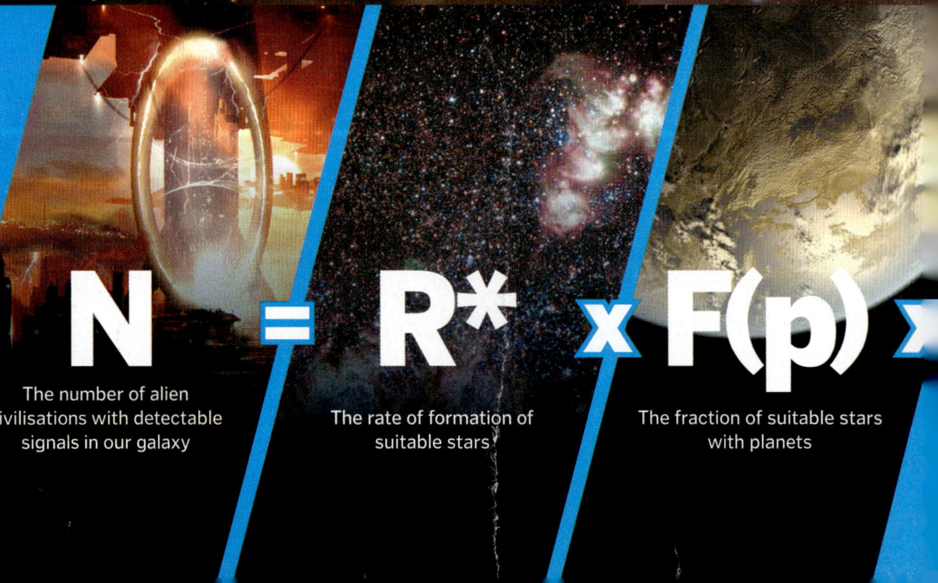

N = R* x F(p) x

N: The number of alien civilisations with detectable signals in our galaxy

R*: The rate of formation of suitable stars

F(p): The fraction of suitable stars with planets

Are we being buzzed?

Fast radio bursts (FRBs) are brief, high-energy pulses of electromagnetic waves that have been appearing in scientific data gathered at the Parkes Telescope since the early 2000s. The bursts contain high and low frequency wavelengths, which travel at different speeds through space, and the delay between the arrival of the highest and lowest frequency waves can be used to calculate the distance to the source. Strangely, the ten FRBs all had delay times nearly divisible by 187.5. There is no natural object known to be able to do this, leading scientists to speculate about a possible alien source. However, other signals, called perytons, have since been found to have much more local origins – scientists discovered that they could produce the same interference patterns by opening the door of the microwave oven.

A Dyson Sphere is one idea for an alien megastructure, designed to capture the energy emitted by a star

Rovers, like NASA's Curiosity, are scouring Mars to see whether it was, or is, capable of supporting life

Every dot in this image is a galaxy with millions or billions of stars

Will we find alien life?

Top scientists think that life is out there, but it could be hard to find

MANY SCIENTISTS BELIEVE THERE COULD BE ALIENS....

- "What is the likelihood that only one ordinary star, the Sun, is accompanied by an inhabited planet? ... To me, it seems far more likely that the universe is brimming over with life." **– *Carl Sagan, Cosmos***
- "To my mathematical brain, the numbers alone make thinking about aliens perfectly rational" **– *Stephen Hawking***
- "I think we're going to have strong indications of life beyond Earth within a decade, and definitive evidence within 20 to 30 years," **– *Ellen Stofan, NASA chief scientist***
- "I think life is common in the universe. We *may* be the only civilisation in the Milky Way. There *will* be other civilisations in the universe" **– *Brian Cox***

...BUT PROVING IT COULD BE A CHALLENGE

- "We have a galaxy full of ten billion planets, in habitable zones, roughly Earth-size... no visits, no communications... How can that be?" **– *William Borucki, ex-NASA Kepler scientist***
- "Life outside of Earth is probably going to be really hard to find... We can't even agree on a definition of what life detection is." **– *John Grunsfeld, NASA***
- "Right now there are maybe only 10,000 civilisations we can detect in the galaxy. That's one in ten million stars. We have to look at ten million stars before we have a good chance of succeeding." **– *Frank Drake***

IT COULD EVEN BE DANGEROUS

- "Active SETI is not scientific research. It is a deliberate attempt to provoke a response by an alien civilisation whose capabilities, intentions, and distance are not known to us." **– *Michael Michaud, International Academy of Astronautics***

N(e) x F(l) x F(i) x F(c) x L

- N(e): The number of planets in each system that could support life
- F(l): The fraction of suitable planets that are actually inhabited
- F(i): The fraction of alien civilisations with detectable electromagnetic signals
- F(c): The fraction of intelligent civilisations that develop technology to send signals
- L: The length of time that the civilisations actually transmit signals into space

Space weather

Get the forecast for the Sun's explosive activity and how it affects us on Earth

The Sun, and the vast vacuum of space surrounding it, may seem pretty peaceful to us on Earth, but it is actually alive with violent activity. Although you might not hear about it on television forecasts, it's the source of a variety of space weather, and there are some very important reasons why we should be aware of it. Throughout its 11-year solar cycle, the big ball of hot plasma at the centre of our Solar System bombards our planet with solar winds. During periods of peak activity, this can disrupt many of the technological systems we rely on for communication, navigation and more. Read on to discover how...

Solar wind

Streams of charged particles called plasma are constantly escaping the surface of the Sun, as the star's powerful gravity fails to contain them. Known as solar wind, it can reach speeds of up to 800 kilometres per second as it hurtles towards Earth, where it continuously batters our planet's magnetic field. Solar wind is so powerful that it is believed to have stripped away the atmospheres of many other planets, such as Mercury, but Earth's relatively strong magnetic field is keeping it at bay.

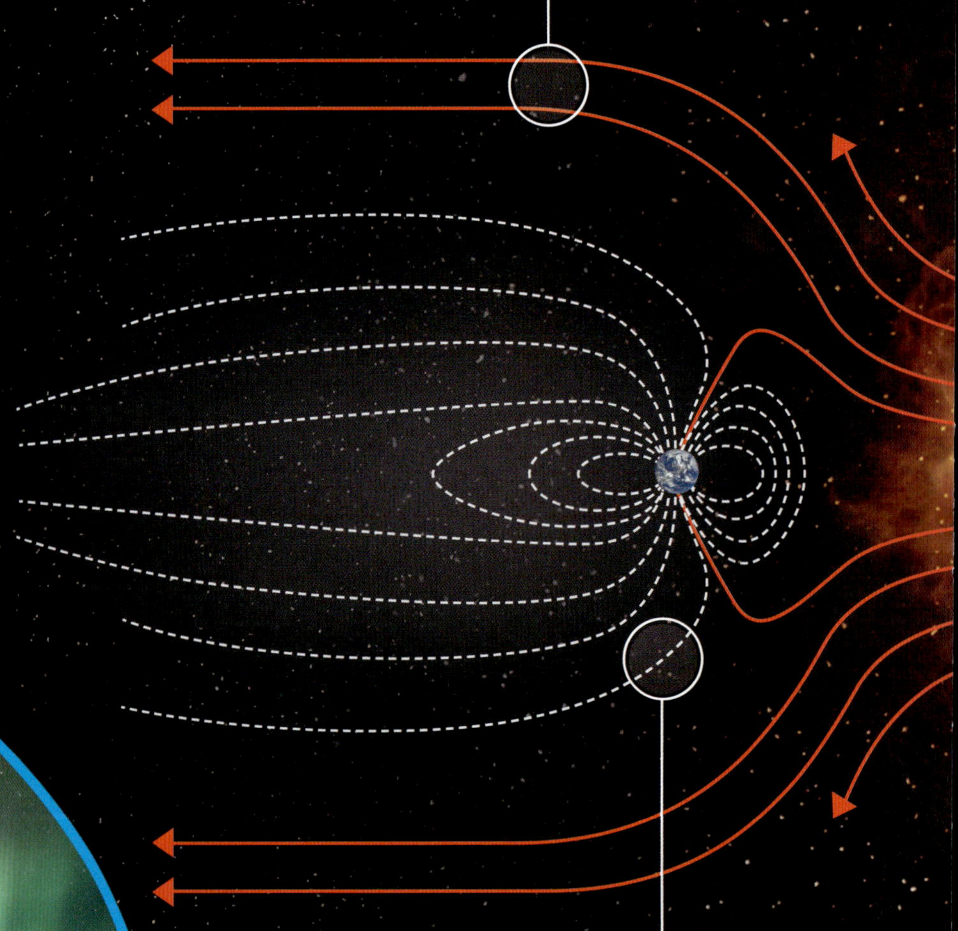

How does space weather affect us?

While the magnetosphere provides us with some protection from space weather, its effects can still impact our daily lives. Geomagnetic storms interfere with Earth's upper atmosphere, interrupting radio communications, disrupting Global Positioning Systems (GPS) and even inducing electric currents at ground level, resulting in disruptions to power grids and widespread blackouts.

Increased levels of solar radiation also pose a threat to spacecraft and astronauts in orbit and can even reach aircraft travelling at high altitudes, presenting health risks for passengers. To minimise these effects, space weather is constantly monitored so that steps can be taken to prepare for extreme events.

Not all of the effects of space weather are bad, though. Auroras, such as the Aurora Borealis (also known as the Northern Lights), are the result of solar wind entering Earth's atmosphere above the magnetic poles. As the charged particles collide with gas particles in the atmosphere, they light up to create a colourful display in the sky.

Auroras are certainly the most visually pleasing effect of space weather

Earth's protection

Earth's magnetic field forms a magnetosphere, which acts as a shield to protect our planet from the effects of space weather. However, the constant battering of solar winds has had a dramatic impact on its shape, compressing the side closest to the Sun and stretching out the other. Sometimes, the solar winds can disconnect the magnetic field lines on the night side, and when they snap back into position, they push charged particles back towards Earth's upper atmosphere.

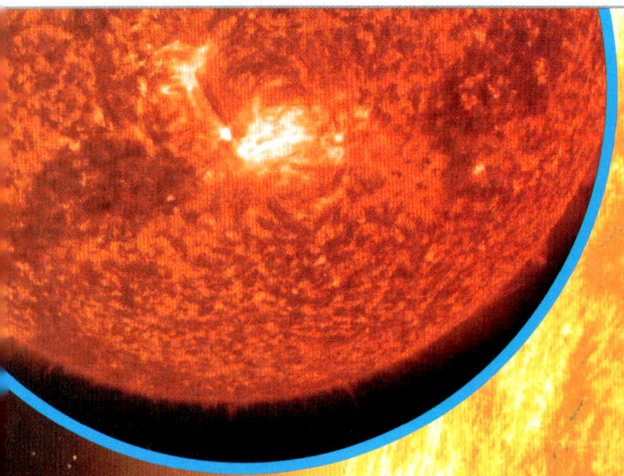

Solar flares

When twisting magnetic field lines in sunspot regions cross and reconnect with one another, they cause massive explosions called solar flares. The energy released is the equivalent of millions of 100-megaton hydrogen bombs exploding at the same time, sending huge amounts of radiation out into the Solar System. The radiation emitted spans across the entire electromagnetic spectrum, from radio waves to X-rays and gamma rays, and travels at the speed of light to reach Earth in just eight minutes.

> "Throughout its 11-year solar cycle, the Sun bombards our planet with solar winds"

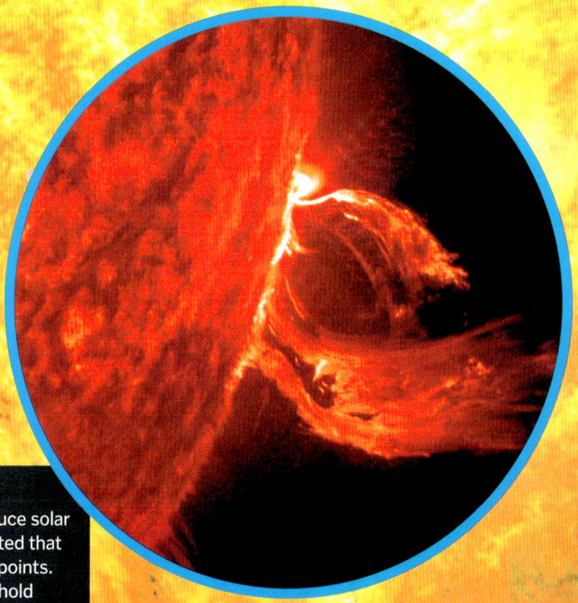

Coronal mass ejections

The magnetic field lines that produce solar flares sometimes become so twisted that they snap and reconnect at other points. The gaps that form can no longer hold plasma on the Sun's surface, and release billions of tons of it into space as a 'coronal mass ejection'. Their speed can vary greatly, meaning they can reach Earth in a matter of hours or days, and when they do their own magnetic field slams into Earth's to generate geomagnetic storms.

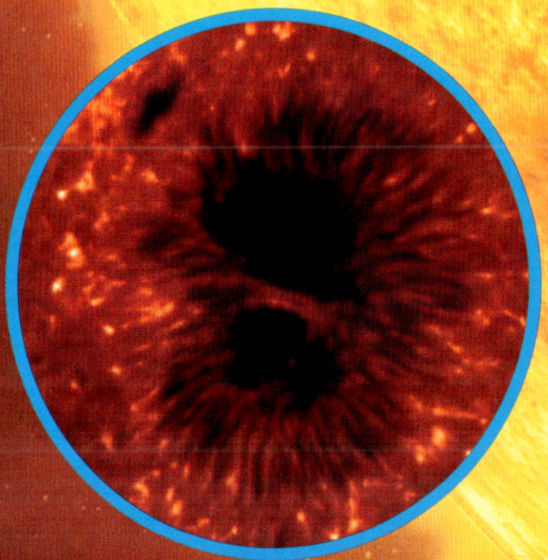

Sunspots

Magnetic field lines breaking through the Sun's surface create dark regions known as sunspots. As heat is inhibited from rising up from the solar interior, these regions are comparatively cooler than the rest of the Sun's surface, but still reach scorching temperatures of around 3,500 degrees Celsius. Sunspots are usually found near to the Sun's equator and are the source of most extreme space weather. The number of them varies throughout the 11-year solar cycle, creating periods of peak activity.

Learn more

Visit **www.spaceweather.com** to get the latest forecast and keep up to date with the current conditions in space. Additional space weather information can also be found at the Space Weather Prediction Center's website, **www.swpc.noaa.gov**.

PARALLEL UNIVERSES

Infinite Earths and alternate realities: does this controversial theory have any scientific basis?

It's an understatement to say that the multiverse theory is one of the most controversial theories in science. In fact, merely putting this in the Space section of the magazine, and not a newly created Theology section, would ruffle a few astrophysicists' feathers. But why is this the case, and is there any basis for suggesting we live in a multiverse?

The origins of the multiverse theory are a grey area. Some, like David Deutsch in his book *The Beginning of Infinity*, point to Erwin Schrödinger and his famous equation. This broadly introduced the idea of quantum mechanics, in which a particle can be in two states at once, in the first half of the 20th century. It would be many years until the broader implications of the theory were given serious thought, though.

You're probably more familiar with the multiverse theory in different terms – parallel universes – so let's begin there. At its core, the multiverse theory suggests that our universe is not alone, but perhaps one of many in some form or another. Just as we discovered Earth was one of many planets, and that the Milky Way was one of many galaxies, some scientists think the same could be said of the universe.

As of yet, we have no direct evidence for multiverses (and even that prospect is contentious, which we'll come on to later). But our best indirect evidence for its existence is a peculiar one. It stems from how exact certain mathematical constants in the universe are. The cosmological constant, for example, is a value for the energy density of the vacuum of space. Its existence explains how the universe is expanding at an ever-increasing speed, something first discovered in 1998.

But the cosmological constant is 120 orders of magnitude smaller (that is, ten to the power of minus 120) than theory predicts it should be. Thus, even a small change in its value would have rendered our universe a mess of nothingness after the Big Bang. So, too, for the values of dark energy. How were these mathematical constants so finely created?

"If [dark energy] had been any bigger, there would have been enough repulsion from it to overwhelm the gravity that drew the galaxies together, drew the stars together, and drew Earth together," Stanford physicist Leonard Susskind told *Discover Magazine* in 2008. "It's one of the greatest mysteries in physics. All we know is that if it were much bigger we wouldn't be here to ask about it."

The multiverse theory has an answer, though. It suggests that in our universe, the cosmological constant is exactly the right value for everything as we know it to exist. But there are an infinite number of other universes, where it is ever so slightly different.

Working on the pretence that this is true, what form would these other universes take? That's the tricky part. There are a large number of theories, from Max Tegmark's four levels of classification (explained later), to M-theory (which encompasses string theory), to cyclic theories, where the universe is in an infinite number of cycles between Big Bangs and Big Crunches.

Tegmark's four levels encompass the broader multiverse theories. The Massachusetts Institute of Technology professor suggested them in 2003, presenting them as a way to classify ideas for the multiverse. "Parallel universes are not a theory, but a prediction of certain theories," he said in his 2014 book *Our Mathematical Universe*. The first level deals with the observable universe, which is the extent to which we can see in the universe. Owing to the finite speed of light, we are only able to see as far as light has been able to travel to us since the Big Bang, 13.8 billion years ago. Due to the expansion of the universe, though, we are able to see light that is now more than 42 billion light years from us, which we call the observable universe. But we cannot see beyond this; what is there, we just don't know.

Tegmark's first multiverse level suggests that there is no end. Instead, the universe just keeps going and going, infinitely. If true, this would create an infinite number of instances for everything to occur. So, at some astronomical distance away from us, we would find an Earth exactly the same as ours, and you would find yourself sitting there reading this very article.

The second level is similar to the first, but proposes that while the whole multiverse is expanding, there are regions within it that expand at different rates, forming bubbles of self-confined space – in other words, bubble universes. Our universe would be one bubble, with an untold number of other bubbles beyond, each with their own laws of physics. In 2015, a later, widely discredited theory suggested

Building a multiverse

Are universes born in black holes?

"As of yet, we have no direct evidence for multiverses"

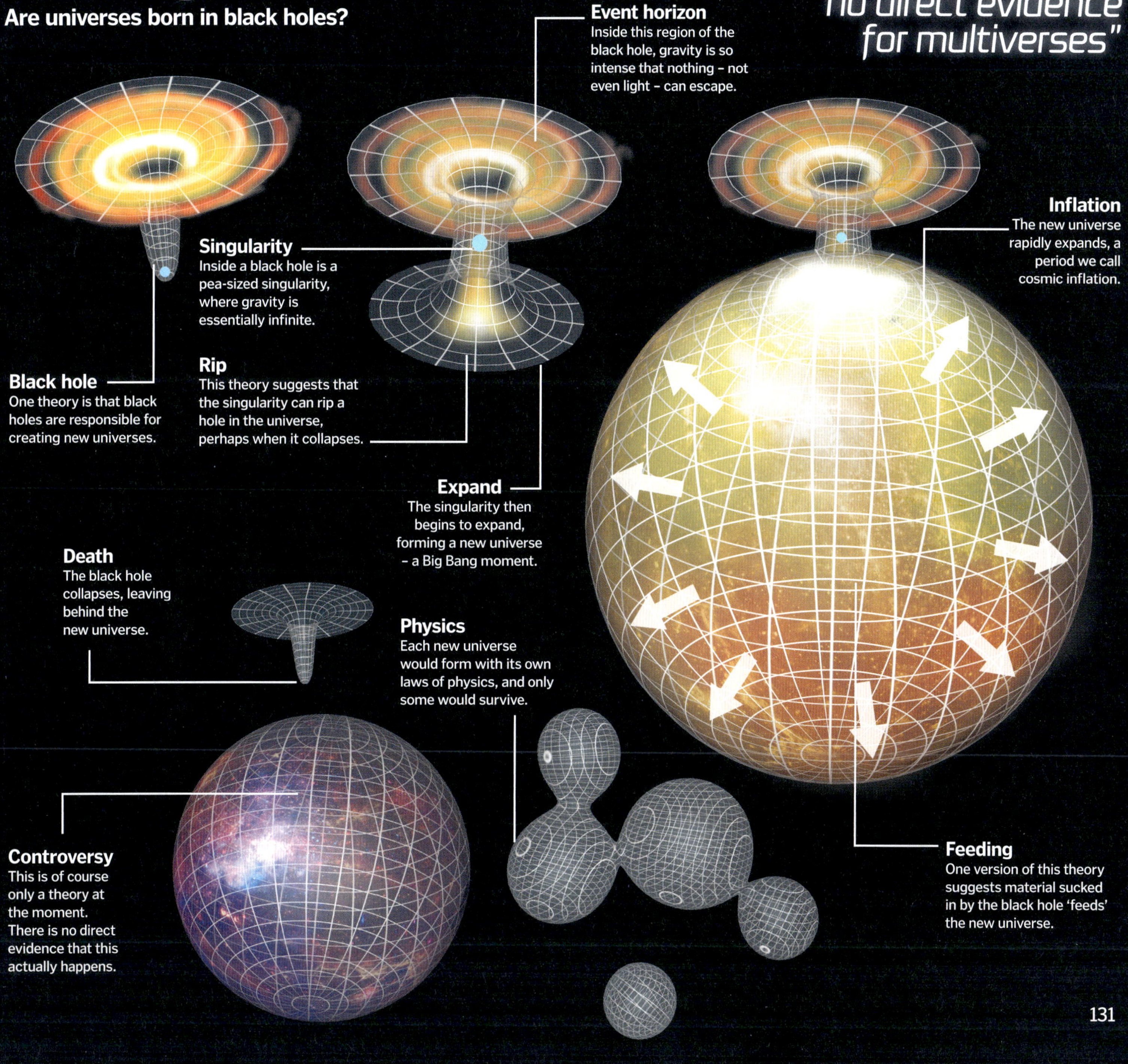

bubble universe had actually 'bumped' into one another, producing a noticeable glow in the far reaches of space.

In the third level, things start to get a little bit strange. Like the first, it suggests that the laws of physics are the same everywhere, but rather than different universes being separated by distance, as in the second level, they are in fact separated by time. The laws of quantum mechanics, as mentioned earlier, allow for a large number of uncertainties and possible futures (for example, whether Schrödinger's famous 'cat in the box' is dead or alive). In this level, all of these possibilities would play out. Every single eventuality would occur, and each time, a new universe would be created along with it. For us as observers, though, we only see one universe – our own.

The fourth and final level, the mathematical multiverse, is fairly difficult to comprehend. It is Tegmark's own theory, presented in *Our Mathematical Universe*. It essentially implies that the universe is composed entirely of mathematics, and we are merely constructs within that. But the book and theory have come under some heavy criticism.

One of the main arguments against the multiverse theory, though, is that it fails one of the very cornerstones of science itself: falsifiability. This is the ultimate test for any scientific theory, namely that it can be proven wrong. For example, if you put forward the theory that every animal on Earth had four legs, someone else could refute that theory by finding an animal with more or less than four.

No multiverse theory is currently falsifiable. We simply don't have the means to disprove some of the claims being made. We will never be able to journey beyond the observable universe, and

DIFFERENT TYPES OF MULTIVERSE

"We have no way of jumping to another universe"

LEVEL ONE:
An extension

Our views into the universe are limited by the age of the universe. We cannot see further than the time light has had to travel to us, which when you take the expansion of the universe into account, comes to 42 billion light years.

But this multiverse theory suggests that, beyond this distance, the universe continues into infinity. And this would mean that eventually, by chance, everything would start to repeat itself – even Earth itself. It will be impossible to ever know what is beyond our observable universe though, without finding some fanciful way to travel faster than light. Until then, we may never know what is beyond our vision.

Learn more

To learn more about multiverse theories, check out Issue 46 of our sister magazine, **All About Space**, which goes into far more detail on the controversial topic.

LEVEL TWO:
The bubble universe

This theory proposes that there are many 'bubble' universes living alongside each other. The key behind the theory is cosmic inflation, which is the period of rapid expansion the universe went through in its first trillionth of a trillionth of a trillionth of a second. This ultimately gave rise to the universe as we know it.

According to this theory, different regions of space expanded at different rates, forming their own 'bubble' regions alongside ours. In theory, there could be an infinite number of these bubble universes alongside ours, with a contentious version suggesting each has its own laws of physics.

thus could never disprove the notion that there are other parallel bubble universes out there, or an infinite universe. As such, many argue that the multiverse theory should not be treated as a theory at all. It should be condemned to the pseudoscience bin.

"The trouble is that no possible astronomical observations can ever see those other universes," said cosmologist George Ellis in an article published in *Scientific American* in 2011. "The arguments are indirect at best. And even if the multiverse exists, it leaves the deep mysteries of nature unexplained."

Of course, falsifiability itself has its detractors. Other more widely accepted theories, such as the existence of dark matter or dark energy, may not be falsifiable. Should we also consign those to the scrapheap? It's fair to say that this is a topic that draws heated debate in the scientific community.

And even aside from falsifiability, we run into a problem. Not only can we not disprove multiverse theories, but we can't currently prove them either. We have no way of jumping to another universe, or even observing one. How are we supposed to sift through the myriad of claims being made when there is no direct evidence available?

The idea of a multiverse is undoubtedly an intriguing one. It has inspired a huge range of science fiction, and has garnered support from some of the most prominent physicists today. "It would not be beyond the realms of possibility that somewhere outside of our own universe lies another different universe," Professor Stephen Hawking said in 2015. But it remains divisive, and will do so for the foreseeable future. For now, it remains a fringe theory in some corners. And perhaps in an issue of **How It Works** in an alternate universe, it is indeed confined to the Theology section.

LEVEL THREE: Many worlds

The many-worlds theory relies on quantum mechanics. The quantum world is odd, in that things such as photons can appear to be in two places, or states, at once. It is only when we observe the photon that its state is decided.

In this theory, though, both states exist. And, in fact, this is happening constantly for everything around us, at all times. Each time there is a 'split', a new universe is created, giving rise to an infinite number of universes. This is probably the closest theory to the idea of 'parallel universes' where one could envision jumping into a nearby universe. It's pretty unlikely that'll ever be possible, though.

LEVEL FOUR: Mathematical universe

This theory is probably the one that is most widely derided. Max Tegmark goes into detail in his doorstop of a book *Our Mathematical Universe*, but in essence, it suggests that our universe, and all other universes, are nothing but mathematical constructs. We are quite simply lumps of mathematics manifested as a consciousness that can perceive this seemingly 'real' world.

It is described by some as the 'ultimate ensemble' and, owing to its nature being everything broken down into mathematics, there cannot be another broader multiverse theory beyond it. As you might have guessed, it's a bit controversial.

Arguments for and against the multiverse

FOR

Cosmic inflation
Our universe grew exponentially in the first moments of its existence, but was this expansion uniform? If not, it suggests different regions of space grew at different rates – and may be isolated from one another.

Mathematical constants
How are the laws of our universe so exact? Some propose that this happened only by chance – we are the one universe out of many that happened to get the numbers right.

The observable universe
What is beyond the edge of the observable space around us? No one knows for sure, and until we do (which could be never), the thought that our universe extends infinitely is an interesting one.

AGAINST

Falsifiability
There is no way for us to ever test theories of the multiverse. We will never see beyond the observable universe, so if there is no way to disprove the theories, should they be given credence?

Occam's razor
Sometimes, the simplest ideas are the best. Some physicists argue that we don't need the multiverse theory at all. It doesn't solve any paradoxes, and only creates new complications.

No evidence
Not only can we not disprove any multiverse theory, we can't prove them either. We currently have no evidence that multiverses exist, and everything we can see suggests there is just one universe – our own.

The Bullet Cluster of galaxies; the blue indicates dark matter, while the pink is normal matter in the form of hot gas and the galaxies themselves

What is the universe made of?

The cosmos is filled with material and energy that we cannot see

If you look up at the night sky, you can see the light of hundreds of stars, as well as nebulae of gas and giant galaxies tens of thousands of light years across. Believe it or not, everything that we can see in the universe emitting light in the electromagnetic spectrum makes up only 4.9 per cent of its total matter and energy. This accounts for all the planets, moons, comets, stars and nebulae, and all the atoms in the periodic table. So what is the other 95.1 per cent?

It was Albert Einstein, with his famous equation $E=mc^2$, who said that matter and energy were equivalent. This allows for most of the universe (68.3 per cent to be exact) to be made from energy and it is causing the expansion of the universe to accelerate. No one knows what it is, so scientists call it 'dark energy'. The remaining 26.8 per cent is made from another dark substance, called dark matter. Astronomers know it exists because its gravity affects the motions of stars and galaxies, and it can bend the light of more distant galaxies. But it emits no light of its own and no one knows what it's made of.

Clean and tidy galaxies

A tidy galaxy allows its stars to sparkle and astronomers to measure its precise distance

Unlike our dusty, dirty Milky Way galaxy, the nearby dwarf galaxy IC 1613 is comparatively clean, sporting very little in the way of cosmic dust.

Galaxies become dusty because their member stars are like cosmic soot machines. When they die, either by expanding into red giants and planetary nebulae, or as explosive supernovae, stars throw out huge amounts of dust into space.

For example, the supernova that exploded in the Large Magellanic Cloud in 1987 produced enough dust to make 200,000 Earth-sized planets! This dust is not like the dust bunnies that collect by your skirting board, but smoke particle-sized grains of heavy elements that go into producing the next generation of stars and planets.

The last main burst of star formation in IC 1613 took place 7 billion years ago. Without many stars forming, dust has not been produced in great quantities. This is an advantage though, because dust tends to scatter blue light, leaving stars and galaxies looking redder than they really are. When this happens, it's hard to judge their distance based on their luminosity.

In the case of IC 1613, however, we can see its stars clearly and measure its distance as 2.3 million light years, which is closer than the Andromeda Galaxy.

The IC 1613 is the Milky Way's clean and tidy galactic neighbour

Taking the Solar System's temperature

How do we know how hot the other planets really are?

Infrared cameras can reveal hotspots on the human body, and the same techniques can be used to take the temperature of objects in outer space. All objects above absolute zero emit infrared radiation, and the hotter they are, the more they release.

Unfortunately, it is not as simple as pointing a detector at the sky. The gases in our atmosphere absorb infrared light, so to get clear data from planets and stars we need to take our equipment out into space. Sensitive infrared instruments can be carried by hot air balloons, probes, and space telescopes, like Hubble and Spitzer, allowing us to detect the radiation emitted and reflected by the planets in the Solar System, and by objects even further away.

It is tempting to assume that the closer a planet is to the Sun, the hotter it will be, but this isn't strictly true. The temperature also depends on how much light the planets reflect (known as the albedo), and how good their atmosphere is at holding on to heat (the greenhouse effect).

Hot or not

The temperature of each planet depends on more than just its distance from the Sun

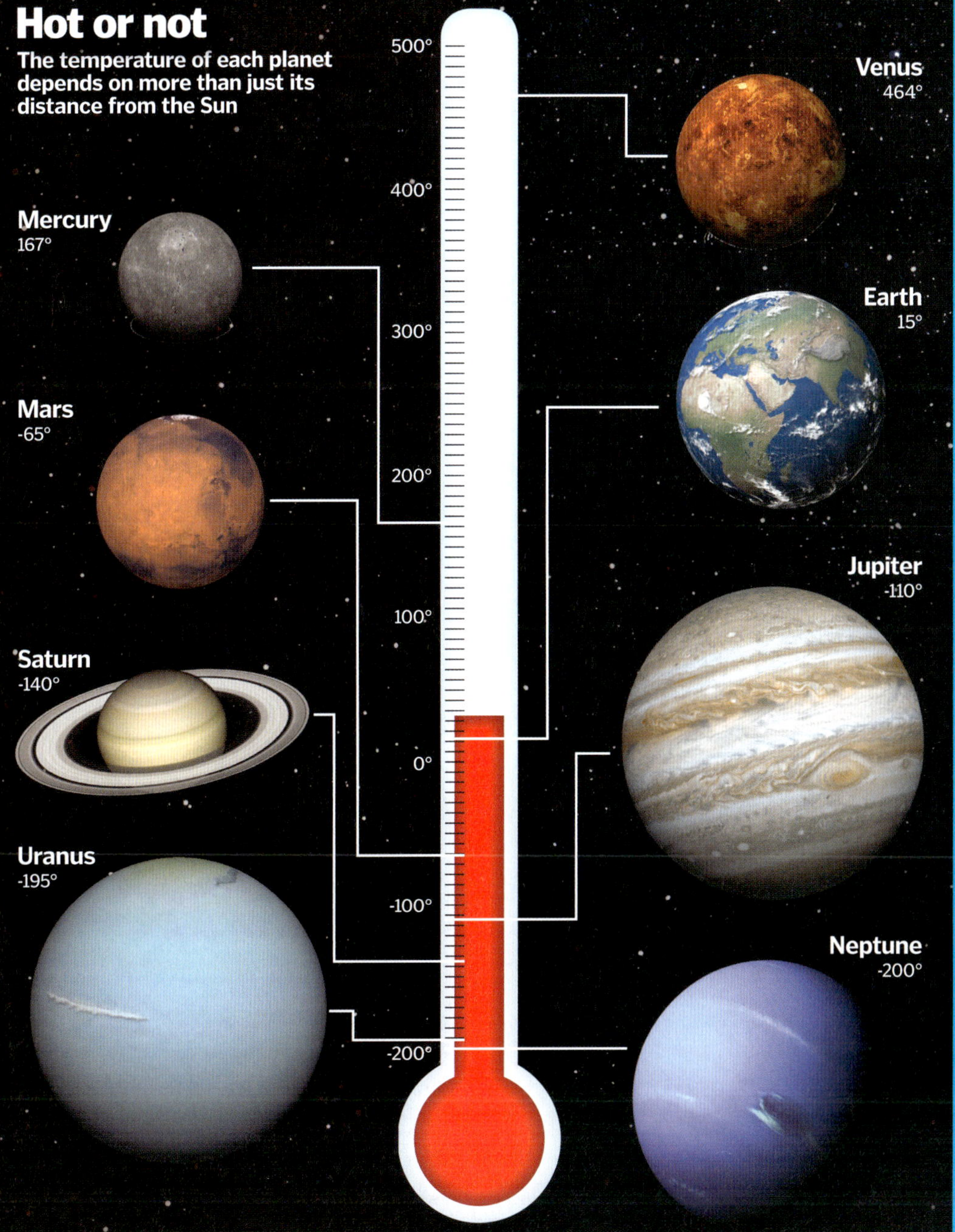

Seeing back in time

When we look into space, we are actually looking into the past

If the Sun suddenly vanished, it would take a full eight minutes and 20 seconds for anyone to notice. This is because sunlight does not reach us instantly; it has to travel through space to get here, and that takes time. Light travels at a speed of just under 300,000,000 metres per second in a vacuum, so the delay when looking at nearby objects isn't noticeable, but when we look out into space, we start to experience some serious lag.

The Moon is just over 384,000 kilometres away, so it takes a bit more than a second for its reflected light to reach us. Light from the Sun, at 150 million kilometres away, takes over eight minutes, while light from our next closest star, Proxima Centauri travels for four years. When light travels from our neighbouring galaxy, Andromeda, it takes an incredible 2.5 million years to reach us.

This effectively means that looking out into space is the equivalent to looking back in time, and the further we look, the further back in time we see. Powerful telescopes, like Hubble, are able to see light released by ancient galaxies more than 13 billion years ago.

When this light was emitted by Andromeda, our ancestors hadn't even learnt to use fire

© NASA

LIVING ON THE MOON

How we could turn craters into colonies for human life

The Moon is our closest neighbour, but only 12 people have ever set foot on its surface. Since 1972, the only visitors have been robots, orbiters and probes. For a long time there was little interest in going back, but at just three days journey away from Earth, the Moon is an obvious target for further investigation. With more countries establishing their own space programmes, and an increasing number of private companies entering the field, interest in the Moon is growing once again.

The environment on the Moon's surface is hazardous, but if we can find a way to construct a base we would gain access to a wealth of off-world resources. It is a prime location for telescopes and communications equipment and its unique environment could hold clues to the history of the Solar System. The Moon's potential has been recognised by organisations across the world, and there are now several exploratory missions in development. At the moment, these are focused around finding out more about the Moon's potential, but over the next few decades, manned missions and even base construction could be on the agenda.

Russia's Roscosmos are planning a series of Luna-Glob missions as a starting point for establishing a robotic base, and in collaboration with the European Space Agency, they are hoping to scope out the Moon's south pole in 2019 and 2020. The China National Space Administration are developing a series of Chang'e probes to collect lunar samples in preparation for future mining missions, and they are building a shuttle capable of lifting human astronauts to the Moon. What's more, in 2007, Google launched the Lunar XPRIZE, encouraging private companies to land rovers on the surface by 2017. Even NASA, who has chosen to focus their resources on manned missions to asteroids and to Mars, are developing a probe to map the water deposits on the lunar south pole.

At the moment, we are just taking our first tentative steps towards further exploration of the Moon, but in the future a science fiction-style base on the surface could become a reality. We explore what such a lunar outpost might look like, and what hazards and challenges could get in the way.

WHY THE MOON?

With preparations already underway for manned missions to Mars, some might question the logic behind a return to the Moon, but a lunar outpost could bring several advantages. A trip to the Moon and back could be completed in under a week, and the surface is rich in resources. Lunar dust contains hydrogen, oxygen, iron and other metals, and if these resources could be mined, it could provide a close off-world source of water and building materials.

The far side of the Moon is shielded from the noise of Earth's communications, providing a quiet vantage point for looking out into the universe, and the near side has a constant view of the surface of our planet, making it an ideal place to set up monitoring stations. Navigational support could also be provided for a variety of operations, from search and rescue on Earth to deep space exploration.

A base on the Moon would also allow us to look closer at its geology, which in turn would help us uncover more about its history and the evolution of the Solar System. Experiments could be conducted, and materials and equipment could be tested, away from the familiar conditions on Earth.

LUNAR HOLIDAYS

With space tourism barely in its infancy, it might seem a bit premature to consider the idea of holidaying on the Moon, but if humanity were to establish a base up there, visitors would almost be inevitable. The company Space Adventures has already sold two $150 million tickets for a trip to visit the Moon in 2018, and more private organisations are looking to set up their own tours. Rules set out in the 1967 Outer Space Treaty state that the Moon cannot be claimed by any country, even if they have set up a base there. However, laws regarding the exploitation of the Moon and its resources for commercial gain have not yet been fully established.

A base on the Moon could pave the way for a new kind of holiday

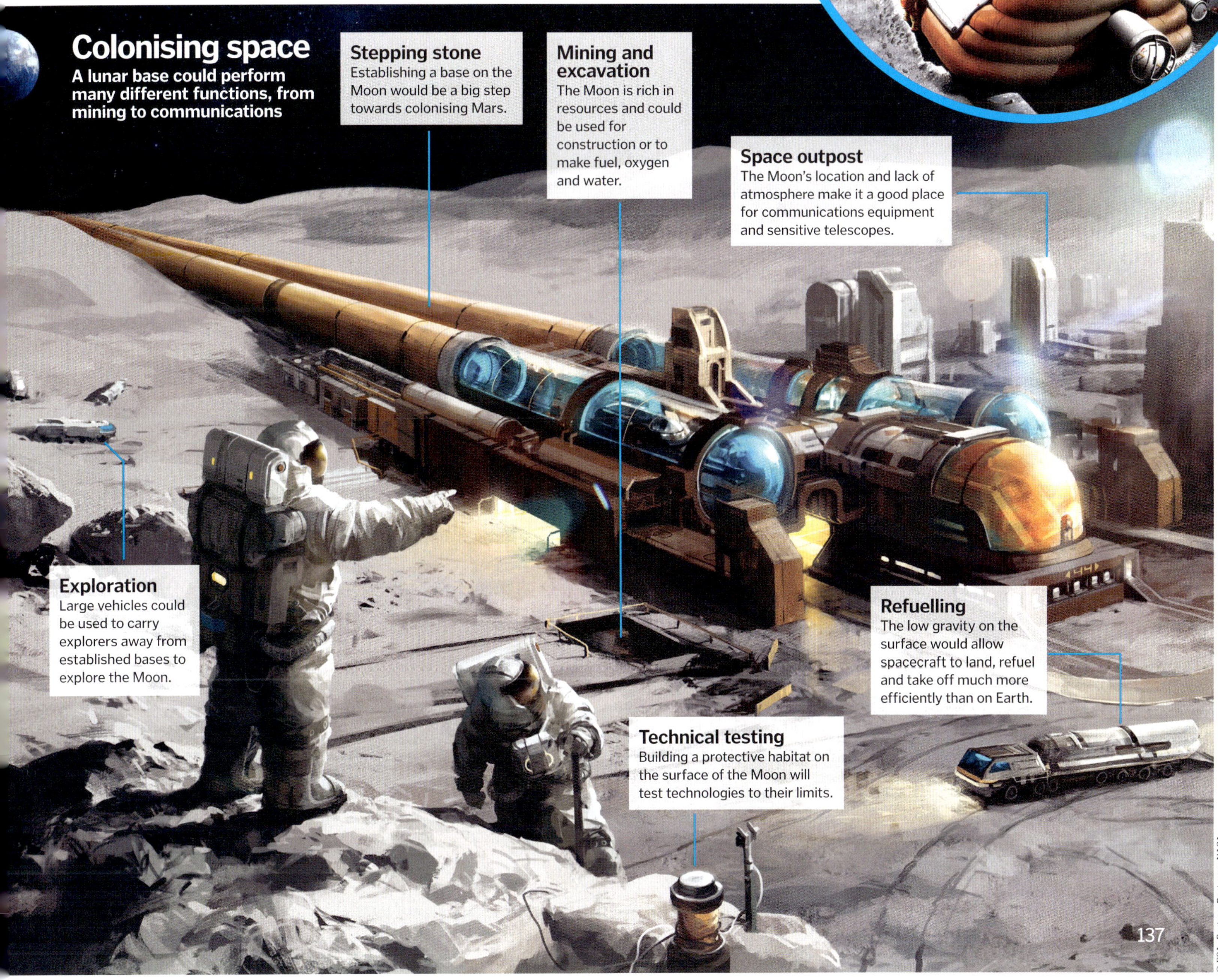

HOW TO BUILD A BASE

The Moon has little atmosphere and none of the protective shielding that we enjoy here on Earth; as a result, the surface is hostile. It is pummelled by solar winds, scorched by radiation, and chunks of rock regularly fall from the sky. The ground is coated in the shattered remains of ancient asteroid impacts, forming a thick layer of sticky dust, and with no atmosphere or weather to wear the particles down, the grains are razor sharp. A successful base would need protection against all of these threats, and, for people to stay there long-term, it would also require a steady supply of food, water, oxygen, power, shelter and rocket fuel.

One of the most popular concepts for a lunar base is inflatable housing – lightweight and easily assembled by pressurising from the inside. With the airlock from the landing capsule used as a door, these structures could provide a quick and simple solution to setting up a base. However, a puncture could prove catastrophic, so the pods would need to be shielded in underground chambers or beneath piles of Moon dust.

Flat-packed panels could also be shipped in from Earth to build sturdier dome or hangar structures, but it would be much more fuel-efficient to use building materials found on the surface of the Moon. When heated, lunar dust can be transformed into a tough solid that could be used to construct buildings and roads, and 3D printers could one day be used to make structures from the regolith.

In the right location, solar panels could provide renewable power for the base, and, if plants are able to grow on the Moon, it could one day be possible to set up a semi-sustainable farming and composting system. Then, if water, oxygen and hydrogen (rocket fuel) could be extracted from lunar dust, a base might even be able to become self-sufficient.

Unfortunately, there are still major challenges to be overcome before we reach this stage, not least the devastating effects of lunar dust. The dust seems to find its way inside even tightly sealed spaces, causing rapid damage to equipment. There are some ideas to get around this, including cable cars or covered transport tubes to minimise the disturbance on the surface, and clean rooms and air locks to keep inside spaces dust-free.

"Solar panels could provide renewable power for the base"

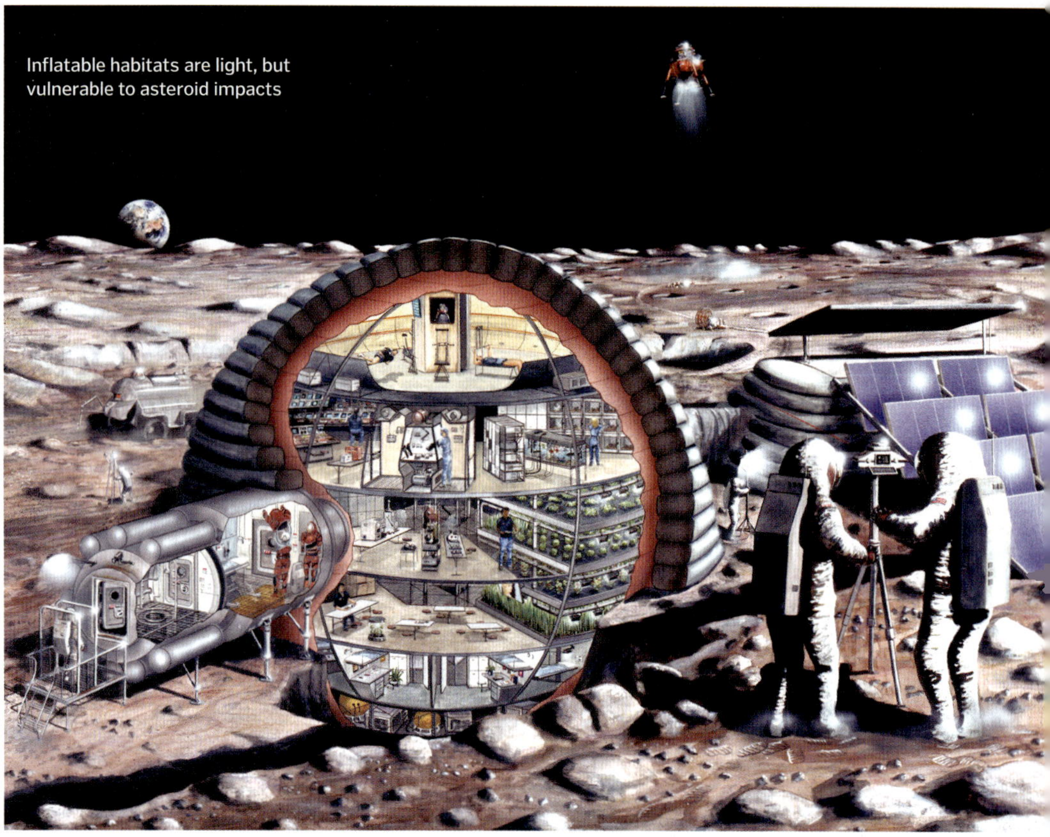

Inflatable habitats are light, but vulnerable to asteroid impacts

Buildings coated in Moon dust would be shielded from impacts and radiation

Dust from the Moon could be used as a material for 3D printing

Excavation equipment would need to resist the damaging effects of fine dust particles

DID YOU KNOW? *NASA held a Regolith Excavation Challenge to encourage engineers to built robots that can dig up lunar soil*

WHERE TO BUILD?

Choosing the right spot could mean the difference between success and failure

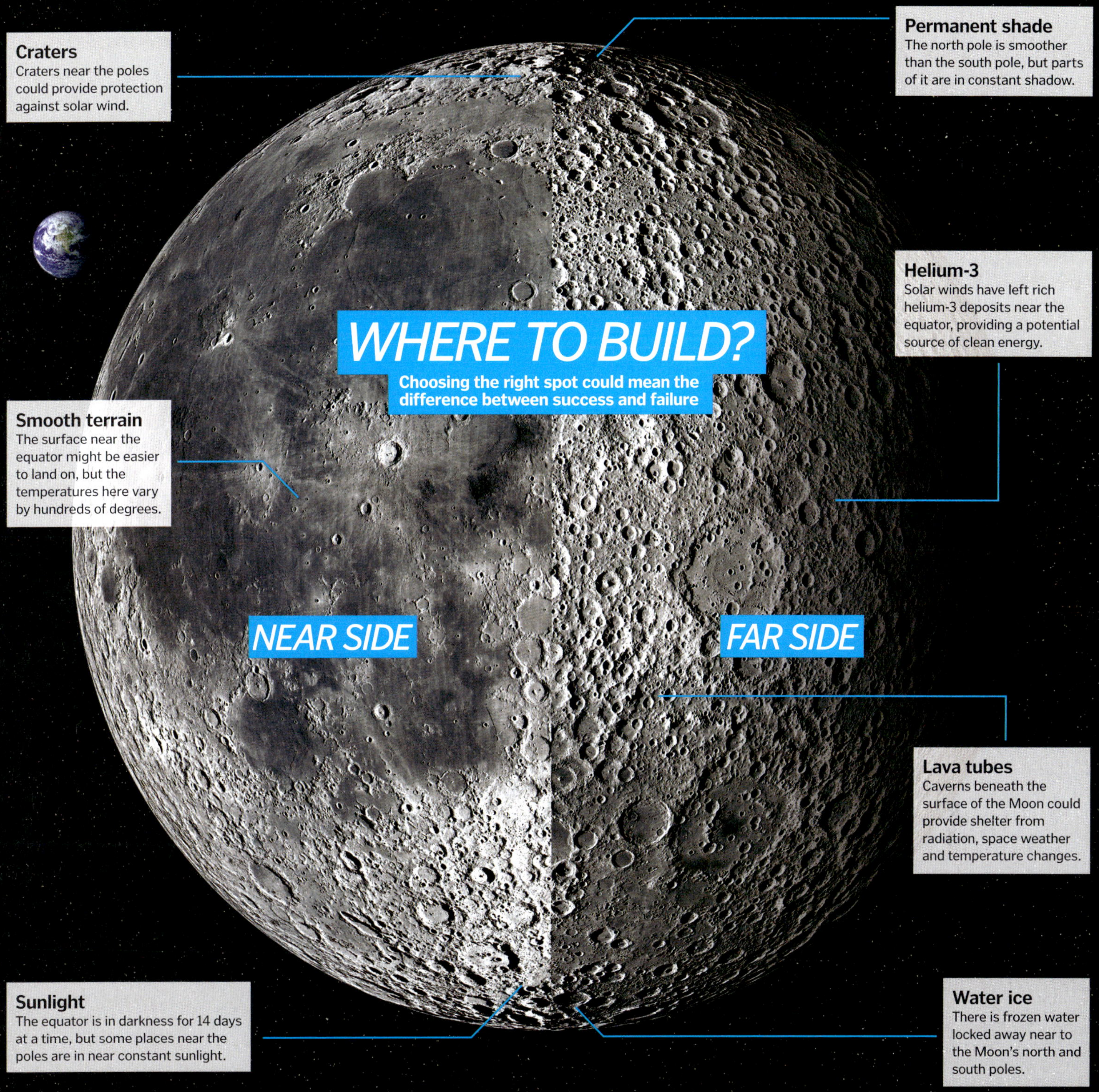

LOCATION, LOCATION, LOCATION

The Apollo missions landed close to the Moon's equator, where the surface is smooth and entering orbit is easy, but these regions have serious problems with temperature control. The Moon turns on its axis once every 28 Earth days, so daytime at the equator lasts for two weeks, and temperatures climb to more than 100 degrees Celsius. For the other two weeks, the same spot is plunged into total darkness and the surface cools to 150 degrees below freezing.

These wide fluctuations could pose real problems for buildings and equipment, and with sunlight absent for days at a time, solar power would be intermittent. Facing head on to the Sun and with little in the way of atmosphere, the equator is also blasted by radiation and solar winds.

At the poles, night and day are less dramatic. The surface is rougher, but certain areas receive sunlight for most of the year, and the temperature remains more stable at around zero degrees Celsius. There is also water ice trapped at the poles, which could provide gases, fluids and even rocket fuel.

One promising location is Shackleton Crater, which is found at the Moon's southern pole. It receives sunlight for around 80 per cent of the year, which could provide a near constant source of electricity from solar panels. Building a base near the equator would be more challenging, but underground habitats could provide enough protection in more exposed locations. Lava tubes like the Marius Hills pit could offer ready-made shelter from temperature fluctuations, solar wind, radiation and surface dust.

WHAT WOULD A LUNAR COLONY LOOK LIKE?

The Moon is not a safe place for humans; the base will be essential for survival

Inflatable habitats
Building materials are heavy, so one option is to use inflatables. These would need to be protected from impacts.

Water supply
Water could be extracted from lunar dust by heating it with hydrogen gas.

Launch and landing
The gravity on the Moon is low, so launching and landing spacecraft requires much less fuel than it does on Earth.

Telescopes and equipment
Away from the interference of Earth's atmosphere, a lunar base could house powerful telescopes.

Radiation shielding
Buildings would need to be protected from radiation. A popular idea is to bury them under layers of moon dust.

"Only a handful of people have visited the Moon's surface, and the longest stay lasted three days"

HOME AWAY FROM HOME

Humans have been living in space since the 1970s, falling around the Earth inside orbiting space stations like Salyut, Almaz, Skylab, Mir and the International Space Station (ISS), but no one has been away from home for longer than a year, making the long-term success of space colonies hard to predict. Over 200 astronauts and cosmonauts have lived on the ISS, and by monitoring them closely we have learnt a lot about the effects of microgravity on the human body, but the Moon is a different environment. Only a handful of people have visited the surface, and the longest stay lasted for only three days.

The Moon has a sixth of the Earth's gravity, and comes with its own unique challenges. The dust that coats the surface could prove one of the most difficult problems to overcome. During the Apollo missions, the sharp particles found their way into equipment, through vacuum seals, and even inside spacesuits, irritating the eyes and lungs of the astronauts.

Permanent settlements on the Moon will only be possible with proper protection

What makes a planet habitable?

Discover what makes Earth so special that it can support life

For life to exist on a planet, there's a bit of a *Goldilocks* situation. The conditions can't be too hot or too cold, with somewhere in the region of -15 and 115 degrees Celsius being about right. Within this range, liquid water can exist, and therefore, in theory, so can life.

In order to be at this optimum temperature, a planet must be the right distance from its host star. This is known as a habitable zone, and lies closer to smaller, cooler stars than large, hot ones. If the habitable zone is too close to a star, stellar flares can destroy the planet's atmosphere, which is needed to keep it warm and protect it from radiation and meteorites. To maintain an atmosphere, a planet must be the right mass to have enough gravity to hold on to it, and needs a magnetic field to protect it from stellar flares. It is believed that Earth's magnetic field is driven by the flow of molten iron in its outer core, so a planet's structure is also a key criterion for supporting life.

Kepler-62f is a super-Earth-size planet in the habitable zone of a star

What is a gravitational well?

How this invisible force shapes the universe

While we are all familiar with gravity being the force that causes a dropped phone to clatter to the ground, Albert Einstein was the first to describe gravity as what happens when space is warped around a mass, creating a dip called a gravitational well. To better understand this, think of a large rubber sheet, held taut. The sheet acts as an analogy for space-time. Then take a bowling ball – which will act as a planet in our example – and place it on the rubber sheet. The sheet will dip and bend with the mass of the ball, forming a concave shape – the gravity well.

Now put a marble on the sheet, which represents a smaller object in space such as a comet or an asteroid. It creates its own gravity well, but it's much smaller than that of the bowling ball. If the marble gets anywhere near the larger gravitational well, it will roll into it – seemingly 'pulled' by gravity.

Everything with mass is able to bend space and the more massive an object is, the more it bends. An object can only escape a gravitational well if it is moving fast enough. Moons and satellites that orbit planets, for example, do not fall any further into the gravitational well of the planet they orbit.

The Solar System's gravitational wells

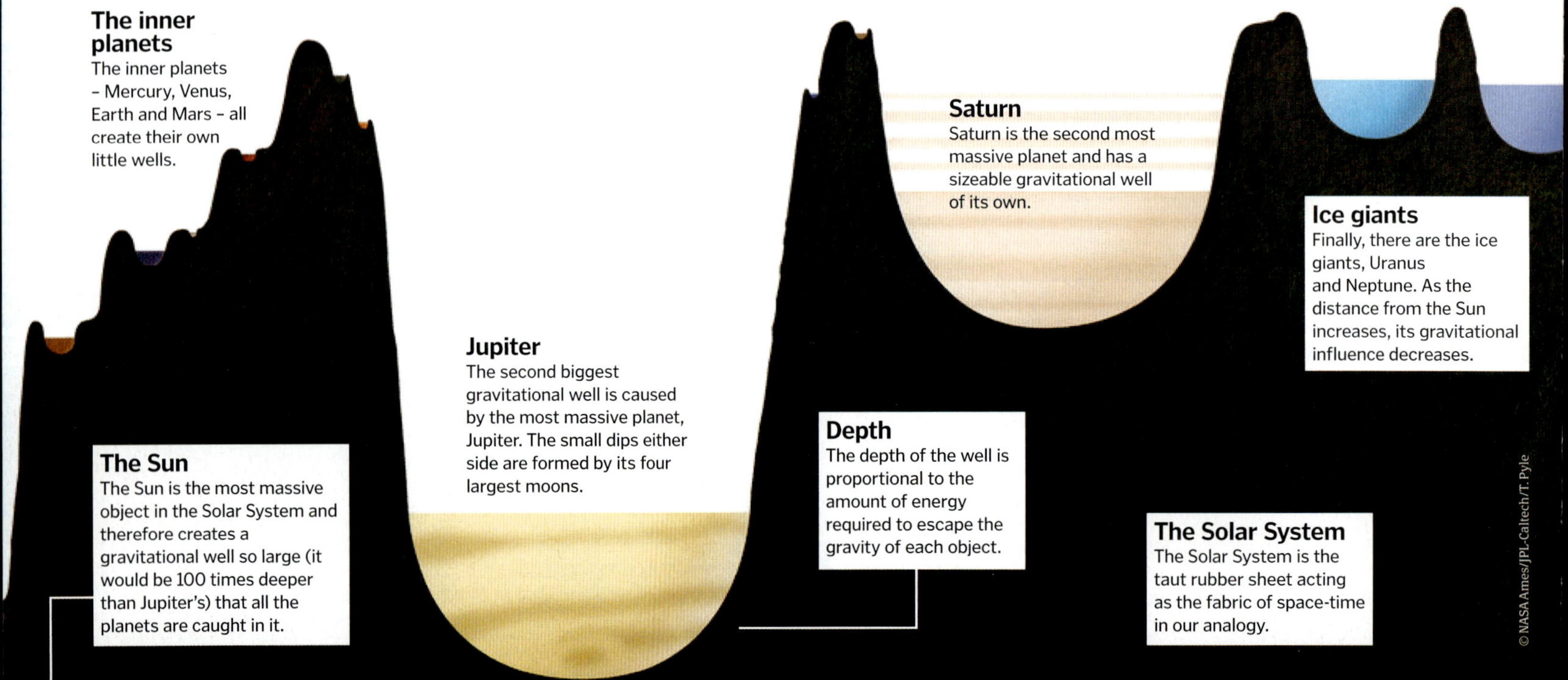

Cannibal galaxies

Inside the galaxy-eat-galaxy world of the cosmic food chain

While small galaxies create new stars from gas and dust, their more massive counterparts grow by gobbling up what's around them. The very strong gravitational forces they exert pull on smaller galaxies that can be millions of light years away, sending the two racing towards each other until they merge in a spectacular galactic feast. This can currently be seen happening between the distant Antennae galaxies, which began colliding a few hundred million years ago.

However, this galactic cannibalism has also been observed much closer to home. A stream of debris, known as the Sagittarius Stream and extending out from our very own Milky Way, is believed to contain the leftovers of its last meal. The stream contains stars that are still travelling in the direction from which they came, creating a trail of breadcrumbs leading to their original source, the nearby Sagittarius dwarf galaxy.

Eventually, it will be the Milky Way's turn to be on the menu, as it is expected to collide with the much larger Andromeda galaxy in about 4 billion years. When this happens, computer simulations have revealed that there is a one in ten chance that our Solar System will be evicted from this new galaxy, making the night sky appear far darker. However, it's more likely that we will end up closer to the core of 'Milkomeda', filling our night sky with even more stars.

Massive galaxies fatten themselves up by feasting on smaller, nearby galaxies

THREE MORE SCARY SPACE OBJECTS

Stellar vampires

Many of the stars in our galaxy share their space with another star, forming a binary system. The one with the lower mass can suck away the other's hydrogen, using the gas to fuel itself. This increases its mass until it strips its neighbour's stellar envelope completely.

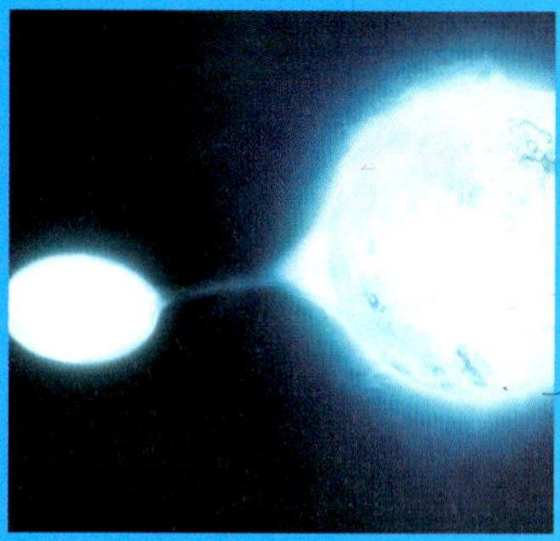

Franken nebula

It may look like Frankenstein's menacing monster, but this is actually the open star cluster NGC 2467, located 20,000 light years away in the Puppis constellation. It contains hundreds of hot, massive stars belching out radiation to sculpt the clouds of the nebula into an eerie, colourful shape.

Little Ghost nebula

When a star the size of our Sun ran out of hydrogen and switched to using helium, its temperature soared. Eventually it expanded and became a red giant, which expelled its outer layers into space, creating a nebula. After about 10,000 years, the stellar remnant in the centre of the Little Ghost nebula will begin to cool off, forming a white dwarf star.

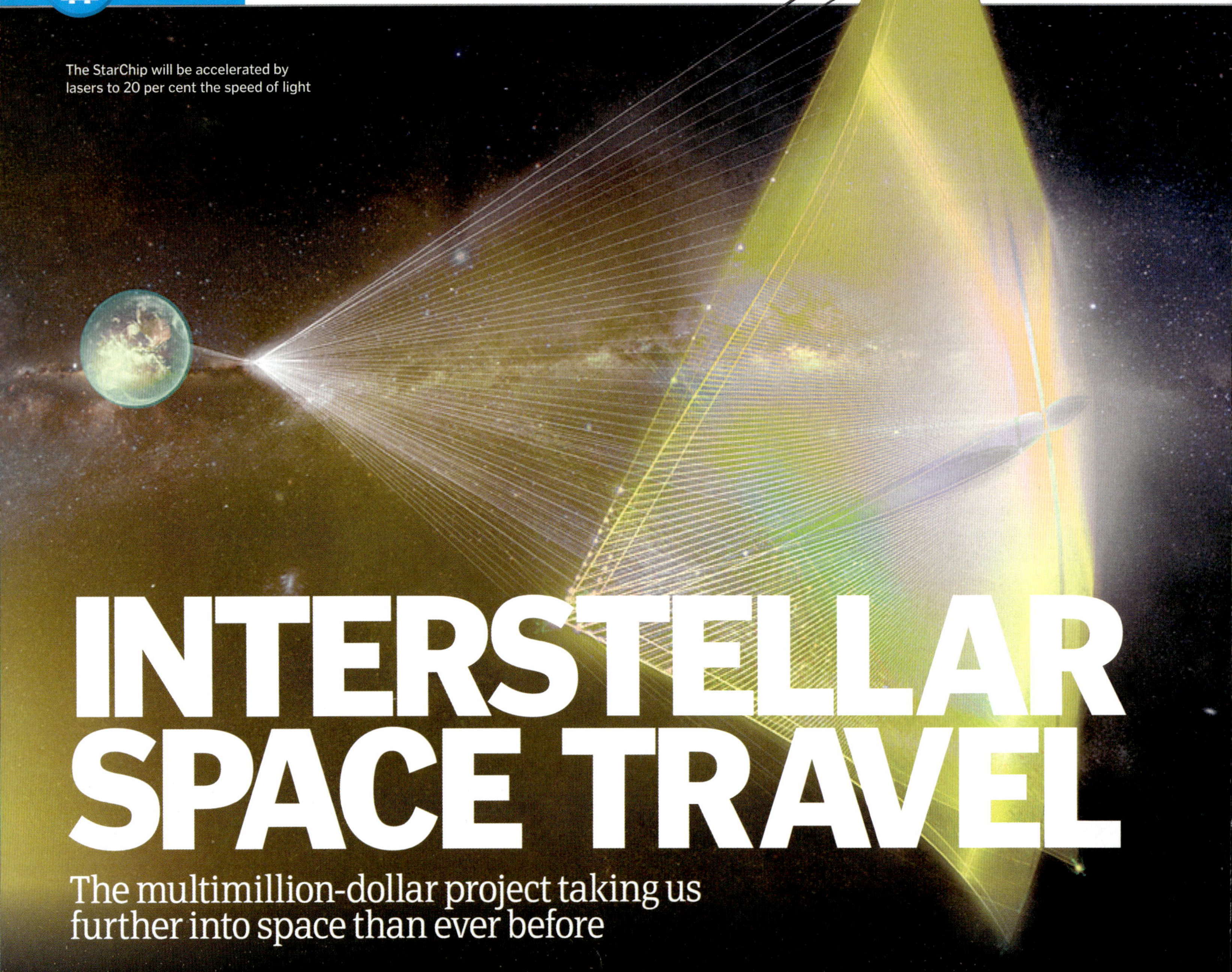

The StarChip will be accelerated by lasers to 20 per cent the speed of light

INTERSTELLAR SPACE TRAVEL

The multimillion-dollar project taking us further into space than ever before

To date, we've done a pretty good job of exploring the Solar System. But in our half a century or so as a space-faring species, we have not yet truly ventured to any of the 100 billion stars in our own galaxy, or beyond. In 20 years, though, that could all be set to change.

On 12 April 2016, Russian billionaire Yuri Milner announced an ambitious project as part of the Breakthrough Initiatives to send a series of small spacecraft to the nearest stars to our own Sun, the Alpha Centauri system. And he wasn't alone; alongside him at this announcement were respected scientists, including Stephen Hawking and Kip Thorne, who have all signed up to help with the project. "The human story is one of great leaps," said Milner. "55 years ago, Yuri Gagarin became the first human in space. Today, we are preparing for the next great leap – to the stars."

So, what's it all about? The project is known as Breakthrough Starshot, and it is utilising an oft-touted – but little explored – technique known as laser sails to reach tremendous speeds, and make a trip to another star possible in as little as a generation.

You've probably heard of solar sails before. These are sheets of thin material that expand to massive sizes in space. Like a wind sail on Earth, these sails then pick up speed not from regular wind, but solar wind, the stream of particles given off by our Sun. The rate of acceleration is very slow but over time, a spacecraft could theoretically reach a significant fraction of the speed of light.

This proposal is slightly different, though. Instead of using solar wind, the team is proposing to fire giant lasers on Earth at sail-mounted spacecraft. These spacecraft, known as a StarChips, would have several instruments packed into them, but be small enough to fit on the palm of your hand, thanks to huge advances in techology. The sail itself would be larger, spanning a metre, although just a few hundred atoms thick. Theoretically, shining a 100-gigawatt laser on one of the sails should accelerate the spacecraft to 20 per cent of the speed of light – or 216 million kilometres per hour – in minutes.

At these speeds, traversing the Solar System would be a breeze. In hours, the spacecraft would reach Mars, a journey that takes several months for conventional spacecraft powered by chemical fuels. In three days, it would reach Pluto, which took New Horizons almost ten years to reach. Most importantly, in 20 years, the spacecraft would reach Alpha Centauri, 4.37 light years (40 trillion kilometres) away.

Existing spacecraft would need to be adapted for interstellar travel

One of the main reasons for going to Alpha Centauri – which is actually a triple system made of three stars – is that it's the closest star system to our Sun. We now think that almost every star plays host to at least one planet, and Alpha Centauri A, B and C should be no exception. The goal of the mission would be to study these planets, returning images and priceless data to Earth. Owing to the distance, this information – travelling at the speed of light – would take 4.37 years to make it back. But a total of less than 25 years for such data is pittance, considering the implications.

"Earth is a wonderful place, but it might not last forever," Stephen Hawking said in a statement from Breakthrough Starshot. "Sooner or later, we must look to the stars. Breakthrough Starshot is a very exciting first step on that journey." So far, so good. But this is just scratching the surface of the technical challenge of this hugely ambitious project. We've never sent a spacecraft beyond 240,000 kilometres per hour before; the StarChip would travel almost 1,000 times faster. There will be a huge number of unknowns of accelerating to and travelling at these speeds. How the spacecraft will hold itself together during the intense acceleration phase, and how it will communicate with Earth at great distances, will also need to be resolved.

Breakthrough Starshot, therefore, is a bid to overcome such hurdles. Milner is investing $100 million of his own money, but he readily admits that this is merely seed funding. The final cost of the mission could spiral into the billions of dollars, and he is hoping for funding from a number of sources in order to support the project. As such, there is no definitive launch date yet, although some time in the next couple of decades is not unthinkable.

One way to overcome some of the challenges facing the project will be to send not just one spacecraft, but to launch a 'mothership' with thousands of StarChips on board. All of them

Sailing to the stars

To travel at high speeds, Breakthrough Starshot's nanocrafts will be propelled by a powerful laser on Earth. Each would be a chip weighing just one gram, with communications, cameras and a battery built in. But expanding from this would be a larger sail spanning a metre. An array of lasers on Earth would shine a combined 100 gigawatts on the spacecraft. Each one would accelerate 60,000 times faster than Earth's gravity, reaching 20 per cent of the speed of light in just two minutes. At these speeds the journey to Alpha Centauri, just over four light years away, would take 20 years.

Yuri Milner (third from left) and other scientists, such as Stephen Hawking (front centre), announcing Breakthrough Starshot

How a laser sail works

The science behind using lasers to reach incredible speeds

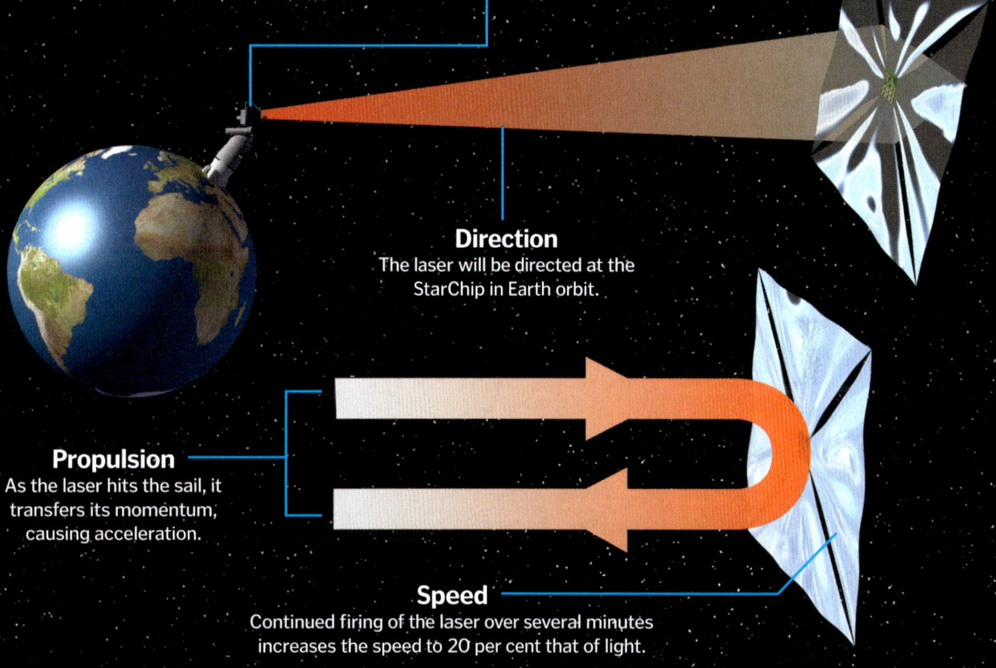

Exploring space

Warp travel
Some theories suggest it may be possible to 'warp' space time, allowing us to travel huge distances in a short amount of time. This is mostly science fiction at the moment, though.

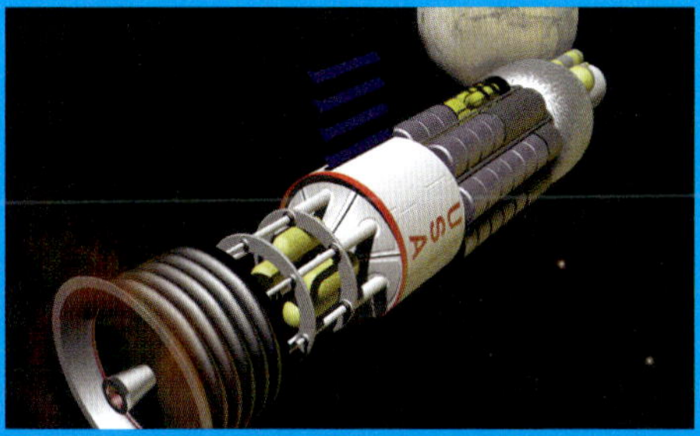

Nuclear power
Launching a spacecraft with nuclear reactors would give it a lengthy source of fuel, allowing it to accelerate and decelerate constantly to reach far-off destinations, but safety is a concern.

Slow and steady
Instead of fast travel, we could send a colony of humans on a 'generation ship', with them travelling for hundreds of years towards a new world.

Breakthrough Starshot timeline

Here's how the spacecraft will make their way beyond the Solar System

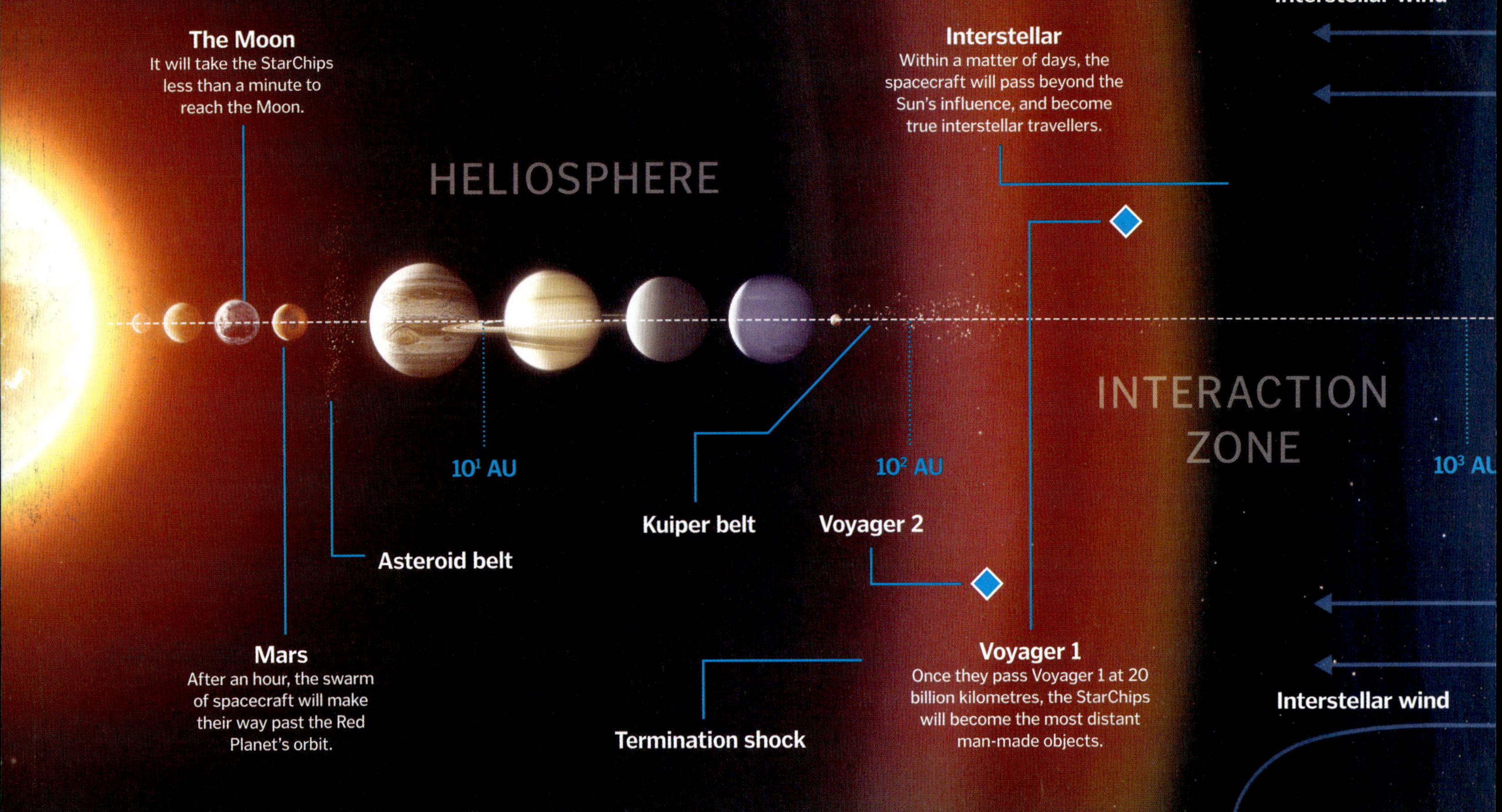

AU = Astronomical Unit, the distance between Earth and the Sun

would be released in orbit, where the powerful Earth-based laser would shine upon them, firing them off in the direction of Alpha Centauri. Think of this mission not as a single man-made vehicle making a lonely journey, but an entire fleet venturing off into the cosmos.

If it works, this form of propulsion could prove invaluable. Not only would it let us reach Alpha Centauri in 20 years, but it would also let us explore destinations closer to home, such as the Moon and Mars, in a tiny fraction of the time that is currently possible. Imagine if, on a regular basis, scientific organisations from around the world could send their own prospecting spacecraft to places all over the Solar System, letting us frequently explore worlds closer to home, rather than sending a mission every few years or so.

Once the spacecraft reached Alpha Centauri, they would not stay for long. Owing to the method of travel, this would very much be a one-way trip. The spacecraft would merely fly by any worlds we discover, snapping as many images as possible and gathering data. They may also collect information on the atmospheric composition of the planets, their temperature, their rotation rate, and so on.

As for Alpha Centauri itself, the system may hold invaluable secrets. At the moment, we're not actually sure if any of the three stars host planets. Previous detections have since been ruled uncertain. But it's fair to assume there are probably some planets in orbit, considering two of the stars are similar to our Sun. We know all stars form in a debris of dust and gas, a planetary disc, which often gives rise to planets. It's hoped the same would be true of Alpha Centauri.

Initially, astronomers had thought that there was a planet orbiting in the desirable habitable zone of one of the stars, Alpha Centauri B, an orbital position that is not too hot nor too cold, where liquid water is able to form on the surface. The nature of whatever planets are there still remains uncertain, but

A giant array on Earth will fire a 100-gigawatt laser at the StarChip

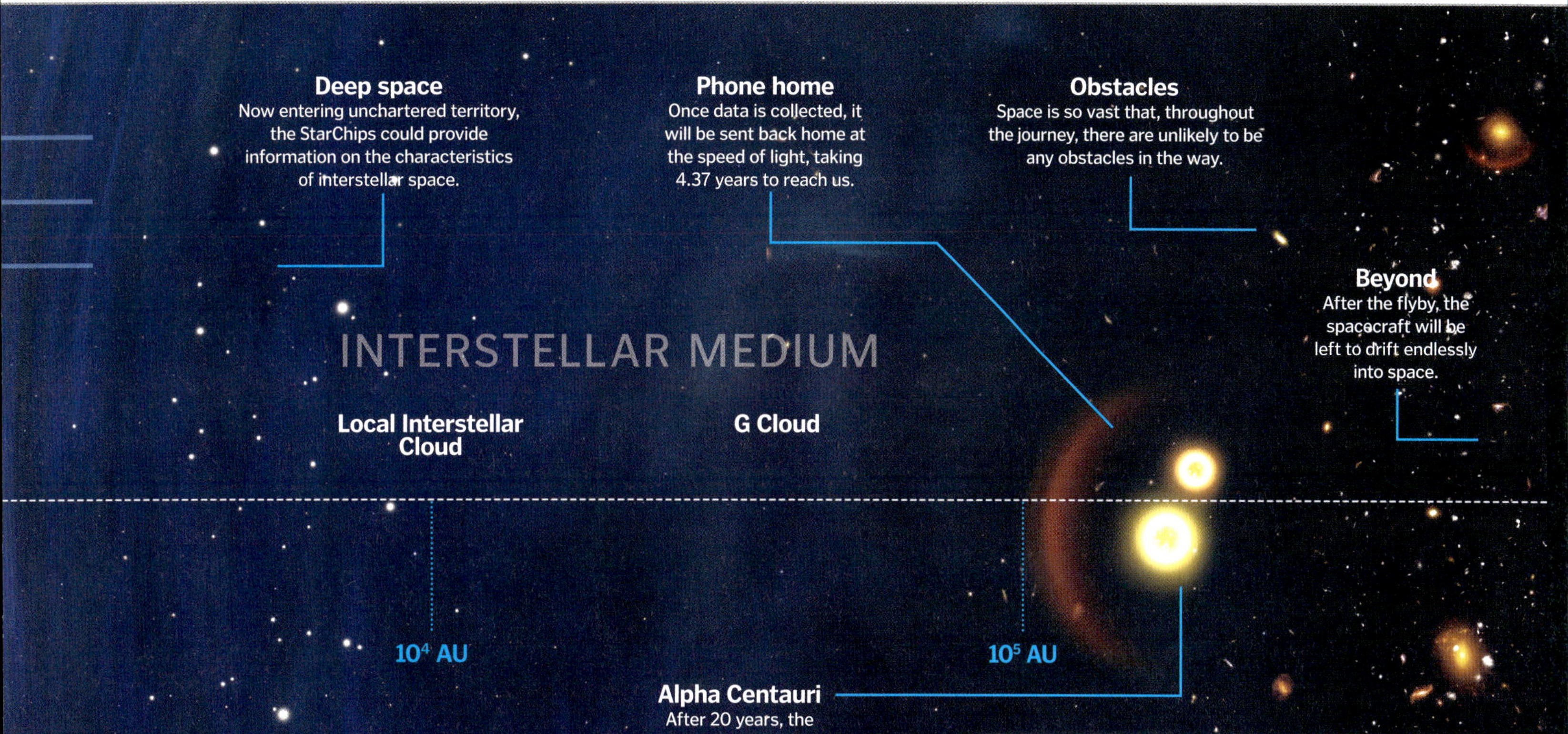

The StarChip is small enough to fit between finger and thumb

the chances that one might be habitable are indeed fascinating.

For decades now, we have been looking for worlds beyond our own that are Earth-like; that is, they have the necessary conditions to host life. After all, we are just one planet orbiting one of 100 billion stars in one of 100 billion galaxies. It seems unlikely that ours is the only planet teeming with life. But so far, finding planets exactly like our own has been difficult, owing to the limited methods of detection we currently employ. However, if we could send probes to a potentially habitable world around Alpha Centauri, we may be able to discover if our planet really is unique – or if there are many others like it. Imagine images being returned of a glorious alien world abundant in water, clouds or perhaps even vegetation. Such a discovery would no doubt change life on Earth forever, with untold money being pumped into missions to find more worlds like our own – and even visit them.

For now, the project is in its infancy, and these dreams are at least 40 years away. But perhaps we'll soon make the first steps to becoming a truly interstellar species, and discover our place among the stars.

> *"Sooner or later, we must look to the stars"*
> *Stephen Hawking*

The Alpha Centauri System

Alpha Centauri is not a single star. The system is actually composed of three stars: Alpha Centauri A and B, which are somewhat similar to the Sun, and Alpha Centauri C, or Proxima Centauri, which is a small and faint red dwarf. It's not known which of the three Breakthrough Starshot would visit yet.

Early in 2015, it was announced that Alpha Centauri B might play host to a planet, dubbed Alpha Centauri Bb, which was thought to be located in a tight and uninhabitable orbit. Later research suggested that Alpha Centauri Bb might not actually exist at all, and could simply have been a blip in observations. But considering how similar two of these stars are to our Sun, it is rather likely that at least one has some planets – and with more powerful telescopes in the future, these should hopefully reveal themselves.

By sending spacecraft there, we could return not only images of these planets, but also information on their atmospheres, and potential habitability. Even if they're molten rocks, images of such alien worlds would be astounding.

It's quite likely there are planets in the triple Alpha Centauri system

HISTORY

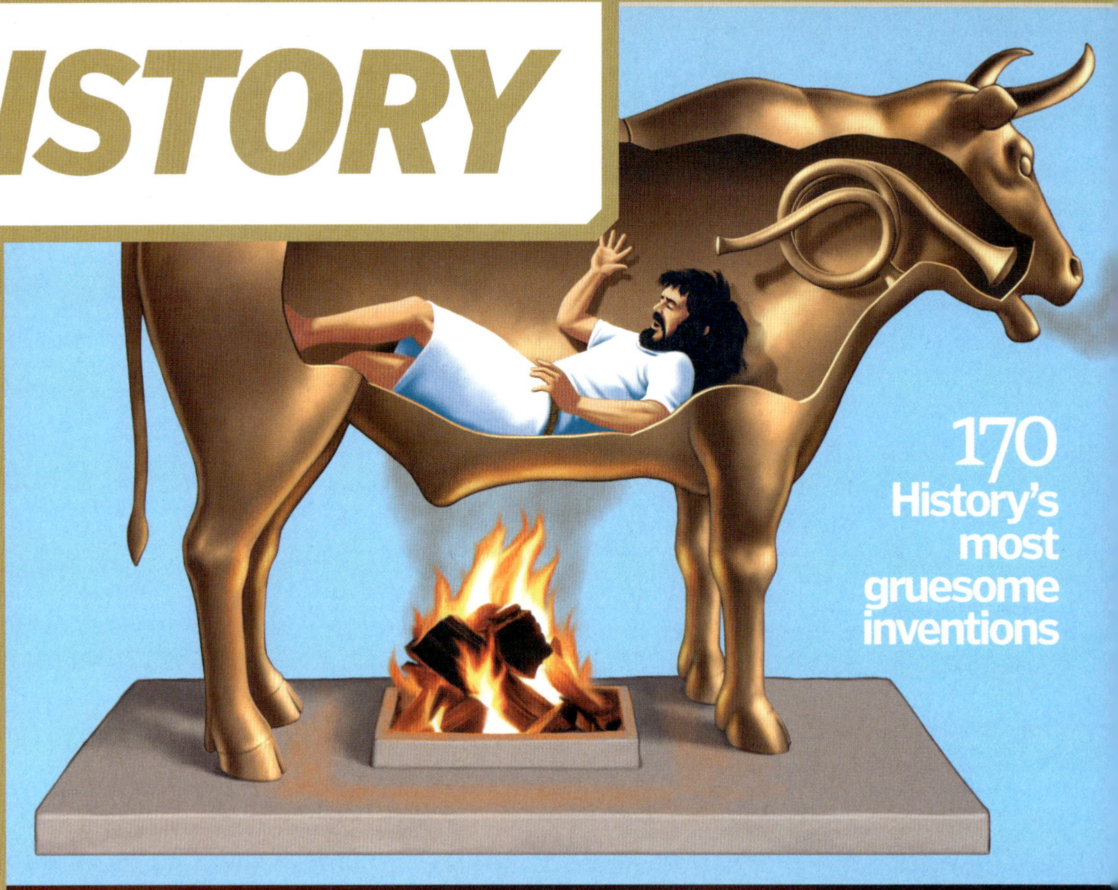

170
History's most gruesome inventions

157
Henry VIII by numbers

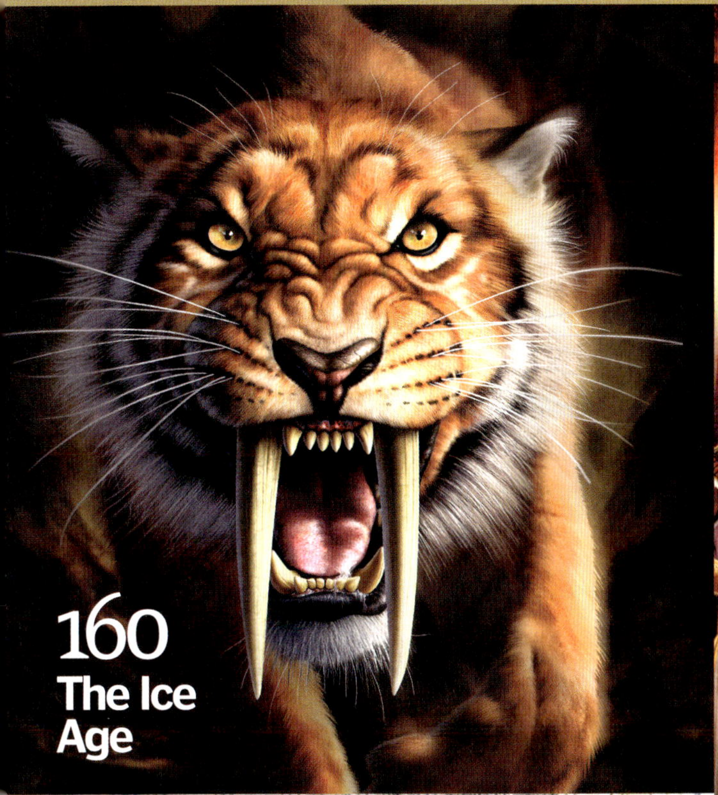

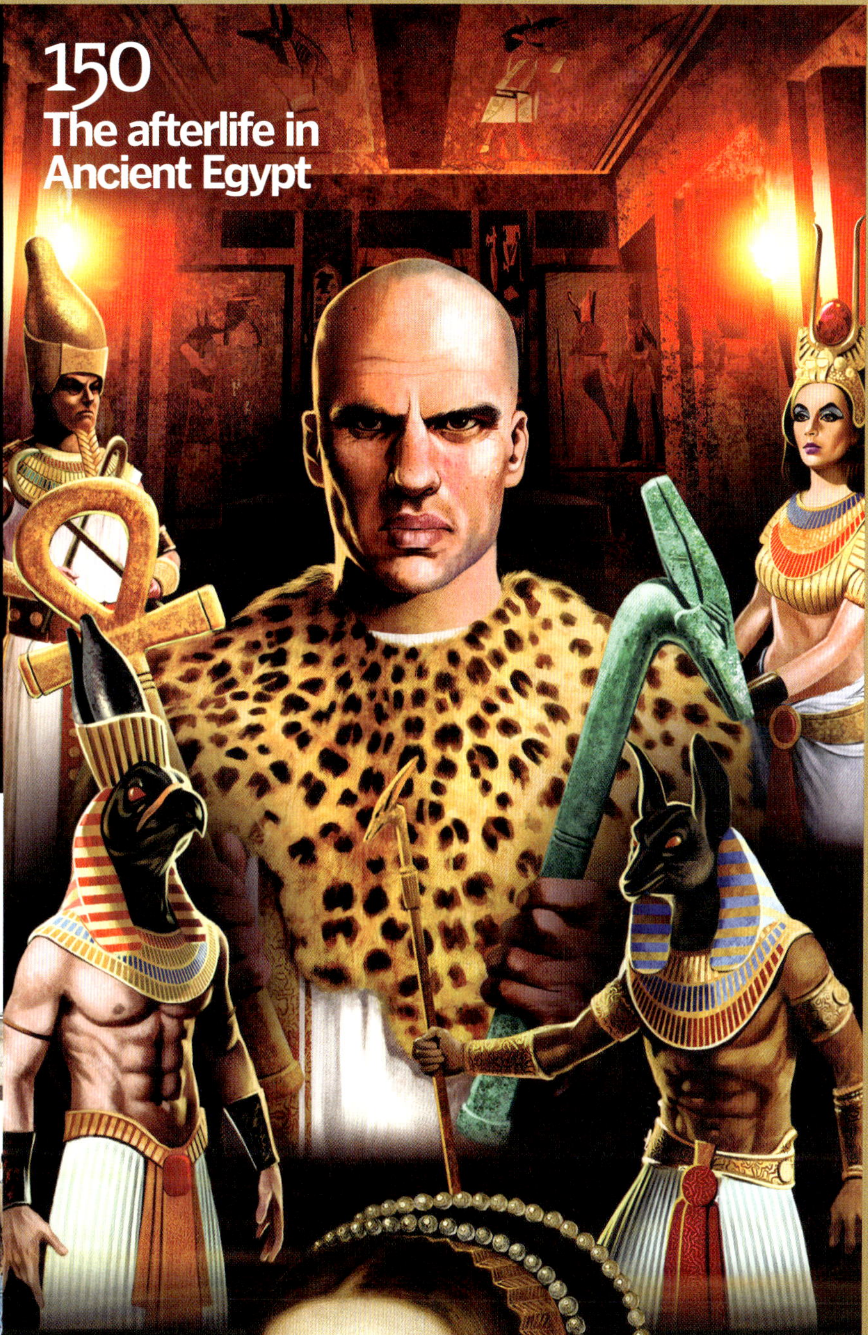

ACHTUNG!
SIE VERLASSEN
WEST BERLIN

The afterlife in Ancient Egypt

Explore the rituals, demons and gods of the underworld

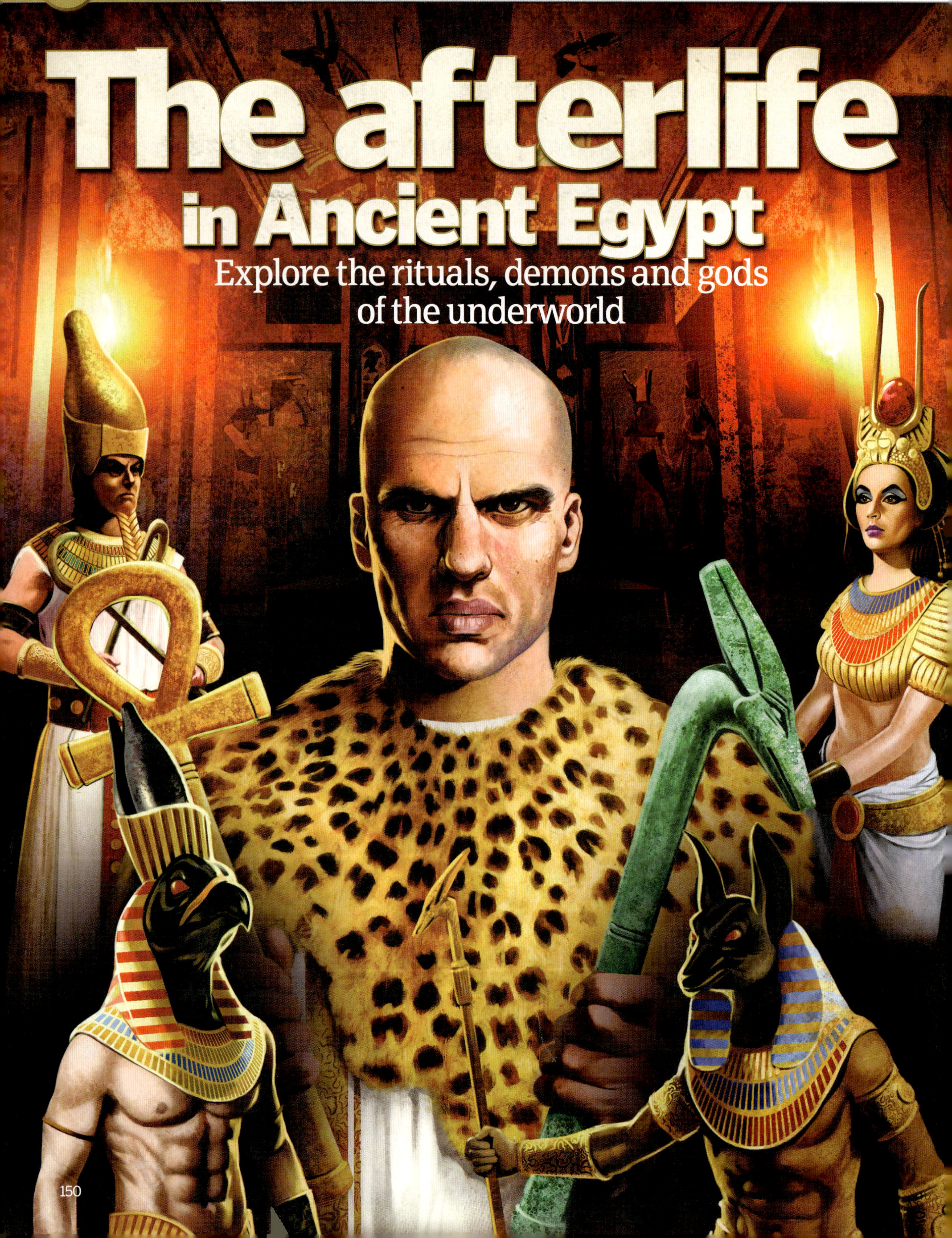

Few cultures conjure as much intrigue and horror as that of the Ancient Egyptians. The civilisation that sprung up along the banks of the Nile around 3000 BCE was among the most powerful on Earth. Though much of Egypt was an uninhabitable desert wasteland, the river was a life source that nourished soil and watered crops.

It gave birth to a society of farmers, doctors, builders and soldiers, whose achievements and inventions were greater than any seen before. They created one of the first writing systems, were among the first to practise science, and their art was a blueprint for the Renaissance masters. But the achievements that the Ancient Egyptians are best remembered for are their towering pyramids and gory mummification rituals. Death was an industry, and a booming one at that.

Religion was the pillar upon which this society was built, and it guided every aspect of life. They believed that there were many gods, each of which had a different role – from Sekhmet, the goddess of war, to Hapi, the god of the Nile, who brought the floods every year. But perhaps the most important element of the Ancient Egyptian religion was the belief in the afterlife. When a person died, it was thought that their soul could live on, but only if it successfully navigated the underworld. First it would have to battle demons and gatekeepers, before arriving at the Hall of Judgement where it would have to prove itself worthy of eternal peace. Those who passed the test could proceed to the Field of Rushes – a heavenly reflection of life on Earth. Those who failed would be forever restless, stuck in a purgatory that was worse than death itself.

Because of these beliefs, the Ancient Egyptians spent their whole lives preparing for their journey through the underworld. Not only did this mean avoiding sin as much as possible, but it also meant ensuring that their physical being had somewhere to rest, and it was accompanied by all of the things their spirit would need to thrive in the afterlife. Wealthy Egyptians spent years building tombs that were often more elaborate than their own homes, and filling them with priceless treasures. In Ancient Egypt, death really was an awfully big adventure.

"Wealthy Egyptians spent years building tombs more elaborate than their own homes"

Pyramids and tombs

In the early days of the Ancient Egyptian kingdom, pharaohs and other wealthy members of society were buried in mastabas. These were flat-roofed, rectangular structures with sloping sides, which helped to protect the grave from scavenging animals and thieves. But during the Third Dynasty, an architect named Imhotep came up with the idea of stacking multiple mastabas on top of each other, creating a much taller structure composed of a number of 'steps'. This would act as a gigantic staircase, allowing the deceased to ascend to the heavens. The first was called the Pyramid of Djoser, and it was built around 2680 BCE.

Over the next few hundred years, pyramids became the norm for pharaonic burials, and eventually the sides became smooth, not stepped. Kings and queens competed to build the tallest, most magnificent monuments, but this came at a cost. Huge amounts of stone were needed to build them, not to mention the costs of labour. Pyramids were also easy targets for gravediggers. By the time of the Seventh Dynasty, it was much more common for pharaohs to be buried in tombs carved deep into the rock.

The first Egyptian pyramid, built by Pharaoh Djoser, is 60 metres high

Nephthys

The mother of Anubis, Nephthys protected the dead as well as the reigning pharaoh.

The Book of the Dead

With so many demons, monsters and gatekeepers to tackle in the underworld, a magic spell or two could always come in handy. The Book of the Dead was a funerary text used from the beginning of the New Kingdom (around 1550 BCE), and contained spells that would help a person on their journey to the afterlife. Only the rich could own a copy, as they had to be specially commissioned and were written and illustrated by many scribes. The book was then placed in the coffin or tomb of the deceased, and extracts were inscribed on the walls, sarcophagi and amulets that were wrapped up with the mummy. Each spell had a different purpose. Some would help the deceased to identify different gods, while others would protect them from evil forces or give them control over the world around them.

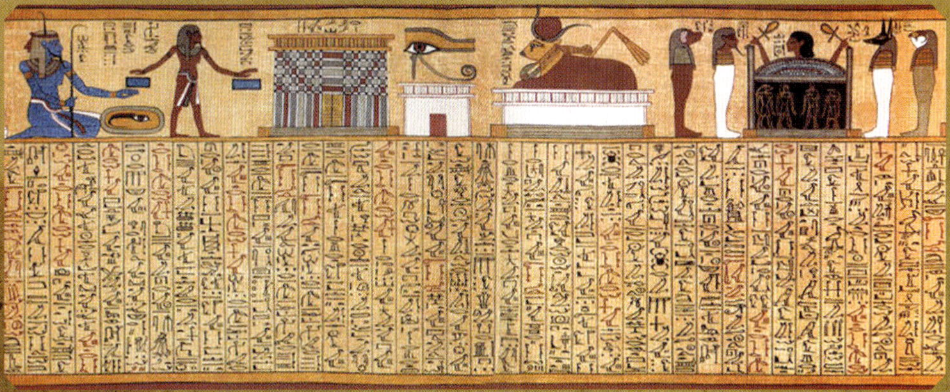

Spell 17 of the Book of the Dead, which helps the deceased to recognise the god Atum

MAKING A MUMMY

The embalming process was long and gruesome, but the Ancient Egyptians believed it was necessary for the soul to survive

The key to eternal life wasn't just preserving the soul. Ancient Egyptians believed it had to return to its body regularly in order to survive, so that too would need to be kept intact. They also believed that the deceased must resemble the living as much as possible in order for the spirit to recognise its physical home. Initially, this was achieved by burying the dead in the desert, where the hot sand would dehydrate bodies and delay decomposition. But over time, the Egyptians developed an artificial method of preservation that would enable their remains to last for millennia. This now-iconic process was called mummification.

The first mummies date back to 2600 BCE, but it wasn't until around 1550 BCE that the most effective and well-known method of mummification was developed. This involved removing the deceased's internal organs, dehydrating the flesh, and then wrapping the entire body in linen bandages. The process took around 70 days and was extremely costly, so only the very rich could afford it. Poorer families were treated with another method of embalmment, which involved liquidising the organs with cedar tree oil and draining them out through the rectum, before placing the body in a salty substance called natron that would help to dry it out.

Because of the climate, embalmment was carried out as soon as possible after death. First the body was taken to an 'ibu', or 'place of purification' – usually a tent close to the Nile. Here it would be 'purified' using water and palm oil, representing the deceased's rebirth, and helping to keep them smelling sweet for longer. Then the body was taken to the 'per nefer', another tent where the embalmment would take place. Only priests were qualified to carry out this procedure, with the chief embalmer known as the 'hery seshta'. This man represented Anubis, the god of embalming and the dead, and often wore a jackal mask to show his importance. The hery seshta was responsible for wrapping the body and performing religious rites over the deceased – an element of the embalmment process just as vital as the physical preservation of the body. Thanks to the ingenuity of the Ancient Egyptians, we can now gaze upon the faces of men, women and children almost exactly as they were 3,000 years ago.

A beginner's guide

Follow these easy steps to create a mummy that will last for eternity

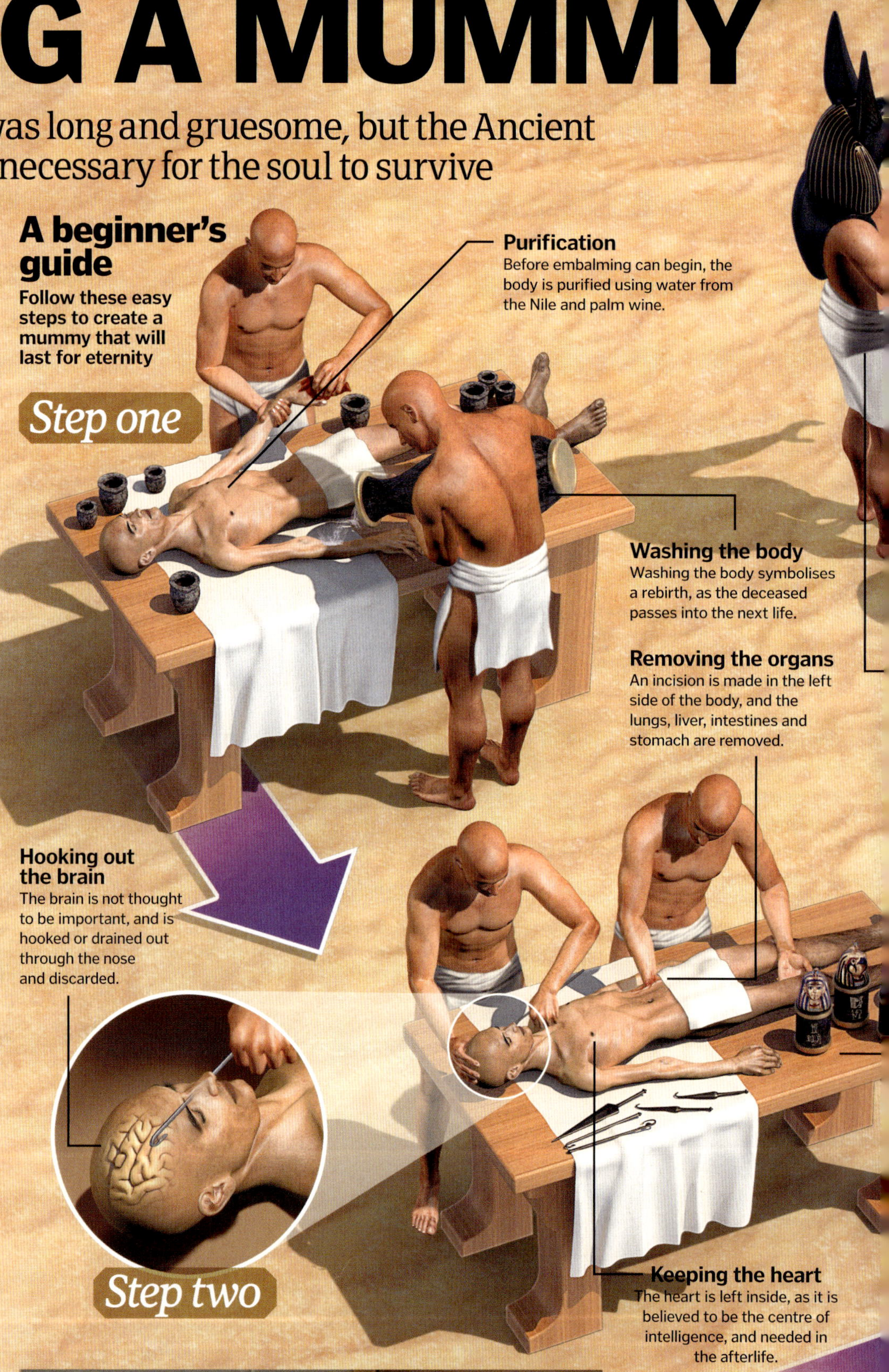

Cats were worshipped by the Ancient Egyptians, so they were also mummified at death

Anubis

The jackal god, Anubis, was guardian of cemeteries and the god of embalming.

DID YOU KNOW? *Many animal mummies have turned out to be empty 'fakes', which some embalmers sold for large profits*

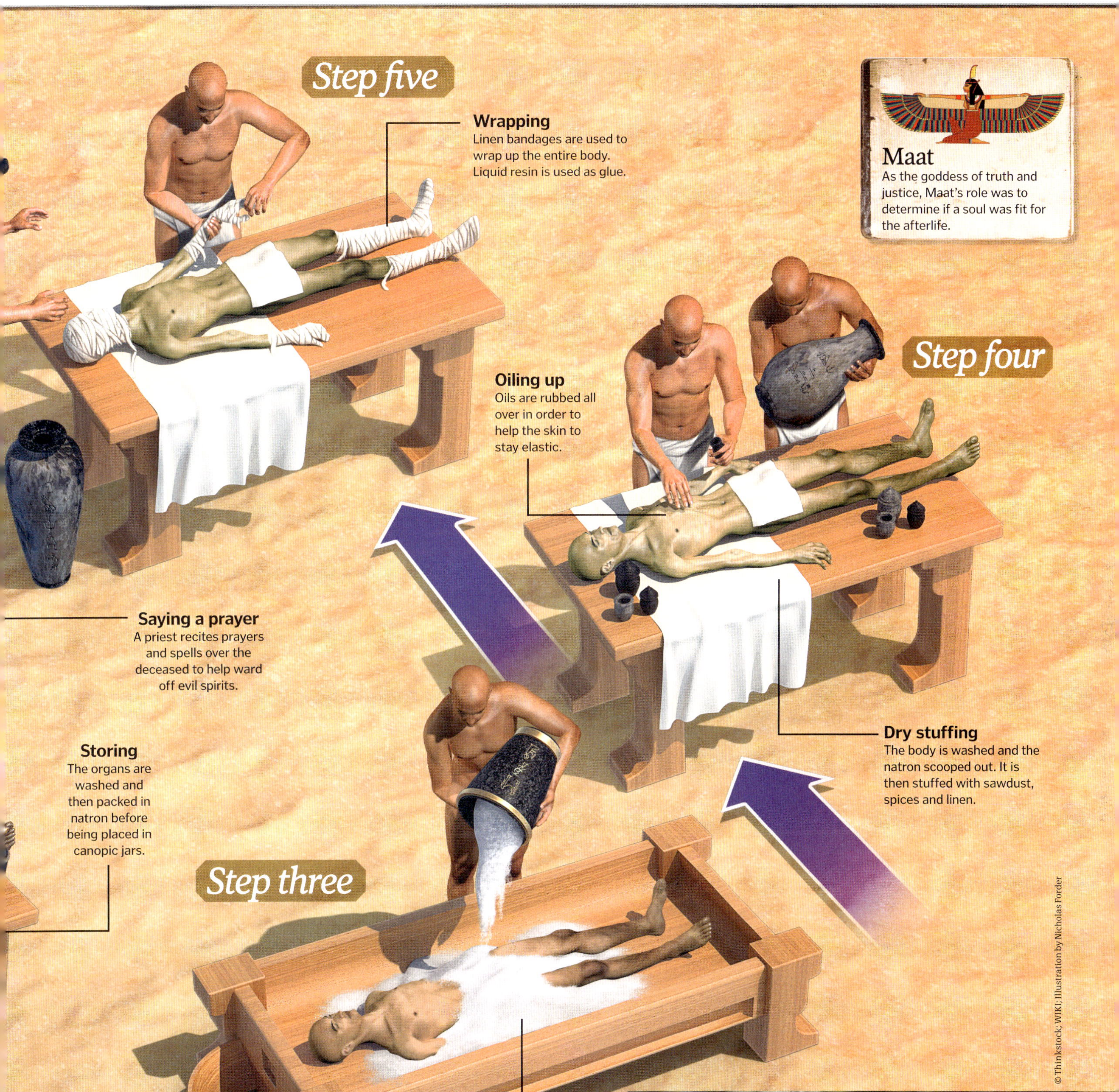

Maat

As the goddess of truth and justice, Maat's role was to determine if a soul was fit for the afterlife.

This mummy, on display in the Louvre, is that of a man who lived in the Ptolemaic period (305-30 BCE)

FUNERALS AND BURIAL

Egyptians departed this world with all their home comforts

Osiris
Osiris, depicted as a mummified pharaoh, was god of the afterlife.

Long before their deaths, wealthy Egyptians would build their tombs and pile them high with things they would need in the afterlife. From tables and chairs to chariots, jewellery and mummified pets, they could guarantee that their spirit would never want for anything. Food was just as important in the afterlife as it had been in their worldly one, so copious amounts of wine, fruit and grains were also buried with the dead. Even meat was included, which was often salted or even mummified to prevent it from rotting. If the worst came to the worst, they could always paint food on the walls – the Ancient Egyptians believed that in the land of the dead, depictions were just as edible as the physical products.

Also placed in the tomb were shabtis. These were small figurines, often made from clay, wood or stone, which would act as servants in the afterlife. Some people were buried with just one or two, whereas others – like Pharaoh Taharqa – were buried with over a thousand.

Poorer Egyptians had less elaborate tombs, while those at the very bottom of society were simply wrapped in cloth and buried in the desert with everyday objects like pots and perhaps a weapon of some kind. But everyone, rich or poor, was given a ceremony, as this was considered necessary in order for his or her spirit to pass to the underworld.

Wealthy Egyptians were given an elaborate funeral, during which the body of the dead was carried to the tomb accompanied by a procession of mourners and dancers. Two women called 'kites' were also present, whose job it was to mourn overtly. According to Ancient Egyptian religion, the greater a showing of grief, the better the soul would fare in the Hall of Judgement.

At the tomb, a priest performed the 'Opening of the Mouth' ceremony, in which the mummy was propped upright and a ceremonial blade pressed against the mouth. This would enable them to breathe, talk and eat in the afterlife. The action was repeated on the eyes and limbs to allow the spirit to see and move. The coffin was placed in a sarcophagus, offerings left, prayers recited and the tomb sealed.

A funeral fit for a pharaoh

These elaborate send-offs prepared the body for the lands of the living and the dead

Death mask
A funerary mask resembling the deceased ensures that the spirit will be able to recognise its body.

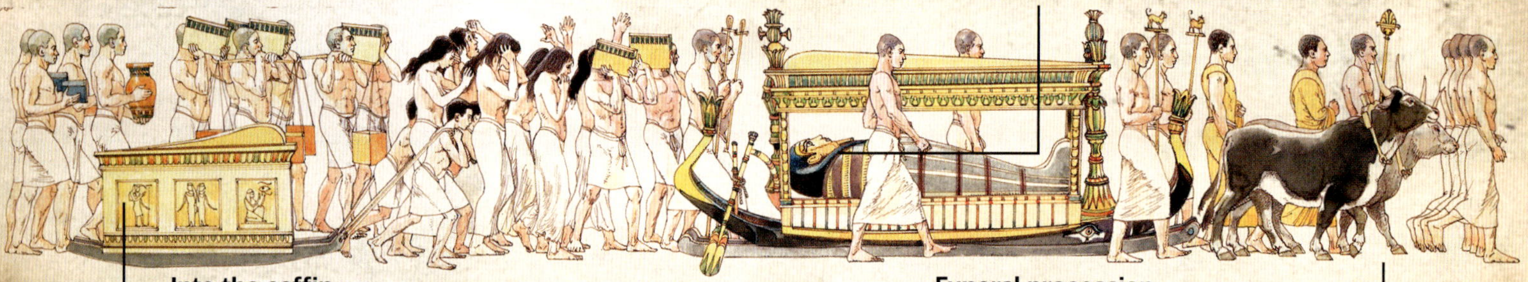

Into the coffin
A painted 'cartonnage' case is attached to the mummy, then it is placed in a 'suhet' (coffin).

Funeral procession
A procession of mourners carries the coffin and grave goods to the tomb. Some of the mourners are paid to weep loudly throughout.

Opening of the Mouth
At the tomb, a priest performs the Opening of the Mouth ceremony, allowing the deceased to breathe and speak in the afterlife.

Sarcophogus
The coffin is placed in a sarcophagus – an alabaster box designed to provide extra protection.

Sealed with a spell
Both the sarcophagus and tomb are sealed before the priest casts a spell to protect them, known as the Curse of the Pharaohs.

Tutankhamun's meteorite dagger

In June, researchers announced that a dagger found by Howard Carter in the tomb of Tutankhamun appeared to be made with iron from a meteorite. The blade had puzzled archaeologists for decades, as ironwork was rare in Ancient Egypt and the metal had not rusted. An X-ray fluorescence spectrometer was used to discover its chemical composition. The high nickel content, as well as the presence of cobalt "strongly suggests an extra-terrestrial origin," and similar levels have in fact been found in a meteorite that crashed 240 kilometres west of Alexandria before or during the time of Tutankhamun.

The iron blade (right) is believed to be made from a meteorite

JOURNEY TO THE AFTERLIFE

Securing an eternal place in the heavens was easier said than done

No amount of money spent on tombs or time spent memorising spells could guarantee an Ancient Egyptian a place in the afterlife. First, their soul would have to conquer the obstacles and demons of the underworld, and then face the judgement of the gods in the 'Weighing of the Heart' ceremony. Only the worthiest souls could then proceed to the Field of Rushes, where they would exist in pleasure for eternity.

The Ancient Egyptians believed that when a person was buried, their spirit departed their body and descended to the underworld (Duat). There, it must pass through 12 gates, each of which was guarded by a different deity, which the spirit must recognise and name. That may sound easy, but there were also monsters, demons and lakes of fire to contend with. The Book of the Dead provided a list of spells that would help the spirit to overcome these obstacles. If successful, the soul would pass into the Hall of Judgement, where it would have to prove its worthiness in front of 42 deities. The Book of the Dead also helped the spirit with the right answers to their questions, so that it could potentially pass this stage of the test without being entirely innocent.

Next, the spirit could proceed to the Weighing of the Heart ceremony. This was overseen by Osiris, the chief god of the underworld. The Egyptians believed the heart contained a record of all of the deceased's actions in life, so it was weighed against the feather of the goddess Maat to determine how virtuous they had been. If the scales balanced, the spirit was welcomed into the afterlife by Osiris. If the heart was heavier than the feather, it was thrown to the crocodile demoness, Ammut, and the soul was cast into the darkness, condemned to an eternity of restlessness. Of course, the dead could always rely on their trusty book for help. A simple recital of spell 30B could help to prevent the heart from giving away their murky past.

Those lucky enough to secure a place in the afterlife would experience the magnificence of the Field of Rushes. The dead would be granted a plot of land on which to grow crops, assisted by the shabtis they had been buried with, and look forward to a future of eternal peace.

Isis

Along with her sister, Nepthys, Isis protected the dead, and was goddess of children.

Egyptians were buried with all their worldly possessions, including beds and chariots

In the underworld, the spirit would have to battle giant serpents and other monsters

The Palais Garnier opera house

Check out the building that inspired Leroux's *Phantom Of The Opera*

Emperor Napoleon III commissioned the construction of the grand opera house

Formally opened in 1875, this grand opera house was designed by architect Charles Garnier. Built in the Neo-Baroque style, the lavish interior sports iconic, gilded staircases and lounges that allow vast numbers of people to flow through the foyer areas into the horseshoe-shaped auditorium. A huge chandelier hangs in the centre of the room, from which a counterweight fell to the ground in 1896, killing a construction worker. This, along with many more of the building's quirks, inspired Gaston Leroux's 1910 gothic love story, *The Phantom Of The Opera*.

When work began on the site in 1861, the workforces cleared hundreds of square metres of ground but were delayed in laying the concrete foundations. Despite many attempts to drain the site, the only way to stem the flow of water was to install a huge stone water tank. The pressure of the tank stops any more water rising, and it also stabilises the building. As well as inspiring Leroux's *Phantom*'s underground lake, Parisian firefighters now use the tank to practise swimming in the dark.

Inside the Palais

Phantom or not, the opera house has plenty of secrets to tell

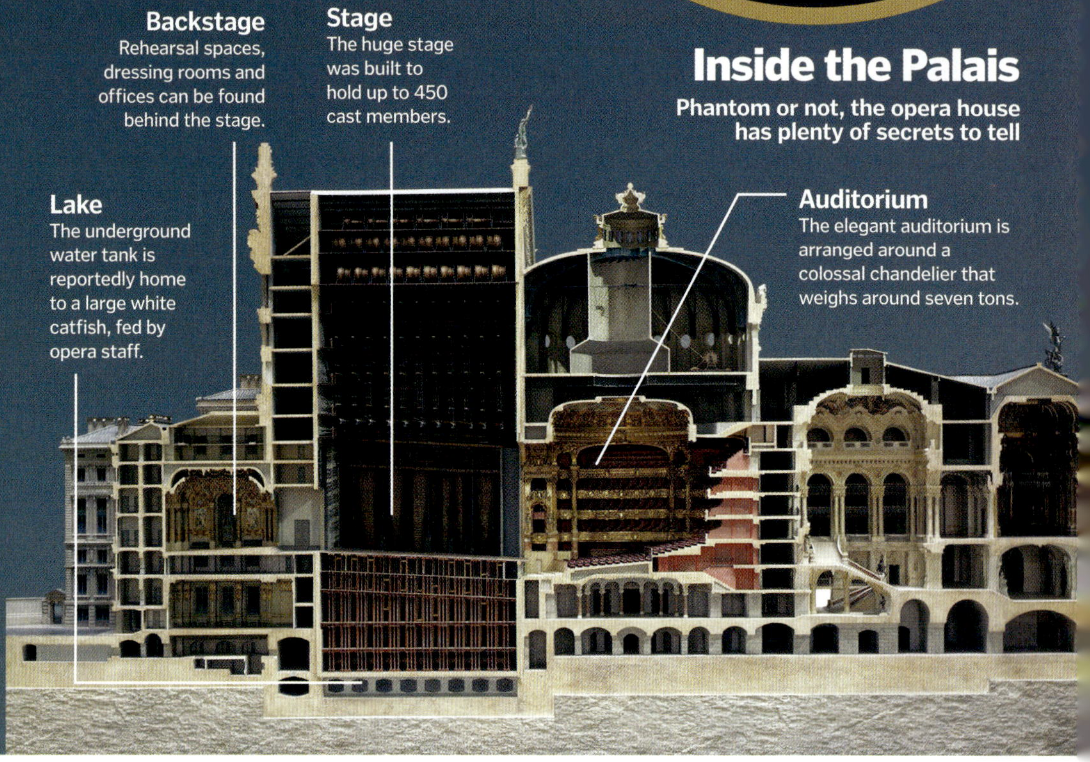

The world's tallest statues

Rounding up some of the most gigantic figures ever built

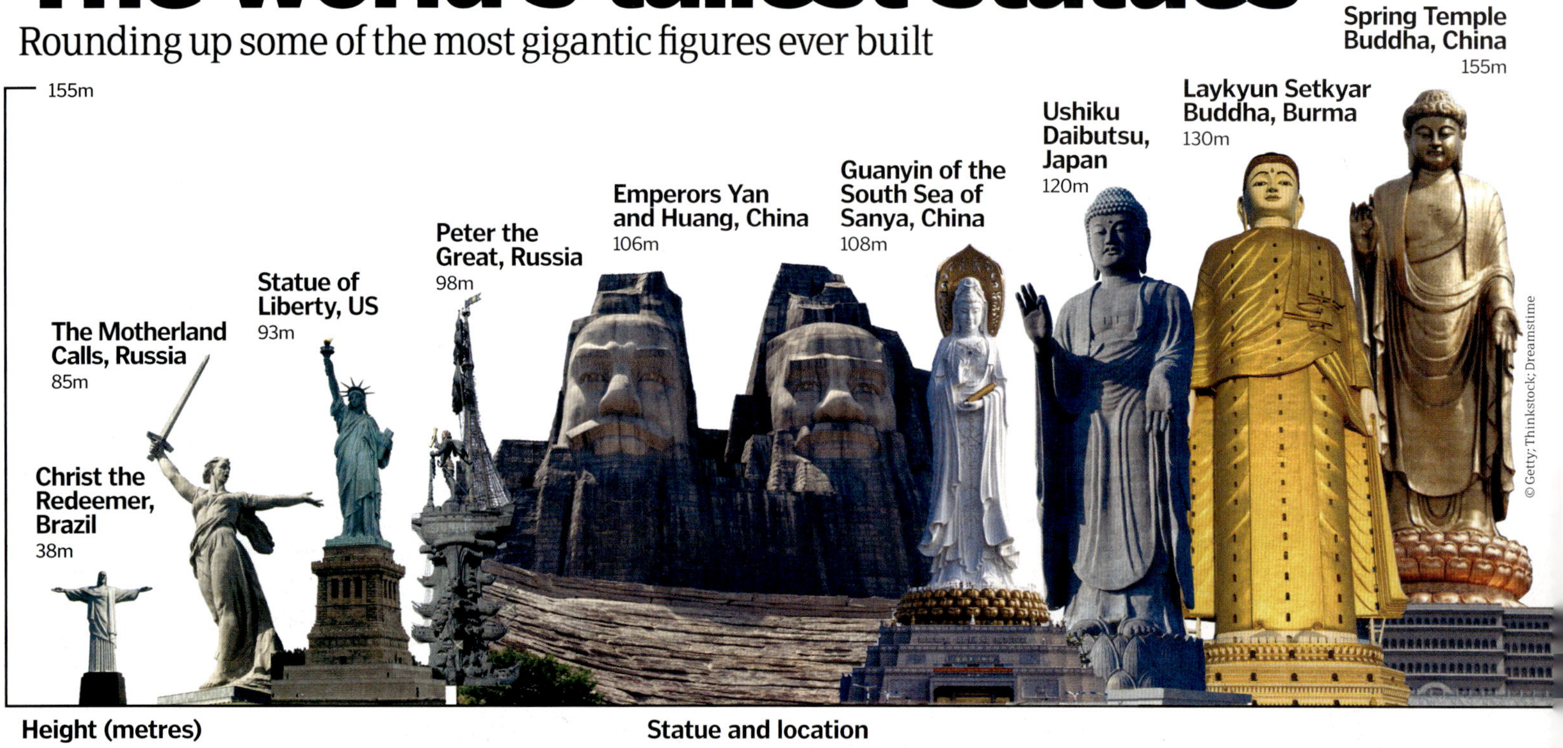

HENRY VIII by numbers

Shocking facts and figures about the infamous Tudor

Adored, feared, respected and reviled, Henry VIII is perhaps the most controversial king to have ever ruled England. He is best remembered for doing the unthinkable and breaking with the Catholic Church, instead declaring himself head of the new Church of England in 1534, in a period known as the English Reformation. The break was down to a dispute after the Pope had refused to annul Henry's marriage to his first wife, Catherine of Aragon, who had been unable to bear him a son. He turned his gaze to Anne Boleyn, and as they say, the rest is history.

Responsible for up to 72,000 EXECUTIONS

Estimates for the death toll vary greatly, but sources claim that anyone who refused to recognise Anne Boleyn as his lawful wife or who didn't agree with his break from the Catholic Church was killed, as well as anyone he took a general disliking to.

60 HOUSES

Henry was a prolific palace builder. His most famous, Hampton Court Palace, had:

- A HUNTING PARK OF MORE THAN 445 HECTARES
- KITCHENS COVERING 3,340 SQUARE METRES
- A GARDEROBE (LAVATORY) THAT COULD SEAT 28 PEOPLE

6 wives

Catherine of Aragon (m. 1509-1533)

Anne Boleyn (m. 1533-1536)

Jane Seymour (m. 1536-1537)

Anne of Cleves (m. Jan-July 1540)

Catherine Howard (m. 1540-1542)

Catherine Parr (m. 1543-1547)

Henry was a well-respected musician and composer. Among his collection of musical instruments there were:

- 26 lutes
- 154 recorders
- 19 viols (similar to violins)
- 65 flutes
- 5 sets of bagpipes

1.88m

Henry towered over most of the other men in his court

1.90
1.85
1.80

Legitimate children 9

Henry's wives bore him many children, but only three survived past their first birthday. He also had an illegitimate child by his mistress Elizabeth Blount.

Mary I (1516-1558)

Elizabeth I (1533-1601)

Edward VI (1537-1553)

17 YEARS OLD

When he came to the throne, Henry was still a teenager. He reigned for 37 years until his death, aged 55.

Weight at death

Henry's appetite and inability to exercise due to ulcerated legs – the result of a riding accident – eventually took a toll on his waistline.

178kg

Medieval siege mining

If a castle proved resistant to attack, every good commander knew he could literally undermine its defences

In Medieval warfare there were many ways to bring a fortress crashing to its knees. Battering rams, trebuchets, ladders, or simply starving the garrison into submission were all perfect tools and tactics for winning a siege. If none of these usual methods worked, however, the attacking force could dig under the walls themselves, and destroy them from beneath. With a huge hole in the castle's defences, the attackers could swarm in and overwhelm the unfortunate defenders.

In 1215 CE, Rochester Castle came under siege by King John, who used mining to bring down the defences

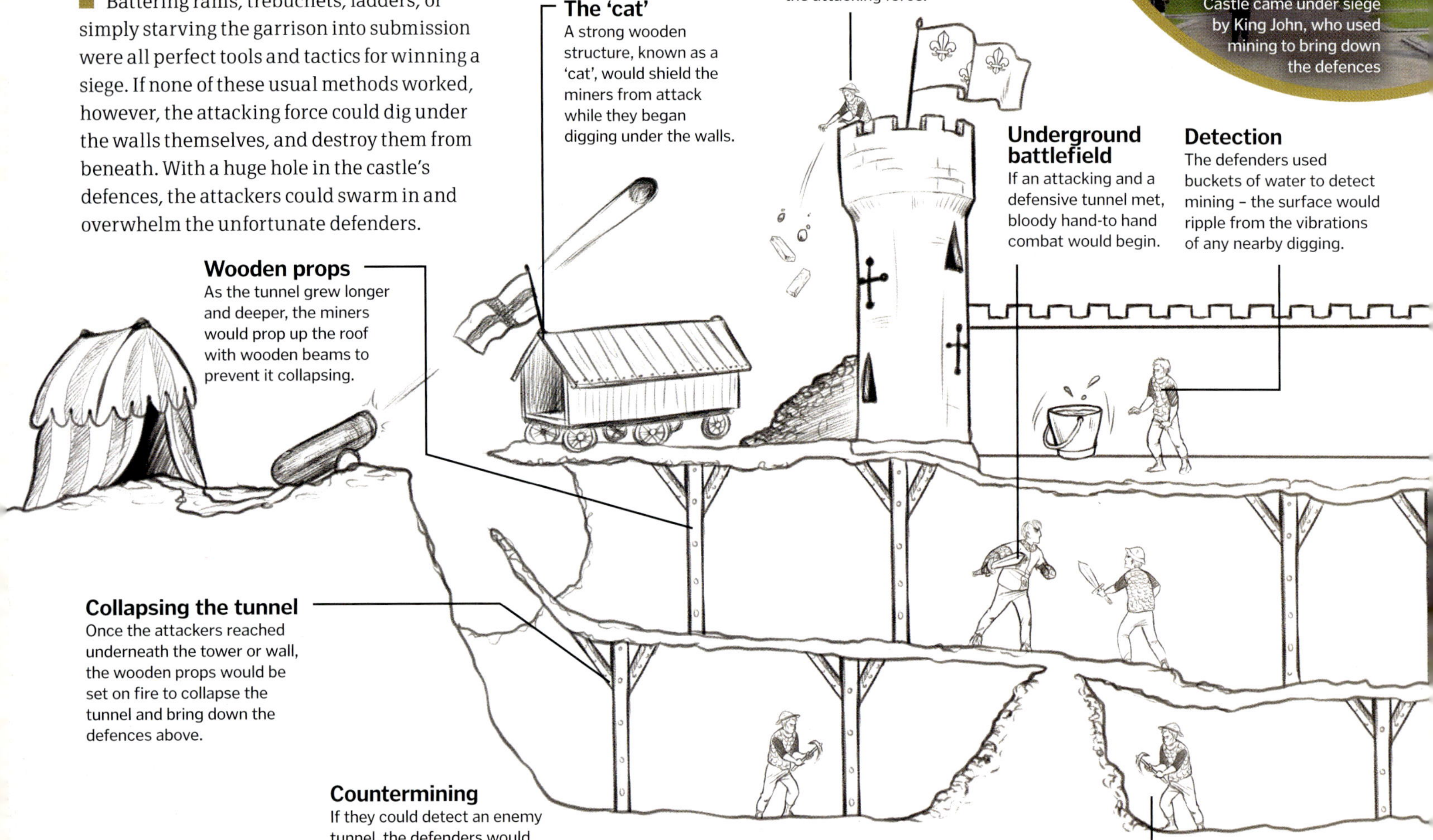

Military acoustic locators

These huge listening devices could hear the enemy coming before they came into view

Before the development of radar, there was only one reliable method for detecting enemy aircraft from far away: to listen carefully. Devices known as acoustic locators were developed to intercept the sound of an approaching aircraft. The sound would travel down an attached cable and into the earphones of the operator, just like a doctor's stethoscope.

Hundreds of different designs were developed during and after World War I, ranging from smaller portable equipment, to devices resembling massive trumpets. At the time, aircraft were relatively slow and their engines loud enough that their approximate direction and elevation could be detected from a distance.

As enemy bombing raids increased over the south of England, huge 'acoustic mirrors' were built to provide early warning of approaching aircraft. These large concrete structures looked like stone satellite dishes, and were designed to capture the engine noise of incoming German zeppelins. However, with the invention of radar and the development of faster aircraft, these structures and acoustic locators became obsolete.

Japan's Emperor Hirohito inspects two Type 90 Large Detectors, nicknamed 'war tubas'

Beer through the ages

The history of the world's most widely consumed alcoholic tipple

1988

PLASTIC WIDGETS

Invented originally for Guinness, plastic widgets are nitrogen-filled spheres. Now common in many lightly carbonated beers, they help release some of the dissolved carbon dioxide bubbles when pouring, creating a frothy 'head'.

1933

BEER CAN

The Gottfried Krueger Brewing Company was the first to produce beer cans, initially creating 2,000 which were given to its customers to trial. The original aluminium design weighed roughly seven times the average beer can today.

1858

FERMENTATION

The French chemist Louis Pasteur demonstrated that yeast was responsible for fermenting sugar into alcohol. He also showed that bacterial life could spoil beer, and invented a method called pasteurisation that killed microbes with heat.

Circa 1500

GROWING POPULARITY

During the Middle Ages, beer became hugely popular, particularly in Europe. In 1516 Germany introduced the first purity law, stating that beer may only be brewed from water, hops and barley.

Circa 800

HOPS

The first written evidence of hops being used as a beer ingredient is from a French monastery. By the 13th century they were used as a preservative, replacing traditional mixes of herbs and spices, and imparting a bitter, tangy flavour.

Circa 9000-7000 BCE

BARLEY

Although beer's true origins are unknown, many believe it was invented by accident during the Neolithic era. Wild yeast may have settled on barley that had germinated, starting the fermentation process and creating alcohol.

Five facts about the Berlin Wall

A few things you didn't know about the defining symbol of the Cold War

1 It fell by mistake

On 9 November 1989, East German politician Günter Schabowski prematurely announced that the Wall's travel restrictions would be lifted immediately. The original plan was for East Germans to apply for a visa to gain access to the West, but once a mob of angry protestors gathered, the gates were opened that very same day.

2 The Wall contained many layers

East and West Berlin were actually separated by two concrete walls, with tall wire fences either side. Between the towering concrete structures was the 'death strip', a gap up to 150 metres wide filled with watchtowers and trip-wire that could trigger automatic guns, all to deter people from crossing.

3 It separated three 'zones' from the Soviet sector

After World War II, Germany was divided into four sections – three of these were controlled by Western countries (Britain, the US and France) while the Soviet Union ruled over the fourth. The Berlin Wall split the three Western sectors from the Soviet-governed fourth, preventing East Germans from crossing into the western part of the capital.

4 5,000 people tried to escape before it fell

Many East Berliners were desperate to escape to the more lucrative West, and would often stow away in cars or dig underground tunnels to try and reach the other side. Some border guards were also keen to flee – among the very first successful escapees was an East German guard, two days after the Wall's gates were sealed.

5 JFK was relieved when the Wall was built

Before the Wall was erected, there was talk of Soviet forces blockading West Berlin if Western forces did not leave. When the Soviet Union announced the construction of the Wall, President John F Kennedy is said to have confided: "It's not a very nice solution, but a wall is a hell of a lot better than a war."

THE ICE AGE

Uncover the lost world & giant beasts of frozen Earth

For most of Earth's history, the planet has been free of ice, even at the poles. However, for the last 2.4 billion years, Earth has been cycling in and out of freezing ice ages. For millions of years at a time, temperatures plummet and large areas of the globe become trapped under sheets of ice. These glacial periods start gradually. Snow falls during the winter, and fails to melt in the summer, and over time, layer upon layer is built up. The white surface reflects sunlight back into space, and a cycle of cooling begins.

Vast glaciers form at the poles, creeping inwards towards the equator, and Earth's water is locked away into slowly moving ice. As it creeps along, it carves great scars into the landscape beneath. When Earth's water freezes, sea levels drop, revealing land once hidden beneath the oceans. Winds and currents change direction, and even those places untouched by ice undergo significant climate change.

There have been at least five ice ages so far, the first of which transformed the entire planet into a giant snowball. However, within these periods of extreme chill, there have been occasional bursts of warmth. During each ice age, the Earth cycles in and out of glaciation, freezing for tens of thousands of years, thawing temporarily, and then freezing again. As the glaciers warm, water floods back across the land, filling valleys and carving out new tracks in the landscape. Sea levels rise, and winds and currents shift. In fact, we are in the middle of an ice age right now – but we are in a temporary thaw that began around 11,000 years ago. These warm periods are known as 'interglacials' and we don't know exactly how long they last for. Ice sheets still cover Antarctica and Greenland, trapping 75 per cent of Earth's fresh water, and when these finally melt, it will mark the end of the current ice age. Until then, join us as we delve into the history of ice on Earth.

"Vast glaciers form at the poles, creeping towards the equator"

DID YOU KNOW? *Around 52 to 57 million years ago, Earth was so warm that there were trees in the Arctic and Antarctic*

TRIGGER POINT

Earth's temperature depends on where it's at in its Milankovitch cycles

The Sun warms our planet, but the amount of heat we receive varies over years, decades and millennia. This is because Earth's orbit, tilt and axis angle fluctuate in three different patterns, known as the Milankovitch cycles.

The first cycle is known as eccentricity. Earth moves around the Sun in an elliptical orbit, coming in close and then moving further away. However, the shape of this orbit changes over time, becoming more elongated (or 'eccentric') and rounder in a cycle that lasts 100,000 years.

The second cycle, known as obliquity, refers to the tilt of Earth relative to the plane of its orbit, which varies from 22.1 to 24.5 degrees over a 40,000-year period. The bigger the tilt, the more extreme the seasons are on our planet. Finally, Earth also wobbles as it spins, a little like a spinning top as it slows down. This wobble is known as precession, and it takes 26,000-years to complete one cycle.

The amount of solar energy that reaches Earth depends on where it is in all three Milankovitch cycles. At times when the planet receives the least energy, summer temperatures are coldest, and an ice age may be triggered. But the planet's fate also depends on the position of continents, ocean circulation and composition of the atmosphere.

The making of an ice age

Several factors come together to tip the Earth into a big freeze

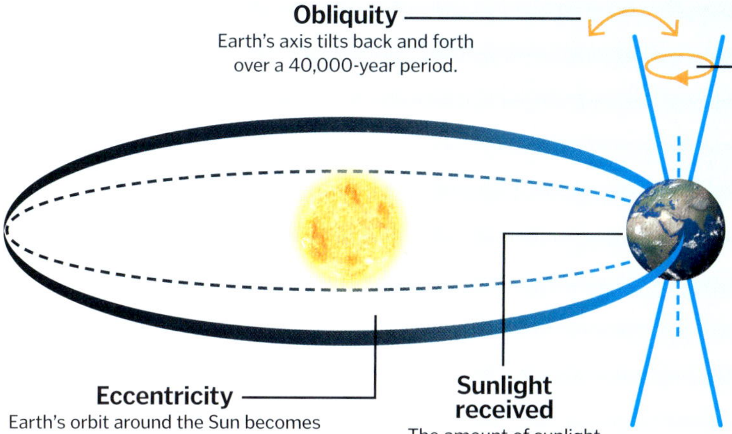

When Earth's water freezes, sea levels drop, and the land beneath is revealed

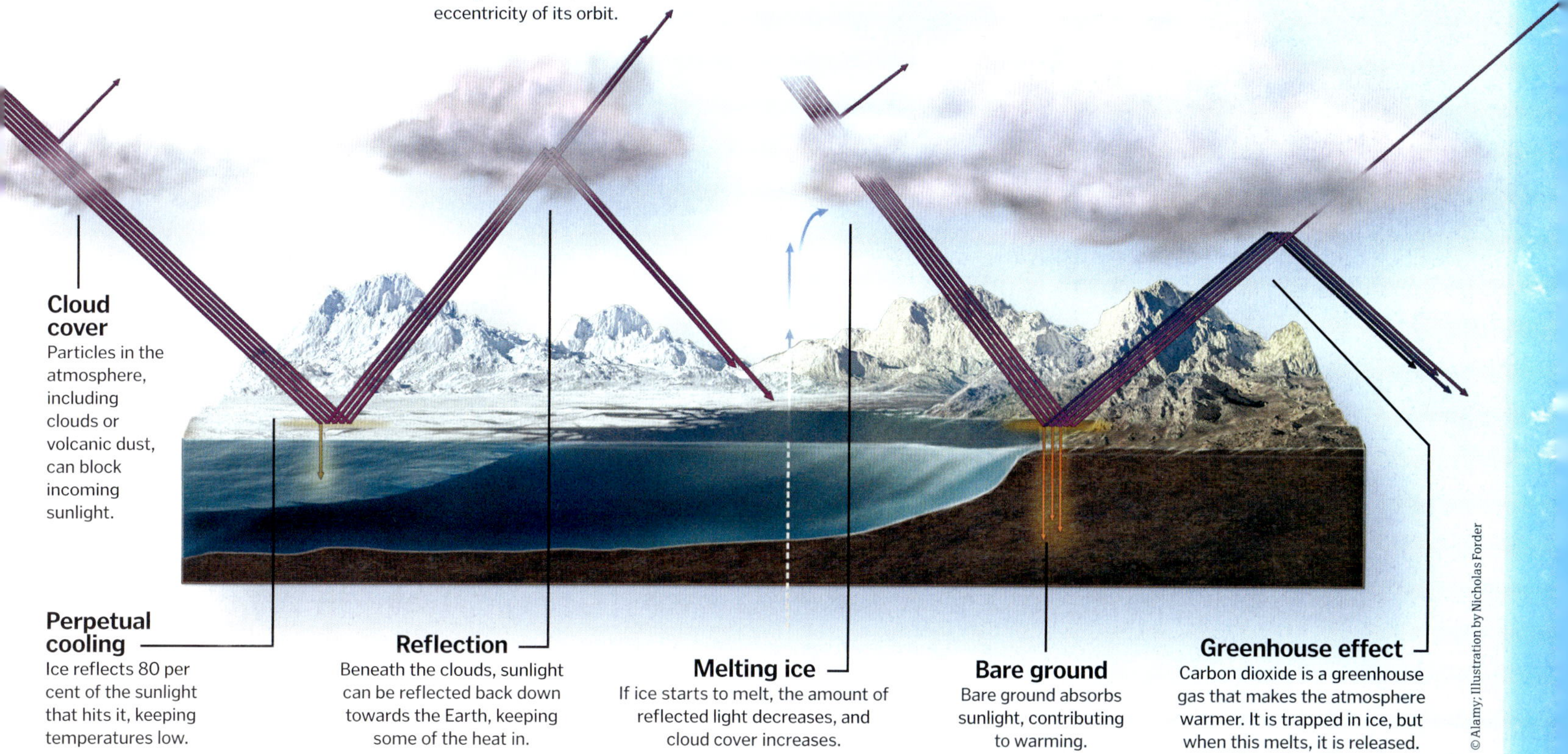

THE LAST GLACIAL PERIOD

What did the world look like at the height of the last ice age?

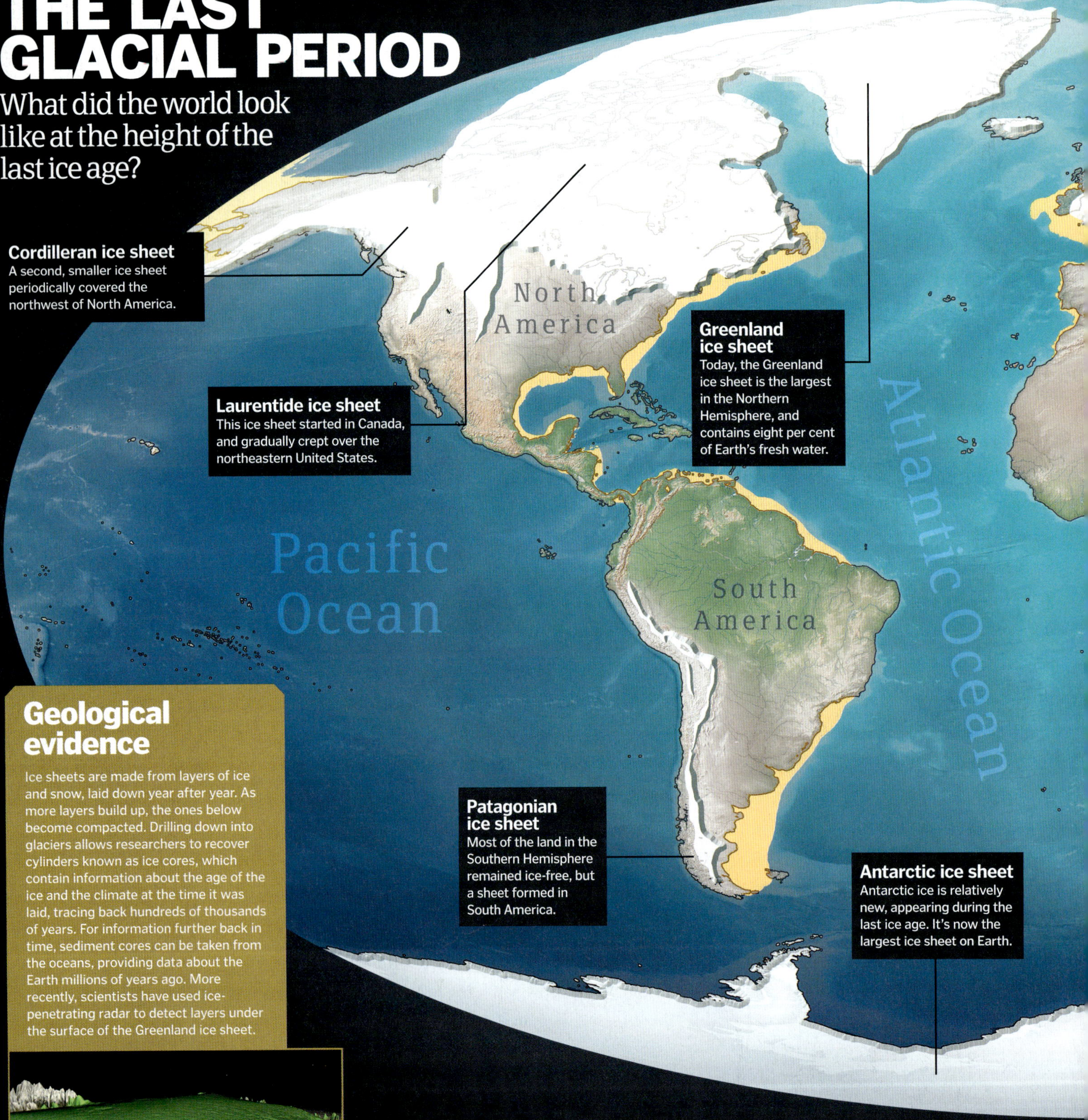

Cordilleran ice sheet
A second, smaller ice sheet periodically covered the northwest of North America.

Laurentide ice sheet
This ice sheet started in Canada, and gradually crept over the northeastern United States.

Greenland ice sheet
Today, the Greenland ice sheet is the largest in the Northern Hemisphere, and contains eight per cent of Earth's fresh water.

Patagonian ice sheet
Most of the land in the Southern Hemisphere remained ice-free, but a sheet formed in South America.

Antarctic ice sheet
Antarctic ice is relatively new, appearing during the last ice age. It's now the largest ice sheet on Earth.

Geological evidence

Ice sheets are made from layers of ice and snow, laid down year after year. As more layers build up, the ones below become compacted. Drilling down into glaciers allows researchers to recover cylinders known as ice cores, which contain information about the age of the ice and the climate at the time it was laid, tracing back hundreds of thousands of years. For information further back in time, sediment cores can be taken from the oceans, providing data about the Earth millions of years ago. More recently, scientists have used ice-penetrating radar to detect layers under the surface of the Greenland ice sheet.

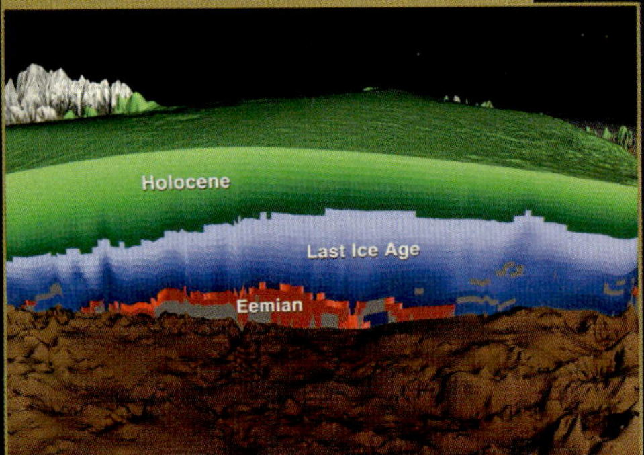

The Greenland ice sheet contains evidence of the last ice age, and the warm period that preceded it

Earth's ice through the ages

Our landscape has changed dramatically over the last 2.4 billion years

3 BILLION YRS AGO — 2 BILLION YRS AGO

2.4-2.1 BILLION YRS AGO
1 Snowball Earth Our entire planet froze over during the first ever ice age, called the Huronian.

850-630 MILLION YRS AGO
2 Slushball Earth During the Cryogenian ice age, a band of liquid ocean remained at the equator.

460-430 MILLION YRS AGO
3 Mass extinction The Andean-Saharan ice age accompanied the second largest mass extinction in history.

"When Earth's water freezes, sea levels drop, revealing land once hidden beneath the oceans"

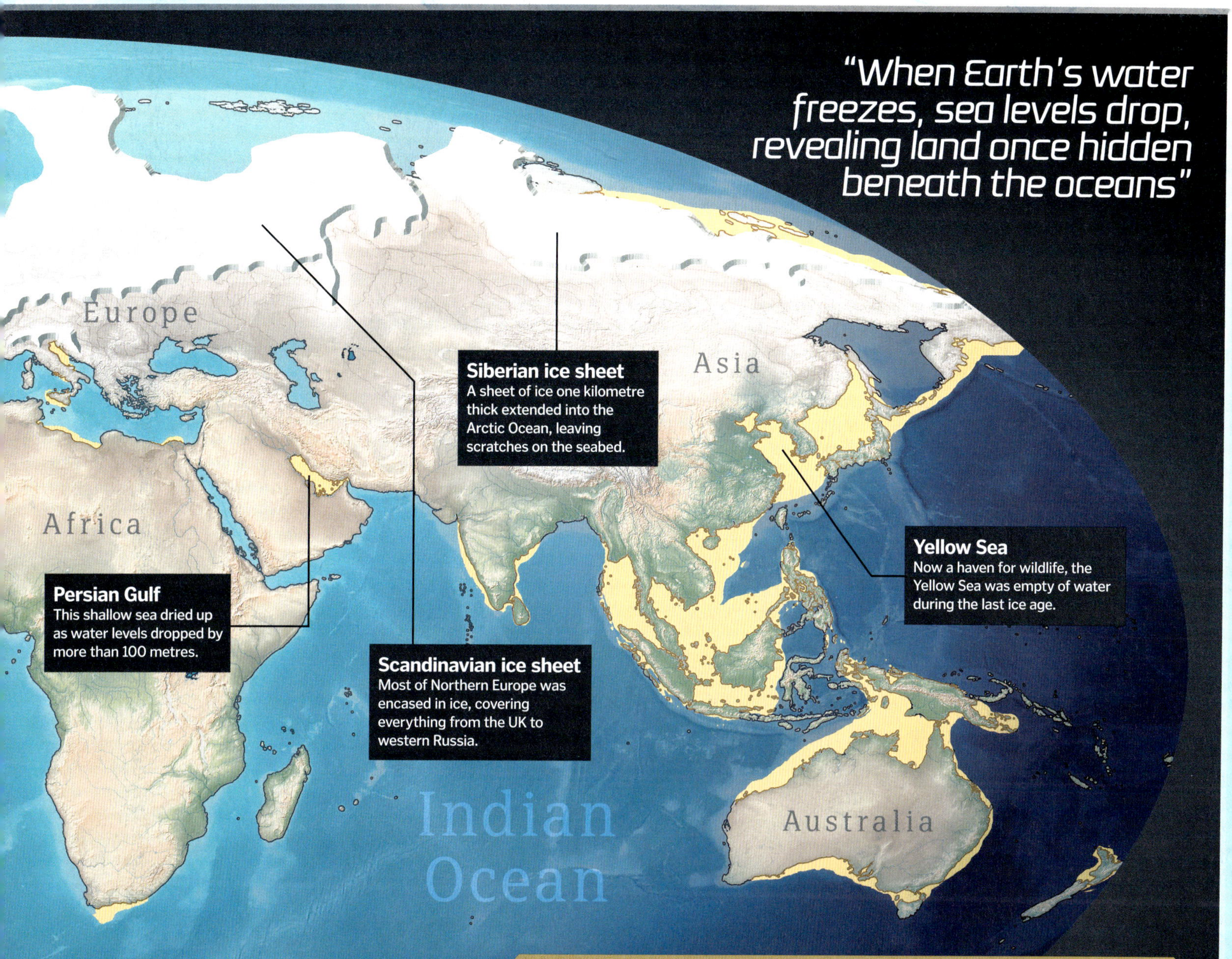

Siberian ice sheet
A sheet of ice one kilometre thick extended into the Arctic Ocean, leaving scratches on the seabed.

Yellow Sea
Now a haven for wildlife, the Yellow Sea was empty of water during the last ice age.

Persian Gulf
This shallow sea dried up as water levels dropped by more than 100 metres.

Scandinavian ice sheet
Most of Northern Europe was encased in ice, covering everything from the UK to western Russia.

Land bridges

When Earth's water freezes into glaciers, sea levels drop, exposing land once hidden beneath the waves. These 'land bridges' connect islands and continents, allowing animals to move from one place to another. The most well-known is the Bering Land Bridge, which once linked Siberia to Alaska, closing the gap between Asia and North America. This bridge provided a sheltered path that took early humans to the Americas. In the past, solid ground has also appeared between the UK and Europe, connecting the islands of the Indonesian archipelago, and linking Australia to New Guinea.

Today, the Bering Strait is flooded with water

360-260 MILLION YRS AGO
4 The arrival of plants
Plants sucked carbon dioxide from the air, causing the Karoo ice age.

20 MILLION YRS AGO
5 The making of Antarctica
The beginnings of the Antarctic ice sheet started to form.

2.5 MILLION YRS AGO
6 Quaternary ice age
The latest cold snap started very recently, and is still going on to this day.

11,000 YRS AGO
7 Interglacial period
We are in the middle of a short intermission in the current ice age.

1300-1800 YRS AGO
8 Little Ice Age
In recent history, Earth experienced a sharp drop in temperature.

THE FUTURE...
9 Next ice age
Human activity is warming the planet, and the date of the next ice age is uncertain.

THE SURVIVORS

Meet the giant beasts that conquered the frozen wilderness

Before the end of the last ice age, Earth was inhabited by weird and wonderful mammalian megafauna. Food was abundant, allowing animals to grow to enormous sizes, and the larger they got, the more protection they had from the cold. Not all of the animals that lived during the ice age inhabited the coldest parts of the planet; many, like ground sloths and sabre-toothed cats, preferred to live in warmer and more temperate regions further south.

There were also many true ice survivors, including fur-covered woolly mammoths, musk oxen, and giant dire wolves. Their stocky bodies helped to minimise heat loss through their skin, and layers of fat and hair provided thick insulation. However, when the temperatures started to rise, these animals began to struggle.

During interglacial periods, glaciers melt and sea levels rise; valleys flood and lakes appear in the landscape. Ocean currents change direction, and winds shift. And as if that weren't enough pressure, at the end of this particular ice age, humans were roaming the landscape with spears. Our ancestors competed with top predators, and hunted some of the largest animals. Mammoths and mastodons were 'keystone' species, so large and numerous that their activities carved out vital niches that other animals needed for survival. But around 50,000 years ago, the ice age megafauna started to die out, and by the time the glaciers had retreated, at least 177 large mammal species were extinct.

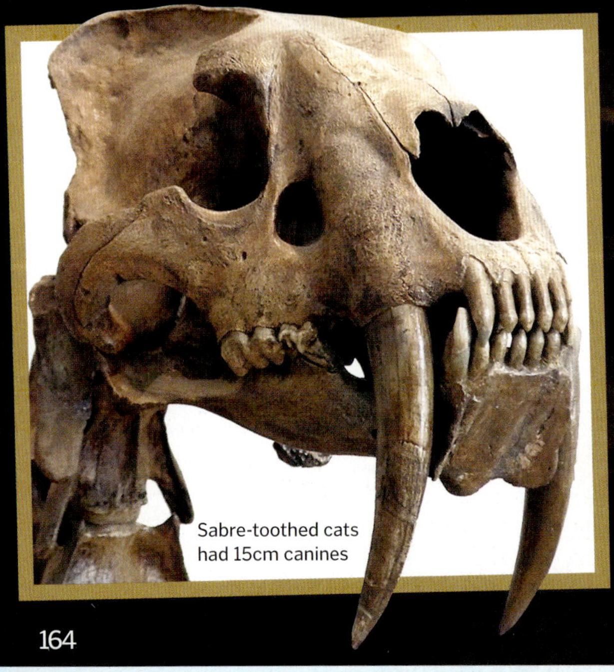

Sabre-toothed cats had 15cm canines

"At the end of the ice age, humans were roaming the landscape with spears"

Sabre-toothed cat

There were three species of sabre-toothed cat, all found in the Americas. They were similar in size to modern lions, but with shorter legs and significantly larger teeth. Their curved canines were over 15 centimetres long, and their mouths opened almost twice as wide as those of modern cats. Surprisingly, however, their bite force was nowhere near as powerful as a lion's. Although they are often called tigers, the colour and patterning of their fur is not known and they are not closely related to modern tigers.

DID YOU KNOW? *The first fossilised mastodon tooth was found by a farmer in 1705 and weighed 2kg – he traded it for rum!*

Woolly mammoth

These iconic ice age animals were covered in thick hair and layers of insulating fat. Unlike modern elephants that have large ears to aid heat loss, mammoths had small ears to conserve heat, and even their blood was adapted to cold weather. Their haemoglobin – the molecule that transports oxygen in the blood – functioned over a much wider temperature range than that of modern elephants, allowing oxygen to reach their extremities even in the freezing cold.

Dire wolf

These prehistoric wolves were slightly larger than their modern counterparts, with short legs, broad heads, and smaller brains. While grey wolves use speed and teamwork to wear their prey down, these snow hunters are thought to have preferred ambush tactics. Grey wolves existed alongside these fearsome hunters but 10,000 years ago, dire wolves had disappeared, along with other ice age predators like sabre-toothed cats and American lions.

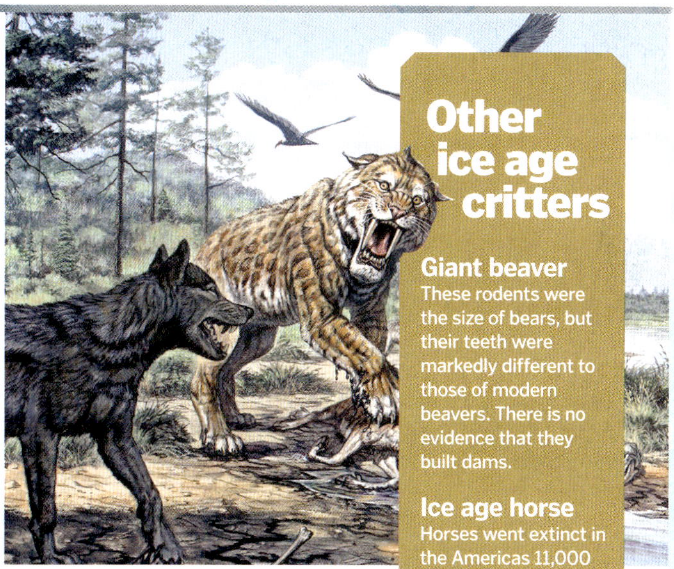

Ground sloths

Megatherium, or ground sloths, were the size of modern-day bison. They lived in the savannahs, forests and grasslands of North America, subsisting on a plant-based diet. They had long hair, huge jaws and powerful claws, which they used for digging and reaching up to tear leaves off branches.

Other ice age critters

Giant beaver
These rodents were the size of bears, but their teeth were markedly different to those of modern beavers. There is no evidence that they built dams.

Ice age horse
Horses went extinct in the Americas 11,000 years ago, but they managed to survive in Eurasia and Africa. Modern horses in the Americas – as well as donkeys and asses – are the descendents of these survivors.

Musk ox
These heavy-set, woolly animals almost went extinct due to hunting during the last ice age, and the warming climate that followed. There are still some musk oxen in Canada today, but their numbers are vastly reduced.

American lion
Larger than modern lions, and with longer legs, these animals would have had to compete with sabre-toothed cats and short-faced bears for prey.

Mastodon
Relatives of mammoths, these elephant-like animals had long trunks and woolly hair. Some fossilised bones show evidence of tuberculosis, which could have been one of the factors leading to their extinction.

Stag-moose
With stilt-like legs, these animals were adapted to pick their way through damp marshland and boggy ground. They had large, complex antlers and faces similar to modern-day elk.

Glyptodonts

These bizarre-looking beasts were the size of a car, and the heaviest weighed more than a ton. Related to modern armadillos, they had a protective exoskeleton made from plates of bone called osteoderms, and a fearsome-looking clubbed tail. While armadillos can flex their armour, glyptodonts had fused bones with rigid shells that turned them into walking tanks.

Short-faced bear

These ferocious bears are thought to have been the fastest of their kind, with front-facing feet that allowed them to reach speeds of more than 64 kilometres per hour. Their blunt snouts are thought to have helped them to get the maximum amount of air into their lungs while chasing their prey.

LIVING IN A FROZEN WORLD

How did early humans survive the ice age?

Early humans had begun to explore Europe, Asia and North America by the time the last glacial period set in around 110,000 years ago – this is what is often referred to as *the* Ice Age. Although many humans lived far enough to the south that they escaped the advancing ice, some had to brave fierce drops in temperature. They had three choices: migrate, adapt or die.

Humans weren't alone in their struggle. Another hominid species, Neanderthals, were also attempting to brave the cold. They were stockier than humans, with shorter forearms and shins, which would have helped to conserve body heat. Neanderthals built simple shelters, used animal skins for blankets, and kept themselves warm beside wood-fuelled fires. In mild conditions, they hunted red deer, and as it grew colder, they switched to reindeer. Eventually, when the landscape froze, they moved south in search of warmth.

However, humans had something that Neanderthals did not: advanced technology and sophisticated communication skills. They moved south to escape the worst of the cold, but some were still exposed to chilling temperatures and challenging environments. They learnt to burn bones when wood was scarce, built more complex shelters, and traded over great distances, thereby making the most of their social networks.

Humans banded together and used sharp tools to hunt large animals like mammoths and mastodons, securing the biggest calorie payoff for their efforts. And when the meat had been consumed, they made needles and stitched the skins into well-fitting clothes. Neanderthals were extinct by the time of the glacial maximum, 20,000 years ago, but humans' intelligence and ingenuity helped them to cling on through the cold.

> "Humans moved south to escape the worst of the cold"

The secrets of survival

Clever thinking and advanced technology allowed humans to make it out alive

THE END OF THE ICE AGE

What caused frozen Earth to thaw?

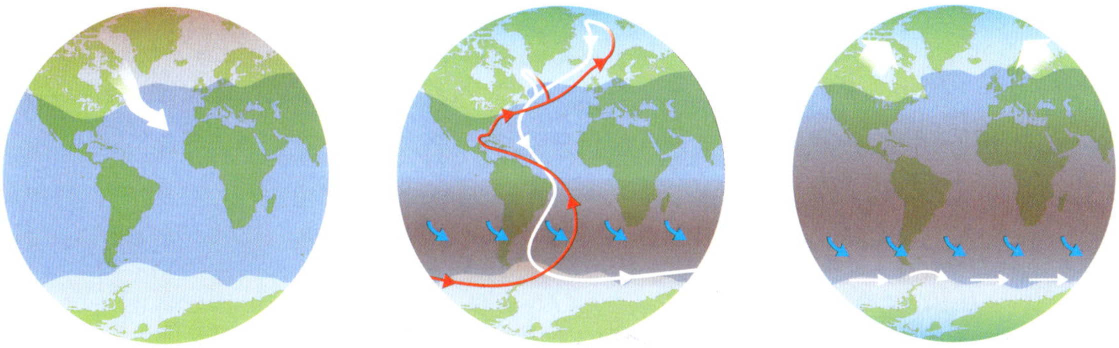

20,000 years ago
Towards the end of the last ice age, Earth tilted on its orbit, pointing the Northern Hemisphere towards the Sun. With more light and more heat striking the frozen surface, ice sheets in this area finally began to melt, and water flooded into the Atlantic Ocean.

19,000 years ago
The influx of cold water into the Atlantic disrupted the ocean currents, slowing the flow of warm water moving up from the south. With nowhere to go, these hot streams remained in the Southern Hemisphere, warming oceans and melting ice.

17,500 years ago
The flow of ocean currents affects the wind, and with the disruption in the north, winds pushed downwards. As the southern glaciers melted, more water was released into the oceans, and with it came carbon dioxide – a greenhouse gas that helps to trap heat.

Is winter coming?

The impact of humans on Earth could affect the forecast

Technically, we are still in the middle of an ice age. The cold period that saw the rise and fall of woolly mammoths has not yet ended. We are in an interglacial period, and if history is anything to go by, these last for around 15,000 to 20,000 years.

11,000 years have already passed, but whether another cold snap is around the corner is a matter of debate. In the late 17th century, there was a Little Ice Age, during which time rivers froze and ice fields refused to melt during the summer. This is thought to have been caused by a period known as the Maunder Minimum.

The Sun's changing magnetic field produces sunspots, which normally increase and decrease in a pattern that repeats every 11 years, but during the Little Ice Age, this cycle all but stopped. For 70 years, there were only around 50 recorded spots, when normally there would have been closer to 50,000.

In 2008, sunspots disappeared again, and when they eventually returned in 2014, they were weaker than at any other time on record. However, since the 17th century, humans have been busy expanding and industrialising, and, at least in part thanks to us, global temperatures are rising. Whether this will have an effect on the ice age cycle remains to be seen.

The Little Ice Age is thought to have inspired tales of white Christmases

Tudor beauty

The dos and don'ts of looking gorgeous in 16th century England

Perception of beauty varies greatly throughout history, and the Tudors went to great lengths to achieve the ideal. They looked to their Queen, Elizabeth I, for inspiration, so it became very fashionable to have fair hair with porcelain skin and blue or grey eyes.

Pale skin was a sign of wealth and relaxation, as by contrast, tanned, freckled or sunburned skin was an indication of hard labour out in the fields. In the early Tudor period, women softened their skin with creams and ointments, but towards the end of the era ladies used ceruse, a cream made of white lead and vinegar, to whiten their complexion. Many suffered from lead poisoning as a result, but they also went to further extremes, such as bleeding themselves to remove any rosy flush.

Darker-haired ladies dyed their locks red with henna, or attempted to lighten it using urine or a mixture of cumin, saffron seeds, celandine and oil. Wigs were also very fashionable, and high-class women would wear these to achieve the desired colour without a messy dye job.

The model queen

The Darnley Portrait of Elizabeth I was completed circa 1575 and shows her as a picture of popular beauty

Anne Boleyn wasn't considered traditionally beautiful, due to her dark hair and sallow skin

Ancient Greek theatre

Uncover the civilisation that invented the play and set the stage for Western culture

We have a lot to thank Ancient Greece for. From democracy to philosophy, this thriving collection of city-states was the birthplace of so many things that we take for granted today – including theatre.

The first mention of it dates back to 532 BCE, when an actor called Thespis performed a tragedy. His name has been immortalised as a term for a performer – a 'thespian'. A few decades later, a festival called the City Dionysia was established in Athens to honour Dionysus, the god of wine. The events centred on competitive performances of tragedies and, from 487 BCE, comedies. Thousands flocked from all over Greece, businesses closed and prisoners were released to take part in five days of festivities.

Performances were staged at the Theatre of Dionysus, considered by many to be the first ever built. This was a huge open-air arena that could seat up to 17,000 people on rows of benches set into a hill. The actors performed in the centre, known as the 'orchestra', while a backdrop was painted onto a building behind the stage known as the 'skene'. This was also where the actors changed into their masks and costumes.

The theatre's acoustics were so well thought out that every single audience member would have been able to hear the actors performing, even in the days before microphones and sound systems. Over two thousand years later, we still base our theatre designs on these incredible ancient structures.

The ruins of the theatre of Dionysus as they appear today

How to put on a play in Ancient Greece

Follow these steps to produce your very own dramatic masterpiece

1 Pick a genre

In Ancient Greece, tragedy and comedy should never mix. The City Dionysia pits the writers of these two genres against each other in its annual theatre competition, so choose a side and get planning.

2 Get funding

Plays in Athens are publicly funded, but you will need to pitch your idea to an official, who is known as the eponymous archon, and get his approval, before you see the colour of his money.

3 Decide your actors

The eponymous archon is responsible for deciding your lead actors, which is done by drawing random lots. The chorus actors are paid for by wealthy citizens looking to win public favour.

4 Start writing

Not only do your plays have to be written in verse, you'll also need to compose the music to accompany them. As for subject matter, the more revolutionary the better.

5 Perform your play

Once rehearsals are over, it's time to bring your work to the stage. The competitions can attract up to 17,000 people and last from dawn until dusk.

6 Collect your prize

The judges write their scores on tablets and place them in urns. The eponymous archon draws five of them at random and the winner is awarded with a wreath and a goat!

History's MOST GRUESOME inventions

From brutal torture devices to bizarre medical treatments, these terrifying contraptions reveal a darker side of innovation

From the wheel to the World Wide Web, we have invented some truly ground-breaking things during our time on Earth. Yet throughout history, inventors have also been known to put their skills to use in horrifying ways, creating contraptions that have caused unimaginable suffering.

In the past, if you committed a terrible crime, a punishment much worse than a long prison sentence awaited you. From boiling people alive to sawing them in half, execution methods were often developed to be as cruel as possible. These gruesome events were usually carried out in public to deter others from following in the footsteps of the accused.

Even if you weren't sentenced to death, there were plenty of ghastly implements that could be used to torture you instead. Typically used to extract a confession or information about accomplices, torture was popular in medieval times, with the screams of victims echoing from castle dungeons across Europe.

War has also inspired a wide selection of horrific innovations. While guns and bombs were designed to kill instantly, chemical weapons could draw out death for several agonising days – thankfully, this form of warfare is now prohibited.

We are also lucky that some medical devices from history are no longer used. Despite being designed with good intentions, many medieval procedures were truly stomach-churning, making a trip to the doctor quite the ordeal.

So as you drive around in your car and browse the web on your phone, be grateful that the inventions you use aren't gruesome like these...

THE BRAZEN BULL

Turning the screams of the dying into the roar of a beast

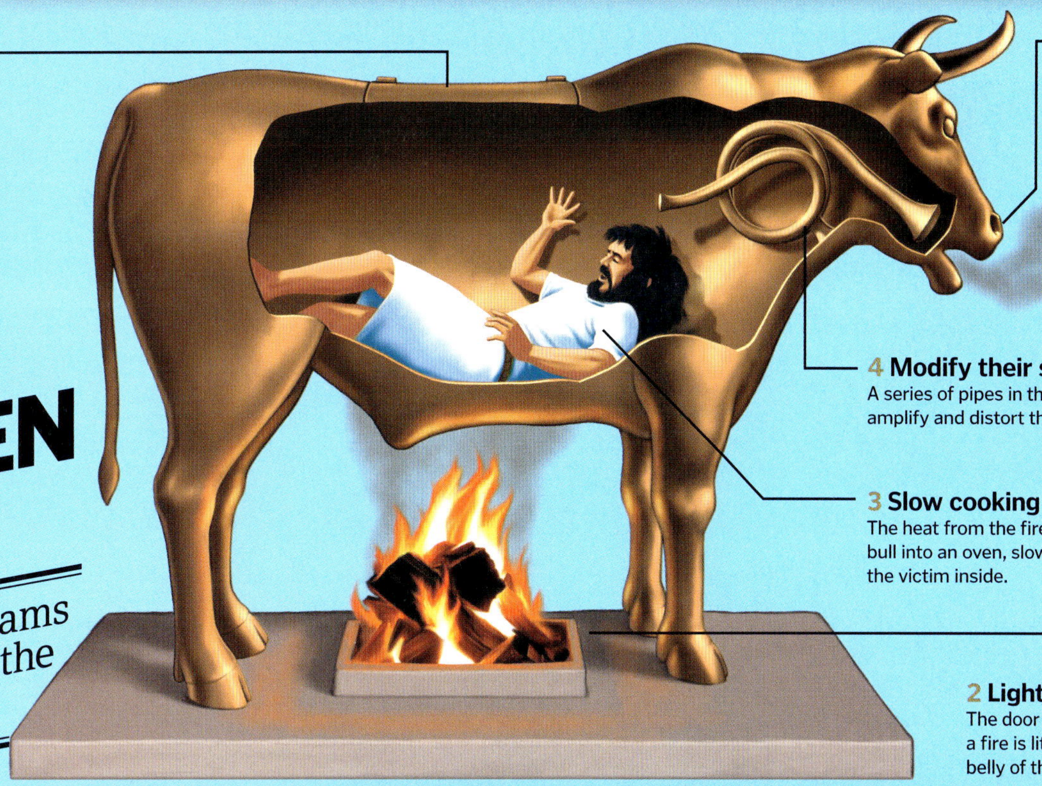

Illustration by Tom Connell / Art Agency

One of the most brutal methods of execution ever created took the form of a hollow bull statue. Invented in ancient Greece by Perillus, a bronze worker in Athens, it was given as a gift to a cruel tyrant named Phalaris of Agrigentum. As well as roasting criminals alive, the device also doubled as a musical instrument, converting the victim's desperate cries into what Perillus described as "the tenderest, most pathetic, most melodious of bellowings". Distrustful of the inventor's claims, Phalaris ordered Perillus to climb inside and prove the device's musical capabilities himself. However, as soon as he was inside, Phalaris shut the door and lit a fire beneath, causing Perillus to scream for real. However, rather then letting him die at the hands of his own creation, Phalaris had him removed and thrown off a cliff instead.

Crucifixion

Devised over 2,500 years ago as punishment for the most serious crimes, crucifixion would kill victims in a horribly drawn-out and painful way. With their wrists and feet nailed or tightly bound to a cross, and their legs broken by the executioners to speed up death, the victim's weight would be transferred to their arms. This would gradually pull the shoulders and elbows out of their sockets, leaving the chest to bear the weight. Although inhaling would still be possible, exhaling would be difficult and the victim would eventually suffocate due to a lack of oxygen. This excruciating process could take 24 hours.

Crucifixion would lead to suffocation and multiple organ failure

Louis XVI and Marie Antoinette were both publically executed using the guillotine

Guillotine

Although beheading methods had already been around for centuries, in 1789 French physician Dr Joseph Guillotin proposed a much more efficient and humane device for decapitation. When the executioner released the rope holding the guillotine's weighted blade in place, it would drop onto the victim's neck, killing them in a fraction of a second. This helped to eliminate the human error that was common with axe and sword beheadings, which sometimes required the executioner to deliver multiple swings to fully remove the head. Although quick, guillotine executions were popular spectator events during the French Revolution and the guillotine operators become national celebrities.

Electric chair

Electrocution was introduced as a quicker and supposedly less painful method of execution than hanging in the 1880s. When brought to the electric chair, a person has their head and one calf shaved to reduce resistance to electricity and is strapped in across their waist, arms and legs. A moistened sponge is then placed on their head and an electrode in the shape of a metal skullcap is secured on top. Another electrode is attached to their shaved leg and then the power is switched on. 2,000 volts pass through their body, paralysing the respiratory system and causing cardiac arrest.

Electrocution is still used as a method of execution in some US states

INSIDE A TORTURE CHAMBER

The terrifying devices that inflicted intense pain

Torture has been used as a method of punishment and interrogation for centuries, with the ancient Greeks and Romans regularly torturing criminals as part of their justice system. However, by the Middle Ages torture had become particularly prevalent, especially in response to crimes of treason. If you had been disloyal to the sovereign and your country, a whole plethora of horrifying torture devices awaited you.

Torture was usually conducted in secret, with most medieval castles featuring an underground dungeon in which these diabolical deeds took place. A great deal of ingenuity and artistic skill went into developing instruments that would inflict the maximum amount of pain. Often simply threatening to use one on a person was enough to get them to confess, while others would quickly give in after seeing it used on a fellow prisoner. Some torture devices were designed to only inflict pain, but others would result in a slow, drawn-out death that prolonged the suffering until the victim drew their last breath.

However, even if a prisoner was lucky enough to survive the torture, they were usually left severely disfigured and often had to be to be carried to their resulting trial, as they could no longer walk on their own. From the mid-17th century onwards, torture became much less common as there was much speculation about its effectiveness. Many prisoners would say anything to end their suffering, so it often produced inaccurate information or false confessions. It wasn't until 1948 that the United Nations General Assembly adopted the Universal Declaration of Human Rights, banning the use of torture.

1 Breaking wheel

With the victim's limbs tied to the spokes of this large wooden wheel, it would be slowly revolved. As it spun, the executioner would bludgeon the victim's arms and legs with an iron hammer, shattering their bones one by one. If the victim survived this, they were placed on top of a large pole, so birds could peck at their body until they eventually died of dehydration, which could take several days.

2 The rack

With their hands and feet tied to rollers at each end of the wooden frame, the torture victim would be subjected to intense interrogation. If they failed to confess to their crimes or give up the information the torturer was looking for, a crank would be turned to rotate the rollers. This would pull on the ropes, gradually stretching the victim's body and causing intense pain, eventually dislocating their limbs.

3 Iron maiden

A series of menacing spikes protruded from the interior of this iron chamber. With the victim inside, the door was closed slowly, causing the strategically placed spikes to pierce their body. However, the spikes were not long enough to be instantly fatal. Instead, the victim would be left to slowly bleed to death.

DID YOU KNOW? *Guy Fawkes was tortured for three days after his failed attempt to blow up Parliament in 1605*

4 Head crusher

With the victim's chin placed over the bottom bar and their head beneath the metal cap, the executioner would slowly turn the screw to bring the two together, only stopping if the victim gave the right answers. As the victim's head was crushed, their teeth would shatter into their jaw and their eyes would pop out from their sockets.

5 Thumbscrew

Used as punishment or a method of extracting information, the victim's fingers, thumbs or toes were placed between two horizontal metal bars. When the screw was turned, the two bars were pressed together, crushing the digits inside. Some thumbscrews even featured metal spikes on the bars to increase the pain.

6 Choke pear

Also known as the 'pear of anguish', this device was inserted into one of the victim's orifices, such as their mouth. When the key or crank was turned, the 'petals' of the pear-shaped end would slowly open up, painfully mutilating the victim's insides, but not causing death.

7 Heretic's fork

Usually reserved for blasphemers, this metal rod with two prongs at either end was attached to a leather strap around the victim's neck. One end would pierce their chin, while the other dug into their sternum, causing immense pain if they attempted to move their jaw or neck, making it more or less impossible to talk.

8 Lead sprinkler

Deceptively designed to look like a holy water sprinkler, this device was actually filled with molten lead, acid or boiling hot oil or water. The long handle was shaken to shower the victim's body with the substance inside. This caused horrific burns and was potentially lethal.

MISERABLE MEDICINE

The medical practices that did more harm than good

Nowadays, when you're feeling unwell, you can visit a clean hospital and receive tried and tested treatments from a doctor with years of medical training. We often take this modern medicine for granted, but our ancestors throughout history were not quite so lucky when it came to health care. In medieval England for example, poor hygiene and filthy living conditions meant that disease was very common. However, with little knowledge of the human anatomy, many illnesses were attributed to witchcraft, demons, the will of god or even the positions of celestial bodies. Trepanning, which involves drilling a hole into the skull, was a popular treatment prescribed to allow the disease-causing evil spirits trapped inside to escape. Others believed that diseases were caused by the fluids in the body becoming unbalanced, and so bloodletting – draining the blood from a particular part of the body – was thought to restore things to normal.

The 'doctors' who carried out these procedures were usually monks, as they tended to have a basic medical knowledge, or barbers or butchers who simply had the right tools for the job. The equipment used was very rarely sterilised, as little was known about contamination, and procedures were carried out with no form of anaesthesia to numb the pain. It's no wonder that people would put off seeking treatment for as long as possible!

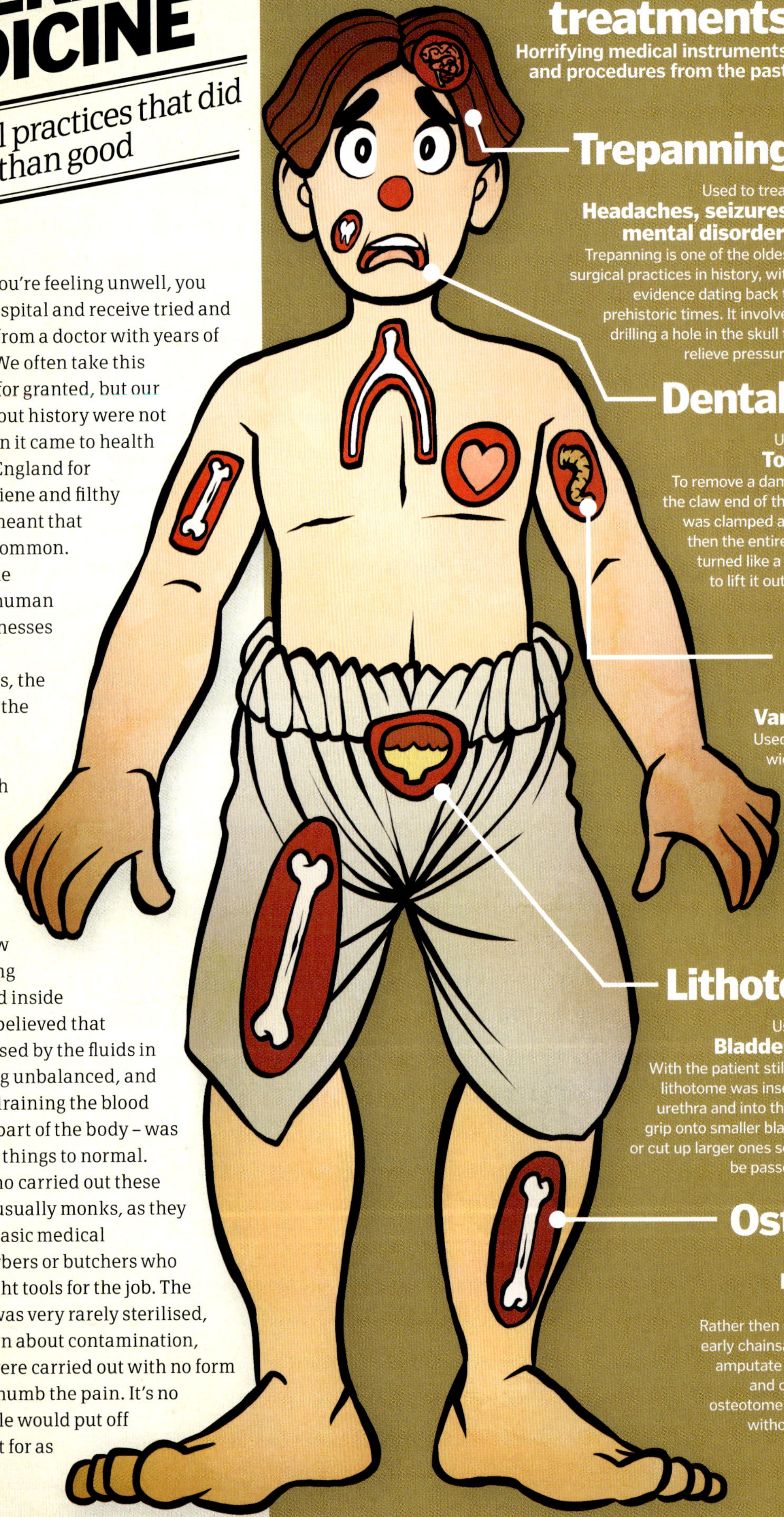

Terrifying treatments

Horrifying medical instruments and procedures from the past

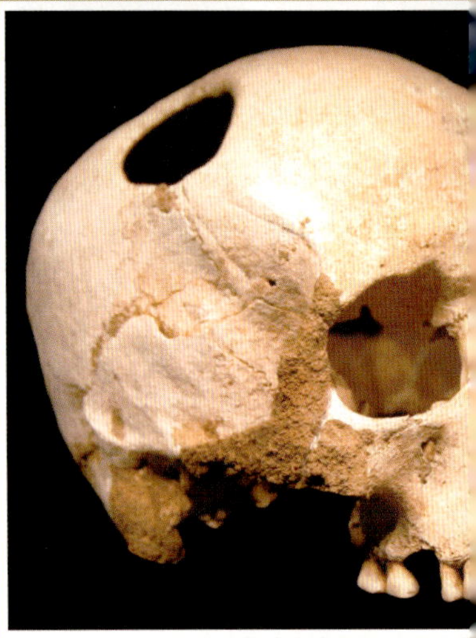

Trepanning

Used to treat:
Headaches, seizures, mental disorders

Trepanning is one of the oldest surgical practices in history, with evidence dating back to prehistoric times. It involves drilling a hole in the skull to relieve pressure.

Dental key

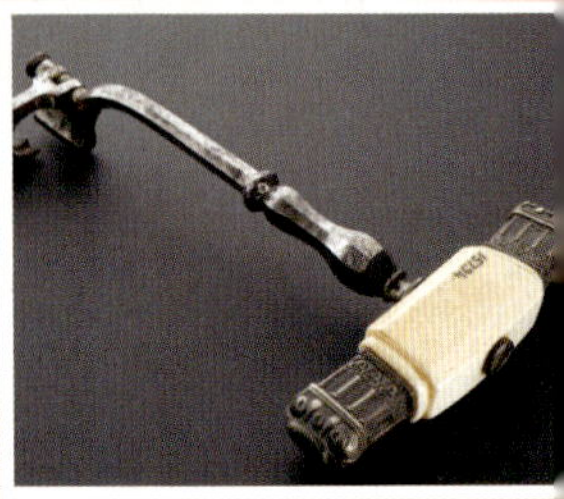

Used to treat:
Toothache

To remove a damaged tooth, the claw end of the dental key was clamped around it and then the entire device was turned like a key in a lock to lift it out of the gum.

Artificial leech

Used to treat:
Various infections and diseases

Used for bloodletting a popular treatment for a wide range of medical conditions, this device mimicked the action of reel leeches, with rotating blades that cut into the skin whilst a vacuum in the cylinder sucked out the blood.

Lithotome

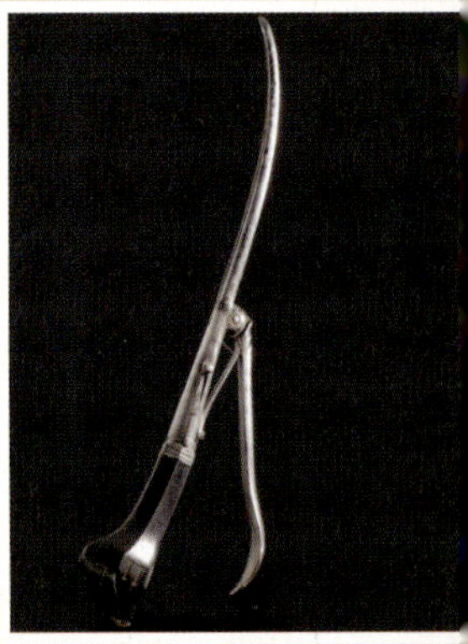

Used to treat:
Bladder stones

With the patient still awake, the lithotome was inserted up the urethra and into the bladder to grip onto smaller bladder stones or cut up larger ones so they could be passed naturally.

Osteotome

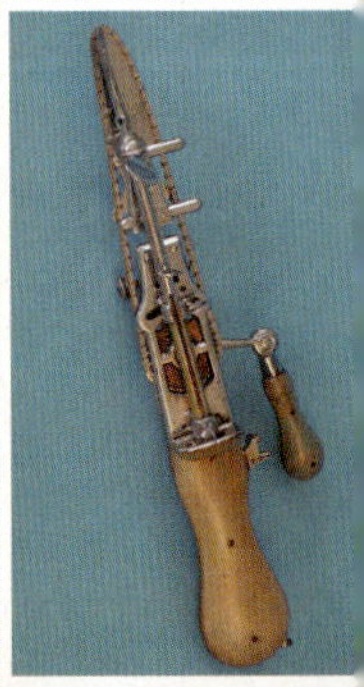

Used to treat:
Infections in the arms or legs

Rather then cutting down trees, this early chainsaw was actually used to amputate limbs. Unlike a hammer and chisel, the hand-cranked osteotome could cut through bone without causing it to splinter.

WEAPONS OF WAR

How the chemical arms race changed the face of conflict

Chemical weapons

On 22 April 1915, Germany shocked the world by launching the first large-scale gas attack in war. After waiting several weeks for the wind to blow in the right direction, German soldiers released clouds of chlorine gas near the enemy trenches in Ypres, suffocating the unprepared Allied troops. Although The Hague Convention of 1899 prohibited the use of poisonous weapons, Germany justified its actions by claiming that France had already broken the ban by deploying tear gas grenades in 1914. The chlorine gas attack kick-started a chemical arms race and by the end of World War I, around 50 different chemicals had been used on the battlefield. The most prevalent were chlorine, phosgene and mustard gas, which would result in slow and painful deaths if soldiers were exposed to large enough quantities. Eventually, gas masks were developed for protection, but chemicals such as mustard gas could still cause horrific blisters if they came into contact with the skin. Among the most devastating chemical weapons are nerve agents, such as sarin, which attack the nervous system. Even small concentrations can be lethal, killing in mere minutes.

Cl_2

Chlorine

Appearing as a pale green cloud with a strong bleach-like odour, chlorine gas reacts with water in the lungs to form hydrochloric acid. This damages the lung tissue, causing coughing, vomiting and eventually death.

$COCl_2$

Phosgene

This colourless gas with a musty odour reacts with proteins in the alveoli, tiny air sacs found in the lungs. This leads to fluid in the lungs and eventually suffocation, but the symptoms can take up to 48 hours to manifest.

$C_4H_8Cl_2S$

Mustard gas

With the odour of garlic, horseradish or sulphur, yellow-brown clouds of mustard gas cause chemical burns on the skin, eyes and respiratory tract, leading to large blisters, temporary blindness and shortness of breath.

$C_4H_{10}FO_2P$

Sarin

Colourless, tasteless and odourless, this gas blocks normal communication between nerves. The nerve signals become stuck 'on', and muscles are unable to relax. This can lead to spasms, paralysis and asphyxiation.

The Geneva Protocol

By the end of World War I, over 125,000 tons of poison gas had been deployed in battle. Although it was only responsible for less than one per cent of the war's total fatalities, the psychological terror it had inflicted on soldiers was immense. On 17 June 1925, seven years after the war had ended, the Geneva Protocol was introduced, prohibiting the use of chemical and biological weapons. 138 states have now signed the treaty.

38 states originally signed the Geneva Protocol to ban the use of chemical weapons

Napalm

Napalm is a flammable liquid with a gel-like consistency, allowing it to stick to surfaces easily. In a bomb, it is combined with gasoline or jet fuel to explode upon impact, capable of burning at more than 2,760 degrees Celsius. Even the slightest contact with skin can result in severe burns and it can also cause death by asphyxiation. When ignited, napalm generates carbon monoxide and removes oxygen from the air, suffocating those in the vicinity.

Napalm fires combust oxygen in the air, turning carbon dioxide into carbon monoxide

Greek fire

Developed by the Byzantine Greeks in the 7th century, Greek fire was a flammable liquid that could burn on water, making it particularly effective for naval warfare. This liquid fire was sprayed at the enemy using early flamethrower devices, or thrown in primitive hand grenades, creating a raging fire that could only be extinguished with sand, vinegar or urine. The true ingredients are a mystery, but scientists believe it could have contained petroleum, sulphur and pine tar.

Greek fire was the napalm of its day, but its ingredients are a mystery